POUND IN PURGATORY

Pound in Purgatory

From Economic Radicalism
to Anti-Semitism

Leon Surette

University of Illinois Press
Urbana and Chicago

Publication of this book was supported by a grant from
the University of Western Ontario.

Library of Congress Cataloging-in-Publication Data
Surette, Leon.
Pound in purgatory : from economic radicalism to anti-semitism /
Leon Surette.
p.   cm.
Includes bibliographical references (p.) and index.
ISBN 0-252-02498-2 (acid-free paper)
1. Pound, Ezra, 1885–1972—Knowledge—Economics.
2. Economics—United States—History—20th century.
3. Antisemitism—History—20th century.
4. Antisemitism in literature. 5. Radicalism in literature.
6. Economics in literature. I. Title.
PS3531.O82Z848   1999
811'.52—dc21   99-6096
CIP

C 5 4 3 2 1

To Valerie,
my life's companion for thirty-five years

Contents

Preface

It is a matter of mild embarrassment to me that this is the third monograph I have produced in which Ezra Pound is the sole or principal figure. The embarrassment arises from a sense that I seem to have always left loose threads in my accounts of his poetry and thought, for this book, like the second one, is an extension of a discussion raised, but not completed, in my first study of Pound, *A Light from Eleusis*, published twenty years ago.

My second study of Pound and his intellectual milieu was prompted by a phone call from Bill French (now deceased), a St. Elizabeths acolyte of Pound and an occultist. The present work was similarly prompted by a communication—though this time from a young(er) scholar, Alec Marsh of Muhlenberg College, who sent me a chapter of what was then a work in progress, now published as *Money and Modernity: Pound, Williams, and the Spirit of Jefferson*.

In responding to that chapter, I sent him a package of articles I had published over the previous decade or so on the topic of Pound's engagement with the dismal science. I was, I must admit, somewhat miffed that he had apparently been unable to discover their existence. Perhaps to make up for his neglect, Alec suggested that I publish those articles in a collection of some sort.

Spurred by this suggestion, I set aside the sabbatical project I had promised to undertake and set about to revise and extend those essays. The issue, as I saw it, was to articulate the relation between Pound's aesthetic, political, economic, and racial views. I had already formed—and expressed in those articles—an opinion on that relationship, but I had a new set of relevant information arising from the edition Demetres Tryphonopoulos and I had prepared of Pound's correspondence with Olivia Rossetti Agresti. Those letters unequivocally demonstrated that during his St. Elizabeths period Pound himself believed that all of his opinions—including anti-Semitism—formed a coherent and indissoluble set.

Given that disturbing finding, I now saw my task differently: it was to discover how Pound could have fallen into such egregious and appalling error. In contrast to some other scholars, I remained convinced at the outset that the Pound of the middle and late thirties was not a natural and inevitable maturation of the young poet who had arrived in London in 1909. Knowing that it was not just Pound that had changed, I sought the explanation in the transformation Europe had undergone. Europe had metamorphosed dramatically and irrevocably between 1909 and 1933—when Pound returned to an active study of economics, an interest he had set aside upon leaving London in 1922.

Instead of retreating into Sibylline detachment in response to the "tragedy of Europe"—like his mentor, W. B. Yeats—Pound once again seized the nettle of economics in 1933 and severely wounded himself. I had not previously examined closely Pound's frenetic engagement in economic journalism between 1933 and 1944—nor had anyone else. It was here that I thought it might be possible to gain some insight into Pound's descent.

Such a study could scarcely have been undertaken without the resource of *Ezra Pound's Poetry and Prose* (edited by Lea Baechler, A. Walton Litz, and James Longenbach), which brings together in ten volumes photostatic copies of all of Pound's periodical publications. Even more important to this study has been the resource of the Beinecke Rare Book and Manuscript Library of Yale University. The library has put its catalog on line, enabling me to follow up newly discovered leads from my home in London, Ontario. Lynn Braunsdorf of the Beinecke was most helpful and courteous in assisting me to purchase photocopies of correspondence without the cost and inconvenience of multiple trips to New Haven. I also want to thank the Lilly Library of Indiana University, the New York Public Library, the Riverside University Library of the University of California at Riverside, and the Humanities Research Center in Austin, Texas.

This has been a largely solitary work, but I want to thank Keith Tuma of Miami University for sharing information and opinion with me and Becky Standard of the University of Illinois Press for her unfailing patience and alarming erudition.

I could not have afforded the costs of computers and associated equipment without a generous grant from the Social Science and Humanities Research Council for the years 1995–98. Finally, this book was written while I was enjoying a sabbatical leave from the University of Western Ontario.

Acknowledgments

Previously unpublished material by Ezra Pound Copyright © 1999 by Mary de Rachewiltz and Omar S. Pound; used by permission of New Directions Publishing Corporation, agents.

Grateful acknowledgement is given to City Lights Books for permission to quote from *The Chinese Written Character as a Medium for Poetry*, ed. Ezra Pound (Copyright 1936 by Ezra Pound).

Ezra Pound's correspondence quoted from John McCormick, *George Santayana: A Biography* (New York: Paragon House, 1988), by permission of James Laughlin, executor, Ezra Pound Literary Property Trust, and of the Humanities Research Center, Austin; *DK: Some Letters of Ezra Pound*, ed. Louis Dudek (Montreal: DC Books, 1974; Copyright © 1974 by the Trustees of the Ezra Pound Literary Property Trust); and *"I Cease Not to Yowl": Ezra Pound's Letters to Olivia Rossetti Agresti*, ed. Demetres Tryphonopoulos and Leon Surette (Urbana: University of Illinois Press, 1998; © 1998 by the Board of Trustees of the University of Illinois; previously unpublished letters of Ezra Pound © 1998 by Mary de Rachewiltz and Omar S. Pound).

Earlier versions of portions of chapter 1 appeared as "Ezra Pound and British Radicalism" in *English Studies in Canada* 9 (Dec. 1983): 435–51 and "Economics and Eleusis" in *San Jose Studies* 12 (Fall 1986): 58–66. An earlier version of portions of chapter 4 appeared as "Ezra Pound's Fascism: Aberration or Essence: The Correspondence with William Bird," *Queen's Quarterly* 96 (Autumn 1989): 601–24. An earlier version of portions of chapter 6 appeared as "Pound, 'guru' economico" in *Ezra Pound: Educatore*, ed. Luca Gallesi (Milan: Terziaria, 1998), 107–28. Earlier versions of portions of chapter 7 appeared as "Pound, Postmodernism, and Fascism" in *University of Toronto Quarterly* 59 (Winter 1989–90): 60–79 and "Modernism, Postmodernism, Fascism, and Historicism" in *University of Toronto Quarterly* 60 (Summer 1991): 476–92.

Introduction

Ezra Pound's affiliation with Mussolini's fascism has placed him in a unique and exposed position amongst English language modernists. Despite many articles and several books devoted to Pound's fascism and anti-Semitism, there is still no consensus on how they fit into his work as a whole or how they relate to his economic radicalism. I offer answers to those questions through a careful survey of Pound's published and unpublished correspondence, his well-known essays and books, and the ephemeral journalism available since 1991 in the ten volumes of *Ezra Pound's Poetry and Prose*. In addition, I examine the state of economic opinion and its evolution during the nearly three decades of Pound's engagement with economic theory.

Discussions of Pound's political and economic views tend to be either denunciations or apologetics. The apologetic literature breaks down into three general types. The New Critical approach—typified by Hugh Kenner—has relied heavily on the principle of aesthetic autonomy, licensing a disregard for the poet's personal opinions, whether economic, political, or racial. As the hegemony of New Criticism waned and the evidence of Pound's "errors" mounted, apologists fell back to the position that these opinions were only briefly held. Others have attempted to characterize the political and racist errors as excesses of an otherwise sound and insightful economic and cultural awareness.

In this study—which focuses on the years 1931 to 1936 during which Pound attempted to educate himself in economics—I concede some economic wisdom to Pound's views, but demonstrate that he never abandoned the political, economic, and racist views for which he is justly criticized. I call into question the presumption of his wisdom and good judgment on economics and politics, while attempting to preserve some fragment of goodwill and honest intention. Even though he had been radicalized by the Social Credit theories of Major C. H. Douglas and A. R.

Orage fourteen years prior to his engagement with fascism, Pound read little, and wrote less, on economic and political topics prior to 1931—as Tim Redman has noted in *Ezra Pound and Italian Fascism*. After that date *The Cantos* began to serve Pound's economic and political agenda rather than merely being informed by it. This shift of focus was undoubtedly in response to the Great Depression, a malaise for which Pound believed Social Credit had a cure. Accordingly he became increasingly preoccupied with the project of capturing political power so as to carry out Social Credit economic reforms.

I do not doubt that his initial motivation was to improve the material lot of humankind. If Social Credit had a simple and practical solution for the economic woes of the world, all right-thinking men and women would be obliged to leave no stone unturned until they had persuaded those in positions of power to adopt it. Unfortunately, the more Pound read in economics, the more confused he became, though his confusion was not entirely his fault. The orthodox economics of his day had no solution for the disaster of the world depression, and his radical allies were at loggerheads amongst themselves and often incoherent and confused in their own theories. When Pound sought guidance through the labyrinth of economic speculation from his mentors, Orage and Douglas, they failed him. They could hardly have done otherwise, for they were themselves quite incompetent and were in addition far more hidebound than was Pound.

The range of Pound's correspondence on economics is truly astonishing. Amongst radicals, in addition to Orage and Douglas, he wrote to the Proudhonian Arthur Kitson and the Gesellites Hugo Fack and E. S. Woodward. Until this study Pound's correspondence with the latter two has not been examined by Pound scholars; the Kitson correspondence has been barely mentioned; and only Tim Redman has given much attention to the correspondence with Orage and Douglas. Shortly after his return to economics, Pound forged a close alliance with Odon Por, an early enthusiast for Mussolini, and—like Kitson—an economic radical who had been associated with Orage and Douglas in the late years of World War I. Tim Redman has made good use of this correspondence in *Ezra Pound and Italian Fascism*, but did not find as much confusion as I do in Pound's exchanges with Por. He did not look at Pound's correspondence with Kitson, Fack, or Woodward. Kitson and Fack were virulent anti-Semites, and Fack—who became a Nazi supporter—was instrumental in pushing Pound toward anti-Semitism. Fack's role in Pound's descent into racism has not been noticed, though it appears to have been pivotal.

In addition to these figures, Pound sought alliances with supporters of the New Deal, notably the historian W. E. Woodward and the Catholic

Chestertonian Christopher Hollis. Pound was unable to persuade Woodward that there was any value in Social Credit, but Hollis was more amenable to Douglasite views. Both men tried to persuade Pound that Roosevelt was on the right track, but unfortunately Pound was more impressed with Fack's anti–New Deal arguments. Pound also wrote to Father Charles Coughlin, the infamous radio priest. Coughlin had initially been a New Dealer, but soured on Roosevelt and campaigned against him in 1936. Coughlin sent Pound only form letters in return, asking for money. Despite such a rebuff, Pound continued to listen to Coughlin's broadcasts and was favorably impressed by Coughlin's exposure of the Jewish conspiracy in *Money! Questions and Answers*—a book Pound mentions only rarely and that therefore has been overlooked by scholars.

With the exception of Por, all of Pound's correspondents stressed that Mussolini's economic policies had nothing in common with the policy prescriptions of any of the economic reformers. But he remained deaf to such comments—whether from Social Crediters, Gesellites, New Dealers, or his old friends William Bird and Wyndham Lewis. Pound was absolutely immovable in his commitment to *both* Social Credit *and* Mussolini. And as if these incommensurables were not enough, Pound added a commitment to Gesellite policies—notably stamp scrip money, or *Schwundgeld*.

Pound also came into contact with two eminent orthodox economists, Irving Fisher and Lionel Robbins. Fisher and Pound shared an enthusiasm for Silvio Gesell's stamp scrip, but nothing else. So Pound soon turned sour on Fisher—egged on by Fack's hostility toward him. Robbins was another matter. He was one of the orthodox economists (a Labourite) to whom Pound sent his handbill "Volitionist Economics" in 1934 (see the appendix). Robbins responded in a most amiable—if rather condescending—manner, attempting to persuade Pound to abandon Douglas and economics and return to poetry. It is a remarkable coincidence that Robbins had been drawn to the study of economics through an enthusiasm for Orage and guild socialism in his youth. He had been instrumental in instigating the Labour party's inquiry into Social Credit. Of course Pound knew nothing of this—nor did Robbins mention it in his letters—but it very likely had something to do with his amiable response. However, Robbins had no luck with Pound, not even getting a polite response.

It is a great misfortune that Pound rejected all overtures from competent academics and economists while responding favorably to the more crankish speculation of Social Crediters and Gesellites. But it must be recognized that those competent economists were wrong on salient points where Douglas—and the Proudhonians—were closer to a correct understanding. Their error—and the correctness of the heretics' insights—was not apparent to anyone until John Maynard Keynes's revolutionary *General Theory of Employment, Interest, and Money* was published in 1936. After its appearance Hollis, E. S. Woodward, and Fack all attempted to persuade Pound of the compatibility of Keynes's views with those of Emile Proudhon, Gesell, and Douglas. But Pound remained implacably hostile to Keynes's theories, following Douglas's lead in this view. Both were quite unable—or unwilling—to see that Keynesianism addressed the same problem of underconsumption as did the "heretics" and like them recommended a solution that would not disturb the status quo.

Much of the discussion of Pound's relationship with economic thought is vitiated by a failure of scholars to recognize that the Keynesian revolution took place in the midst of Pound's economic evangelism. The Keynesian reforms in the postwar period achieved much of what Douglas and Pound had desired—that is, a technical rather than a revolutionary solution to the economic woes of modern industrial economies. Of course, Milton Friedman has since led a successful reaction against the Keynesian reforms, but those developments in economic thinking lie outside the purview of this study.

The answer, then, to the much discussed question, Was Pound really a Social Crediter? is yes and no. He was loyal to the movement and put up with Douglas's egregious rudeness in responses to his queries. Pound even offered to go to Alberta to advise the newly elected Social Credit government of William Aberhart in 1935. He also refused to give up either Gesell's stamp scrip money or Proudhon's commodity money despite Douglas's insistence that he do so. (Douglas erroneously believed that either policy would lead to uncontrollable inflation.) On theoretical grounds, then, Pound was not an orthodox Social Crediter, but he never disassociated himself from the movement nor did he ever give up the thoroughly quixotic hope that he could convert Italian fascism to Social Credit.

It is generally agreed that Pound's affiliation with fascism and his anti-Semitism are related to his economic radicalism, but there is no consensus on just what that relationship is. Most studies rely on perceived affinities between Pound's views on poetics, religion, and culture, on the one hand, and his economic and political views, on the other. Such an a priori approach is not without merit, but it does assume a consistency and coherence of views that needs to be demonstrated, and not just assumed. The evidence does not support the presumption of consistency in Pound's views on economics, politics, or racial prejudice. Of course, there is an underlying consistency in Pound's goals, modes of procedure, and beliefs, but these "strategic" positions do not map smoothly on to "tactical" decisions. For example, Pound's undoubted archaism in religion would not predict his support for Mussolini's fascism. His adoption of a Social Credit economic analysis is inconsistent with his later advocacy of Gesellite stamp scrip, and both are at odds with Proudhonian commodity money, which he also recommended.

Pound's views are neither static nor perfectly consistent. They are more like a snowball picking up bits of detritus and dropping other bits as it rolls along. To be sure, there is an underlying pattern and motivation, and I have spoken of those in my two earlier studies, *A Light from Eleusis* (1979) and *The Birth of Modernism* (1993). In the case of economics, his motivation throughout was to ensure economic welfare for everyone. Another—and less happy—consistency was his belief that fundamental reform in human affairs could be brought about only by a stroke of genius. He believed that Douglas had struck such a blow in 1917 and prided himself on having been among the first to recognize it. Mussolini's corporate state was another such stroke of genius in Pound's view. In this case Pound was a little slower, not recognizing Mussolini's genius until 1931, nine years after his rise to power and seven years after Pound's move to Rapallo. Pound's self-assigned role as an artist was to communicate the wisdom of such developments to others. Unfortunately for Pound neither economics nor politics is a field of endeavor that lends itself to resolution through the Alexandrian gesture of cutting through the Gordian knot. As a result Pound became increasingly confused and conflicted as he attempted to cut through the tangle of conflicting and incommensurable analyses and nostrums found in economic theory.

Repeatedly failing to convince others of Douglas's wisdom and unable to persuade Douglas or Orage to adopt the ideas of Gesell and Proudhon, Pound became increasingly frustrated and eventually muddled. This muddle became so apparent that his loyal Social Credit associate, Odon Por, complained that even he could not understand Pound's economic prose. I will demonstrate that Pound's descent into the paranoia of conspiracy theory and anti-Semitism was in great part a consequence of this muddle. Unable to see his way through the dark wood to the clear light, he persuaded himself that the fault was in those who found his arguments unconvincing. And he further concluded that their fault was willful. Seeking a motive for that willful incomprehension, he found it in conspiracy theory. The descent worked itself out in a remarkably short time—fewer than six years.

There is a tendency of scholars to assume that if Pound was ever an anti-Semite, then he must always have been one. In the following pages I trace Pound's exposure to anti-Semitic opinion from economic radicals with whom he corresponded. Though Douglas betrayed anti-Semitic views in his earliest writings, Pound never shared that sentiment in his correspondence with Douglas, as he did, for example, with Fack. And when Kitson invited Pound to join him in denouncing Jews, he did not bite. Similarly, when Bird floated the notion of a Masonic conspiracy, Pound mocked him for such foolishness. But when he encountered an anti-Semitic article by William Pelley in 1934, he reacted very differently. He then began to take the possibility of a Jewish conspiracy seriously and set John Drummond to work researching the subject. At about the same time, he initiated a correspondence with Fack, a blatant anti-Semite, and was listening over shortwave radio to the broadcasts of Coughlin, an uncompromising anti-Semite. Listening to the broadcasts led him to purchase and read *Money!* a work published under Coughlin's name but actually ghostwritten by Gertrude Coogan, a follower of Arthur Kitson and also an anti-Semite and conspiracy theorist. By 1936, when Pound read this work, his manner and message had changed radically for the worse.

It is a common error to equate fascism with anti-Semitism, but in fact Mussolini's adoption of anti-Semitic policies was primarily a consequence of his alliance with Hitler's Germany and not a constituent element of Italian fascism. When Pound recommenced his economic studies in 1931, he was already committed to Mussolini as a "factive personality," that is, someone who gets the job done without worrying too much about ideology, principles, or, indeed, broken heads. But neither Mussolini himself nor any of the leading Fascists was anti-Semitic. Nor did a commitment to Mussolini in 1931 put Pound at odds with his fellow Americans, many of whom admired the Italian dictator (Diggins). Indeed, Mussolini was a syndicated columnist for the Hearst newspaper chain from 1931 to 1935, when he (not Hearst) broke off the arrangement. When Roosevelt was elected in 1932 Pound was not the only observer who saw the New Deal as an American version of fascist state intervention in the economy (Diggins). Pound even dreamed that Roosevelt could be persuaded to adopt Social Credit policies. However, he was ultimately disappointed in Roosevelt, whose fiscal and monetary policies did not conform to Social Credit prescriptions. (Nor did Mussolini's, but Pound would not hear any criticism of him.)

Although random anti-Semitic remarks can be found in Pound's poetry, prose, and correspondence prior to 1936, it is only after his contact with Fack and Coughlin that the vituperative and obsessive targeting of Jews is found—and it is then found everywhere, including in *The Cantos*. In this study I conclude that Pound's anti-Semitism was driven by his paranoid belief in a Jewish conspiracy rather than by simple racism or even an antipathy for Hebraic religion and culture. This is not to say that racism and anti-Hebraism cannot be found in his correspondence and prose, but rather that those attitudes are found both before and after he evinces paranoid obsession with the "Jewish problem." The finding that Pound's anti-Semitism has a conspiracy theory provenance in no way excuses it. On the contrary, it reveals it as an intellectual failure rather than some mental tic or emotional aberration. Though I would not endorse Massimo Bacigalupo's very harsh judgment in the preface to *The Formèd Trace* that *The Cantos* "belong in those shops that sell swastikas and recordings of Mussolini's speeches," this study does lend support to that view (x). On the other hand, my investigation tends to contradict Robert Casillo's judgment in *The Genealogy of Demons* that Pound's anti-Semitism derived from prejudices imbibed in his youth. Yet the intermediate position—that Pound's anti-Semitism was a brief and regrettable aberration—cannot be maintained, for his correspondence reveals that he remained anti-Semitic and profascist throughout his incarceration at St. Elizabeths Hospital.

The motivation for this study was to sort out Pound's hubristic engagement with economics. I had supposed that his anti-Semitism was essentially traceable to the error of identifying bankers with Jews, but the relation between his economic views and his adoption of conspiracy theory was more contingent than I had imagined. The discoveries I have made about Pound's descent into anti-Semitism are the most striking and most accessible aspects of this study, but most of it is devoted to a discussion of economic theory and Pound's engagement with it.

No scholar has traced the development and alteration of his views on the topic. Everyone acknowledges that Pound mixes Douglas and Gesell, but the Proudhonian component—which he takes from Kitson and the Gesellites—has not been adequately appreciated. Even more importantly, previous studies have failed to place Pound's self-education in economics in the context of the great transformation in economic thinking wrought by Keynes's *General Theory*.

Keynes's book modified equilibrium theory—which had dominated economic thought since the early nineteenth century—and made underconsumption theoretically possible, that is, a state in which aggregate goods and services on offer exceed aggregate purchasing power. Unrevised equilibrium theory (alternatively called "quantity theory") holds that such a condition is impossible. Though equilibrium theory had been put under severe strain in the 1930s by the persistence of the Great Depression, economic luminaries such as A. C. Pigou and Robbins clung to it in the face of the massive contradictory evidence of persistent world surpluses of both goods and labor. Even Fisher recommended only a temporary and partial expansion of the money supply through Gesell's stamp scrip rather than a radical rethinking of equilibrium theory.

Virtually all of the economic radicals—from Ruskin and Proudhon to Gesell, Kitson, and Douglas—were what Keynes called "underconsumptionists," that is, they believed that industrial economies suffer from a disequilibrium between productive capacity and purchasing power that blocks the distribution of goods and services. Since equilibrium theory holds that purchasing power and productive capacity are always and necessarily in balance, all varieties of underconsumption were dismissed as ill-informed at best and subversive at worst. The prescription these reformers offered for the ills of underconsumption was usually some variety of monetary reform whose purpose was to increase purchasing power so as to bring it into balance with productive capacity. Social Credit was distinct on this point. It recommended a kind of negative tax, called the national dividend, to make up the shortfall in purchasing power and was opposed to expansion of the money supply. This posture was shown again and again to be incoherent, but nothing could move Douglas from it.

Marx and the Communists, it should be noted, were not underconsumptionists. Like Robbins and Pigou after him and David Ricardo before him, Marx adhered to equilibrium theory and also to the labor theory of value, in which precious metals were thought to embody labor value. In such a view, monetary reform could never be anything but a placebo for the disease of the maldistribution of wealth within an economy. All of the underconsumptionists, in contrast, held to a fiat theory of money and saw adherence to a commodity theory of money—which underpinned the gold standard—as the principal cause of underconsumption. (Today all Western currencies are avowedly fiat money, the last link to gold having been abandoned by the Nixon administration on 15 August 1971.) Pound was theoretically insulated from Marxism by his adherence to fiat money, as he frequently observed in remarks on Marx's failure to recognize the importance of money.

When in 1931 Pound began his study of economics in earnest, nothing had changed in mainstream economics since his first exposure to the subject in 1917. Equilibrium theory still held sway, and gold still bottomed all major currencies. His studies soon led him to the monetary ideas of Gesell and Proudhon (the latter indirectly through both Gesell and Kitson). Although Gesell's stamp scrip money and Proudhon's commodity money were both underconsumptionist prescriptions like Social Credit, Douglas thought they were erroneous. He thought so because—though an underconsumptionist himself—he clung to equilibrium theory. Such a posture was entirely incoherent, since equilibrium theory demonstrates the impossibility of underconsumption. The incoherence of his position and his economic incompetence is manifest in Douglas's testimony before the Macmillan Commission of 1930 examined below—a commission, incidentally, on which Keynes sat.

Pound was less doctrinaire than Douglas and Orage, and his understanding of the issues was marginally better than theirs, but he placed complete confidence in their judgment, as can be seen in the correspondence. Pound brings criticism of Social Credit theory to Douglas and Orage in hopes of clarification, but he gets only injunctions to ignore them. As a result Pound disobediently recommended Gesellite and Proudhonian policies—putting his good relations with Social Crediters under severe strain. Pound followed Douglas's adherence to equilibrium theory absolutely, even though it is clearly at odds with the monetary solutions offered by Proudhon, Kitson, and Gesell, to which Pound also subscribed.

It cannot be said that Pound's grasp of economic theory was competent or even coherent. Nonetheless, current economic wisdom concedes that the underconsumptionists were correct in their conviction that the orthodox economists of their day had got it wrong. Keynes showed that underconsumption was possible under certain circumstances and—in contradiction of equilibrium theory—prescribed an expansion of purchasing power through fiscal policy as a remedy for economic slumps. Keynes's insights have permanently altered economic opinion and the behavior of monetary authorities, even though the "Keynesian" policy of active management of the money supply is currently in eclipse. Although Pigou and Robbins both rejected Keynes initially, they eventually ate crow on this point. Surprisingly, Pound and the Social Crediters also rejected Keynes— and for the same reason Pigou and Robbins did, that his policy flouted equilibrium theory. Unlike the orthodox economists, Pound and Douglas never admitted—nor, indeed, recognized—their error.

E. S. Woodward, Fack, and Hollis all praised Keynes's *General Theory* to Pound early in 1936, but to no avail. As a Social Crediter he was convinced that interest charges were the cause of the shortfall in purchasing power and that the remedy was for the state to issue money directly through the national dividend, instead of indirectly through private banks (as it is still done today). Proudhon, Kitson, and Gesell preferred a less statist solution. Their remedy was to permit companies and municipalities to issue their own currency instead of borrowing from banks. But they all agreed that the solution was to remove the monopoly of credit and currency from the banks. Keynes recommended no such course. His policy prescription was to expand the money supply through lower interest rates, but to leave the banks as the issuers of credit, that is, as the agents who effectively expanded the money supply.

Pound was fixated on the role of the banks, and that fixation certainly contributed to his descent into violent anti-Semitism between 1931 and 1936—a descent mirrored in the course of Fascist Italy during those same years. Mussolini's invasion of Ethiopia in 1935 and his alliance with Nazi Germany in the following year isolated Italy from the democracies and destroyed any hope of forging an alliance between Communists, Fascists, and other conservatives in Italy, France, the United States, and Britain against liberalism and usury, as Pound had quixotically hoped to do. The new society that Pound had hoped to bring about would have been right-wing, elitist, and antidemocratic, but there is no reason to believe that it would have been racist, bellicose, and vicious on the model of Nazi Europe.

Like Pound, Mussolini had also imagined the possibility of an alliance with Britain, France, and the United States, but in the end threw in his lot with Hitler, thereby transforming himself from a bellicose Italian dictator into a Nazi toady. The transformation was complete by 1936, by which date Pound had found his own route to admiration of Hitler's Nazism. Unlike Mussolini, however, Pound continued to suppose that there was a constituency in the United States to which he could appeal. His 1939 visit was posited on such a belief, as were his radio broadcasts. He honestly believed that he was the true American patriot and Roosevelt the traitor— a view shared by many right-wing Americans until Pearl Harbor.

Clearly Pound was a babe in the woods in his engagement with economics and politics. He imagined that sound aesthetic perceptions could be mapped straightforwardly onto the practical world of politics and economics. Such a belief has a long provenance in literary culture. Certainly, Pound's early mentor, William Butler Yeats, held such a view and derived it explicitly from Blake and Shelley. Yeats, however, had the wisdom to couch his political advice in the elaborate fiction of *A Vision*. Had Pound isolated his beliefs and predictions in *The Cantos* he would have escaped much grief. Instead, from 1931 to 1945 his poetry took a back seat to his activities as an economic reformer and propagandist for the corporate state.

Pound's story is a cautionary tale. A major factor contributing to his embitterment and hatred was his belief that all difficulties must yield to bold, simple solutions. Wyndham Lewis's characterization of him in *Time and Western Man* (1927) as a "revolutionary simpleton" seems to have been right on the mark. In Social Credit economics he had got hold of a half-truth, but his epistemology committed him to a holism that does not allow for half-truths. Incapable—despite heroic efforts—of untangling the

Gordian knot of economic theory, Pound chose the Alexandrian solution of the simple stroke of the sword—all the while imagining himself an opponent of violence. Even in 1953, on reading Hitler's *Table Talk*, he was still capable of seeing Hitler and Mussolini as victims—an opinion he confided to Olivia Rossetti Agresti. We can perhaps excuse Pound his intellectual and moral failure, but we ought not to deny or obscure it. There is too much at stake to give artists a license to preach vicious nonsense just because they are a precious adornment to society. All that can be said of a positive nature of Pound's political involvement is that he clung to his convictions—false as they were—and took his punishment like a man.

Well-intentioned though he was, overweening self-confidence led Pound into error and sin. (I can think of no more appropriate term for his moral failure.) Perhaps Dante would have been merciful enough to place him in purgatory rather than hell, perhaps in the first Terrace of Love Perverted, which is reserved for the Wrathful. I do not think Pound is entitled to place himself in the third heaven of Venus, below the spirits of divine judgment, or Thrones (*Paradiso* 9.61–63), as he perhaps intended when he chose the title *Thrones* for the last section of *The Cantos*.

CHAPTER 1

Banking and Social Credit

T. S. Eliot's conversion to Anglicanism has long been perceived as a watershed in his literary career. His announcement that he was classicist in art, royalist in politics, and Anglican in religion was not only a dramatic event at the time, but academic opinion has persisted in dividing his poetic canon on both expressive and thematic grounds at "Ash Wednesday," his first overtly Anglican poem. Even Lyndall Gordon's demonstration that Eliot was, from his youth, a religious sensibility in search of an acceptable creed has not displaced his religious conversion from its defining spot on the curve of his literary career.

No such neat bifurcation is to be found in the academic formulation of Ezra Pound's literary career. On the contrary, the thrust of Pound criticism has been to articulate a continuity of expressive features and thematic concerns even though at first glance his career appears to run off in several directions at once. It is not my intention to deny the continuities perceived by Hugh Kenner and the mainstream of Pound commentary that descends from him. I have, myself, argued elsewhere for such continuities. Nonetheless, the effort to discover coherence in an apparent crazy quilt of verse styles, critical principles, crankish economic theories, and distasteful political affiliations has made it difficult to perceive the genesis and development of any of these components of Pound's career. In particular, his economic and political opinions have not been properly dated, nor has the suddenness of his radicalization been appreciated. Pound *had* a conversion experience—in 1919—but it was ideological, not religious.

Any consideration of the shape of Pound's literary career must, of course, begin with the inescapable and seemingly incommensurable datum of his lifework, *The Cantos*. Begun in 1915, *The Cantos* absorbed virtually all of Pound's original composition of poetry from 1920 until his death in 1972. Never finished, the poem was, however, never abandoned. Pound intended it to be the epic of the Modern Age, a poem worthy to take its place alongside Dante's *Commedia* and Virgil's *Aeneid*, if not the Homeric epics.

Pound believed that the epic genre is, at its heart, ideological in the sense that it must offer answers to questions about the beliefs of men and women, their institutions, and their collective behavior. All of the epics of the past, he thought, had expressed some widely held belief, ideology, or *paideuma*, as he liked to call it, adopting the German version of the Greek *paideia* from the German anthropologist Leo Frobenius. The Homeric epics express or instantiate the Greek *paideia;* Virgil's *Aeneid* expresses the Roman or Augustan Imperium; Spenser's *Faerie Queene* manifestly expresses the English Reformation; and Milton's *Paradise Lost* is arguably an expression of the failure of the Puritan revolution to establish God's kingdom on earth. In 1915 the dominant ideology in the English-speaking world was the matrix of democratic liberalism, post-Christian utilitarian morality, and free enterprise economics. It was the ideology in which Pound—like most Americans and Britons—had grown up. But World War I shook confidence in that faith. The interwar period, as we now call it, seemed to be a time for elegy, jeremiad, or mockery, not a time for epic. *The Waste Land, Women in Love, Ulysses, The Great Gatsby,* and Yeats's late poetry were the sorts of works that bespoke the spirit immediately following the war. It was not a time for the celebration or proclamation of a *paideia* or *Weltanschauung*. Or if it was, it could only be of some new, not yet realized *paideia*.

The Russian Revolution provided Marxists with a *paideia* and an optimistic outlook. But English literature had no Berthold Brecht or Sergei Eisenstein, though there were many English Marxist writers of the interwar years. Pound and his cohort group were not pulled in that direction, though he did try to co-opt Marxists for his own vision of the future. Even Continental artists born in the 1880s were not much drawn to Marxism, though the painters Pablo Picasso (b. 1881) and Diego Rivera (b. 1886) are prominent exceptions. Brecht and Eisenstein were both born in 1898, Sartre in 1905, and Auden in 1907. These younger men came to maturity during or immediately after the 1914–18 conflict that changed Europe forever and saw Marxism as the natural alternative to the old regime. But Pound's cohort group was nearly thirty in 1914. Imagining itself the herald of a new age, it was confronted with the full force of the disillusioning "shock of modernity" that World War I represented and was permanently scarred by the experience.

A major cultural consequence of the war was profound disillusionment with the hope of a new age that had infused nineteenth-century America and Europe and was continued in the prewar period by Filippo Marinetti's futurism. This general cultural malaise, however, did not divert Pound from his overweening literary ambition. It may be that he was insulated against the general despondency by the prevailing artistic doctrine of the time, *ars victrix,* which considered the artist a person set apart, an "unacknowledged legislator" who saw clearly where others were muddled, blind, or hypocritical. In such a view, the confused states of people's minds was a challenge and an opportunity for the poet to show the way. Although no one knew what the Modern Age was, or would be, they *would* know when Pound finished his epic. That this was his attitude is—somewhat facetiously—corroborated by an anecdote Pound recounted to Donald Hall in a 1960 interview. A little boy is engaged in drawing a picture of God. In response to an adult's observation that no one knows what God looks like, Johnny replies: "They will when I get through" (Hall 241). Pound recounted this anecdote to characterize his own confidence as an epic poet.

There is another probable reason for Pound's persistence in his epic ambition in the face of a general pessimism—such as that expressed by Spengler in *The Decline of the West* or Yeats in *A Vision.* In addition to the exalted, Shelleyan sense of the artist's role and capacity that Pound held, he also believed that he had discovered a means to save Western civilization from the malaise into which it had sunk. That means was economic reform along the lines laid out by Douglas and Orage, which they called Social Credit. As Spenser sang the birth of the Elizabethan *paideia* and Milton the loss of a Puritan paradise on earth, so Pound would sing the birth of a Social Credit paradise on earth. As it turned out, he picked a particular expression of that earthly paradise, Fascist Italy, which was not Social Credit, was very unlike an earthly paradise, and proved to be a dead end.

Pound began composition of his epic in the second year of the war, but for a good many years he was not at all sure what shape and direction it should take (see Surette *Light*). Indeed, he did not publish any section of it—as opposed to individual cantos or small groups of cantos—for ten years after he began. Even then, he entitled the first installment *A Draft of XVI Cantos* (1925), suggesting that he had still not resolved the problems of writing a modern epic. He continued to publish such parts of the poem—which he began to call "sections"—every few years until in 1941 he had published 71 cantos. In the end, the poem attained the length of 109 cantos before he (or his publishers) terminated it with *Drafts and Fragments* in 1968. The poem simply kept on going because he could find no way of concluding it. In his seventy-seventh year—fifty-three years after beginning his epic—Pound did not know what the Modern Age would or should look like, though he had believed that he had known for a time.

The tenor of my remarks so far would suggest that Pound was a kind of literary Don Quixote attempting to act out the fantasies of nineteenth-century utopian dreamers like Coleridge and Shelley. Indeed, the analogy is not a bad one. It can serve to shape the sharply divergent response that Pound and his poetry prompt. Like Don Quixote, he was prepared to do real harm in the real world in pursuit of his ideals, and like him— though less innocently—he chose his ideals unwisely. Both the real and the fictional man selflessly pursued an ideal of conduct to which most people pay only lip service. In Pound's case that ideal was the artist as hero. It would not be too much to say that Pound's career debunks the ideal of the artist as hero as effectively as Cervantes's great parody debunked the chivalric ideal.

If we are to understand the strange, quixotic career of Ezra Pound, it is not enough to analyze his character and intellect, we must also understand the intellectual climate in which he formulated his epic, the same climate in which one of the most evil of all ideological movements was born— fascism/Nazism. Pound scholars now acknowledge—though with much special pleading—that Pound attached himself to Italian fascism in the early thirties and persisted in that attachment for the rest of his life. When Pound came to London in the autumn of 1908, shortly before his twenty-third birthday, such developments were still unimagined. In hindsight we can perceive their genesis in the speculation of such authors as Julien Sorel. Sorel's infamous 1908 celebration of violence, *Reflections on Violence,* was translated by T. E. Hulme, a fellow Imagist, and published in 1915. Pound, however, seems not to have been interested, since the only mention of him I have found is dismissive ("Le Major C. H. Douglas").

Fascism is Mussolini's label for his own party, which was initially no more than his personal political vehicle. *Fascio* is an innocent Italian word meaning *bundle* or *group,* and—before Mussolini adopted it for his movement— was used for any association, such as a club. (It was only later that Fascist ideologues stressed the connection with the Roman *fasces,* a bundle of sticks symbolizing the power to inflict corporal punishment.) However, I use the term in its now standard general sense to include the right-wing totalitarian regimes of Europe modeled on Mussolini's. Sir Oswald Mosley, for example, called his own party the British Union of Fascists. Hitler's party was called the National Socialist or Nazi party, but I include it as well as Franco's party under the label *fascism*.

On the other hand, I restrict *fascist* to those European regimes of the 1920s, 1930s, and 1940s and would not extend it to include all nonsocialist authoritarian regimes before and after World War II, as some current writers do. Nor would I consider the Japanese regime of the same period to be fascist even though it was clearly authoritarian and allied itself with the Axis. Japan was a military oligarchy under a compliant emperor, not unlike the Kaiser's Germany of World War I. In any case, the Japanese were never obliged to rationalize a departure from liberal democracy or to articulate an alternative to communism. And both of these negative necessities go a long way to account for the ideological component of fascism in its historical sense.

Because of the horrors of Nazism, *fascism* has become a synonym for *monstrosity*. Quite naturally, scholars in history, political science, and philosophy have not devoted much attention to exploring the cognitive content of fascism; instead they have described it by its most offensive features: racism, bellicose nationalism, and tyranny. If we remain blind or indifferent to its other features, we are condemned to suppose that all its adherents were attracted to its offensive traits, and no doubt that is true for some. But fascism did not achieve its political success exclusively through bullying and terrorist tactics, nor did it appeal only to bullies and sadists.

Thanks in large part to the Israeli scholar Zeev Sternhell, fascism has begun to receive serious scholarly attention that is neither an apologetics nor a demonization of the movement. His project is to place fascism within European political and cultural history. He believes that "the marginalization of fascism relieves those that deal with it of the necessity of relating to the broad cultural context, which was its true intellectual seedbed." Sternhell's view is that fascism expressed the "opposition to optimism, universalism, and humanism [which] developed into a general struggle that affected all areas of intellectual activity." For him, fascism was the political expression of the effort "to rescue Europe from the heritage of the Enlightenment," a heritage characterized by "rationalism and humanism" (Sternhell 249–50). In this view fascism can be seen as a political expression of cultural and political values that have a long history in Europe and not just of hooliganism, racism, and bellicosity, as it is commonly perceived.

Of course, to argue that the fascist movement grew out of authentic European social, political, and religious roots is not to say that it remained faithful to those roots. However, it does permit one to suggest that the undeniable criminality and brutality of the German Nazi regime and its puppets, which ultimately included Mussolini's Italy, was not an authentic expression of those roots. The standard view—that fascism is defined by nationalism, antimodernism, the *Führer Prinzip*, and the totalitarian state—is not wrong, but rather incomplete or insufficiently specific. In particular, it has to be admitted that Leninism and Stalinism are also characterized by the absolute dominance of a great leader—even to the cult of personality—and totalitarianism, that is, the suppression of individual liberties in the name of the collectivity, embodied in the party and the leader. This leaves nationalism and antimodernism as the only distinguishing marks of fascism. But these are not new features of the European political landscape. Nationalism goes back at least to 1789, and antimodernism has roughly the same birth date—if I can be permitted such a label for Burkean Toryism.

The point I want to make is that if we are to avoid demonizing those who embraced fascism—a very large proportion of the population of Europe from the straits of Gibraltar to the Baltic Sea—we must make the imaginative effort to see what fascism looked like from the other side of World War II and the Holocaust. Certainly the core of Fascist parties everywhere were brutal young men licensed to beat and even kill those they disliked or opposed. But most—even bourgeois Jews, who were amongst the targets of such violence—thought such lawless brutality would soon be suppressed by fascist governments once consolidated in power (see Rubinstein 19–25). Many—perhaps most—supporters of Mussolini and Hitler feared communism more than they welcomed tyranny. They saw communism as a threat to the status quo, a division of property and wealth that favored large, influential segments of the population. Even the working classes, who did not benefit from the status quo, contained many who abhorred communism as atheistic and internationalistic. World War I had shown the fragility of Marxist internationalism among the working classes of the combatants, almost all of whom remained loyal to their *patria* (see Schorske). The history of fascism and Nazism confronts the cultural historian with the phenomenon of the most "advanced" and "civilized" societies in the world spiraling downward into a brutality that arguably exceeds that of any previous society. The overwhelming question is, How could such a thing happen? It is clearly ludicrous to suppose that only depraved individuals participated in, approved, or silently endorsed the brutalities of the period. It would be too much to argue that Pound's case can be taken as paradigmatic for those who embraced fascism and Nazism, but his descent from political conservatism and fashionable aesthetic-pagan religiosity into raging antiliberalism, antidemocracy, and anti-Semitism reflects—though in an exaggerated form—a path many of his contemporaries in Europe traversed or at least entered upon.

Sternhell's assessment fits Pound and his Social Credit friends almost perfectly. At least it does if one accepts the view of Pound's cultural project that Demetres Tryphonopoulos, Akiko Miyake, myself, and others have articulated. In this view Pound is not avant-garde in the sense that he himself pretended and that has been accepted for the most part by the Pound industry. Pound is not an adherent of Enlightenment progressivism, rejecting the past and looking to a perfected future, as he is often portrayed. Although he presents himself as avant-garde, an innovator in art, and a believer in technological progress, he is better understood as an evangelist of archaism than as a Futurist. His slogan, "make it new," should not be interpreted to mean "throw away the old and adopt the new," but rather—and quite literally—to "pick up the old, repair, refurbish, and reuse it." His well-documented hostility toward the past is directed only toward the immediate past—the nineteenth century and its alleged materialism. Like the fascist movement as understood by Sternhell, Pound saw the nineteenth century as the age of commerce, exploitation, and war, of positivist skepticism, of anti-aesthetic, anti-imaginative, and anti-erotic suburban bourgeois culture. In this respect he belongs to the broad cultural movement of which fascism and Nazism were late and pathological expressions.

One last cavil is perhaps worth making. All fascist regimes of the period were authoritarian, but not all authoritarian regimes were fascist; Primo de Rivera's Spain, Pilsudski's Poland, and Stalin's Russia were nonfascist authoritarian regimes. Though the first two might be considered protofascist, Stalinist Russia certainly cannot. It does not contribute to our understanding of fascism to lump together Mussolini, Genghis Khan, and the Ayatollah Khomeini as fascists just because they were all authoritarian and two of them were anticommunist. Though it is inappropriate to equate tyranny with fascism, that is not to deny that all historical instances of fascism were tyrannical and authoritarian or that fascism as an ideology justifies and institutionalizes tyranny in the *Führer Prinzip*. Fascist ideology—ragtag and ad hoc as it was—represented tyranny as the price of saving European civilization from the threat of modernity, that is, secularism, materialism, technology, and egalitarianism. Though fascism's claim to be the savior of European civilization is patently grotesque to any observer today, its grotesquerie was not so obvious in 1933, though its brutal methods caused many to shun it.

Our own perception of fascism and Nazism as self-evidently evil is a historical perspective that no one could possibly have had in the 1930s.

Sternhell's characterization of the conservative Right's reaction to Germany's conquest of France in 1940 can help us to gain some historical perspective and imagine how fascism could have been mistaken for a benign movement:

> In the view of the people who came to power in the summer of 1940, France had been overcome not by the most perfect and effective war machine ever known in military history, but by a political culture that sprang out of the soil of the eighteenth century. The materialism and egoism underlying liberalism and socialism, the principle of equality introduced by the revolution—these had been roundly defeated by a political culture based on the organic conception of society and its definite priority with regard to the individual. The victorious ideology refused to define society as a collection of individuals, regarded only blood relationships as natural to human beings, and denied the validity of relationships deriving from the will and decisions of the individual. (256)

Pound's cultural posture was, from the beginning, friendly to most of this, though not to the priority of blood relationships or to the insignificance of the will and the individual. He, too, looked forward to the fall of France in an April 1940 letter to Odon Por: "When did you say France wd/ throw in her hand? I fergit whether you counted on our spending the Fourth of July in Paris: or whether the burning of the Brite=yittisch Embassy is due for le QUATORZE JUILLET of this year" (22 Apr. 1940, Pound Papers). France did capitulate on 22 June, so they could have celebrated Independence Day in German-occupied Paris—but they did not.

No one can explain how so many intelligent and otherwise decent men and women could have been led to follow Hitler and Mussolini despite the unspeakable crimes against humanity committed at their instigation. But we should not pretend that only the morally depraved or mentally challenged embraced fascism. We have a duty to seek to understand how entire nations could succumb to such moral and intellectual failure. One route toward such an understanding is to trace the path of an individual into the heart of darkness. In Pound's case we have not only an extraordinary individual but also one who copiously articulated his views in poetry, cultural analysis, journalism, and private correspondence. The poetry will not receive much attention in these pages, for it is the final, richest—and therefore most ambiguous—product of Pound's interaction with his times.

When Pound arrived in London in 1908, he was narrowly focused on aesthetic matters. He quickly established an impressive network of contacts in the literary world. He became an intimate friend of the elder writers William Butler Yeats—at that time the preeminent poet writing in English—and Ford Madox Ford and was well known amongst the English writers of his own generation. His most fateful encounter, at least for this story, was with A. R. Orage, editor of a weekly journal of the arts, the *New Age*. Orage and his friend Holbrook Jackson had taken over the journal in 1907 with financial assistance from wealthy Fabians, among them George Bernard Shaw and the Theosophist Lewis Wallace. However, the journal was never an organ of Fabian or Theosophical opinion. It aspired to be open to all stripes of political and cultural opinion, but tended to espouse radical movements. It was not obscure. Frequent contributors included Shaw, H. G. Wells, Arnold Bennet, G. K. Chesterton, Hilaire Belloc, T. E. Hulme, Herbert Read, Katherine Mansfield, and Edwin Muir as well as Ezra Pound.

The *New Age* paid for contributions. Pound had no income except from his literary work and small sums from his parents. As a consequence, between 30 November 1911 and 13 January 1921 he contributed some 260 articles, poems, and letters. He wrote weekly reviews of painting using the name B. H. Dias and of music as William Atheling. Clearly the *New Age* was a very large part of Pound's life during those ten years, years that include World War I and the immediate postwar period. It was in these years that he reformed himself. He arrived in London as a late symbolist singer of the erotic sublime and left as an Imagist satirist of the modern world. It was also in this period that he began his epic poem, though it did not take its definitive shape until he had moved to Rapallo, Italy.

The *New Age* was the crossroads for the two dominant—and mutually hostile—radical ideological postures of prewar Britain. On the Left were the Fabians, democratic socialists whose political arm reached into the Labour party. They drew their inspiration primarily from the Utilitarians, but joined the collectivist propensities of socialist thinkers such as Proudhon and Marx to that resolutely individualistic doctrine. Like other socialists, they were forward-looking, placing their faith in technological progress as a cure for most social ills. The political Right, of course, distrusted technology and tended to look to the Middle Ages for their social and economic models. The Right was a less cohesive group. Its intellectual leaders were G. K. Chesterton and Hilaire Belloc, who drew their inspiration from Thomas Carlyle, John Ruskin, and—to a lesser extent— William Morris. They were "reactionary" or backward-looking in their social and political thinking, as opposed to the Fabians and most Marxists. Belloc and Chesterton were vigorous Catholics. The Fabians were, on the whole, militant atheists. There were few Marxists among British socialists. Though William Morris as a self-declared Communist was an exception, he was co-opted both by conservative reformers like Chesterton and Belloc and by Fabians (see Weinroth).

The issue between the two radical camps was put very succinctly—and very influentially—by Hilaire Belloc in his 1912 book, *The Servile State*. There were, he wrote, only three possible solutions to the inherent instability of free enterprise capitalism:

a) Collectivism, or the placing of the means of production in the hands of the political officers of the community.

b) Property, or the re-establishment of a Distributive State in which the mass of citizens should severally own the means of production.

c) Slavery or a Servile State in which those who do not own the means of production shall be legally compelled to work for those who do, and shall receive in exchange a security of livelihood. (5–6)

Belloc further argued that socialism (his collectivism) would eventually produce a condition of slavery equivalent to the servile state of free enterprise liberalism. He painted a portrait of the apprehended servile state from which George Orwell could have drawn much of *1984*—though, of course, by that time Orwell had the Communist Soviet Union and fascist regimes as models of totalitarian states as well as Yevgeny Zamyatin's dystopic novel *We*.

The Servile State was unquestionably the most successful polemic ever produced by the British radical Right. Its power rested upon Belloc's appeal to the common ground of all colors of British political opinion—the belief in the priority of individual liberty over all other political rights. British socialists have always been embarrassed by the necessity to relegate this Lockean principle to a secondary position behind the guarantee of economic liberty to all through collective action and the agency of the state. The "conservatism" of the radical Right consisted in its followers' passionate adherence to the priority of individual rights over collective rights—a passion they shared with liberals *and* anarchists. But unlike adherents of those ideologies, Belloc and the radical Right also wished to protect spiritual values. Belloc and Chesterton were militant Catholics, but Christians generally were drawn to the radical Right; so, too, were Theosophists, spiritualists, and those like Pound who believed that art expressed spiritual values. Both the radical Right and liberals—unlike anarchists, syndicalists, and Marxists—wished to preserve the social order. But whereas liberals were committed to individual rights and enlightened self-interest, those on the radical Right stressed collective rights and sought to achieve "rule by the enlightened." Thus it can legitimately be charged with elitism—or at least of paternalism. Like Nietzsche, those on the radical Right were overtly hostile to popular democracy, which they saw as the rule of the average over the exceptional.

Orage and the *New Age* circle—George Russell, William Penty, T. E. Hulme, and Pound—could not swallow the Catholicism and Medievalism of Belloc and Chesterton, but they agreed with their assessment and analysis of the outstanding social and economic issues, including the sacrosanct nature of individual rights. As a Theosophist and later as a follower of G. I. Gurdjieff, Orage valued the spiritual and abhorred the atheism of the socialists as much as the Catholics did. The *New Age* crowd thought that there must be some middle ground between the stifling consequences for intellectual, artistic, and social liberty of collectivism and the cruelly wasteful misallocation of resources within capitalist free enterprise and liberal states.

The *New Age* gang also agreed with the radical Right's Ruskinian perception that the arts were always one of the first casualties of the free enterprise economic order. Because he earned his living as a poet and literary journalist, Pound had long been sensitive to this aspect of political economy. It was, he passionately believed, intolerable that artists should have to depend upon the sale of their wares in a market economy. *Hugh Selwyn Mauberley* contains perhaps his most eloquent, but by no means his first, expression of this view:

> The age demanded an image
> Of its accelerated grimace
> Something for the modern stage,
> Not, at any rate, an Attic grace:

> Not, not certainly, the obscure reveries
> Of the inward gaze;
> Better mendacities
> Than the classics in paraphrase!

> The "Age demanded" chiefly a mould in plaster,
> Made with no loss of time,
> A prose kinema, not, not assuredly, alabaster
> Of the "sculpture" of rhyme.
>
> (*Personae* 188)

Shaw and Wells, as eminently successful writers in a market economy, were less sensitive to such arguments.

The principle thrust of Ruskin's economic criticism had been that the free enterprise economy, organized by the free market rather than by regulation, produced a large and harmful misallocation of resources:

there are two kinds of true production, always going on in an active State: one of seed, and of food; or production for the Ground, and for the Mouth; both of which are by covetous persons thought to be production only for the granary; whereas the function of the granary is but intermediate and conservative, fulfilled in distribution; else it ends in nothing but mildew, and nourishment of rats and worms. And since production for the Ground is only useful with future hope of harvest, all *essential* production is for the Mouth; and it is finally measured by the Mouth; hence, as I said above, consumption is the crown of production; and the wealth of a nation is only to be estimated by what it consumes. (*Unto This Last* 104; Ruskin's emphasis)

Production for the ground is what economists call "investment." Within classical economics, the wealth of a nation is a function of the level of investment. Given that investment must be drawn from savings—that is, from what is left over after distribution and consumption—the wealth of a nation is a function of the excess of production over consumption. On these grounds the aristocratic virtue of magnanimity becomes the vice of wastefulness, and bourgeois "meanness" becomes the virtue of thrift. The thrifty have no money to spare for the arts and precious little for the poor, the sick, or those otherwise unproductive. This apparent stinginess is— in the view of orthodox scarcity economics—prudent and wise and will in the long run benefit the poor as well as the wealthy, for the invested savings will create greater aggregate wealth. Charitable assistance given to the poor, in contrast, would be immediately squandered on food, shelter, and clothing—or, worse, on debauchery.

The special status ascribed to savings derives from Adam Smith, who first made the point that savings created wealth. He showed that savings are consumed just as surely as largesse, and nearly as quickly, but largesse is consumed by the unproductive aristocracy and their servants, whereas savings are consumed by productive bourgeois merchants and entrepreneurs: "That portion of his revenue which a rich man annually spends is in most cases consumed by idle guests and menial servants, who leave nothing behind them in return for their consumption. That portion which he annually saves, as for the sake of the profit is immediately employed as capital, is consumed in the same manner, and nearly in the same time too, but by a different set of people, by laborers, manufacturers, and artificers, who reproduce with a profit the value of their annual consumption" (438). This point is crucial for the whole debate about scarcity and plenty. Ruskin and all of the so-called "underconsumptionist" critics of laissez-faire economics foundered on it.

Ruskin's first series of economic articles, entitled *Unto This Last,* was published in *Cornhill Magazine* in 1860, seven years before *Das Kapital* (though a dozen years after the *Communist Manifesto*). The articles caused an immediate outcry, and the editor was forced to ask Ruskin to discontinue them. Ruskin's argument that the determining variable in an economic formula should be consumption rather than savings offended against the principle of equilibrium, crudely sketched by Adam Smith in the paragraph above. The consequence of Ruskin's starting point was that cheap and rapid production (which minimizes consumption) is not desirable. Instead high-cost production—as with labor-intensive craft techniques—should be fostered on the grounds that it would distribute more purchasing power amongst the masses, thus encouraging consumption *and* stimulating the production to meet such "effective demand"—as it later came to be called.

The underconsumptionist argument, plausible as it seems, is open to the objection that machine production, by producing more with less labor, increases the aggregate wealth of the nation. Hence, the nation as a whole benefits, and the greater wealth must eventually improve the average lot of its people. Marx's answer to this objection was that the capitalist seized most or all of this "dividend," or "surplus value" as he called it. Ruskin's answer was less technical, but more appealing to an aesthetic temperament. Observing the squalor and shoddy merchandise of industrial England, Ruskin asserted that much of this new "wealth" was in fact undesirable and coined the term *illth* for it.

Ruskin's arguments had no impact on economic thought in Britain or elsewhere, but his impassioned plea against the widespread poverty and misery of the British proletariat was not without consequences. The English Arts and Crafts movement derived directly from his economic writing, and the Co-operative movement did so more indirectly. In addition, the radical Right drew political and social conclusions from his economic perceptions. Ruskin's influence has been so pervasive and varied that such a summary does not begin to do it justice. He is frequently cited by radicals of both the Left and the Right, each of whom took from his extensive writings what they wanted. The point to be borne in mind is that although he profoundly influenced economic and political thinking in Britain, his influence remained largely outside professional economics and political science.

Ruskin's strongest appeal—at least within the *New Age* circle—was that he provided an economic justification for expenditure on the arts. In a Ruskinian analysis, the commission and purchase of works of art are a form of consumption and therefore an addition to the wealth of the nation. His economic model, had it been fully worked out, would have promoted the slow and costly modes of production appropriate to the fine arts rather than the rapid and cheap modes of production required by Smithian laissez-faire economics. Long before he encountered Douglas's Social Credit theories, Pound was expressing Ruskinian sentiments: "I don't care whether or no the capitalist system decays, but for the good brothers [socialists] who hope that it is decaying, I can only say 'be of good cheer.' One of the finest symptoms of its rottenness is that the care of the arts has been given over to the poor, and to the just-above-poor. And the balance of power rests with the arts" ("On the Imbecility of the Rich" 389–90).

Twenty-three years later, Pound retained this Ruskinian view of the arts and economics, but had changed his focus to the evil of interest charges on loans (usury):

> With usura hath no man a house of good stone
> each block cut smooth and well fitting
> that design might cover their face,
> with usura
> hath no man a painted paradise on his church wall
> *harpes et luthes*
> or where virgin receiveth message
> and halo projects from incision.
>
> (canto 45/229)

Pound's point is that we can longer afford these fine things even though the modern industrial world is far richer than the medieval craft world, which *could* afford them. When he found out why the twentieth century had less money for the arts than the fifteenth, then he would have the analytical key that would make it possible to write an epic of the Modern Age. The key was "underconsumption," and Pound found it under his feet in the pages of the *New Age*, which launched Social Credit during World War I.

Although Pound took no direct part in the war, he repeatedly took his compatriots to task for their tardiness in joining in (see "American Chaos" 449, 471; and "What America Has to Live Down" [22 Aug. 1918]: 266–67, [27 Aug. 1918]: 281–82). He even attempted to enlist, but was thirty-two years old in 1917 (when the United States entered the war) and not wanted by the military. However, once the war was safely won and the liberal democracies settled back once more into their apparently natural state of widespread poverty and unemployment, a powerful revulsion against the war and its pointless massacre of young men set in. Pound registered this revulsion with uncharacteristic lucidity and elegance in *Hugh Selwyn Mauberley* 4 (1919):

Died some, pro patria,
> non "dulce" non "et decor" . . .
walked eye-deep in hell
believing in old men's lies, then unbelieving
came home, home to a lie,
home to many deceits,
home to old lies and new infamy;
usury age-old and age-thick
and liars in public places.

Daring as never before, wastage as never before.
Young blood and high blood,
fair cheeks, and fine bodies;

fortitude as never before

frankness as never before
disillusions as never told in the old days,
hysterias, trench confessions,
laughter out of dead bellies.
> (*Personae* 187–88)

Similar sentiments can be found in many other documents of the period. In 1914 Wells had trumpeted that this war was the war to end wars, and Woodrow Wilson told his reluctant countrymen that it would make the world safe for democracy. But even though Britain and France won, their victory was pyhrric. Few came through it with their faith in the meliorist doctrine of liberal capitalism intact. Nothing had been saved; many had died:

There died a myriad,
And of the best, among them,
For an old bitch gone in the teeth,
For a botched civilization,

Charm, smiling at the good mouth,
Quick eyes gone under earth's lid,

For two gross of broken statues,
For a few thousand battered books.
> (*Personae* 188)

Only two years before he wrote these lines Pound had offered the following sentiments to his compatriots, on the occasion of the American entry into the war: "England is our noble ally, she has saved civilization (along with France, Italy, Portugal, Japan, Serbia, Montenegro, Belgium). She has been perhaps more splendid, in so far as she could have kept out.

So could we have kept out, to the eternal loss of our position, as England to the ultimate loss of her Empire" ("What America Has to Live Down," 22 Aug. 1918, 267). The point to be taken from this account is that from his arrival in England through to the immediate postwar period, Pound was conventional in his political and economic opinions. He was far less radical than the *New Age* itself. According to his own testimony he took no notice of the guild socialist movement launched in the *New Age* in 1912, which carried on a vigorous existence until it finally fizzled out, like so much else, in the face of the war. It was the arrival of Douglas that changed everything:

> The actual battle with ignorance, in the acute phase wherein I shared, began with Douglas's arrival in Cursitor Street. The earlier Guild Social-ism, and all other political or social theory had lain outside my view. (This statement is neither boast nor apology.) I take it I was present at some of the earliest talks between the two leaders. At any rate my economic study dates from their union, and their fight for its place in public knowledge. ("He Pulled His Weight" in *Ezra Pound's Poetry and Prose* 6:213–14)

Douglas was an industrial engineer and quite innocent of any training in economics or journalism. But while reorganizing the Royal Aircraft Works at Farnborough, he claims to have made a startling discovery. He found that the wages, salaries, dividends, and retained profit of the factory added up to a smaller sum than the aggregate price of the goods it produced—the aircraft. From this observation he drew the conclusion that it would be impossible for the workers, managers, and owners of any factory to purchase the product of that factory with their collective incomes. If this were true, there would be a chronic, structural shortfall of purchasing power in the economy. Pound incorporated this *aperçu* into canto 38 (published in 1933 in Orage's new journal, the *New English Weekly*):

> A factory
> has also another aspect, which we call the financial aspect
> It gives people the power to buy (wages, dividends
> which are power to buy) but it is also the cause of prices
> or values, financial, I mean financial values
> It pays workers, and pays *for* material.
> What it pays in wages and dividends
> stays fluid, as power to buy, and this power is less,
> per forza, damn blast your intellex, is less
> than the total payments made by the factory
> (as wages, dividends AND payments for raw material,
> bank charges, etcetera)
> and all, that is the whole, that is the total

of these is added into the total of prices
caused by that factory, any damn factory
and there is and must be therefore a clog
and the power to purchase can never
(under the present system) catch up with
prices at large.

(canto 38/190)

Pound's rhetorical heat reflects the frustration of a man unable to convince others of the truth of a self-evident observation. Pound, like Douglas an economic naïf, assumed that people would automatically be converted to his economic analysis once it had been clearly explained to them. As Douglas put it: "I had the idea that I had got hold of some specific technical information and I had only to get it accepted; I had the idea that I was like a clever little boy and that I had only to run to father and he would be very pleased about it" (Macpherson 120).

Douglas did please one man—A. R. Orage. Douglas came to the *New Age* in 1918 and spent many months discussing his theories in the journal's Cursitor Street office and the ABC Restaurant nearby. Pound was a fascinated participant in these discussions. He recalled them in his memorial of Orage: "Those of us who saw the Major's point in the first weeks of his first declarations find it rather difficult to unsee it, or to put ourselves in the role of non-perceivers" (*Impact* 161).

Out of these discussions was born Social Credit, a movement based on Douglas's technical explanation of the phenomenon of underconsumption, for which Ruskin had been unable to account. As with Ruskin, Douglas's analysis was designed to serve conservative social and political goals. In effect, Social Credit was a technologized version of Belloc's distributism (which descended directly from Ruskin). Social Credit placed its emphasis on an alleged structural flaw in the bookkeeping of industrial-commercial economies, rather than on the production of useless or harmful consumables, as Ruskin and the distributists had done, or on the capitalist's profit, as Marx had done.

The heart of Social Credit theory is the A + B theorem. In a nutshell, the theorem holds that aggregate payments to individuals in wages, salaries, and dividends (A) plus aggregate costs of materials, bank charges, royalties, and taxes (B) produce aggregate price (P). Obviously P will always be larger than A, since it must include B. The theorem shows that the income of all citizens (the A figure) will be insufficiently large to buy the produce of the nation—a classic underconsumptionist argument (Douglas, *Economic Democracy* 28–29). There are many difficulties with the theorem. Most glaringly, it is simply an application of double-entry bookkeeping in a case where it is inappropriate. It is entirely inadequate to categorize aggregate transactions as either revenues or disbursements, since every disbursement is a revenue for some other economic agent, and vice versa. But it had the virtue of providing a simple and comprehensible account of the undeniable fact of endemic underconsumption.

Though it is common to deride Social Credit economics as foolish as well as erroneous, its failures were not as obvious as all that. It was apparent to everyone—even economists—that industrial economies suffered from recurrent collapses of purchasing power called "the business cycle." Britain and Germany experienced a down swing in the cycle immediately after World War I, giving economic heretics an eager audience, which evaporated when prosperity returned. Interest revived only with the worldwide depression of the thirties. Douglas's great merit for the noneconomist seeking an explanation of the business cycle was that the A + B theorem led to a simple and plausible explanation for the shortfall. Douglas believed that interest charges caused the shortfall in purchasing power more than anything else.

Douglas's belief does not follow obviously from his own analysis, however, since taxes are an equally plausible villain. There were plausible reasons for singling out interest charges based on the peculiarity of paper money. From Roman times, coinage has been the prerogative of the state—usually of the Crown. The Crown or state received a significant revenue, called "seigniorage," from the coining of the precious metals and could also expand the money supply somewhat by debasing the coinage—reducing its weight below its nominal weight or reducing fineness. Debasing the coinage was a hidden tax as well as an expansion of the money supply. It was universally condemned by moralists throughout the period when money and precious metals were synonymous. However, debasement of the coinage was probably unavoidable because the European economy gradually outgrew the supply of precious metals—until the discovery of Aztec gold.

In contrast to coins, paper money began as bank notes, paper issued by private banks and not state currency. For a century or so after their introduction, bank notes were not regarded as money, but as certificates for "real money"—gold or silver. Until very recently the paper money of most countries bore the inscription, "Will pay to the bearer on demand" such and such an amount in gold or silver. Today many currencies retain this formula but promise to pay the face amount in currency, not precious metal. Since paper currency is not money, the state had no special prerogative over its issue. Nonetheless, most nations eventually restricted the issue of paper money to one central bank, commonly still a private institution operating for profit. The granddaddy of all of these state-sanctioned banks is Bank of England, founded as a private institution in 1694 and given the charter to issue sterling for the Crown. It remained a private institution until 1946. One of the results of this practice was that the Crown surrendered the profits, or "seigniorage," accruing to the issue of paper currency to the shareholders of the Bank of England.

The way the system works is roughly as follows. When tax revenues do not meet the government's fiscal obligations, the treasury borrows money from the central bank by selling treasury bills, that is, government promissory notes. The central bank buys the treasury bills by the simple expedient of entering the equivalent amount on its books as a debt owing to the bank. Thus the state pays interest on money that the bank has created out of nothing. Douglas was scandalized by this practice—which was certainly a sweet deal for the Bank of England, though the profits were not nearly as large as Douglas imagined.

Standard banks of discount, as opposed to banks of issue, also create money in that they are legally entitled to lend more money than they have on deposit. The amount is limited by the "discount rate"—commonly about 10 percent. Thus if I deposit $1,000 in my bank, it can lend my neighbor $1,100 and charge interest on the full amount. That extra $100 is what Douglas called "credit," that is, the newly created or "fiat" money. Central banks, as banks of issue, are not restricted by any such discount rate and can extend "credit" to any amount and collect interest on it. (Of course, if it extends too much credit—as the German Bundesbank did quite deliberately in the 1920s—there will be consequences.) This "credit," Douglas believed, properly belonged to the citizens of the nation, hence the name "Social Credit."

Except for the United States, which has a Reserve System made up of private banks (see chapter 5), all major industrial nations today have a central bank that is an instrument of the state, and the state retains the profits accruing from the issue of treasury bonds, which are grounded on the credit of the nation and not on a hoard of precious metals. To that extent, history has vindicated Douglas's judgment that the state, not private corporations, should reap the profits of the issue of currency. However, he wildly overestimated the size and importance of central bank profits, believing that they were so large that if reclaimed by the state, taxation would no longer be necessary and the government would be able to hand out money to its citizens as the national dividend. Pound was completely persuaded by Douglas's analysis. In fact, in an excess of vanity, he even claimed in a letter to Orage to have been the first to announce this consequence: "As far as I remember the first man to say in yr/ late

lamented pyper the Noo Age: Any govt. That wasn't god damned (or words
to that effect) bloody inefficient could pay dividends and NOT need to
collect any taxes. Was NOT the noble Maj. But yours truly" (29 Jan. 1932,
Pound Papers). No doubt Pound's conviction that he was a cofounder of
Social Credit contributed to his loyalty to it through thick and thin.

The Social Credit movement was launched in a series of articles by
Douglas published in the *New Age* in June, July, and August 1919 entitled
"Economic Democracy" and published as a book under the same title in
1920. A second, longer series soon followed—running from February to
August 1920—called "Credit Power and Democracy." This series ran con-
currently with one of Pound's called "The Revolt of Intelligence." In the
sixth essay of his series (15 January 1920) Pound first delivered himself
of an economic opinion in print. He was in his thirty-fourth year, and had
been wrestling for five years with the difficulties of writing an epic poem.
The remark is worth quoting for its impatient and accusatory tone, so
characteristic of his economic prose. He registers—rather verbosely—his
irritation at the resistance of the Catholic radicals, Belloc and Chesterton,
to Douglas's revelation:

> In THE NEW AGE one's ruminations appear side by side with "modern
> thought"; that is to say, I can on one page refer to some statement already
> a platitude in the eighteenth or seventeenth century on the next page
> some fellow-contributor puts forth the comparatively insolite suggestion
> that a steam plough or a dynamo is as good a basis of credit as a lump of
> gold which possibly does not exist. Of course, a belief in infant damna-
> tion or Papal infallibility may not prevent a man from grasping "new"
> ideas on economics, or production or distribution or credit or any other
> live issue; but, on the other hand, one may question whether an
> embeddedness in ancient superstitions, in modes of mentality, errone-
> ously said to be obsolete—to the dead issues—does or does not predis-
> pose men to examine new ideas, or any ideas, with fair and open intelli-
> gence. (177)

But despite the reluctance of Belloc and Chesterton to get aboard the
Social Credit bandwagon, they were potential allies worth wooing. In June
1936, when Pound was attempting to forge an alliance with Catholic reformers, he complained to Odon Por about a piece on Social Credit by a
journalist named Carmagna: "Failure to mention Chesterton politely great
mistake. IF he dont recognize C's fight vs. league etc// how the hell can
he hold C's following" (Pound Papers). In the previous year he had written "The Root of Evil" for *G. K.'s Weekly,* Chesterton's journal (*Ezra Pound's
Poetry and Prose* 6:249–50) and a friendly obituary on the occasion of
Chesterton's death in which he claims that Mussolini's Milan speech of 6

October 1934 aligned him with Chesterton's distributism ("Un Compianto Amico: Gilbert Chesterton" in *Ezra Pound's Poetry and Prose* 7:63).

Social Credit failed to attract its natural constituency—the radical Right—and remained a fringe movement in Britain, rejected by both the Left and the Right, though it was the official policy of the Scottish National party until the late 1960s. It took hold as a political movement only in Canada and New Zealand. In Canada it found its first constituency in the flock of a fundamentalist preacher, William Aberhart, who founded a Social Credit party and was premier of Alberta from 1935 to his death in 1943. The Social Credit party continued to govern Alberta under his successor, Ernest Manning, another Baptist preacher, and retained power until 1971, though it had long since abandoned Douglas's economic principles. Social Credit also had electoral success in British Columbia, where a small-town hardware merchant, W. A. C. Bennet, was premier from 1952 to 1972, though—unlike Aberhart—there is no evidence that he had any interest in the economic theories of Douglas. Réal Caouette, a small-town Quebec car dealer, was federal leader of the Social Credit Party of Canada during its most successful years (1971–76).

After he was elected in September 1935, Aberhart cabled Douglas, inviting him to advise the new government. Unaccountably Douglas stalled and in the end did not go. Pound, who was very keen on the Alberta experiment, offered to go himself—even before Douglas had been invited. He cited as qualifications his birth in Idaho on the same longitude as Alberta and his ability to speak French (Pound to Douglas, 2 Sept. 1935, Pound Papers). (There are very few francophones in Alberta. Pound seemed to think that the capital of Canada was Quebec. Perhaps that is why he thought his capability in French would be of service.) Douglas responded with characteristic disdain: "With the aid of a wet towel I seem to get the idea that you are suggesting that you stand for a Federal Constituency! If that is not the idea, please correct me" (4 Sept. 1935, Pound Papers). In any event nothing came of it. Neither of them went to Alberta (Finlay 140). John Hargrave, the founder of the fascist-style movement Kibbo Kift and a Social Crediter, went in Douglas's stead—though without his blessing and uninvited by Aberhart—in December 1936. Hargrave was allowed to sit in on cabinet and committee meetings, but eventually discredited himself and returned to England with his tail between his legs (E. S. Woodward to Pound, 27 Jan. 1937, Pound Papers).

The Alberta Social Credit government proved to be a total failure so far as monetary reform was concerned. Aberhart vacillated on policy, met stiff legal and political obstacles, and revealed himself to be incompetent as an economic reformer, though a successful demagogue. Douglas, for his part, was seriously damaged by his refusal to seize the proffered opportunity. Though well informed about the Alberta disaster through letters from E. S. Woodward, a Canadian Gesellite, Pound chose to cling to the unreliable and vacillating Douglas, turning his back on Alberta and continuing his evangelism for a movement whose ragged theory and incompetent leadership was becoming increasingly apparent. A Social Credit government was also elected in New Zealand in 1935. It was less of a disaster than the one in Alberta, but Pound's enthusiasm did not extend to an offer to go down under (Pound to Odon Por, 8 Feb. 1935, Pound Papers).

The political appeal of Social Credit was that it promised the resolution of the endemic problems of capitalism—notably the business cycle and maldistribution of wealth—without any significant alteration of prevailing social and political structures. In Canada it occupied the same political space as populism had occupied in the United States—independent farmers, small business owners, and the xenophobic. Social Credit survived in Canada by ceasing to be a movement of economic reform and settling into the role of a right-wing parliamentary political party. Its fate in Britain was very different. Never able to achieve a political presence in the British parliament, it remained a fringe movement, moving further and further from its roots in conservative collectivism toward extremism of the Right, competing with Fascists and attracting anti-Semites. Douglas himself was anti-Semitic, a prejudice that no doubt colored his economic analysis as well as clouded whatever political acumen he may have possessed.

Social Credit's intellectual weakness was twofold. First, Douglas and Orage—the principle "theoreticians" of Social Credit—were incompetent as economists. Quite apart from their crude understanding of the nature and function of a national economy, they simply did not do the numbers, never descending from a general and abstract level. Had they done the numbers—even very roughly—their errors would have been exposed immediately. In 1937 E. S. Woodward provided Pound with a trenchant critique of Douglas's advice to Aberhart:

> Aberhart was badly betrayed by Major Douglas. Douglas refused to come to Alberta despite a generous financial contract and he gave fantastic long range advice. Two pieces of advice stand out as mad-house concentrate. 1. To ask the chartered banks to supply $3,200,000 without interest or promise of repayment, and 2. Alternatively to place $3,200,000 to the credit of bondholders on the books of the Province for use by them in the purchase of Alberta products. He conveniently forgot that . . . no farmer in Alberta would part with one bushel of wheat for the whole of the $3,200,000 credit entry. The Social Credit government of Alberta has no credit standing even among its social credit supporters. (E. S. Woodward to Pound, 27 Jan. 1937, Pound Papers)

Even earlier, as will be discussed below, the American historian W. E. Woodward had similarly exposed the impracticality of Douglas's scheme.

The second weakness was independent of the frailties of Social Crediters. As an underconsumptionist theory, it sinned against equilibrium theory, the first axiom of classical economics, which holds that the redistribution of wealth is immediate and automatic. The underconsumptionist heretics did not know how to disprove that wonderfully counterintuitive axiom. They simply mocked equilibrium theory as obviously at odds with the facts. Such an approach got them nowhere with the economically literate.

As I observed in the introduction, equilibrium theory is equivalent to "quantity theory." An influential articulation of it is Say's law. It ruled economic thinking until the revolution brought about by Keynes's *General Theory*. John Kenneth Galbraith's assessment of the power of Say's law gives some indication of what these economic radicals were up against:

> Until Keynes, Say's Law had ruled in economics for more than a century. And the rule was no casual thing; to a remarkable degree acceptance of Say was the test by which reputable economists were distinguished from the crackpots. Until late in the '30s no candidate for a Ph. D. at a major American university who spoke seriously of a shortage of purchasing power as a cause of depression could be passed. He was a man who saw only the surface of things, was unworthy of the company of scholars. Say's Law stands as the most distinguished example of the stability of economic ideas, including when they are wrong. (*Money* 218–19)

In a 1934 lecture Keynes said much the same about the power that Say's law held over people's minds:

> Say's Law [holds that Demand equals Supply] for all values of N. However many men you employ there is no danger of [Supply] being greater than D[emand]. There is therefore never any obstacle to full employment. . . . All classical theory is based on this vital assumption. . . . Malthus opposed this classical assumption, and said the trouble arose because effective demand was deficient, which Ricardo said was impossible. Malthus was swept out of the way and Ricardo was completely victorious. The controversy disappeared from economic discussion or was ignored, except by the underworld of Marx, Gesell, and Major Douglas. This has given an unreality to economics . . . hence the lack of respect of the common man. (qtd. in Skidelsky, *Keynes* 511)

And it should not be forgotten that Keynes also paid Douglas left-handed tribute in his *General Theory:*

> Since the war there has been a spate of heretical theories of under-consumption, of which those of Major Douglas are the most famous. The strength of Major Douglas's advocacy has, of course, largely depended

on orthodoxy having no valid reply to much of his destructive criticism. On the other hand, the detail of his diagnosis, in particular the so-called A + B theorem, includes much mystification. . . . Major Douglas is entitled to claim, as against some of his orthodox adversaries, that he at least has not been wholly oblivious of the outstanding problem of our economic system. Yet he has scarcely established an equal claim to rank—a private, perhaps, but not a major in the brave army of heretics—with Mandeville, Gesell and Hobson, who, following their intuitions, have preferred to see the truth obscurely and imperfectly rather than to maintain error, reached indeed with clearness and consistency and by easy logic but on hypotheses inappropriate to the facts. (370–71)

Keynes's use of the terms *heretic* and *orthodox* has been adopted by the discipline, indicating more clearly than any argument the dependence of economic theory on consensus rather than rigorous demonstration or empirical verification. Economic theories are rather more like doctrines than they are like hypotheses to be tested. Today, as in 1920, there are competing economic theories: Keynesianism, monetarism, rational expectationism, new classical, and new institutional are competing doctrines within Anglo-American liberal capitalist economics—leaving out of account the many varieties of socialist and Marxist economic doctrines. Robert Heilbroner's and William Milberg's survey of the schismatic state of late-twentieth-century economics suggests that economic theories are not so much true or false as they are convenient or inconvenient. They say that dominant or classical theories "attain their importance not because they can lay claim to some objective truth, superior accuracy, or usefulness in the constructs they use, but because, for reasons that may be very difficult to defend on 'scientific' grounds, they command something like universal assent" (15). Of course, Pound and Douglas would agree whole-heartedly with this view—when applied to their opponents.

When Douglas and Orage attempted to launch their new economic doctrine, the dominant theory was still classical laissez-faire capitalism, descending from Adam Smith through David Ricardo, J. S. Mill, and Alfred Marshall. Orthodox economics was thought to be just as authoritative as physics, chemistry, or biology. Keynes describes its hold over people's minds with caustic wit and graceful eloquence:

The completeness of the Ricardian victory is something of a curiosity and a mystery. It must have been due to a complex of suitabilities in the doctrine to the environment into which it was projected. That it reached conclusions quite different from what the ordinary uninstructed person would expect, added, I suppose, to its intellectual prestige. That its teaching, translated into practice, was austere and often unpalatable, lent it virtue. That it was adapted to carry a vast and consistent logical super-structure, gave it beauty. That it could explain much social injustice and apparent cruelty as an inevitable incident in the scheme of progress, and the attempt to change such things as likely on the whole to do more harm than good, commended it to authority. That it afforded a measure of justification to the free activities of the individual capitalist, attracted to it the support of the dominant social force behind authority. (32–33)

The war, and the disruptions of the peace, offered a brief opportunity for open debate, but that was closed when Britain—on the advice of the Cunliffe Committee (1918–19)—went back on the gold standard in 1925. (The pound sterling's convertibility to gold had been suspended during the war. It was restored to convertibility at prewar levels, which occasioned a great constriction of the money supply in Britain and a subsequent de-pression.) According to Irving Fisher this report "furnished the basis for the monetary policies which were subsequently followed, not only in Great Britain, but in the entire world" (*Stable Money* 277–78). The depression and the British General Strike of 1926 polarized public opinion and left little space for the radical Right. Socialists rallied to the side of the strik-ers, and the liberal supporters of the status quo marshaled public opin-ion on their side by holding up the specter of violent Bolshevik revolu-tion. Social Credit could not make itself heard in the midst of the melee.

Though it was naive, amateurish, and technically crude, the Social Credit economic analysis was not as crackpot as is commonly believed. There was enough merit in Douglas's thought for Galbraith to claim (somewhat mischievously) that Douglas anticipated Keynes: "by the time of Keynes [1936], Major C. H. Douglas had, for some years, been winning lowbrow converts to the concept of Social Credit. The operative feature of Social Credit was a social dividend, meaning the equivalent of cash payable to citizens at large—a reprise of the pioneering idea of colonial Maryland. The social dividend would surely be spent. It involved none of the passiveness of monetary policy. So Douglas anticipated Keynes—as Keynes himself observed" (*Money* 223–24).

Social Credit, then, was correct enough that one ought not to seek rea-sons for Pound's adherence to it in psychological pathology, ideological commitment, or even in anti-Semitism as is done all too frequently (see Bacigalupo; Casillo; Chace; and Lauber; for a contrary view see Redman). Its appeal to Pound was twofold: in contrast to the impotence of ortho-dox economics on this point, it accounted for the inability of the citizens of a nation to purchase their own produce, and it provided a "conserva-tive"—that is, nondisruptive—solution to the problem. Even though xe-nophobia, anti-Semitism, and conspiracy theory took hold of Pound in the late 1930s, his radicalization by Douglas and Orage need not have led to those later reprehensible views. The leading cause of this descent into paranoia was the economic incompetence of Douglas, Orage, and Pound himself.

Pound's conversion to Social Credit was sudden and complete. He reviewed Douglas's first book, *Economic Democracy*, in the April 1920 issue of the *Little Review*. His review appeared immediately before episode 13 of James Joyce's *Ulysses*. Thus the first readers of Gerty McDowell's girlish erotic fantasies were also treated to the announcement of a new heresy, another triumph of reason over ignorance and superstition: "Universitaire economics hold the field as non-experimental science and catholicism held the fields in Bacon's day and in Voltaire's, and I have no doubt that the opposition to Major Douglas' Statements will take the tack of making him out a mere Luther. Humanism came to the surface in the renaissance and the succeeding centuries have laboured, not always in vain, to crush it down" ("*Economic Democracy*" 40). Pound noted that Douglas's thought was "directed to the prevention of new wars, wars blown up out of economic villainies at the whim of small bodies of irresponsible individuals." The notion of conspiracy, then, was present in the very earliest version of Pound's economic radicalism, as was his recognition that Social Credit offered "an alternative to bloody and violent revolutions," that is, to communism or Belloc's servile state: "He is a humanist, which is a blessed relief after humanitarians; he is emphatically and repeatedly against the demand to subordinate the individuality to the need of some external organization, the exaltation of the State into an authority from which there is no appeal" (40–42).

The political posture of Social Credit was virtually identical to Belloc's in *The Servile State*. Both stressed individual liberty and the threat of increasing centralization of power in the state. But, unlike Belloc's distributivism, Social Credit did not propose any dismantling of the capitalist structure and was in no way hostile to modern industrial technology. Both movements were paternalistic; Douglas is not coy on this point:

> The essential feature of a sound democracy is not at all that the will of the majority shall prevail; that is simply mob law; but it is that the welfare of the individual shall be the primary consideration of the community. We put it forward as an article of personal faith that the welfare of the community cannot possibly involve injustice to the individual; and that it is the erection of a system of thought, action and politics in the form of an impersonal State to be used for personal or class interests which has made the conflict between the state and the individual the feature of the present crisis. Just so long as the thing called the State is

determined to march to its ends over the rebellious individuality of even the smallest section of its components, just so long is its policy unsound. ("Notes of the Week" 270)

This posture is one that any American populist of the 1920s or right-wing democrat of the 1990s would readily endorse. It can claim—with reasonable legitimacy—a provenance in Lockean liberalism as well as in Smithian laissez-faire economics.

With Douglas's economic analysis in hand Pound had an intellectual tool that he believed was the key to an understanding of history—a necessity for the would-be epic poet. Douglas drew two important conclusions from his analysis: that the application of prevailing economic doctrine in the government of nations would lead inevitably to trade competition and war (*Control* 79); and that the key to political and economic control of any nation was control of that nation's financial credit (*Social Credit* 100–101). With respect to the first point, Pound highlights the manufacture of armaments in *The Cantos* as an obvious inducement to war:

> "Peace! pieyce!!" said Mr. Giddings,
> "Universal? Not while yew got tew billions ov money,"
> Said Mr. Giddings, "invested in the man-u-facture
> Of war machinery."
>
> (canto 18/81)

Douglas's second conclusion is a little more complicated and more fundamental to *The Cantos*'s ideology. We have already discussed his concept of credit and the bank's control of it. He believed that credit represented a lien on future production. So understood, any debt would automatically be canceled when the future production came on line. However, that is not what happens in the banking system. The banks collect principal *and* interest. Douglas believed that the interest represented an excess over production, and hence could not be met. To cover the interest charges, new debts had to be contracted, and so on, until the banks swallowed up the entire wealth of the world.

He believed that his analysis explained the business cycle of boom and bust. The periodic busts wiped out debts through bankruptcies, thus permitting the system to continue to function, though at the cost of tremendous social dislocation. Exports were another means of making up the shortfall in domestic purchasing power caused by interest charges, since exports are paid for by foreigners. However, since every nation is in the same sinking boat, every nation does whatever it can to force its neighbors to absorb its unpurchasable product. The obvious consequence of such competition was international conflict and war. (Douglas's analysis of foreign trade is not his own, but is adapted from J. A. Hobson's *Imperialism: A Study.*)

It is now generally believed that the business cycle was caused by the restriction of money supply largely as a result of adherence to the gold standard. Interest rates are largely a function of the rate of growth of the money supply. A high rate of growth produces low interest rates, and a low one, high rates. As economic activity expanded and more goods and services were on offer, for nations on the gold standard, either the value or the supply of gold had to rise. Since the supply of gold was inelastic, its value tended to rise. A rise in the price of gold is the same thing as a fall in the value of money, or inflation. Hence every economic boom was accompanied by a rise in prices, and since the money supply could not be expanded to match increased economic activity, booms invariably collapsed through a failure of liquidity.

The standard view was that the rise in prices was caused by shortages in supply. Fisher debunked that standard view, calling it "the money illusion," the belief "that money is in itself stable," causing people to "look to the goods for the cause of all price fluctuations" (*Stable Money* 2). Douglas is less measured, but he made essentially the same point in a 1920 article:

> Money is only a mechanism by means of which we deal with things—it has no properties except those we choose to give to it. A phrase such as "There is no money in the country with which to do such and so" means simply nothing, unless we are also saying "The goods and services required to do this thing do not exist and cannot be produced, therefore it is useless to create the money equivalent of them." For instance, it is simply childish to say that a country has no money for social betterment, or for any other purpose, when it has the skill, the men and the material and plant to create that betterment. The banks or the Treasury can create the money in five minutes, and are doing it every day, and have been doing it for centuries. ("The Mechanism of Consumer Control" 78)

Keynesian policy—the manipulation of the money supply through central bank manipulation of interest rates and the sale or purchase of treasury bonds—is an application of the view of the role of money that Douglas expressed in this article. But in 1920 such remarks were perceived as mischievous madness.

Despite the affinities of Douglas's and Keynes's analyses, neither Douglas nor Pound accepted Keynes as an ally. I have been unable to find any direct comment on Keynes by Douglas, even though the fragmentary correspondence between Douglas and Pound that has survived suggests that they both read Keynes's *General Theory* shortly after it appeared in

February 1936. Pound alludes to Keynes's praise of Gesell in a letter to Douglas of March 1936. However, neither of them has a good word for Keynes. They do not even comment on his remarks on Douglas. In *The Brief for the Prosecution*—his last book—Douglas does refer to Keynes, uncompromisingly rejecting his policy of a managed money supply. It is, Douglas says, "simply a vicious form of managed theft, ultimately accompanied of necessity by cumulative industrial waste. Assuming that it is understood by its sponsors, it is an attempt to perpetuate government by finance" (66). Many conservative thinkers in the 1990s would agree wholeheartedly with Douglas's first sentence, though not with his ascription of conspiracy in the second sentence.

Keynesianism has been largely displaced as a policy guide in the Atlantic community by varieties of monetarism. Monetarists and Keynesians agree that an increase in the supply of goods and services must be accompanied by an increase in the supply of money and credit if stable prices (or "stable money," as Fisher preferred to say) are to be maintained. If the money supply does not expand, then prices will fall, that is, there will be a rise in the value of money, or deflation. Conversely, if the growth of the money supply outruns the supply of goods and services, there will be a drop in the value of money, or inflation. The monetarists—like Douglas—are opposed to *management* of the money supply so as to either "dampen" or "stimulate" economic activity according to perceived requirements. Instead they recommend an invariable rate of expansion of the money supply sufficient to support an expanding economy, while also maintaining stable money. Such policies have been followed since approximately 1980 in most of the industrial nations. So far the results have been gratifying for the proponents of such policies: mild inflation, a burgeoning stock market, and high real interest rates. The accompanying rather high rates of unemployment, though regrettable, bring "discipline" into the labor market.

In the immediate postwar period two mechanisms were available for the expansion of the money supply of a nation. One was the accumulation of larger gold reserves through trade surpluses or gold mines. The other was through an essentially autonomous private banking system. All banks in the West are banks of discount, that is, they are permitted to lend some multiple of their deposits. Bank credit has the same function and powers as the coins and bills issued by the government. Though bank credit played a crucial role in financing the Industrial Revolution, it did so at the cost of a volatile and unstable monetary environment. Nervous bankers could easily precipitate a crash by calling in debts. And, since by the nature of banking no bank had sufficient funds to cover all of its deposits, nervous depositors could push a bank into insolvency by panic withdrawals. Franklin Delano Roosevelt was confronted by such a panic immediately after his election in 1932, as we will see below.

The world had always depended on gold and silver as the only "currency" in which international accounts could be settled. Hence the *world* supply of currency could be increased only by metal discoveries or improved recovery techniques applied in existing mines. Fisher explains that it was just such circumstances that rescued the United States from a severe currency shortage in the late nineteenth century. His comments allude to William Jennings Bryan's failed presidential campaign of 1896 on the platform of bimetallism, that is, the monetization of silver as well as gold. The effect of bimetallism would have been to expand the money supply: "Had not the increased supply of gold, beginning in 1896, broadened the basis of the currency, the bimetallists would have had a better chance of winning the next election in 1900. But rich gold mine discoveries in South Africa in 1889, the opening of the Klondike and Alaskan Mines, the discovery of the cyanide process of extracting gold from formerly unusable residues, soon quadrupled the annual gold production" (*Stable Money* 57).

The state of opinion about currency and banking in the early years of the twentieth century is indicated by the fact that the entry under "Banking Credit" in editions of the *Encyclopedia Britannica* prior to 1929 did not draw attention to the fact that bank credit was an addition to the money supply. The fourteenth edition is quite straightforward on this point: "Banks create credit. It is a mistake to suppose that bank credit is created to any important extent by the payment of money into the banks. . . . The bank's debt is a means of payment; it is credit money. It is a clear addition to the amount of means of payment in the community." Even today, most people think that banks make money by lending depositors' money at a higher interest rate than they pay. Of course, there is a "spread" between what they pay and what they charge, but they also benefit from the discount rate, that is, from lending more than they have on deposit. A bank's assets are its loans, and its liabilities are its deposits. When its assets become too much greater than its liabilities—in contrast to non-banking enterprises—a bank is dangerously "exposed" and may succumb to a "run."

Even though Social Credit had some things right that more orthodox opinion at the time had wrong, Douglas's model of the British economy, which he called Britain Inc., was inadequately developed and quite unworkable. And he proved incapable of learning from criticism and commentary, even from friends and allies like Pound and Orage. His fatal flaw as a reformer—apart from his economic naiveté—was his inability to believe that people could in good faith hold views *he* thought erroneous. His analysis of the cause of the British depression of 1920 was not wildly incorrect, but his presumption that the banks deliberately caused it was a paranoid fantasy:

> There is no doubt whatever, and I do not suppose that anyone at all familiar with the subject would dispute the statement for a moment, that the present trade depression is directly and consciously caused by the concerted action of the banks in restricting credit facilities, and that such credit facilities as are granted have very little relation to public need; that, whatever else might have happened had this policy not been pursued, there would have been no trade depression at this time, any more than there was during the war; and that the banks through their control of credit facilities, hold the volume of production at all times in the hollow of their hands. ("The Mechanism of Consumer Control" 87)

Pound accepted Douglas's conspiratorial analysis as early as his 1920 review of Douglas's book cited above. If there is any factor of overriding importance in Pound's slide into extremism, it is this conviction that sinister forces are controlling events.

The issue was simple for Douglas. Credit was the rightful possession of the community because it represents the capacity of the community to deliver goods and services *in the future*. The orthodox view is that credit represents the accrued capital of the saver, that is, goods and services *already produced* but not consumed. Savers, Smith argued, are morally entitled to interest as a reward for their abstinence. But if credit is a lien on the future capacity of the community to deliver the goods, then there is no moral justification for interest. As Douglas put it: "The community creates all the credit there is; there is nothing whatever to prevent the community entering into its own and dwelling therein except it shall be by sheer demonstrated inability to seize the opportunity which at this very moment lies open to it" (*Control* 55). Although it was clear that the problem could be solved only by political action, Douglas and Orage did not envision revolution. They believed that since no fundamental alteration of social arrangements would be required to implement Social Credit policies, persuasion and education should soon produce the entry of the people into their birthright—a fair share of the wealth of an industrial economy. He called the wealth of an advanced industrial society the "increment of association" and thought it was sufficient to make everyone comfortable if only fairly distributed.

All that was needed was to abolish private banks and have the state lend money without interest charges: "Now, it must be perfectly obvious to anyone who seriously considers the matter that the State should lend, not borrow, and that in this respect, as in others, the Capitalist usurps the function of the State" (Douglas, *Economic Democracy* 124). It is important to recognize that the banking system does in fact create credit, and profits from it. Today when governments wish to expand the money supply, one technique is to purchase securities on the open market, thereby increasing the aggregate supply of money, since the purchases are made with fiat money created by the central bank. Douglas believed that this indirect system—which amounted to the state borrowing from commercial banks—was indefensible. He recommended a direct payment to individuals to make up the perceived shortfall in purchasing power. He called these disbursements the "national dividend." Inexplicably, he did not think such payments would represent a net increase in the money supply—a consequence he denounced as inflationary.

Though Douglas's grasp of the banking system was imperfect, it was not wildly incorrect. The private banks as a collectivity did not in fact control credit to the extent he believed. However, Britain's central bank was until 1946 a private bank and retained the profits of monetary issue. Douglas—not implausibly—believed that it was morally wrong that private banks should control the community asset of credit and reap profits from it. Even worse, he believed that through control of credit the banks directed—or, rather, misdirected—the allocation of the resources of the community. A glance at the allocation of resources in any capitalist democracy in 1920 led many to conclude that far too many resources were allocated to armaments, the production of useless or harmful articles of consumption, and leisure services; and not enough to education, health, public amenities, the arts, and those sciences that have little military application. Of course, countries following socialist, Marxist, fascist, monarchist, or whatever other doctrines one can think of have not been distinguished by a more humane allocation of resources.

This ideological neutrality of Douglas's analysis was a feature that appealed very strongly to Pound, but it might be seen as a flaw. If all political systems suffered from the same malaise, the cause had to be in some common feature. Since private banks did not exist in socialist states, some other cause must be found. Douglas did not hesitate to identify an international conspiracy of Jews as the culprit—thereby discrediting himself to anyone of understanding. As we will see, Pound ignored Douglas's anti-Semitism and conspiracy theory for nearly twenty years until he eventually succumbed to that intellectual pathology. That Pound ignored it instead of shunning Douglas and his theory because of this irrationality is a measure of his lack of independence in economic opinion. Having accepted Orage and Douglas as his mentors, he was unable to challenge their

authority, despite his own best efforts to chart an independent course—
an effort I will examine in the following pages.

Pound's 1921 review of Douglas's *Credit-Power and Democracy* in William
Carlos William's short-lived periodical, *Contact,* announces his abandon-
ment of the symbolist doctrine of *l'art pour l'art* and his commitment to
Douglas's analysis:

> A moderate reform is necessary if any civilization is to be kept up. I don't
> care if so moderate a system as Douglas's go through in its entirety, so
> long as his ideas become known, and thereby act as a deterrent, i.e., pre-
> vent those who now hold the credit Power, from flagrant use of it—war
> making etc.
>
> The symbolist position, artistic aloofness from world affairs, is no good
> now. It may have assisted several people to write and work in the 80's,
> but it is not, in 1921, opportune or apposite. (Review n.p.)

For the rest of his life Pound tried to juggle these two overpowering concerns—economics and art.

Hugh Selwyn Mauberley is his poetic statement of his conversion from an
aesthete to an engaged political writer. It was the last shorter poem he was
to write. The rest of his career was devoted to his epic, *The Cantos*—though
he published many translations and some doggerel. Pound described
Mauberley as his farewell to London. It is a sort of threnody for a fictional
aesthete, Hugh Selwyn Mauberley, a synecdoche for the aesthetic movement, which Pound traces back to the Pre-Raphaelite Brotherhood of the
1850s. Pound's place in the poem is enigmatically marked by the opening poem, "E.P. Ode Pour l'Election de son Sepulchre," which "buries"
Pound. The balance of the sequence is a half-nostalgic, half-satirical portrait of the British literary scene from about 1850 to 1920.

Mauberley has drawn a great deal of critical attention—as much because
of its opacity as its wit and elegance. In contrast to the sprawl of those
cantos that precede and follow it, *Mauberley* is tight, condensed, "sculp-
tural." The eponymous Mauberley is probably a medalist, and the rhetoric of the poem mimes the condensation and precision of the medalist's
art. But the sequence is so cryptic that no real consensus has yet been
reached (three-quarters of a century later) by its readers as to what it is
all about. Its obscurity renders it a suitable marker of Pound's move away
from the aestheticism of his first mentor, Yeats, toward the political activism of Orage and Douglas. Pound's inability—or unwillingness—to make
his poetry comprehensible augured ill for his success as an evangelist of
economic reform. Nonetheless, at about this time he set himself the task
of presenting to the world—in both polemical prose and epic verse—the

new age of Social Credit, expressed in the archaic rhetoric of China that he had made new in the "ideogrammic method."

Although thoroughly radicalized by Douglas and Orage, economics did not preoccupy Pound until the "dirty thirties." Economic discussion is rare—both in publications and correspondence—between 1921 and 1931. But in January 1931 he reestablished contact with Douglas and began to read widely in economic literature. His engagement in economic journalism reached the point that he had little time for literary activity—even for *The Cantos*. Pound was conscious of the turn he had given to his career, but regarded it as a necessary and temporary diversion. He wrote to Odon Por, his closest ally in the effort to capture fascism for Social Credit, early in 1936: "1937!!! do you expect ME to be still an economist by 1937? It ought to be DONE by then, and civilized blokes like us, bein Kultur Mensch or something tony. I xxxspekk to be ritin muzik and poesy by 1937. hell thazz anno XV and then some. econ/ shd/ by then be handed over to arkin's trained staff of accountants" ([May 1936], Pound Papers). Though these remarks are somewhat facetious, Pound clearly regarded his foray into economics as a temporary diversion from his artistic métier. However, he did not finish with economics in 1937—or ever.

CHAPTER 2

Economics and Mythopoeia

Since I have written two books that focus on the place of myth and occult-ism in Pound's work, it might be expected that I would find some rela-tion between Pound's economics and his *arcanum,* or interest in myth. And, indeed, I believe the two to be intimately related—although perhaps not quite in the way that might be expected. I do not believe that Pound's interest in myth—or, rather, *mythography*—and his interest in mystery re-ligion, cultural history, and poetry can be isolated from one another. Pound regards the stories we call myths as esoteric writings containing the fundamental revelations that define particular cultures, as records of the psychic experiences of the most perceptive and intelligent minds. Cultures are understood as the aggregations of the insights of artists (for a fuller discussion of these issues see Surette *Light* and *Birth*).

In the modern world we no longer have myths in the restricted sense of stories about divinities; we have art instead. It is this view of culture and revelation that informs this well-known paragraph from "Psychology and Troubadours":

> I believe in a sort of permanent basis in humanity, that is to say, I believe that Greek myth arose when someone having passed through delightful psychic experience tried to communicate it to others and found it nec-essary to screen himself from persecution. Speaking aesthetically, the myths are explications of mood: you may stop there, or you may probe deeper. Certain it is that these myths are only intelligible in a vivid and glittering sense to those people to whom they occur. I know, I mean, one

man who understands Persephone and Demeter, and one who understands the Laurel, and another who has, I should say, met Artemis. These
things are for them *real*. (*The Spirit of Romance* 92)

I have often wondered who the friend of Artemis and the initiate of
Eleusis might be. But even though I can only guess at their identity, it is a
safe bet that Pound could have met them in the *New Age* offices on Cursitor
Street just as easily as at the meetings of the Theosophical Society in whose
journal (*The Quest*) these remarks were first published. As it happens
Pound's occult friends (who informed his understanding of myth) and
his *New Age* friends (who formulated his understanding of economics)
were not two sets, but a single set. The man who most fully exemplified
the union of these two seemingly remote spheres of interest is the editor
of the *New Age*, A. R. Orage.

Orage was some twelve years Pound's senior. Born 22 January 1873 in
Fenstanton, Yorkshire, to a family impoverished by an improvident father,
who also inconveniently died soon after A. R.'s birth, he was educated as
a schoolteacher through the good offices of the Coote family. While a
young teacher in Leeds he developed a keen interest in the mystical specu-
lations of Madame Blavatsky and became an active member of the Leeds
branch of her Theosophical Society. His closest friends at Leeds were
Holbrook Jackson and Arthur J. Penty, both also Theosophists. Jackson
introduced Orage to the work of Nietzsche and Penty to socialism and
economics. Together they formed the Leeds Arts Club and held lectures
on religious, philosophical, social, and economic subjects (Mairet).

Penty was the first of the three to depart for London, where he established handicraft workshops as part of a Ruskinian craft movement. Orage
and Jackson followed Penty in 1905, and all three were active in the foundation of the Fabian Arts Group in that same year. Two years later, in May
1907, Orage and Jackson purchased a failing magazine, the *New Age*, with
money donated by a prominent Fabian, George Bernard Shaw, and a
wealthy Theosophist, Lewis Wallace—who also later contributed as "M. B.
Oxon" (Selver *Orage;* Webb 207). The *New Age* had been founded in 1894,
bearing the subtitle *A Weekly Record of Christian Culture, Social Service, and
Literary Life*. Four years later it was taken over by Joseph Clayton, a fierce
and aggressive socialist (Finlay 63). Just before Orage and company took
it over Clayton had announced that it would be the voice of the Labour
movement, the New Theology movement, and the Woman movement
(Finlay 241). Thus, even before Orage and Jackson, the journal had
blended religious and socialist interests. The joint editorship of Jackson
and Orage did not last out the year, and Orage was in full control from

late 1907 until his departure for Gurdjieff's School of World Harmony at Fontainebleau in 1922.

Before the *New Age* absorbed all of his energies, Orage had written three books on religious and philosophical subjects. The first two, *Friedrich Nietzsche: The Dionysian Spirit of the Age* (1906) and *Consciousness: Animal, Human, and Divine* (1907), were lectures he had delivered at the Leeds Theosophical Society. The third, *Nietzsche in Outline and Aphorism* (1907), was a selection of passages from Nietzsche's writings. Jackson published nothing at this time and remained the least radical of the three, though he kept in touch throughout Orage's London years. Penty published the first of his many Ruskinian socialist studies, *The Restoration of the Guild System*, in 1906. Although Orage opened the pages of the *New Age* to his occultist friends, its content was primarily social and political commentary with considerable attention to the arts—mostly from Pound's pen. Under Orage's editorship it was a journal of radical or avant-garde political, economic, and cultural opinion, eventually becoming the organ of Social Credit.

To understand the strange and potent mix of Orientalism, radical underconsumption economics, mythography, right-wing politics, and avant-garde poetry that make up Pound's career, we need to know something of the kind of education Pound received in the *New Age* offices at 38 Cursitor Street. He became a contributor late in 1911, having been introduced to Orage by F. S. Flint. Pound and Orage were at that time poles apart in both style and interest so far as one could judge by their writing. In fact, Beatrice Hastings claims in her memoir, *The Old "New Age,"* that "Orage . . . said, so late as Oct. 1913, nearly two years after Pound's debut: 'Mr. Pound's style is a paste of colloquy, slang journalism and pedantry. Of culture in Nietzsche's sense of the word, it bears no sign'" (7).

Hastings was Orage's mistress from 1907 to 1914, but at the time she wrote her memoir, their relationship had long since ended, and Orage was married to Jessie Dwight of New York. It is clear from her memoir, and the later *Defence of Madame Blavatsky*, that Hastings was an occultist. In an effort to discredit Orage, she accuses him of sorcery and links him with the notorious Aleister Crowley: "I first met Orage at a theosophical lecture he gave in 1906, when on a visit to London from Leeds. Afterwards in the smoking room I rallied him on his perverse loquacity (of the which I later detected every trick). A year or so after, when Aphrodite had amused herself at our expense, I found in his rooms a collection of works on sorcery. Up to this time, Orage's intimate friend was not Mr. Holbrook Jackson, who thought he was, but Mr. Aleister Crowley" (19). Though one cannot entirely trust Hastings's memoir, that she should attempt character assassination by the charge of sorcery reveals that her target audience was the London occult circle. Theosophists of the day regarded sorcery (or theurgy) with pious horror (see, for example, Huysmans).

We must suppose that Pound acquired some Nietzschean culture in Orage's estimation since he continued to publish him for the entire period of his editorship of the *New Age* and immediately opened the pages of the *New English Weekly* to Pound after he broke with Gurdjieff in 1931 and returned to London and journalism. (Unable to regain editorship of the *New Age*, Orage founded the *New English Weekly* in 1932.) To learn what Hastings meant by "culture in Nietzsche's sense" we need only turn to Orage's *Friedrich Nietzsche: The Dionysian Spirit of the Age:*

> Every organism, whether an individual, a people, or a race, belongs either to an ascending or a descending current. And its morality, art, form of society, instincts, and in fact its whole mode of manifestation, depend on whether it belongs to one or the other order of being. The primary characteristic of the ascending life is the consciousness of inexhaustible power. The individual or people behind which the flowing tide of life-force moves is creative, generous, reckless, enthusiastic, prodigal, passionate: its virtues, be it observed, are Dionysian. Its will-to-power is vigorous; in energy it finds delight. And the moral code of such a people will reflect faithfully the people's power.
>
> But the prevailing characteristic of the descending life is the consciousness of *declining* power. The individual or people in whom the life-force is ebbing instinctively husband their resources. They are preservative rather than creative, niggardly, careful, fearful of passion and excess, calculating and moderate. And, in turn, their code of morality faithfully reflects their will. (50–51)

Readers of *Patria Mia* (first published as a double series of articles in the *New Age*) will recognize these sentiments. Possibly these Oragean views are the "neo-Nietzschean clatter" for which Mauberley's mildness was "quite out of place," a supposition supported by Pound's description of the Mauberley sequence as "a farewell to London"—most particularly occult Kensington.

Mauberley is portrayed as belonging to the "descending life." He is conservative, niggardly, careful, fearful of passion and excess, calculating, and moderate. He can be seen as an amalgam of the rather precious crowd of preening superior consciousnesses amongst whom Pound had been pleased to number himself. A sample of that earlier preening is Pound's review of Allen Upward's *Divine Mystery:* "He thinks, *il pense*. He is intelligent. Good God! is it not a marvel that in the age of Cadbury and Northcliffe, and the 'Atlantic Monthly' and the present 'English Review,' etc., etc., ad nauseam, is it not an overwhelming wonder that a thinking sentient being should still inhabit this planet and be allowed to publish a book!!" ("The Divine Mystery" 207).

Allan Upward is an interesting character in his own right. An undoubted occultist, he was a member of the *New Age* circle, but also an enthusiastic amateur Sinologist. He wrote for the *New Age* when it was a journal of Christian socialism. It is probably to Upward that we owe Pound's interest in things Chinese, for in 1904 Upward and a man named Byng established the Primrose (later the Orient) Press to publish the series Wisdom of the East. Its first title was Upward's translation of some Confucian wisdom, entitled *Sayings of Confucius*. After the demise of the Orient Press the series was continued by John Murray. Upward published Chinese translations in both the *New Age* and the *New Freewoman* during Pound's association with those journals, and Pound included him in the first Imagist anthology (Upward). Although Upward had no particular interest in economic theory, he helped to formulate Pound's general social and political postures—in particular his elitism and his tendency to entrust political power to the exceptional individual. (Upward has received some attention from Pound scholars; see Knox; Moody; and Surette *Light*.)

In contrast to Upward, Orage always maintained an interest in social issues, and hence economics, along with his occultism. Indeed one can perceive the economic metaphors in his characterization of the "ascending life" as generous and prodigal while the "descending life" is parsimonious and moderate. Except for the ten-year period that he was a Gurdjieffian evangelist, Orage looked to economic reform as the key to an improved society.

Gurdjieff was an Armenian guru and the inventor of the technique of "encounter groups." His London missionaries were P. D. Ouspensky (a Russian brought to London in August 1921 by Lady Rothermere) and Dimitrij Mitrinovic (a Serbian with the nom de plume M. M. Cosmoi). Orage rewrote into better English Mitrinovic's column called "World Affairs" for the *New Age*. In 1922 Orage left London to join Gurdjieff's Institute at Fontainebleau at an old monastery Gurdjieff had purchased called Le Prieuré. He remained there until December 1923, at which time he sailed to New York as a Gurdjieffian missionary. He remained the American head of the movement until 1931 when he broke with Gurdjieff. Among the attenders of his sessions in New York were Gorham Munson, Elinor Wylie, and Jean Toomer (Welch 38–39, 61–62; Toomer 106–9). Orage did not entirely abandon his Social Credit interests while in New York. Gorham Munson's *New Democracy* was directly inspired by a series of talks on Social Credit that Orage gave in New York in April 1931, just before his return to London (Welch 120, 127; Munson 281–83). The New York Gurdjieff group was still active in 1982 (Welch 138).

Orage returned to London expecting to take back the editorship of the *New Age*, which had continued to be a Social Credit organ under Arthur Brenton, but Brenton was unwilling to surrender his post—largely because of his coolness toward Orage's occult interests (Finlay 168). Accordingly Dimitrij Mitrinovic, Maurice Reckitt, Travers Symons, Philip Mairet, and Alan Porter—the "Chandos Group"—financed the founding of the *New English Weekly* (Finlay 173). It began publishing on 23 April, and Pound very soon became a regular contributor.

Shortly after his return to London, and even before he had secured an editorship, Orage got in touch with Pound. They corresponded regularly from 15 December 1931 until Orage's sudden death on 16 November 1934. In the letters that have survived, at no time do they discuss Orage's occult or religious interests. Orage appears to have had more respect for Pound as a poet than as an economist. Early in their renewed collaboration Pound takes a rather superior attitude and quibbles with some of Douglas's views. Orage replies with a mixture of flattery and scolding:

> Instead of trying to prove—what needs no proof—that your intuitions have always been right in economics as in aesthetics, why dont you—if you must—get all the damned books by Douglas & see for yourself how many of your questions have long ago been fully considered & answered. . . . Do you really think that, at a glance & with all your flair, you can detect a gap which none of us have ever seen? I'll say, quite seriously, that the points you raise have been treated ad nauseam; & that all you have to do is to refer to text. (6 Feb. 1932, Pound Papers)

Though the correspondence is mostly about proselytizing for Social Credit, in one of the last letters he wrote Orage does encourage Pound to concentrate on poetry: "I'm not setting up to give you advice; but the continuation of your Cantos would give *me* a stimulant satisfaction. . . . With submission, again, my dear E. P., your Cantos are your greatest contribution to the cause; & if only you could make *them* the vehicle of your *total being*, their effect would be that of artillery. *Don't* agree with me; still less don't assume I think I'm right. Take it as my sincere opinion" (22 Aug. 1934, Pound Papers).

Unfortunately, Pound did not take Orage's advice, but continued to expend his energy on economic research and proselytizing. Though I have found no evidence that Pound was interested in Orage's occultism, there is ample evidence that he responded with enthusiasm and credence to the theosophy—or "speculative occultism"—that he encountered at the *New Age* offices, in the circle of Yeats, and at the Theosophical Society lectures he attended. Pound published one article ("Psychology and Trouba-dours") in the Theosophical Society's official journal, *The Quest,* edited by G. R. S. Mead. Other contributors included Jessie Weston and Evelyn Underhill, both authors of importance to Pound's friend, T. S. Eliot. Yeats, Pound, Wyndham Lewis, and T. E. Hulme all attended the society's lec-tures in the Kensington town hall, though Eliot does not appear to have done so. Of course their attendance and (for Pound and Lewis) partici-pation as speakers does not mean that they were Theosophists or even interested in religious speculation. It does, however, suggest that they were not embarrassed to be associated with such occult speculation. Theoso-phy and the occult were no more disreputable in Edwardian and Geor-gian London than Jungianism is today—and not so very different, either. (For more detailed discussion of the relations of the occult and the arts see Surette *Birth;* for Jung and the occult see Noll *Jung* and *Aryan*).

It is not so odd that this community of harmless eccentrics should have involved itself in economic reform. Poets, artists, and scholars have been in the forefront of radical or reform economics in Britain virtually since the birth of the discipline of economics in the eighteenth century. Notable names on the artistic side are Bernard Mandeville, John Ruskin, William Morris, Charles Dickens, George Bernard Shaw, and G. K. Chesterton, to mention only the most prominent. As we have seen, this "aesthetic" branch of economic theory is "underconsumptionist" with the exception of Mor-ris, a Communist.

Underconsumption numbers among its theoreticians Thomas Malthus, Simonde de Sismondi, Proudhon, Kitson, J. A. Hobson, S. G. Hobson, Douglas, Gesell, and perhaps Keynes. By his own account, Keynesianism can be seen as a cleaned up, and technically sophisticated, version of Malthusian underconsumptionism, and Social Credit as an unrecon-structed and technically naive version. Here is how a Marxist scholar char-acterizes the error of underconsumptionism:

> we can see that the justification for this singling out of consumption demand is the idea that the object of production is to provide consum-ers with "utilities and conveniences." This is a point of some importance, because it seems to me that this is an idea which is subconsciously active in the heads of most underconsumptionists, inducing them to believe that the demand provided by immediate consumers as opposed to other purchasers occupies some special role in the economy, although there is no reason why this should be so in a capitalist society in which produc-tion depends upon the expectation of private profits. (Bleaney 151)

The idea that the purpose of production is to generate wealth in the form of desirable goods or consumables is hardly "subconsciously active in the heads of most underconsumptionists." It is the fundamental principle upon which the whole edifice is raised. Ruskin's term *illth* very nicely demonstrates an articulate awareness of this point among underconsumptionists. In contrast, Marx's analysis of capitalism is based on his acceptance of classical equilibrium theory—both Say's law and the quantity theory of money. Keynes makes the point in a 1934 Cambridge lecture: "The Marxists have become the ultra-orthodox economists. They take the Ricardian argument to show that nothing can be gained from interference. Hence, since things are bad and mending is impossible, the only solution is to abolish [capitalism] and have quite a new system. Communism is the logical outcome of the classical theory" (qtd. in Skidelsky 511).

Galbraith notes that orthodox economics adheres to "the belief that an economy would find its equilibrium at full employment," a belief grounded on equilibrium theory, which holds that there "could not be a shortage of purchasing power in the economy" (*Money* 218). Equilibrium theory is a corollary of the "quantity theory" of money, "the notion that expansion or contraction of the money supply—other things being equal—will lead to an equiproportional change in the price level" (Green 1). In other words, money does not matter. In theory there can be neither a shortage of purchasing power nor a glut of unsalable goods because an increase in the money supply will simply cause a rise in money prices—inflation. Underconsumptionists believe the contrary—that a shortage of purchasing power will cause a glut of unsalable goods. Roy Green notes that "the problem facing the critics of classical quantity theory . . . is that, due to the universal acceptance of Say's law, they lacked a theory of output comparable with their theory of value and distribution. As a consequence, however sound their policy prescriptions, their theoretical analysis was fatally flawed, and seen to be so" (xi). This circumstance persisted until 1936 when Keynes provided a theory of output in his *General Theory* (Galbraith, *Money* 219), and hence was still very much the case when Orage and Douglas launched Social Credit in 1917.

Curiously, Douglas himself clung to equilibrium theory, affirming it in his testimony before the Macmillan Committee (1 May 1930). When asked, "is it the purchasing power which is wanting or is it the production which is wanting; which of the two sides of the balance has got to be dealt with?" he replied: "if by some process, crude or otherwise, you increase the units of money in people's pockets, and you leave everything else untouched, you get a general rise of prices which will defeat the end you have in view" (Hiskett 32). Quite unjustifiably, Douglas thought that he could get around Say's iron law with the mechanism of direct payments to individual consumers, either by means of the national dividend or by a system of rebates paid directly to the consumer. It was the latter he attempted to articulate before the Macmillan Committee, but—as we will see below—he ran into great difficulty.

The classical equilibrium model, expressed by Say's law, legitimates laissez-faire policies, since in this view economies are self-regulating. Obviously any effort to interfere with an automatically equilibrating mechanism is liable to exacerbate whatever problem is being addressed. Therefore economists always counseled inaction in the face of any economic crisis. To put it another way, classical economic theory rests on two fundamental assumptions: that distribution is automatic and immediate and that the level of output of an economy is inelastic upward, though elastic downward. Malthus notoriously accepted that the level of agricultural output was inelastic upward, but denied that distribution was automatic and perfectly equilibrated. Of course, all of the early economists thought in terms of agricultural and staple production (mining, lumber, trapping, etc.), neither of which could be increased without heavy investment. They were not confronted with the sudden shifts and rapid increases in output characteristic of industrial economies. Since orthodox economics has been very slow to accommodate its theoretical models to a world of innovative technology, the heretics addressed the problem as best they could.

Already in the late nineteenth century, some observers had concluded that the productive capacity of an economy was limited only by the ingenuity and inventiveness of its citizens. One of the first to articulate this view in English was Kitson, who complained in A Scientific Solution of the Money Question (1895) of the failure of economists to adjust to the abundance made possible by industrial production: "There can be no question that the production of wealth during the past century has been enormously in excess of any, within a similar period, that the world has ever known. But with the production of wealth, economics has had comparatively little to do. The growth of production has been due to invention, discovery, and the physical sciences. It is with the distribution of wealth the science [of economics] is chiefly employed, and it is in this particular where it has failed" (27–28). These latter-day underconsumptionists believed that production would take care of itself since the desire for consumer goods is virtually insatiable and the ingenuity of men and women incalculable. In short—in direct contradiction of classical equilibrium theory—they believed that abundance rather than scarcity was the natural condition for a modern, scientific, and industrial economy. Such a belief seems plausible, though it goes against millennia of human culture founded on a very real scarcity of virtually everything.

Most of us react to such claims with skepticism, and some of us with outrage. Our culture—and in many cases our life experiences—affirm that scarcity rather than abundance is the natural state. Our moral codes are designed to make such scarcity and poverty bearable, and even to legitimate them. As a result most of us are inclined to reject such claims as pie-in-the-sky, naive wishful thinking, or charlatanry. Marx called such established beliefs "false consciousness" and believed that they held the proletariat in thrall. Pound, by contrast, was all too willing to believe in the possibility of a utopian world. When E. S. Woodward objected to his rosy view of a world without toil, Pound responded vigorously: "You are as bad as the bloody working man/ [who] conceives a Marxist community everybody WORKING/ blind to fact that in Bali they DONT and that machines make human work weekly less USEFUL. Also you talk as if nobody had any habits and customs, as we/ welcome your damn galloping consumption alias tubercular 'money' [Gesell's stamp scrip]." Pound believed that, when relieved of the necessity to work for survival, people would turn to more creative endeavors: "You feel people GOT to be idle, with machine potential 9000 times human energy. Dont be so fuckin MORAL? Nobody ever did ANYTHING of interest while being *forced* to sell their energy" (Pound to E. S. Woodward, [Dec. 1936], Pound Papers).

It may be that economic radicalism and occultism are found together just because occultists are less constrained by prevailing beliefs and attitudes and are therefore more likely to accept idiosyncratic views on their own merits—or perhaps just because they are unconventional. Because Marx, who was neither an underconsumptionist nor an occultist, accepted classical economical equilibrium analysis and its guarantee of scarcity, he sought a political solution to the maldistribution of scarce resources. Marx thought that the dispossessed proletarian class must seize the means of production, if the product were to be shared according to need instead of birth, ability, or other privilege. The underconsumptionists had an even more radical analysis, believing that scarcity was entirely avoidable. Scarcity was at best the result of poor management, and at worst, of criminal conspiracy.

Pound's circle was constitutionally antipathetic toward Marxism because of its militant materialism. Though his analytic technique is Hegelian dialectics, Marx explicitly discarded Hegel's *Geist* (spirit), calling his system "dialectical materialism." Where Hegel saw history as the working out of *Geist,* to be understood only in terms of ideas, Marx saw it as a product of material conditions. For Marx, Hegel's ideas are merely artifacts of those base conditions—merely "ideology." To alter beliefs and ideas (the superstructure) in a Marxist analysis, one must first change the physical and economic conditions (the base) that they express. Using this analysis many Marxists believed that violent revolution alone could effect the necessary changes in the base so as to bring about a change in the superstructure. Marxists divide on whether it was proper to hasten the revolution by subversion—Leninism—or to await its gradual and peaceful supervention—revisionism or reformism (see Schorske 1–27). Marxist materialism offended all those who placed stock in "spiritual" values, which included Yeats, Pound, and Eliot—indeed most artists born before 1900.

In contrast to Marx and his followers, underconsumptionists were conservative to the extent that they wished to preserve the cultural heritage and social structure in which they found themselves. Of course, they were not conservative in the political sense of the term in 1990s North America, where it means an adherence to laissez-faire policies and a rejection equally of the Keynesian managed economy and of the socialist welfare state. Throughout the nineteenth century and up to the cold war, that set of views was called "liberalism" and was the target of criticism from both conservatives and socialists, who shared common ground with collectivist political philosophies. The conservatives—unlike the socialists—sought to retain private property and traditional spiritual values. Somewhat antinomially, both the conservatives of the first half of the century and those of the last quarter represent themselves as agents of change. (American populism is a late-nineteenth-century variety of conservative opposition to liberal laissez-faire individualism that shares many of the collectivist features of European radical conservatism. It will be discussed below.)

Pound's variety of conservatism rests on the assumption that human behavior is rational in that it is guided by a reasoned analysis of circumstances, goals, and the methods of achieving them. In their naiveté he, Orage, and Douglas thought that to reform society, all they had to do was present a cogent analysis of the issues, identify goals, and specify methods of achieving them. In contrast to the Marxists, they saw no need to shatter a mesmerizing false consciousness, but sought only to persuade a rational public to their views. To this end they wrote letters, articles, and books; edited journals; and formed associations and movements. Pound's behavior in the thirties and forties is perfectly typical of these reformers.

I do not meant to suggest that rationalism is equivalent to occultism or mysticism, though hard-nosed materialists, Marxists, and deconstructionists might so regard it. But the sine qua non of occultism and mysticism—as of religion itself—is belief in an immaterial realm. Occultists, in the West at least, are very much inclined to the idea that our intellects are capable of far more than we suppose, if only we could escape the constrictions and constraints of habit. Occultists treasure the "Ah Ha!" experience, when the scales fall off the eyes and everything becomes plain in a flash. Pound articulates this tendency to rely on sudden insight or revelation—albeit somewhat facetiously—in canto 39. After explicating Douglas's A + B theorem in very flat, prosaic lines, he adds: "and the light became so bright and so blindin' / in this layer of paradise / that the mind of man was bewildered" (canto 39/190).

The link, then, between underconsumptionism and occultism or mythopoetics is to be found primarily in a shared faith in human beings as essentially profligate, creative, generous, and generative. Underconsumptionists believe that incentives (such as profit), compulsion (such as vagrancy laws and hunger), and moral suasion (such as slogans like "the greatest good for the greatest number") are unnecessary inducements to human productivity. The thought that if people were free from want and restraint, the profligate creative forces of the human spirit would be released without further ado drives them. It was Pound's view that the artist above all embodied and articulated those generative and explosive forces, those procreative violations.

Orthodox economics is also grounded on a belief in the rationality of human conduct, but it presumes that possessiveness, not creativity, is the fundamental human passion. Marxism, by contrast, rejects rationalism and its posit of a free, autonomous *cogito,* though it accepts the orthodox finding of inevitable scarcity. In place of the rational agent, Marxism has false consciousness or ideology, a passive reflection of the material conditions in which the individual is nurtured. From a Marxist perspective, there is little to choose between the radical conservatism of Ruskin or Douglas and reforming liberals like Keynes, for both quixotically assume rational economic agents.

There is still another point of resemblance between underconsumptionism and occultism. Both are fringe "movements" or activities rejected by mainstream society and scorned as soft-headed or lunatic. At no time and in no place in the West since the advent of Christianity has either posture enjoyed respectability. Although such a nonsubstantive resemblance would not account for any shared opinions, it is an important sociological or ethnological factor that might help to account for the historical fact that in the interwar period, underconsumptionists and occultists frequently made common cause. In the case of Orage, Gorham Munson, and Pound occultism and underconsumptionism went hand-in-hand. But Ruskin, G. K. Chesterton, and Belloc were not occultists, though all were believing Christians. So far as I know J. A. Hobson, Kitson, and Douglas had no strong religious beliefs, and certainly no interest in the occult.

John L. Finlay provides ample details of the close ties that English theosophy had with Social Credit in *Social Credit: The English Origins* (138, 232–34, 243–44, 249), beginning with Orage himself. According to Finlay the Theosophical Order of Service and the Centre party (a Theosophical organization) were both keen supporters of Social Credit. John Hargrave's Kibbo Kift, a sort of adult—and protofascist—Boy Scout movement, adopted Social Credit and was also Theosophical in bent. Some Social Crediters were drawn to Steiner's Anthroposophy, but many more were old-style Blavatsky Theosophists, among them C. F. J. Galloway, A. E. Powell, Oscar Köllerström, George Hickling, and T. Kennedy. Finlay recalls that J. M. Cohn, "speaking in 1967 and looking back to the mystical circles in his Cambridge of the early twenties, made a special point of connecting Theosophical and Social Credit thinking" (232).

Finlay himself is friendly to both Theosophy and Social Credit. He sees an affinity in a particular cast of mind, which he calls "non-sequential thinking" (much like the "Ah Ha!" experience or satori Pound describes in canto 39): "Many instances of the non-sequential may be found in Social Credit and its associated patterns of thought. A good example would be in Theosophy. The aim of that philosophy is to bring the initiate to a sudden awareness of the truth which lies beyond the veil of appearances. In a slightly different way, Theosophy showed its non-sequential character in the ready way in which it took to the theory of relativity. For people used to Theosophical thinking, Einstein was not so revolutionary" (249). Such a comment may seem unremarkable—even banal—in these post-Derridean days when logocentrism is so widely pilloried by literary cognoscenti. However, it was already a commonplace amongst the occult in the early decades of the century. For example, Moina Mathers alluded to the increasing affinity between the occult and the physical in her introduction to the 1926 edition of her husband's translation of *The Kabbala Unveiled*: "Material science would appear to be spiritualising itself and occult science to be materializing itself. If not clasping hands, they are certainly making tentative attempts in that direction. The Ancient Wisdom, the Sacred Books taught . . . that Matter and Spirit are only opposite poles of the same universal substance" (viii). No doubt she had in mind the equivalence of matter and energy in Einstein's special theory of relativity, which occultists generally (though unjustifiably) take to be a corroboration of their spiritual monism and immanentism.

Finlay also documents the appeal of fascism to those underconsumptionists whose careers he traces, among them Pound and A. J. Penty. For example, the notorious Duke of Bedford (Lord Tavistock) was a Social Crediter as well as a friend to Hitler and the Nazis (for Tavistock see Finlay 132, 138, 177, 222). (Tavistock is the real-life model for the Nazi-loving Lord Darlington in the 1989 novel *Remains of the Day* by Kazuo Ishiguro.) Finlay argues that Social Credit is not fascist in political philosophy, but anarchist. However, as already noted, Social Crediters are typically conservative with respect to culture and social structure. As Finlay puts it: "The only step necessary to usher in the utopia [Social Crediters believed] was the removal of the exploiters, and given the feudal background [of Orage and company], this was held to mean a struggle against the state rather than against any class as such. Finally, the attraction of a feudal past led anarchists [of Eastern Europe] to ignore the methods and preoccupations of the liberal era which they had never known" (240).

Whether Social Crediters and underconsumptionists were fascist or anarchist may be disputed, but there is no doubt that they tended to be anti-Semitic. As already noted, Kitson and Douglas were unabashed anti-Semites and believers in the Zionist conspiracy—a vicious error Pound ultimately embraces. Kitson was an early admirer of Hitler. Penty, Chesterton, Belloc, and Orage all betray some degree of anti-Semitism, though none found Hitler to their taste. The prevalence of anti-Semitism amongst underconsumptionists tends to reinforce the presumption that there must be some common ground between economic heresy and Nazism. But the affinity ran only one way. No fascist or Nazi regime ever adopted, or even showed any interest in, underconsumptionist policy prescriptions. It seems that what they share is the perception by their adherents that they are unjustly neglected, exploited, and reviled, and a strong sense of collective loyalties, which perhaps accounts for the tendency to xenophobia and anti-Semitism.

Zeev Sternhell contends that fascism is characterized by a hostility to Enlightenment values that produced capitalism, liberalism, and popular democracy. He portrays it as arising amongst leftist socialists disappointed at the proletariat's failure to place class interests above national ones during World War I:

When these [the German, French, and Italian] leftists of all shapes and colors came to the conclusion that the working class had definitely beaten a retreat, they did not follow it into this attitude. Their socialism remained revolutionary when that of the proletariat had ceased to be so. Having to choose between the proletariat and revolution, they chose revolution: having to choose between a proletarian but moderate socialism and a non-proletarian but revolutionary and national socialism, they opted for the non-proletarian revolution, the national revolution. (27)

Thus, although fascism and Nazism have leftist roots, in Sternhell's opinion, all they retained of those roots was a belief in revolution. His analysis fits Mussolini and Hitler very well and can be adapted to fit Pound. Although Pound was never drawn to socialist revolution, he became revolutionary or avant-gardist in his aesthetics.

Mussolini's revolutionary rhetoric, anti-statal tendencies, and Caesarism were clearly attractive to Pound. Certainly Pound was not drawn to fascism because of any shared anti-Semitic sentiments, for anti-Semitism was not a component of Italian fascism until several years after Pound committed to Mussolini, as will be discussed below. But even though Pound adopted fascism when it was not anti-Semitic, to his shame, he followed Mussolini down that vicious road. Once infected by anti-Semitism, Pound's intellectual system proved incapable of producing an antibody. Even the horrors of the Holocaust—of which he learned while at St. Elizabeths Hospital (Hall 148)—were insufficient to cause Pound to rethink his conviction that the Jews were conspiring to control the world. It was only in extreme old age that he renounced his "error," very inadequately characterizing it (to Allen Ginsberg in 1967) as a "stupid, suburban prejudice" (Reck 29).

In the shadow of the Holocaust, it borders on the offensive to make distinctions about the motivation for such abominations, but it is on the distinct motivations for anti-Semitism that Pound and other anti-Semites often protest their innocence. Perhaps the most common motivation is simple xenophobia. But underconsumptionists, like Marxists, tended to be internationalists and were therefore not especially susceptible to xenophobia. Certainly Pound was not narrowly xenophobic.

Another—and pathological—motivation for anti-Semitism is the belief in a Jewish conspiracy to overthrow the gentile nations and to control the world. This particular motivation is peculiar to the modern world and is attached to the forged *Protocols of the Elders of Zion,* an early twentieth-century document. Underconsumptionists were much more vulnerable to this motivation—thought by Norman Cohn to be the most dangerous and ubiquitous of motivations for anti-Semitism (20–24). Even though Nazi anti-Semitism was fundamentally racist and biological in expression, Cohn believes that even it was fundamentally motivated by a belief in a Jewish conspiracy to control the world. Pound's radio broadcasts exemplify all three motivations, but we will see that it was conspiracy theory rather than xenophobia or racism that drew him into anti-Semitism.

For all his insistence on the individual and his admiration for Gesell's Proudhonian economic analysis, Pound was no anarchist. His enthusiasm for Confucian political philosophy is incompatible with anarchism of any sort. However authentic it may have been, Pound's Confucianism was so strongly held that he declared his translation of the Confucian *Ta Hio* "the most valuable work" he had "done in three decades"—that is, more important even than *The Cantos* ("Immediate Need of Confucius" in *Impact* 197). Pound saw fascism as fulfilling Cocteau's "rappel à l'ordre"—a return from liberal laissez-faire individualism to order and authority. This preference for order is abundantly clear in *Jefferson and/or Mussolini:*

> The "Will to power" (admired and touted by the generation before my own) was literatureifyed by an ill-balanced hysterical teuto-pollak [Nietzsche]. Nothing more vulgar, in the worst sense of the word, has ever been sprung on a dallying intelligentsia.
>
> Power is necessary to some acts, but neither Lenin nor Mussolini show themselves primarily as men thirsting for power.
>
> The great man is filled with a very different passion, the will toward *order.* (99)

A more uncompromising rejection of anarchism is hard to imagine.

CHAPTER 3

Modernism and Fascism

Although no one in possession of the facts could ever have doubted that Pound's loyalties were with Italy and not with his native country during World War II, Pound apologists have long denied it. They did so because it was not thought possible to admit such a thing without risking the exclusion of Pound from the literary canon. The situation is little different today when—in the wake of a powerful academic surge of neo-Marxism in the American academy—fascism is once again a common topic of academic discussion. The "Manichean" opposition, dating from the Spanish Civil War, between Communists and Fascists, with no room left in the middle for any alternatives—whether liberal democratic capitalism or Social Credit—is once again in vogue. The binarism of fascism versus Marxism has substantially displaced the equally oversimplified one of democracy versus totalitarianism that had dominated cold war rhetoric.

The neo-Marxist critique of modernism contrasts strongly with the older liberal-democratic critique, represented by John Raymond Harrison and William M. Chace. In his 1966 study, *The Reactionaries*, Harrison identified nationalism, corporatism, and elitism as the touchstones of modernist reaction. He, quite appropriately, saw them as the contrary of those liberal democratic attitudes of which he approved. Chace, in *The Political Identities of Ezra Pound and T. S. Eliot* (1973), identified radicalism as the root cause of modernists' failure to adhere to liberal democratic values and threw doubt on the supposition of any fundamental affinity between modernism and fascism. He also maintained that we must put Pound and Eliot into historical perspective if we are to understand the place and weight of their political affiliations, and I agree fully.

Peter Nichols adopts a neo-Marxist assessment of Pound's Fascist sympathies, regarding notions such as authority, reason, and philosophy as bourgeois illusions equally proper to fascism and liberalism (79–103). In support of this he points out that Pound's oft-admired distinction between "ideas in action" and mere abstract principles can be traced to Giovanni Gentile's *Dottrina del fascismo* (97–99). Gentile is certainly the source of the phrase, but Pound expressed much the same notion as early as the 1912 *New Age* series "Patria Mia." It is an idea that was endemic in the Kensington of Allan Upward and G. R. S. Mead.

The American Marxist critic Fredric Jameson, examining modernism through the rather eccentric lens of Wyndham Lewis in *Fables of Identity*, typifies Pound's position as protofascism and links it with American populism: "Protofascism may be characterized as a shifting strategy of class alliances whereby an initially strong populist and anticapitalist impulse is gradually readapted to the ideological habits of a petty bourgeoisie, which can itself be displaced when, with the consolidation of the fascist state, effective power passes back into the hands of big business." However well this characterization may fit Lewis, Mussolini, and Hitler, it certainly does not fit Pound so far as "the hands of big business" are concerned. Jameson assigns protofascism four characteristics: anti-Marxism, antiliberalism, petit bourgeois values, and statism (*Fables* 15–16). Only the second and fourth fit Pound, who was not particularly anti-Marxist. Like Wyndham Lewis and T. S. Eliot, Pound was stoutly antiliberal, but he was a Caesarist long before he had even heard of Mussolini.

As any Marxist would, Jameson regards the belief in the efficacy of persuasion—shared by liberal and conservative reformers—as a bourgeois illusion. On those grounds Pound is certainly bourgeois and is nicely picked out by the canny distinction Jameson draws between liberals and conservatives on this point: "Liberal or left-oriented idealism, from Godwin and Schiller to Charles Reich, aims essentially at the transformation of the self, at some fundamental transformation of our own consciousness (which will then make an external revolution in the institutions unnecessary): the culture critique of the Right, however, takes as the basic object of its diagnosis the consciousness of other people" (130). This observation certainly fits Pound, who has to be the least introspective major English-language poet. His entire career was devoted to the transformation of the consciousness of others, and—unlike Jameson's liberals—he believed that a transformation of his audience would be a sufficient condition for institutional reform and the consequent resolution of many of the world's problems.

But the difference between the liberal and the conservative on this point is not as sharp as Jameson would have it. After all, the transformation of society has to begin with the personal revelations that transform an individual such as Douglas, Orage, or Pound.

Marxist critiques of modernism are much more common now than the liberal critique mounted by Harrison and Chace (see also Kuberski; Morrison; and Wolfe), but both share the assumption that Pound's fascism represents a natural and coherent consequence of his views on other matters. They reject the defense that it was merely an "aberration," an inexplicable tic like Yeats's occultism or Joyce's superstitious attitude toward dates, and they are right to reject such a defense. On the other hand, it is difficult to be entirely comfortable with analyses of Pound and modernism from both ends of the political spectrum that agree only in condemning modernism as a faulted cultural moment (for a spirited defense of Pound's politics, see Scott).

Marjorie Perloff takes on the neo-Marxist condemnation of Pound and modernism by pointing out that American Marxism, at least, did not distinguish itself by opposition to fascism, but followed the Stalinist policy of appeasement until 1941. She concedes that the modernist doctrine of aesthetic autonomy may have contributed to the failure of modernists to respond more appropriately to the crises of midcentury, but she denies that political virtue and vice can be cleanly divided between Marxists and non-Marxists of the period:

> The poetics of Modernism, as Alfred Kazin rightly argues, must undergo severe scrutiny, for the Modernist (which is to say, late Romantic) subordination of life (and hence political consciousness) to "art," its insistence that the artist has no responsibility to anything but his or her art, has had serious consequences. But, and here I part company with Kazin, the implication that Marxist Modernists were immune from this particular historical dilemma, that it was a dilemma of the Right, is simply not so and contemporary Marxists have no reason to feel superior when they examine the Modernist ethos. (19)

In these remarks Perloff offers, I think, a wise and cogent assessment of the nature of the issue at stake—responsibility for the collective violence that has so marred this century. It is important to recognize that World War II and the Nazi death camps were neither the first nor the last—though the largest—of almost innumerable acts of collective violence both before 1939 and after 1945. It is difficult to make this next observation without engaging political or nationalist passions that one would wish to keep in abeyance, but it must be said that all ideological sides and many nations on all sides have been guilty of appalling acts of violence. Perhaps one of the greatest distortions of the history of this century is the notion that all human evil was concentrated in German Nazis between 1933 and 1945. So long as we suppose that opposition to Hitler and the Axis powers is enough to certify one a saint, and association with them enough to certify one a monster, we must disown Pound and all his works.

Such a supposition has long prevented cool discussion of Pound's politics. That it is erroneous should be obvious to anyone in possession of a little historical information. The Soviet Union entered into an alliance with Hitler's Germany despite the implacable hostility of Nazism toward communism and their surrogates' shooting war in Spain. On the other hand, Stalin's alliance with Britain and the United States after Germany invaded the Soviet Union did nothing to help the millions of victims of his regime. Within the United Sates, Franklin Delano Roosevelt was regarded as a war monger and almost a traitor by many Americans—not just Ezra Pound—because of his eagerness to enter the war on Britain's side (Hofstadter, *Progressive* 328–39). Postwar history in the Far East, North Africa, equatorial Africa, Central America, and the Middle East has surely taught us that human evil is widely distributed and respects no ideological or national boundaries.

The vast majority of us choose sides on subrational, emotional, and historical grounds—on grounds of loyalty and patriotism. Ideology and morality commonly serve only to rationalize choices made on those other grounds. Indeed, the traitor is by definition one who changes his or her natal loyalties. Pound certainly did remove his loyalties from the United States and gave them to Italy. The pertinent question is, Why did he do so? It may have been for ideological, personal, cultural, intellectual, or psychological reasons or any combination of them. All five factors played a role. The psychological reasons were not insanity, but arrogance, impatience, and frustration. The intellectual reasons were not quite stupidity, but certainly include a failure to understand the true nature of the Fascist regimes he approved and the liberal democratic regimes he denounced.

Burton Hatlen in a 1985 article, "Ezra Pound and Fascism," concedes Pound's fascism and argues that his anti-Semitism followed from it. Hatlen accepts Noel Stock's chronology, which places Pound's turn to anti-Semitism in 1939, which is several years late,[1] but the major difficulty with Hatlen's argument is that Pound was Fascist in sympathy from at least 1933. He needs some story to account for the delay, but he provides none.

Another difficulty is that he conflates fascism, Nazism, and anti-Semitism as if they came as a set. But fascism was very different from Nazism, and not at all anti-Semitic from 1919 to 1935. It seems to have been the Italian disasters of 1935 in the Spanish Civil War that first prompted Fascist scapegoating of "Bolshevik Jews" (Cannistraro and Sullivan 488–89). Even then, there was no official anti-Semitism in Italy until the passing of the racial laws in 1938.

Hatlen's article sets out to answer the questions, "To what extent did Pound commit himself during the 1930s not only to Mussolini as a leader but also to Fascism as an ideology? And to what extent do the cantos which he wrote during this period serve as a vehicle for such an ideology?" Boldly abandoning earlier apologetic postures of Pound scholars, he adds: "the statement 'Ezra Pound was a fascist' seems to me indisputably true." His resolution of the dilemma is to argue that fascism "blended an authoritarianism usually associated with the 'right' and a 'populism' usually characteristic of the 'left'" (145).

It seems to have become a truism that Pound's fascism was an outgrowth of the American populism in which he was ostensibly raised. Hatlen regards populism as an American equivalent of European socialism. But twentieth-century populists like Huey Long and Father Coughlin, both of whom Pound admired, were ideologues of the Right, not of the Left. It is true that, like the populists, they were antistatist, and on those grounds might be seen to have had some affinity with anarchism, but hardly with socialism. And it is not clear that they were any less "authoritarian" than Mussolini or Hitler, though, of course, Long had less opportunity than they, and Father Coughlin had none at all.

The strongest affinities between Pound's political posture and populism are not those one would wish to promote. Indeed, Richard Hofstadter invokes Pound and some of his heroes in his characterization of American populism's anti-Semitism: "It is not too much to say that the Greenback-Populist tradition activated most of what we have of modern popular anti-Semitism in the United States. From Thaddeus Stevens and Coin Harvey to Father Coughlin, and from Brooks and Henry Adams to Ezra Pound, there has been a curiously persistent linkage between anti-Semitism and money and credit obsessions. A full history of modern anti-Semitism in the United States would reveal, I believe, its substantial Populist lineage" (*Age* 81–82). And there is a strong similarity between Pound's attitude to war and those Hofstadter attributes to American populists: "The Populists distinguished between wars for humanity, and wars of conquest. The first of these they considered legitimate, but naturally they had difficulty in discriminating between the two, and they were quite ready to be ballyhooed into a righteous war, as the Cuban situation was to show" (86). Pound's response to Mussolini's adventures in Ethiopia and Spain, for example, is a mirror image of the jingoistic response of Richard Hovey (a poet admired by the young Pound) to the Spanish-American War expressed in "The Word of the Lord from Havana," which Hovey wrote after the destruction of the *Maine* and published in the New York *World* (Macdonald 203). Although Pound preached isolationism to his American compatriots, he supported Italy's military adventures just as uncritically as Hovey had supported American imperialistic belligerence.

In any case, the opposition Hatlen sets up between authoritarianism and socialism is hardly persuasive, since they are not proper contraries. Lenin and Stalin were just as authoritarian as Hitler, Franco, and Mussolini. Mussolini's fascism was, indeed, superficially like American populism, but neither were "left wing" in the standard sense of public ownership of the means of production and state regulation of the economy. American populists were—and are—opposed to "big government" and state enterprise. By contrast socialists tend to regard the state as the principal instrument of social and economic justice and hence favor "big government." Like the populists, Fascist rhetoric also castigates big government, substituting the intimacy of the party for the cold, remote state.

In his study of Mussolini's reception in America John P. Diggins notes that though they were initially warm, most Americans turned hostile toward Italian fascism by the late twenties (498). Always out of step, Pound's own interest began just as his compatriots' interest was waning. Diggins documents fascism's appeal to a broad range of American political opinion:

> We would do well to bear in mind that Fascism, because of its novelty, eclecticism, and ambiguity, drew admiration from conservatives as well as from liberals, from Christian disciples of natural law, from humanist advocates of ordered hierarchy, and from nervous defenders of private property, not to mention the general public, whose understanding of Fascism was shrouded by a fascination with Mussolini and his cult of personality. In the end it was, after all, not [John] Dewey and [Horace] Kallen but Santayana and Pound who found their spiritual home in Italy. (505)

Fascism and Nazism were little more than old-fashioned tyrannies. They both replaced the rule of law and institutional government and regulation with the personal rule of a tyrant—though Mussolini's hold on the state and party apparatus proved to be much less firm than Hitler's. The *Führer Prinzip* was really nothing more than tyranny dressed up in the mystical notion that the Führer embodies the will of the people. American populism can, I think, be regarded as the indigenous expression of the same antiliberal, antimaterialist, conservative, and xenophobic nationalism that was expressed in Europe by fascism and Nazism. American populism was certainly less given to violence, but it was by no means immune to racism and xenophobia (see Casillo 380–82; and Hofstadter, *Age* 77–91). Political movements are seldom clear or pure expressions of political, economic, or social theory, but tend to be heteroclite coalitions of political activists with ill-defined and often inchoate objectives.

Nonetheless, some affinities between European fascism and American populism are apparent. For example, the Populist party presidential candidate in 1904, Thomas E. Watson, published virulent attacks on Roman Catholics, blacks, Jews, and socialists. He was prosecuted, though not convicted, for *The Roman Catholic Hierarchy* (1910), a diatribe against Catholics. Benjamin Ryan Tillman, governor of South Carolina (1890–94), is another populist whose record is not encouraging. He disenfranchised most of South Carolina's black population in 1895 and defended the use of force to prevent those blacks who retained the franchise from voting.

It is true, however, that both the Populist party and the Social Credit movement advocated monetary reform. The Populists backed William Jennings Bryan in his bimetallist campaign of 1896. After he began corresponding with Arthur Kitson, Pound began to express an interest in Bryan's bimetallism, but that was not until after 13 January 1933. In any event, Hatlen argues for a benign similarity between fascism and populism, not between Social Credit and populism. In the thirties, when Pound became a Fascist, populism was long dead as a national political force, and individuals such as Huey Long and Father Charles Coughlin who donned the populist mantle were not left-wing as Hatlen's argument requires. In fact, Coughlin was a virulent anticommunist and anti-Semite and a paid propagandist for the Axis powers (Warren 233–38).

Discussion of Pound's political loyalties is constrained on the one hand by the requirement that culture heroes cannot be wrong about cultural and political matters and on the other by everyone's unwillingness to argue that Pound's fascism was wise—or even tolerable—after 1936. As a consequence it has been necessary for apologists to deny the plain facts or, alternatively, to isolate Pound's Fascist sympathies by construing them as an unfortunate consequence of his commitment to Social Credit. Neither of these arguments quite fits the facts as they are now available to us.

Although C. David Heymann's printing of English translations of the letters Pound sent to Mussolini and Ciano in two appendixes to *Ezra Pound: The Last Rower* in 1976 (317–31) failed to persuade Pound scholars, Tim Redman's careful and sympathetic study, *Ezra Pound and Italian Fascism,* has surely removed all reasonable doubt that Pound's relationship with Mussolini and Italian fascism was close and friendly—at least from Pound's side. (The regime itself was not at all sure that Pound's message was one it wished to foster.) But if Pound's Fascist loyalty cannot be denied, the role that economics played in determining his political allegiance is still in dispute. We do know that he was radicalized by Social Credit economics more than a decade before he expressed any interest in fascism—in 1933, the year he wrote *Jefferson and/or Mussolini.*

A careless assessment might lead one to suppose that Pound's move to Rapallo from Paris in 1924 was inspired by Mussolini's installation as premier two years previously (October 1922). Pound's own testimony belies such an interpretation: "Life was interesting in Paris from 1921 to 1924, nobody bothered much about Italy. Some details I never heard of at all until I saw the Esposizione del Decennio [of 1932]" (*Jefferson* 51). Pound had no reason in 1935 to deny an early interest in Mussolini, and I have been unable to find any praise of Mussolini earlier than a 30 November 1926 letter to Harriet Monroe in which he says that he thinks "extremely well of Mussolini" (Paige 279).

Though he praises the Fascist state in "The State," an article of 1927, he is still leaning toward the Chestertonian feudal state. But he ultimately retreats to the principle of aesthetic detachment, incompatible with fascism:

> Both Fascio and the Russian revolution are interesting phenomena; beyond which there is the historic perspective. . . .
>
> The capitalist imperialist state must be judged not only in comparison with unrealised utopias, but with past forms of the state; if it will not bear comparison with the feudal order; with the small city states both republican and despotic; either as to its "social justice" *or* as to its permanent products, art, science, literature, the onus of proof goes against it.
>
> The contemporary mind will have to digest this concept of the state as convenience.
>
> The antithesis is: the state as an infernal nuisance.
>
> As to our "joining revolutions" etc. It is unlikely. The artist is concerned with producing something that will be enjoyable even after a successful revolution. (*Selected Prose* 214–15)

Pound had responded favorably to Gabriele D'Annunzio's Fiume adventure of 1919, in which Mussolini embroiled his still marginal Fascist party. D'Annunzio, a Futurist poet, had seized control of the Yugoslavian city of Fiume in September, claiming it for Italy. In "The Revolt of Intelligence" Pound interprets D'Annunzio's adventure—rather implausibly—as symbolic of the struggle of the individual against an oppressive bureaucracy, displaying a tendency to depoliticize the event, very much in contrast with his later habits:

> The D'Annunzio matter is almost wholly a duel between the type

D'Annunzio and the type Woodrow Wilson. D'Annunzio is, unfortunately for our little demonstration, not a pure type, but in the main he represents art and literature. . . . He represents the individual human being, the personality as against the official card-index and official Globe Wernicke system. And this being so, Fiume represents and precedes more important, if less melodramatic, conflicts between art, literature, intelligence, and card-index and officialdom. (13 Nov. 1919, 21)

Little troubled by D'Annunzio's resort to violence as a political instrument, Pound used him as an instance of a politically engaged intellectual.

The Fiume adventure came to an ignoble, and rather bloody, end when Italian forces stormed the city and drove out D'Annunzio's unruly gang in January 1921. Permitted to retire to a retreat on Lake Garda, D'Annunzio declined all future offers to play a political role (Cannistraro and Sullivan 234–36). All in all Pound seems not to have been terribly impressed by D'Annunzio, who rates only three mentions in *The Cantos* and only the last is of much interest. There the poet-revolutionary is memorialized for his rhetorical powers and juxtaposed with Amphion, whose lyre magically caused the stones to build the walls of Thebes:

> & there is no doubt that D'Annunzio
> Could move the crowd in a theatre
> or that the stone rose in Brescia,
> Amphion.
> (93/650)

Pound began to seek an audience with Mussolini in April 1932 and was eventually received on 30 January 1933 (Zapponi 48–49). According to Pound's own testimony, he wrote *Jefferson and/or Mussolini* in February 1933, immediately after the interview. The meeting with Mussolini seems to have been the catalyst that made Pound a Fascist. Pound had sent Mussolini a version of his "Volitionist Economics" handbill and a copy of *The Cantos*. He was so impressed with Mussolini's noncommittal remark on *The Cantos*—"But this is amusing!"—that he cites it in canto 41: "'Ma questo,' / said the Boss, 'e divertente.' / catching the point before the aesthetes had got there" (41/202). He did not have so much luck with the eight points he raised in his handbill.[2]

It is difficult to resist the conclusion that Pound was simply flattered out of his senses by this man who, it must be conceded, had charmed an entire nation, much of Europe, and a good deal of the United States: "His confiding, ingenuous manner, his voice, low-pitched and melodious, made most people take to him on sight. No less a being than Mahatma Gandhi lamented: 'Unfortunately, I am no superman like Mussolini.' The Arch-

bishop of Canterbury saw him as 'the one giant figure in Europe.' Banker
Otto Khan declared: 'The world owes him a debt of gratitude.' 'He was,'
avowed Thomas Edison, 'the greatest genius of the modern age'" (Collier
93). Admittedly—with the exception of Gandhi's undoubtedly facetious
remark—these testimonies come from those already disposed to a conservative ideology.

Mussolini did not appear to the world in the twenties and thirties as the
clownish and ineffectual figure that subsequent events and commentaries have made of him:

> In the thirteen years between the March on Rome in 1922 and the out-
> break of the Ethiopian War in 1935, Mussolini enjoyed a highly favor-
> able image in the foreign press. There were a few journalists and anti-
> Fascist exiles who had witnessed Blackshirt brutalities and wrote highly
> critical accounts of Mussolini's dictatorship. Certain liberal or leftist jour-
> nals and newspapers reminded their readers of the beatings, tortures,
> imprisonments, and murders by which the Fascist regime had come to
> power. Their message went largely unheard. Even in Western democra-
> cies the majority of news publications depicted Mussolini as a necessary
> antidote to the chaos that had plagued Italy. He was the man who chased
> the beggars off the streets, introduced respect for law and order, and
> saved Italy from bolshevism. (Cannistraro and Sullivan 350)

Jefferson and/or Mussolini presents Mussolini as a wise and benevolent
tyrant and aligns him with Lenin and Jefferson. Aware that Mussolini's rule
was dictatorial, Pound claims, quite implausibly—in an effort to make the
the democrat look like a tyrant—that Jefferson ruled the United States for
twenty-four years, "eight years as President and the sixteen wherein he
governed more or less through deputies, Madison and Monroe or 48 if
you count Van Buren's presidency and discount John Quincy Adams" (14–
15). The tyrant rules by force of personality rather than duly constituted
authority. The claim that Jefferson "governed with a limited suffrage and
by means of conversation with his more intelligent friends" (15) is less far-
fetched, but is also transparently designed to make dictatorship appear
more palatable.

Pound also contrasts Mussolini's achievements with the failures of the
democracies. His hope is to make Mussolini's self-declared dictatorship
palatable on a great man, or Caesarist, view of historical causation—a view
Pound had already articulated in the Malatesta cantos (composed in
1922–23). (Hitler, who had just become German chancellor on 30 January 1933, is spoken of disparagingly [127].) At this date, Pound was tout-
ing Mussolini, not the entire right-wing movement we now lump together
as fascism.

Even though Mussolini was widely admired in the early thirties, when Italy was suffering much less from the Great Depression than other nations, *Jefferson and/or Mussolini* does nothing to enhance Pound's reputation as a judge of talent. However, we should not judge Pound's error with the advantage of hindsight. A *London Times* editorial on the strong showing of the Nazis in the German election of 1930 reveals that he was not alone in his misreading of the rise of fascism: "The Nazis have scored their overwhelming success because they have appealed to something more fundamental and more respectable. Like the Italian Fascists they stand for some national ideal, however nebulous and extravagantly expressed, to which personal and class interests shall be subordinate" (qtd. in Meyers 191). Even Jean Paul Sartre, who is at the other end of the political spectrum from Pound, reports that he was quite unaware at this time of the threat that Nazism and fascism represented. He recalls that though he "studied Husserl and Heidegger in Berlin when Hitler was already in power," "until the Munich Agreement [of September 1938 he] was hardly aware of what Nazi rule meant" (qtd. in Meyers 192). Sartre's remark is all the more astonishing when we remember that the Nuremberg racial laws were promulgated on 15 September 1934.

There is little in *Jefferson and/or Mussolini* that we would normally identify as Fascist. There is no mention of racism, no legitimation of violence—either of political assassination or of military adventures—and no talk of grandeur. Even anticommunism, the stock-in-trade of all European varieties of fascism, is not invoked. Instead Pound continues the praise of Lenin that dates to Lincoln Steffens's lecture he heard in Paris in 1924, to which Mary Colum says he listened "with rapt attention, his eyes glued to the speaker's face. . . . And after Steffens was finished he rose to his feet and started talking about the Douglas plan" (*Life and the Dream* 18, qtd. in Norman 272). Pound remembers this lecture in cantos 19 and 84, and boasts in 1930 that he knew of Steffens's "results" by word of mouth before they were published (*Ezra Pound's Poetry and Prose* 5:200–201).

He claims a superiority of fascist over communist revolution for the rather whimsical—but *echt* fascist—reason that "it is not a revolution according to preconceived type" (*J/M* 24). Viewed dispassionately, *Jefferson and/ or Mussolini* is a rather silly book arguing for a primitive political tyranny in which a worthy leader has absolute power. It is evident that Pound is a babe in the political woods, praising innocuous but misguided policies such as Mussolini's drive to increase the Italian population (*J/M* 71–73; cf. Parker 161) and denying the facts of Fascist state censorship of the press.

But there is no reason to doubt that *Jefferson and/or Mussolini* represents Pound's true political beliefs at the time. *The Cantos* also canonizes authoritarian leaders beginning with Sigismondo Malatesta and ending with a motley collection of obscure and semimythical characters such as Abd-el-Melik and the San-ku. Since the Malatesta cantos were composed in 1922–23 *before* Mussolini had made any impression on Pound, we can safely conclude that Pound's preference for benevolent tyranny over democracy was a cause, not an effect, of his infatuation with Mussolini, and although such a preference is obviously undemocratic, it is not fascist in any determinative sense—unless we are willing to make Alexander, Caesar, and Napoleon fascists.

A more accurate description of Pound's ideological posture in 1933 would be Douglasite in economics, modernist in aesthetics, and Platonic in politics. The last epithet is somewhat honorific but not inaccurate, even though, so far as I can determine, Pound never appeals to the *Republic* to support his views. Instead he turns to Confucius and Mencius. Confucian political theory legitimates tyranny in that the just ruler reigns with "the mandate of heaven," not of the people. Pound's earliest political pronouncements, found in *Patria Mia,* celebrated the "imperium," strongly suggesting that his distrust of democracy was not newly acquired in 1933, but was part of the baggage of symbolist elitism that he brought with him from the United States. A letter of 2 June 1934 to Douglas leaves no doubt about his approval of tyranny: "Note that a DICTATOR has damn well GOT to represent the will of the peepul to a much greater degree than any MP or any god damn shitten aggregate of elected blow pipes" (Pound Papers). The Fascist Il Duce or the Nazi Führer, of course, does not *represent* the will of the people in the standard meaning of political representation, but rather *embodies* it in some quasi-mystical manner.

Those in Pound's London circle—Yeats, Ford, Orage, Hulme, Douglas, and Wyndham Lewis—were also antidemocratic and elitist. But Pound alone of that group succumbed to the "temptation" of fascism. Despite his constant praise of Mussolini to Orage and Douglas, neither man saw anything to admire in Mussolini or fascism.

Although an open anti-Semite, Douglas was not attracted to either fascism or Nazism, an anomaly of which Pound complains to Gerhart Münch in a letter of 11 November 1939 (by which date Pound had fully succumbed to paranoid anti-Semitism:

C. H. Douglas is steaming away on six cylinders every week damning jews. BUT he knows nothing of Italy. I have hammered fascism at him for years. If there were more German EDUCATION, if instead of Russian propaganda we had had more EDUCATION, a man like Doug/ wouldn't be going on as if the Nazi land tenure didn't exist.
    All this inalienable minimum holdings, indivisible etc. ought to have been advertised.

The Social Crediter IS explaining in words of one syllable HOW the Jew got his power, and how he goes on gettin it.

What we need FROM Germany is clear text books written on one text of *Mein Kampf/* namely the passage on *LEIHKAPITAL* [loan capital]. (Pound Papers)

Douglas's case demonstrates that underconsumptionism, conspiracy theory, and anti-Semitism do not inevitably produce fascist sympathies. It may seem fussy to stress that one set of beliefs and attitudes do not lead inevitably to identification with groups that hold similar beliefs and attitudes or to approval of their actions, but current critical commentary is so thoroughly a priori in its analysis of political postures that I feel obliged to stress the role of the contingent in human action. Philip Kuberski and Paul Morrison, for example, explain Pound's fascism and anti-Semitism as the inescapable consequence of his aesthetics and poetics. Kuberski's semiotic analysis is the most uncompromising:

> Not only does writing lead Pound to espouse currency reform and to argue for the rightness of fascism for Italy, it also leads him to anti-Semitism. Like his other interests, anti-Semitism is an anachronistic aspect of the political anachronism of fascism. It suggests Pound's nostalgia for an enclosure like the medieval church that could bind history, language, politics, and art into an apparently cohesive ideology. . . . So Pound's anti-Semitism is not an imitation of fascist policy or simply a prejudice; it is an elaboration of the poetics that he displaced into social issues. (18–19)

Although such an assertion is not susceptible of proof or disproof, the fact that others who shared Pound's nostalgia did not embrace fascism at least counts as a counterexample to the inevitability of Pound's "case."

Morrison's take on the Pound case is subtler—and more opaque—than Kuberski's, but participates in the same neo-Marxist apriorism: "But Pound's anti-Semitism and fascism are best understood not as resistance to metaphor but as a failure to read or critique the culture of metaphor other than metaphorically. Pound's hell betrays a thoroughly tropological relation to the actual. And in this we are still his contemporaries" (Morrison 20). Both comments can be placed under the rubric of Walter Benjamin's notion, which they both cite, that fascism is the "aestheticization of politics," that is to say, an application of the aesthetic principles of coherence, comeliness, and closure to political ideology. Though this assessment might apply to D'Annunzio's Fiume adventure, it seems to me woefully inadequate when applied to the behavior of Fascist and Nazi regimes. One wonders if Benjamin would have revised his view in the light of later events, had he not taken his life in 1940.

Wendy Stallard Flory adopts a less opaque apologetics in *The American Ezra Pound*. She takes the view that his anti-Semitism was a psychosis: "Pound's perceptions of the political world and his relationship to it were so at odds with the real situation as to be genuinely psychotic." However, she wants to isolate this "psychosis" from the rest of Pound's intellect, in which "an intuitive sense of moral responsibility and moral decency seems to have been preserved intact" (144). This defense is perilously close to pointing out that the staff of Buchenwald and Belsen were loving parents and loyal spouses. Certainly Pound believed that he was acting morally when he denounced the Jewish conspiracy and endorsed Nazi racial policies, but surely we cannot regard that delusion as exculpatory.

Pound's movement from an understandable, if rather foolish, admiration for Mussolini in 1933 to a full endorsation of the international gangsterism and racism of the Nazis by 1939 is difficult to reconcile with the picture of Pound as a decent and intelligent human being. The enormity of Pound's intellectual failure is somewhat mitigated by a reconstruction of the complexity of the political scene in the 1930s, when the democracies were mismanaging their economies disastrously.

Liberalism, closely identified with laissez-faire economics, was seriously discredited in everyone's minds. Socialism and Marxism seemed almost inevitable alternatives, but many saw them as leading inevitably to Belloc's servile state. The brutal collectivization begun by Stalin in 1928 and the purges beginning in 1934 did little to mitigate such fears. Mussolini and Hitler seemed to offer an alternative. These circumstances made it difficult to see a clear political route and make Pound's political errors somewhat more comprehensible. I can think of nothing, however, that would excuse his failure to deplore political assassination, racism, and mass extermination.

G. K. Chesterton is an interesting case in point. He was openly anti-Semitic for most of his career—in the Christian version, which condemns the Jews for stubbornly rejecting the Messiah who came among them. But he renounced his anti-Semitism in the face of Nazi atrocities in a letter to the *Jewish Chronicle* published in September 1933. Chesterton was brought to this change of heart by the harassment of Jews by Nazi thugs. Of course things were to get much worse. Most of those who held "genteel" anti-Semitic views did not recognize the evil of Nazism until the Nuremberg race laws of September 1934 or Kristallnacht of November 1938. Of course, neither of these outrages compare to the genocidal policies Germany adopted in 1941, but the genocide was a closely guarded secret—though rumors abounded—until the truth was revealed when the allies overran extermination camps in 1945 (Rubinstein 84–86).

Though Chesterton's renunciation of anti-Semitism is far from complete, his rejection of Nazi brutality is perfectly clear and contrasts favorably with Wyndham Lewis's response to it two years earlier in *Hitler* (1931)— not to speak of Pound's fulminations at about the same time as Chesterton's letter:

> In our early days Hilaire Belloc and myself were accused of being uncompromising anti-semites.
>
> Today, although I still think that there is a Jewish problem, and that what I understand by the expression "the Jewish spirit" is a spirit foreign to Western countries, I am appalled by the Hitlerite atrocities in Germany. They have absolutely no reason or logic behind them, and are quite obviously the expediency of a man who, not knowing quite what to do to carry out his wild promises to a sorely tried people, has been driven to seeking a scapegoat, and has found, with relief, the most famous scapegoat in European history—the Jewish people. I am quite ready to believe now that Belloc and myself will die defending the last Jew in Europe. Thus does history play its ironical jokes upon us. (*Jewish Chronicle*, 23 Sept. 1933, qtd. in Rubinstein 58)

One can see Chesterton's basic morality overcoming his bigotry toward a culture and religion he regards as alien and hostile. Pound seems to have lacked such a sheet anchor to keep him from the excesses into which his passionate espousal of an economic scheme he believed would guarantee peace and social justice led him.

Oddly, Pound's "treason" seems to generate more heat than his fascism and racism. On that point, we should remember that Fascist Italy was a trusted ally of Britain and France until Mussolini's invasion of Ethiopia (1934–35) strained relations and drove Italy closer to Germany—leading ultimately to the Axis alliance of October 1936. Nor was Mussolini the only dictator in Europe in 1933. Spain was ruled by the military dictator Miguel Primo de Rivera until his overthrow in 1930 by a monarchist regime, which was in turn displaced by a Republican regime two years later. General Francisco Franco rose up in rebellion against the Republicans in 1936 and took power in 1939. Poland was ruled by another military dictator, József Pilsudski, for virtually the entire interwar period (see Parker). Weak democratic governments—notably the Weimar Republic of Germany—were proving unable (or unwilling) to govern. Strong men like Mussolini, Primo de Rivera, and Pilsudski seemed to many a necessary evil in the face of economic collapse, social unrest, and the Communist threat.

In contrast to Primo de Rivera and Pilsudski, military dictators with scant public relations skills, Mussolini was a journalist and intellectual whose success was a consequence of such skills. Like Hitler, he was a spellbinding orator who represented his movement as a middle ground between liberal democracy and communism. Though we can now see that he was little more than an opportunistic demagogue, he did not seem so to many sensible people at the time, including the renowned Italian philosophers Benedetto Croce and Giovanni Gentile, who gave fascism intellectual respectability. They represented it as an alternative to the godless materialism of communism, to liberal skepticism, and to anarchist disorder.

Although sharing Sorel and Proudhon as precursors with communism, fascism represented itself as the contrary of communism:

> Such a conception of life [love of neighbor and vigilance against the other] makes Fascism the resolute negation of the doctrine underlying so-called scientific and Marxian socialism, the doctrine of historic materialism which would explain the history of mankind in terms of the class-struggle and by changes in the processes and instruments of production, to the exclusion of all else.
>
> That the vicissitudes of economic life—discoveries of raw materials, new technical processes, scientific inventions—have their importance, no one denies; but that they suffice to explain human history to the exclusion of other factors is absurd. Fascism believes now and always in sanctity and heroism, that is to say in acts in which no economic motive—remote or immediate—is at work. Having denied historic materialism, which sees in men mere puppets on the surface of history, appearing and disappearing on the crest of the waves while in the depths the real directing forces move and work, Fascism also denies the immutable and irreparable character of the class struggle which is the natural outcome of this economic conception of history; above all it denies that the class struggle is the preponderating agent in social transformations. (Mussolini 20)

Though Pound assigned much greater importance to "economic life" and scientific inventions than did Mussolini, he ignored that disagreement, presumably because their agreement on the centrality of human agency, of "sanctity and heroism," was of overriding importance.

As early as 1918, Pound had seen himself as occupying a beleaguered middle ground between Bolshevik communism and Christian superstition:

> AT PRESENT the intellectual sees himself threatened by bolshevism on one side and the Y. M. C. A. on the other, while the raging three-headed Kultur-bitch devastates things in the middle. Is it any wonder he is indifferent to the speeches and essays of Missouri professors, that he is self-absorbed, or despondent, or busy with attempting computations for the salvage of some scraps of civilisation?
>
> He does not want labouring men and their families mowed down by the machine-guns of militia subsidised by the capitalist.

He does not want labour to bull-doze civilisation, he does not want bolshevism, he does not want Whitechapel to sack the West End. He does not want the Y. M. C. A. erected into an American national church, and erecting an inquisition more tyrannous and less systematised than that which catholicism revived as recently as A. D. 1824.

He does not want reactions into outworn superstitions. He has his hands and his mind full. He does not want his papers suppressed. He does not want a censorship of literature and the arts placed in the hands of the ignorant and of fanatics. ("What America Has to Live Down" 314)

This position is distinctly at odds with fascism, which was to present itself as the champion of Christian spirituality and truth against the godless materialism of the Communists and the relativism of the liberals. Moreover, when Pound looks to the past, it is primarily to the late Middle Ages and the Italian Renaissance—to the Troubadours, Cavalcanti, Dante, and the Medicis. Fascism, by contrast, looked to the Enlightenment and classical Rome.

Sixteen years later, when he declared his Fascist sympathies in *Jefferson and/or Mussolini,* Pound praised Lenin—along with the arch capitalist Henry Ford—but saw Mussolini's fascism as the heir to the Italian renaissance: "Henry Ford and Mussolini may have done more than any two men save Lenin himself toward damning and breaking up the bankers' stranglehold on humanity, but they are at absolute opposites on MAN. One of the most vigorous sinews of the fascist doctrine is that the MAN shall not be reduced to the status of mere mechanism. This is Italian, Italianissimo and fibre of Italian Anschauung since the renaissance" ("Declaration" 5).

Pound's belief that fascism was a bulwark defending the individual against dehumanizing technology is hardly justified and was remote from Mussolini's stress on the discipline that fascism imposes on the individual, replacing the flabby indulgence of the liberal state:

The key-stone of the Fascist doctrine is its conception of the State, of its essence, its functions, and its aims. For Fascism the State is absolute, individuals and groups relative. Individuals and groups are admissible in so far as they come within the State. Instead of directing the game and guiding the material and moral progress of the community, the liberal State restricts its activities to recording results. The Fascist State is wide awake and has a will of its own. For this reason it can be described as "ethical." (Mussolini 27)

This sounds very much like the vigorous Christianity of the YMCA, which Pound had found thoroughly undesirable in "What America Has to Live Down."

Fascism was antimaterialistic, and to that extent opposed to the technological imperatives that Marxist materialism and laissez-faire liberalism both regarded as inescapable. Its antimaterialism is one component that merited Pound's admiration, given his own rather special form of idealism. Pound's Crocean slogan, "ideas in action," expresses the political form of his idealism. Croce, like Pound, thought fascism could be an instrument of his idealist philosophy, and Mussolini tolerated his illusion. This form of idealism maintains that actions are the output of freely formed true beliefs and rational desires. It is directly contradictory of dialectical materialism's false consciousness. Pound ties this dynamic Crocean idealism to Social Credit, calling the amalgam "Volitionist Economics":

> Ideas are true as they go into action. I am not resurrecting a pragmatic sanction, but trying to light up pragmatic PROOF. . . .
> The moment man realizes that the guinea stamp not the metal, is the essential component of the coin, he has broken with all materialist philosophies. . . .
> I repeat: this view repudiates materialism. It is volitionism. It inheres and adheres in and to certain kinds of thinking, certain systems of values. (*Guide* 188–89)

His point is that an understanding of monetary value as conventional or ideal entails a rejection of materialism. The contrary, gold standard view is materialistic.

Pound's use of the word *pragmatic* here may well have been motivated by Mussolini's habit of allying his Fascist movement with American pragmatism, particularly as articulated by William James. Indeed, in the preface to *All the King's Men* Robert Penn Warren claimed that James lay behind both Mussolini and Huey Long—the model for "the King" of the novel—an opinion shared by many thoughtful Americans in the early twenties (Diggins 493–98). However, when questioned about James by Horace Kallen, "Mussolini could make only vague references to titles of books" (Diggins 489). Fascism was "pragmatic" only in the general sense that it was not guided by principle or plan, but by the necessities of the moment. Indeed, the notion of "ideas in action" is more like Hegelian idealism than pragmatic Darwinism.

As a materialist Marx found Ricardo's labor theory of value congenial: "The recent scientific discovery, that the products of labour, so far as they are values, are but material expressions of the human labour spent in their production, marks, indeed, an epoch in the history of the development of the human race, but by no means, dissipates the mist through which the social character of labour appears to us to be an objective character of the products themselves" (Marx 1:79). Marx's meaning is that our attachment of value to the "objective character of the products them-selves"—such as beauty or utility—is an illusion. In reality that value is what he elsewhere calls "congealed" labor. Things are valued because of the labor embodied in them, not because of any intrinsic features they may possess. Marxists call the latter view "essentialism," since it supposedly assigns some Aristotelian essence to a merely phenomenal object. For Pound a beautiful object or action is beautiful because it is an embodi-ment of intellect, not of labor. Pound expressed this view most succinctly and beautifully in canto 51: "That hath the light of the doer, as it were / a form cleaving to it."

Marx also adhered to the commodity theory of money, a carryover from mercantilism retained by Adam Smith and congenial to his materialism:

> Money, like every other commodity, cannot express the magnitude of its value except relatively in other commodities. This value is determined by the labour-time required for its production, and is expressed by the quantity of any other commodity that costs the same amount of labour-time. Such quantitative determination of its relative value takes place at the source of its production by means of barter. When it steps into cir-culation as money, its value is already given. In the last decades of the 17th century [Marx is referring to the mercantilists] it had already been shown that money is a commodity, but this step marks only the infancy of the analysis. The difficulty lies not in comprehending that money is a commodity, but in discovering how, why, and by what means a commod-ity becomes money. (Marx 1:95)

The infant analysis to which Marx refers was completed by Ricardo and expressed in his labor theory of value.

In his review of *The Natural Economic Order,* Pound pretends boredom with Gesell's refutation of Marx—no doubt in an effort to bring his So-cial Credit audience on board—but is struck by Gesell's observation that Marx overlooked the importance of money:

> I find it hard to read "straight along" because, having known Douglas for 16 years, there is a lot in the Natural Economic Order that I do not need to learn. On the other hand, if one browses about in the book, there are a great number of entertaining passages. There are a number of things "put the other way on."
>
> "Marx finds nothing to criticise in money." That is a beautiful sentence. (Over on 222, Gesell's criticism of Marx rather escapes the stricture I have made on his earlier chapter.) (*Ezra Pound's Poetry and Prose* 6:241)

Strikingly, Keynes also notes in his *General Theory* that Gesell is more radi-cal than Marx: "the purpose of the book . . . [was] the establishment of an anti-Marxian socialism, a reaction against *laissez-faire* built on theoretical foundations totally unlike those of Marx in being based on a repudiation instead of on an acceptance of the classical hypotheses, and on an unfettering of competition instead of its abolition. I believe that the future will learn more from the spirit of Gesell than from that of Marx" (Keynes 355). The "classical hypotheses" are Say's law and the quantity theory of money.

Despite Pound's best efforts to find some affinities between Fascist economic policy and Social Credit theory, there is precious little indication that any exist. He knew perfectly well that Mussolini was indifferent to Social Credit economic theory, as he was to all speculation, being resolutely anti-intellectual. Pound seems to have believed that a man of ideas like himself could influence a man of action like Mussolini, thereby achieving government by an enlightened elite on vaguely Confucian lines:

> Fascism and Economic Democracy converge to a point of believing that a responsibility for financial action exists. That is to say, that men exercising great power owe something to those by whom the power exists and who are affected by the functioning of that power. . . .
>
> The economics of C. H. Douglas, as distinct from the mechanism he suggests for causing the economics to function is not incompatible with Fascism. . . .
>
> As a simple problem in instruction, I am all for leaving out the questions of political mechanism until there is a better distribution of economic understanding. I don't care a hoot whether a particular country is run by a man or by a committee so long as it isn't run by a crook, or crooks, or by a damn fool or fools. ("Presenting Some Thoughts on Fascism" in *Ezra Pound's Poetry and Prose* 6:99)

Even though these remarks are intended for an American audience predisposed to regard fascism as tyranny, they are characteristic of Pound's repeated assertion that Social Credit is a technical solution to a structural problem in the monetary and banking system of industrial economies and therefore is quite indifferent to political system or ideology. For example, he told Odon Por:

> As for propaganda here/ Dougs economic ideas (as distinct from his political) superstitions would fit perfectly well into fascism. They are no more anti-fascist that a Zeiss gun-sight.
>
> Their place in Italy is as 'useful mechanism for distribution'// on same plane with electric centrals. ([prior to 14 Apr. 1934], Pound Papers)

As we will see, Pound often claimed that one or another of Mussolini's policies were Social Credit in spirit, but such remarks are clearly motivated by a desire to forge an alliance between fascism and economic reform rather than by disinterested analysis. His letters to Mussolini and Ciano reveal quite clearly that Pound knew perfectly well that Fascist economic policy was not in conformity with Social Credit prescriptions, otherwise he would not have repeatedly recommended their adoption as cures for whatever ills he was addressing in a given letter (see esp. 22 Dec. 1936, Heymann 323–24).

It is quite possible that Pound first regarded fascism as a means to the end of economic reform, rather than as an end in itself. This was certainly true of his early enthusiasm for Roosevelt. But when the New Deal failed to meet his expectations, he turned from support for Roosevelt to implacable hostility. In contrast, he stuck to Mussolini in spite of his failure to adopt Social Credit policies—not to mention his brutality, tyranny, bellicosity, and alliance with Nazism.

With respect to Mussolini's economic policy Pound knew perfectly well that it was not Social Credit in any way. He knew because his correspondents repeatedly confronted him with Mussolini's failure to follow Social Credit prescriptions. The most important of these was Douglas himself, who was unkind enough to remind Pound of his incompetence. The first surviving letter from Douglas (21 January 1931, Pound Papers) opens condescendingly, "I am always glad to receive your wild, untutored communications," and he maintains this tone throughout the correspondence. Though most of his letters are just brief notes that do not deign to acknowledge Pound's observations and queries, on 16 October 1933 he was sufficiently irritated by Pound's praise of Gesell and Mussolini to respond at unusual length:

> I am surprised that a man of your moderate intelligence should make such an elementary mistake. Your arguments merely prove that your local Works Foreman [Mussolini] is successfully carrying out a number of Five Year Plans better than his Russian Opposite number.
>
> If you have not realised that the problem is not to carry out Five Year Plans, then all I can say is that your proper place is at the "better, bigger, and brighter business" meeting of the Rotary Club at Oshkosh, Indiana!" (Pound Papers)

No doubt Douglas's irritation was exacerbated by Pound's closing remark, which implied an inadequacy in Douglas: "The efficient value of an idea depends not only on its validity but on WHO has it . . . . that's fairly platitudinous" (13 Oct. [1933], Pound Papers).[3] If only Pound had paid more attention to this principle.

Though incompatible on economic policy, Social Credit and fascism did share some political objectives and did appeal to the same petit bourgeois stratum of society. No doubt it is this class solidarity that accounts for the fact that Social Crediters as a group were strongly attracted to fascist-style movements. However, in Pound's case it is not necessary to remain at such a general level of analysis because we have his correspondence with Odon Por, which is primarily concerned with their joint effort to capture Italian fascism for Social Credit.

Por was a freelance journalist and economic radical who had been special correspondent in London for the Milan socialist paper *Avanti* during the first Miner's General Strike of 1912 and had been associated briefly with the *New Age* group in the immediate postwar years (Por to Pound, 28 Mar. 1935, Pound Papers). An early supporter of Mussolini's Fascist government, Por wrote two books outlining the affinities between guild socialism and fascism in 1923, *Guilds and Co-operatives in Italy* and *Fascism*, both translated by E. Townshend and published by the Labour Publishing Company. The former had an introduction by Yeats's mystical friend George Russell and an appendix by the prominent guild socialist G. D. H. Cole.

Surprisingly, neither Pound nor Orage had any particular recollection of Por when he made contact with Pound in 1934. His first letter leaves no doubt of what he hoped from the association: "Perhaps you know my name as an old New Age–Orage man. I am just back from London after 4 months there. (And glad to be back!) I am trying to begin to propagate Social Credit etc.—here. (See my article in *Gerarchia* March 34 [Mussolini's journal]). Orage told me that you had some contact with Mussolini on this matter. Now you know how difficult it is to discuss such matters in Italy. What is M's attitude—if he has any—In this matter?" ([prior to 14 Apr. 1934], Pound Papers).

Pound's response is enthusiastic and indicates that he is more committed to Mussolini than to Douglas, considering John Hargrave's fascist-style Green Shirts as potentially more reliable allies than Social Crediters:

> My belief is that the DUCE understands more REAL econ/ than Doug/ He (the Duce) not giving a damn about slips of paper (as an autotelic end).
>
> Anything you can do to get Gerarchia or any high ups to see that AT ROOT the Green Shirts are probably nearer the real *spirit* of Italian fascism than are any of the chaps that are merely wearing clothes . . . wd/ I think be useful/
>
> The other useful line is to wear down IDIOTIC prejudice against Fascism. I MEAN ITALIAN as distinct from fake fascism. The weakness of Douglas as a movement has been that no emphasis was put on the underlying

ETHOS the new real BASIS of value. That fits with M's objection to everything "anti-storico" [antihistorical]. (undated, Pound Papers)

As late as 1943 Pound equated Social Credit and the Green Shirts in a "Service Note" to Mussolini (28 October 1943) in which he also claimed credit for arranging a meeting between Douglas and Oswald Mosley, the leader of the British Union of Fascists (Mullins 325).[4]

He continues the topic of affinities between Social Credit and fascism in the next letter to Por (14 April 1934, Pound Papers), now numbering five points of agreement. The first is a putative equivalence between Douglas's "cultural heritage" and Mussolini's historicism: "Doug's 'Cultural heritage' as true foundation of valu/ of/ Duce's objection to everything anti-storico." It is difficult to see what Pound means. He explains in the preface to *Jefferson and/or Mussolini* that he takes "historical" to mean "historic process," that is, a kind of destiny like the "manifest destiny" of the Yankees to overrun the North American continent (v). Hence Mussolini's objection to "everything anti-storico" would seem to be a left-handed assertion of a historicist belief in destiny—that the future determines the present. But Douglas's cultural heritage is founded on the contrary belief that the past determines the present.

The second alleged affinity is that both advocate "state control of financial system." However, Mussolini neither advocated nor carried out such a policy. He *was* obliged to nationalize the Italian banks in 1936 so as to rescue them from bankruptcy, but had not touched the banks at the time Pound was writing. The third affinity is fascism's "great elasticity," an attribute truly possessed by Italian fascism, but not at all by Douglas's Social Credit, which Pound knew to be inflexible and hidebound. His fourth point is just a claim that fascism could and should adopt Douglas's economic policy prescriptions.

His fifth point is a summary of the first four: "5.(to repeat) the COMMON AIM of doug/ and the Boss. keep off particular details. Hammer on the a plus b/ theorem in various verbal forms. that is the diagnosis of DISEASE. That and the cult/ herit/ as source of values/ give a common line of departure." He concludes with a claim that Mussolini's incentives for private housing are equivalent to Douglas's national dividend, though he knows they are not: "Note new housing campaign/ CONCRETE dividend. (My use of this term may horrify you as an ECONOMIST. or book keeper. And I suppose Doug's hair wd/ rise . . . but nevertheless. the AIM, gordamn it the AIM// the constructive spirit." All of this is desperate special pleading. Even in a private letter to a fellow Social Crediter and Fascist Pound was unable to find any important common ground between fascism and Social Credit.

It is difficult to know what to make of Pound's stubborn adherence to the fiction that his two enthusiasms were mutually supportive in the face of compelling evidence to the contrary. For whatever reason, he persisted to the bitter end in the belief that fascism was the political instrument that would bring about those economic reforms which would ensure the peace and prosperity of the world. His efforts to reconcile the conflict demonstrate that he was aware of it, but he proved to be emotionally incapable of surrendering either his economic radicalism or his hero-worship of Mussolini. It seems probable that this conflict contributed to his increasingly irrational and irascible behavior. A case in point is his reception of his old mentor, Yeats, at about this time.

Yeats had traveled to Rapallo specifically to get Pound's opinion on his latest play, *The King of the Great Clock Tower,* and invited him to supper at his hotel. Yeats asked him for his "opinion on some verse I have written lately." But Pound "would not speak of art, or of literature, or of anything related to them." Instead "he said apropos of nothing 'Arthur Balfour was a scoundrel,' and from that on would talk of nothing but politics. All the other modern statesmen were more or less scoundrels except 'Mussolini and that hysterical imitator of his, Hitler.'" Yeats left him the manuscript of the play, and "next day his judgement came and that in a single word 'Putrid'" (Yeats, *King* vi–vii). Pound recalled this incident in Donald Hall's 1962 *Paris Review* interview. His recollection is silent on the political dimensions that Yeats stressed: "Once out at Rapallo I tried for God's sake to prevent him from printing a thing. I told him it was rubbish. All he did was print it with a preface saying that I *said* it was rubbish" (Hall 227).

The tension created by Pound's divided loyalties was slight in 1934 compared to what it would become. Mussolini's invasion of Ethiopia in October 1935, the Axis alliance of October 1936, and the beginning of the Spanish Civil War in July 1936 enormously exacerbated the strains to which Pound was subjected. He interpreted these events in the light of underconsumptionist arguments—as the predictable results of economic injustice and mismanagement. He completely failed to see the more mundane causes of national rivalry, historical grievances, and national ambition, which surely drove the belligerence of Germany, Italy, and Japan more than any ideological commitments. Blinded by a half-baked economic theory and an uncritical hero-worship of Mussolini, Pound descended, cursing and flailing, further and further into the heart of darkness.

But again, we should remember that things were not so clear in the thirties as they are in the nineties. Many observers at the time saw the developing conflict as just another manifestation of the long-standing rivalries of France, Britain, Germany, Russia, and Italy. Pound always saw it as an ideological conflict, as both Fascist and Communist propaganda presented it. Fascism and communism agreed that the liberal democracies were corrupt, wasteful, and usurious and represented themselves as honest, efficient, and just. It is easy to see the grotesque falsity of that picture today, but it was not so obvious in the depths of the depression and before the wars of aggression. I would not endorse a view that portrays the liberal democracies as the principal villains during the depression, but they certainly failed to protect the economic interests of their citizens. In short, Pound's political posture in 1933 was not unreasonable or vicious. But as the evil of Hitler's regime and the venality of Mussolini's became apparent to most observers, Pound failed to adjust his political analysis.

The Spanish Civil War had encouraged many intellectuals to read the growing conflict as one between reactionary fascism and progressive communism, with the liberal and imperialistic democracies shamefully standing by on the sidelines. But the German invasion of Poland in 1939 and the fall of France in 1940 changed that perception. Now many of those same intellectuals saw the struggle as one between fascist totalitarianism and liberal democracy. Whereas liberals had been embarrassed by the inaction of the democracies in the face of the Fascist alliance in Spain, after 1939 it was the Communists who were embarrassed by Stalin's non-aggression pact with Hitler, which enabled Germany to invade Poland, risking war with Britain and France. Stalin quickly took his reward—annexing eastern Poland and invading Finland.

Pound's native land stood aside throughout, leaving Britain and the Commonwealth to confront Hitler and Mussolini alone (see Parker). Though divided before the fall of France, after that disaster American opinion was firmly behind the British. The failures of the democracies to deal with the economic problems of the thirties were quickly forgotten or forgiven—even by the seriously disenchanted—in the midst of the crisis. The moral superiority that the Communists had been able to claim in Spain was now seriously compromised. Pound's response to all of these shifts was to cling firmly to Mussolini and his version of economic reform. His failure to recognize that all bets were off after the fall of France was probably the second of his great political errors (his first was to pick Mussolini over Roosevelt as his hero and guiding light).

Hitler's invasion of the Soviet Union on 22 June 1941 and Japan's attack on Pearl Harbor on 7 December of the same year once again changed the nature of the conflict, particularly for an American national like Pound. Once again he failed to adjust his behavior appropriately. Having spoken on shortwave radio from Rome on 11 January 1935, he was keen thereafter to take advantage of this new tool for his economic evangelism (Pound to Douglas, 25 Feb. 1935, Pound Papers). However, he did not begin regular broadcasts until January 1941 (Redman 158, 208). At that date he might reasonably have supposed that the war had been won by the Axis powers and that he could serve the cause of peace by persuading the British to seek an armistice. He also desperately needed new sources of income because the war had cut off much of the old ones (Redman 204).

It is truly astonishing that none of the changes in the alignments of world powers led Pound to reconsider his reading of contemporary events or, indeed, his future personal welfare and security. The conclusion he had reached—that a conspiracy of ignorance controlled the democracies—was not patently absurd in the light of the foolish and cruel behavior of many democratic governments in the thirties. However, it is difficult to think of a polite epithet for his persistence in a conspiratorial view of history in the light of the transparently belligerent, racist, and tyrannical behavior of Nazi Germany and its subservient ally, Fascist Italy. Despite being advised repeatedly of the folly of his position by individuals he had reason to trust, he clung stubbornly to his fallacious analysis of geopolitics. He was alone, even amongst those who shared one or more of his economical, political, and anti-Semitic views. In the face of the conflict, virtually everyone with whom Pound was associated clung to their national loyalties; that Pound did not perhaps speaks to the strength of his ideological commitment, but it also reflects his alienation from his American roots.

It would be dishonest to claim that Pound was simply confused. He *was* confused, certainly. But he was drawn to tyranny on ideological principles that he had long held and that are embedded in *The Cantos*. It is true that in that work he praises benevolent dictatorship and not brutal tyranny, but he proved incapable of recognizing that Mussolini and Hitler were brutal tyrants and not benevolent dictators. On this point I agree with Massimo Bacigalupo's and Michael Bernstein's insistence that *The Cantos* reflects and expresses Pound's political loyalties (Bacigalupo 64–66; Bernstein 114–19), and I made much the same point in my own study of *The Cantos* (*Light* 178).

A case can be made for the view that his commitment to the Axis powers—as opposed to his attraction to plausible tyrants—was a historical accident consequent upon his residence in Italy, but it does not do much to rehabilitate his political acumen. Having chosen Mussolini as his philosopher king, he flattered himself that he was a player in the historical drama and labored tirelessly to further the cause of fascism and economic reform. He was clearly deluded on both counts. On the evidence of his correspondence with Por, the Fascist regime neither trusted nor understood him, though it granted him generous access to the press and to radio. And neither fascism nor Nazism had any interest in economic reform along Social Credit—or any other—lines. And even if they had, Pound's policy recommendations were a dog's breakfast—impossible to implement and based on a faulty economic analysis.

Once Pound had committed to fascism and Mussolini, he remained loyal to that error in spite of everything. His letter to the Canadian poet Louis Dudek of January 1953 is typical of many letters of his St. Elizabeths period:

> leave MUS [Mussolini] as Mus/ conditioned by circs/[. . . .]
> the final filth is E. W. Morrow [probably E. R. Morrow, American journalist], blasting of "totalitarian" fascist or bolshoi/ OMITTING the fact that his pewk and Roosevelt brought in the goddam savages. It was Oooze and Winston, who betrayed civilization. Not Mus/ Moscow Ally
> (of course they make no distinction between Mus and Hit [Hitler].)
> another squalor.[5] (Dudek 95)

Pound was wildly wrong in his estimate of where the preponderance of virtue lay in World War II, and he was equally wrong in his reading of the politics of the postwar period.

While the objectionable nature of Pound's political allegiances is beyond dispute, the relation between them and his other views remains moot. If we concede, as we must, that he espoused evil, are we obliged to reject his art? Can we isolate the poetry from the beliefs? I think we cannot—at least not for *The Cantos,* since that poem is overtly ideological. However, I hope to show that Pound's errors were *his* errors, and not an inevitable consequence of this or that opinion or general belief.

To put it bluntly, not everyone who, in Kuberski's words, has a "nostalgia for an enclosure like the medieval church that could bind history, language, politics, and art into an apparently cohesive ideology" becomes a fascist and an anti-Semite. In fact, Kuberski's portrait would fit any nationalist, including Zionists. Are all those who love their country, their nation, their language, their faith to be condemned?

Because literary modernism, despite all its talk of objectivity and textual autonomy, remained fully committed to the genius theory of artistic creation, it has not been possible to mount a defense of Pound's behavior on grounds of stupidity without a drastic devaluation of everything else he did. And because of his pivotal position in the history of literary modernism in English—as the theorist of Imagism, "discoverer" of Joyce, editor of *The Waste Land,* and a continuing source of poetic inspiration to subsequent generations of poets—it has not been possible simply to expunge Pound from literary history. Literally dozens of books and chapters of books have been devoted to the expulsion of Pound from his allegedly important role in each of the literary moments listed above, but all have failed, no doubt because of a plethora of good evidence to the contrary.

If we abandon the naive notion that an important poet must be a font of wisdom in all fields, then we can admit that Pound was simply stupid and arrogant on political matters and out of his depth on economic matters. Such an explanation is not a "defense" in the sense that it implies that we ought to excuse him from the consequences of his errors, but it is an explanation as opposed to either an indictment or an indulgence.

Within the Romantic and modernist doctrine that a work of art—or an artist's oeuvre—is a single, organic whole, Pound's political opinions cannot be isolated from his poetry. In such a doctrine any imperfection in its message is like an infection or poison that will inevitably spread to the entire organism. Such a Romantic presumption is resisted by Marjorie Perloff in her response to the assessment of modernism itself as fascist— that is, as violent, racist, and authoritarian. The "case" of Pound is instructive because he was indubitably modernist and (also indubitably) a defender and even proponent of violence, racism, and authoritarianism. He has long been an irritant galling the tender parts of the theory of aesthetic autonomy. Perhaps the poet can be saved only at the sacrifice of the theory.

Even though Pound endorsed the racism and false history of the Nazis, other economic heretics did not follow this route, and neither the Nazis nor the Fascists adopted the underconsumptionist heresy. In the following pages I will trace the development of Pound's economic views in the years following *Jefferson and/or Mussolini.* They were undeniably just as fateful years in the history of the world as Pound expected they would be when he began his epic in 1915, but they were too fateful even for a poetic genius to encapsulate. We will see that his adoption of fascism led Pound to engage in a course of self-education in economics that led him away from Douglas's inadequate analysis and ultimately into confusion.

Notes

1. Tim Redman also sees the outbreak of war in 1939 as a watershed in Pound's growing anti-Semitism: "Some restraint gave way in Pound's psyche with the onset of the second World War, for his anti-Semitism suddenly becomes a more pronounced feature of his letters" (194). I concur with Redman's judgment, but, as

we shall see, Pound began to take the notion of a Jewish conspiracy seriously even before the outbreak of hostilities, though he does not express any credence in *The Protocols of the Elders of Zion* until 1940.

2. The eight points he mentions in the letter were presumably some version of the eight points later published in a handbill entitled "Volitionist Economics." See the appendix.

3. Pound frequently employed ellipsis points in varying number and with variable spacing in his correspondence. I have rendered them exactly as he did. If I have made an elision in a quotation from one of his letters, I have placed the ellipsis points in brackets. Unless otherwise noted, ellipsis points in all other quotations are mine and will not appear in brackets.

4. Pound carried on a considerable correspondence with Hargrave. They were friendly enough that he suggested Pound write a book of Green Shirt cantos (Flory 76–77). Like Douglas and Orage, Hargrave tried to dissuade Pound from his infatuation with Mussolini and dissociated himself from Mosley's enthusiasm for Hitler (Hargrave to Pound, 8 Sept. 1939, qtd. in Flory 112–13).

5. "Ooze" is undoubtedly Roosevelt, but I don't know what Pound is referring to in the remark that Roosevelt brought in the savages. Given that Pound was involved with American racists at the time, he may be referring to the presence of blacks in the American armed forces. His remark that it was not Mussolini who was an ally of Moscow reflects the hysterical anticommunism of the fifties and does nothing to enhance any estimate of his political sagacity.

CHAPTER 4

Social Credit and Fascism

Pound made his situation especially difficult because his Rome radio broadcasts looked very much like "offering aid and comfort to the enemy," leading to his indictment for treason. Pound never admitted—and presumably did not believe—that he had chosen the wrong side. But even if he had reverted to American loyalties (or just kept prudently silent) after the invasion of Poland or after Pearl Harbor, he still would have behaved very differently than his friend and fellow vorticist Wyndham Lewis. At the outbreak of war Lewis abandoned his earlier support for Hitler and, fearful of reprisals—such as Oswald Mosley's arrest—fled to Canada. Pound chose to remain in Italy, though he might have fled. In fact he wrote to Por on 29 September 1939 that he was not going to Switzerland because the border might be closed: "in which case I prefer to be on THIS side of it" (Pound Papers). Even after Badoglio's coup in 1943, when it was clear that Mussolini's days were numbered, Pound continued to publish journalism in support of the Salò Republic and even mailed several "Service Reports" to Il Duce (Heymann 325–26)—though he might have lain low. Whatever Pound's moral failings may have been, cowardice and self-service were not among them.

Lewis and Pound had been allies in the cultural wars of the prewar and early postwar years beginning with *Blast,* the satirical review of 1914, and continuing virtually to Lewis's death in 1957 (for the early period see Materer *Vortex*). But they were also longtime antagonists. Lewis attacked both Pound and Joyce as "time philosophers" in his 1927 monograph,

Time and Western Man, and seemed to regard Pound as an amiable fool on political matters: "Pound is not a vulgar humbug even in those purely propagandist activities, where, to my mind, he certainly handles humbug, but quite innocently, I believe. Pound is—that is my belief—a genuine *naïf.* He is a sort of revolutionary simpleton" (38). Lewis's assessment has, I think, been borne out by events.

It is instructive to compare Lewis's 1931 monograph, *Hitler,* with Pound's *Jefferson and/or Mussolini* written a couple of years later, though Pound did not read Lewis's book until late in 1937 (Materer, *Pound/Lewis* letter 166). Lewis is clearly a much more competent observer of the political scene than Pound. In contrast to Pound's silence on the strong-arm tactics of the Fascists, Lewis declared himself willing to tolerate the violence and racism[1] of the Nazis because they countered the greater danger posed by Marxism. By contrast Pound praised Lenin as well as Mussolini, arguing for the benevolence, efficiency, and intelligence of a totalitarian system as compared to the allegedly corrupt liberal and capitalist democracies.

At the time he wrote *Hitler* the Nazi party was only the official opposition in the Reichstag. However, *Mein Kampf* and many political speeches by Hitler and Göring made the Nazis' position on racism and German expansion clear. And the thuggish behavior of the SA, or Brownshirts, left no doubt about Nazi willingness to employ violence to achieve political ends. Indeed, the attitudes Lewis strikes in *Hitler* are much closer to those Pound later expresses in his radio speeches than to those in *Jefferson and/ or Mussolini.*

Like Pound, Lewis was persuaded by Douglas's analysis of the economic situation in the thirties. Pound recommended *Hitler* to Douglas in a letter of 13 November 1936. Douglas promptly read it and found it "absolutely first class," adding that he had been reading Lewis in Mosley's *British Union of Fascism Quarterly* (16 Nov. 1936, Pound Papers). Pound suggested that Douglas invite Lewis to write for the Social Credit journal, *The Fig Tree,* but nothing came of it.

In the later *The Hitler Cult* (1939) Lewis retracts his support for Hitler, attributing his earlier sympathy to the appeal of Nazi economic policies and claiming that his motivation in *Hitler* was a mischievous political vandalism: "I was, above all, glad the stupid French chauvinists were about to have their noses rubbed in their handiwork. And the views on finance of Herr Feder[2] were not without a certain appeal—they reminded me of our Major Douglas. . . . The idea of a 'credit crank' being let loose in the second greatest industrial country in the world recommended itself to me. That would brighten things up! I thought Europe had asked for that, too" (26–27).

The French "handiwork" to which Lewis refers is the Treaty of Versailles. Keynes's assessment of the reparations in *The Economic Consequences of the Peace* (1919) as vindictive and a sure cause of German grievance set the tone for British opinion. Lewis was reflecting mainstream British opinion that the reparations were unjust and contributed to the rise of Nazism. The French had a different view, attributing the return of German bellicosity to the lack of British support for the terms of the treaty. In defense of the French, it should be noted that although the British considered French efforts to collect compensation from Germany malicious, they did not criticize the Americans for their refusal to forgive the war debts owed to them by Britain and France (see Parker 244–45).

Even in his *apologia, The Hitler Cult,* Lewis cites strongly anti-French British opinion on this point—an opinion that persisted even after the outbreak of war in 1939 (28–29). Though hostile to Britain, Pound reflected British anti-French sentiment in his journalism: "Obviously the 'cursed Hun' has been driven nearly distracted by the greed of the overstuffed frog" ("By All Means Be Patriotic" in *Ezra Pound's Poetry and Prose* 5:377–78).

But Lewis's retraction in *The Hitler Cult* is evasive, for in *Hitler* he had endorsed more of the Nazi program than just Feder's economic policies. Nevertheless, his retraction is illustrative of the ideological and political mood of the early thirties, when many reasonable people thought that something was radically wrong with liberal democracy and capitalism:

> Now, in the light of the beliefs I have been exposing, this "misery" is purely and absolutely *artificial.* It is the result not of an *actual,* a natural, want, but of an artificially-fostered, sedulously-contrived want. Obviously there is no real want: there is an enormous abundance of everything, if men's technical power to produce were made use of and put at the disposal of all. But for some reason or other we have slowly been conducted into such a state of affairs that, in the Lap of Plenty, we have agreed to starve. And the "Science" of Economics, as usually practised, does certainly seem to be there merely in order to confuse us, and to throw dust in our eyes. (186)

Lewis's claim that the depression was entirely avoidable and easily curable is straight out of Douglas and implies that some group must wish the misery to continue. This logic was also part of the antidemocratic rhetoric of Mussolini, Hitler, and Oswald Mosley, all of whom accused politicians of being in the pay of malign forces.

On this point, Chace's argument that it was radicalism itself—by which he seems to have meant a distrust of existing institutions—that drew the Modernists to fascism is plausible. But there is also in Lewis, as in Pound, a strong "conservative" motive, a desire to preserve and maintain values and mores that he thought "civilized" and to which Mussolini and Hitler appealed by presenting themselves as a bulwark against materialistic Marxism. While there is no hint of anti-Semitism in *Jefferson and/or Mussolini*, that is not true of Lewis's *Hitler:*

> It is a subject of constant speculation how the Roman Empire came to collapse. . . . There is no mystery at all—it is an "open conspiracy"—about the Fall of Europe. In a word, it is the result, in the first instance, of an enormous new factor—machinery and industrial technique. In the short space of a century science turned our world upside-down. Secondly, the world being upside down and inside-out, the shrewd parasite (existing in all times and places) psychologically an outcast as regards our settled structure, took advantage of this disorder and consequent bafflement to sting us all to death. (73)

While this statement avoids naming the "shrewd parasites," no one reading a book in praise of the Nazi party would fail to identify them as the Jews.

Though Lewis believes in a Jewish conspiracy, he explicitly rejects the racist theory of a superior Aryan race and says that anti-Semitism is appropriate for the Germans but unsuitable for the British (35–43). Nonetheless he endorses racism as an antibody that could protect Europe from infection with Marxist theories of class conflict: "The 'Class'-doctrinaire has no greater enemy than Race. And it is natural therefore that he should seek every opportunity of belittling Race. It is also natural that the Nationalsocialist, persuaded that the 'Class-war' propaganda is one of the main factors in the present disintegration—for it sets friend against friend—should insist upon Race—and he has done that to some purpose" (84). Such brutal cynicism is perhaps more culpable than Pound's misguided conviction.

Lewis's *Hitler* is not only more objectionable from either a liberal or a Marxist perspective than Pound's *Jefferson and/or Mussolini* but it is also far less naive and sophomoric. Lewis's analysis is better informed and more cogent than Pound's, and in fact reflects the mainstream British reading of political events of the day. Pound's analysis is eccentric and eclectic—an indigestible mixture of Social Credit, fascism, Marxism, and Jeffersonian democracy.

Lewis sees France as the bad actor in Europe between the wars because of its allegedly vindictive attitude toward the unfortunate Germans. He agrees with Mussolini and Hitler that, with its doctrines of class conflict and internationalism, communism represents the principal threat to European security. Like them he thinks the best defense against communism—as World War I had shown—was nationalist loyalty. He accepts the German view that the Versailles treaty had not honored "self-determination" for the Germans, as it had for others, isolating as it did many German speakers in Poland, Hungary, and Czechoslovakia. His conclusion that France's insistence on the strict application of the punitive measures against Germany in the treaty was the principal destabilizing factor in Europe is widely at odds with opinion today, but not out of step with the British policy of appeasement followed by Neville Chamberlain.

None of this pro-German *Realpolitik* is reflected in *Jefferson and/or Mussolini*. Of course the Italians viewed matters rather differently than the British and Germans, and Pound in part reflects that difference. Italy had been an ally, albeit a somewhat reluctant one, of France and Britain in World War I. Nonetheless, it, too, felt cheated by Versailles, which denied it the promised Fiume and gave it none of the spoils of the Ottoman Empire and nothing in North Africa. Pound, however, does not invoke European national rivalries and grievances or the Communist threat. His whole focus is on Mussolini as a remarkable man comparable to Jefferson, John Adams, and Lenin—pointedly including the whole political spectrum of the day. His message was that neither ideology nor institutions matters; only the quality of those who govern does: "Jefferson thought the formal features of the American system would work, and they did work till the time of General Grant but the condition of their working was that inside them there should be a *de facto* government composed of sincere men willing the national good. When the men of understanding, and then the nucleus of the national mind hasn't the moral force to translate knowledge into action I don't believe it matters a damn what legal forms or what administrative forms there are in a government" (*J/M* 94–95).

The idea that it is people, not institutions, that matter is driven home again and again in *The Cantos*. While such a view seems plausible, it is an extremely crude and dangerous political doctrine—as the history of the period emphatically demonstrates. Both Fascist Italy and Nazi Germany were ruled by the leader and his party quite outside the institutional framework of the state. The Italian state was governed by the party's *gerarchia* (hierarchy) and its self-appointed Grand Council, which bypassed the legislative mechanisms that were nonetheless left in place. Though Mussolini could be removed—and was—his word was law so long as he was Il Duce.[3] Nazi Germany followed much the same pattern, as did the Soviet Union, though all had constitutions, legislative bodies, and popular elections.

Pound's belief that the best government is a benevolent tyranny or a self-selected aristocracy does not entail an approval of oppression, political violence, racism, and genocide. Pound always assumed a benevolent tyranny, though it must be admitted that he was blind to Mussolini's excesses. We are entitled to deplore his lack of trust in common human nature and to rebuke him for his political naiveté, but Pound's political incorrectness was well within the range of tolerable eccentricity in a poet in the early thirties. And it is evident that his devotion to economic reform was based on a genuine desire to reduce human suffering and want and to restore a social order in which the artist held a place of honor. But it all went terribly wrong. Unable to understand the great events unfolding around him and unable to admit—even to himself—his incomprehension, he could only denounce those he could not persuade.

Redman argues (116–17) that Pound's failure in this regard was a technical one, an excessive reliance on "efficient cause" to the exclusion of "sufficient cause" (he does not mention the third Aristotelian category, "final cause"). He cites the epigram from *Jefferson and/or Mussolini* ("Nothing is without efficient cause") to support his case. My view, however, is that Pound's appeal to the Aristotelian causal category is little more than protective coloring for a primitive—and Carlylean—historical analysis that attributes historical events to the actions of voluntary agents. Good agents (benign heroes) produce good effects; bad agents (evil exploiters) produce bad effects.

Lewis was much less protected by political naiveté than Pound. Where Pound completely ignores the unsavory tactics of Mussolini's Brownshirts, Lewis acknowledges the violence and racism of the Nazis. Nonetheless he holds up Hitler as potentially the savior of Europe: "It would be a great mistake to regard him as merely just another 'dictator': for he is a very different person to Mussolini, Pilsudski, or Primo de Rivera and we must expect very different behaviour to ensue upon his accession to power" (*Hitler* 51). On this last point history has proven Lewis correct, though not in the way he expected.

Pound's backing of Mussolini in 1933 was a mistake that "anyone could have made," and many did. It was an error that pales beside Lewis's backing of Hitler. But Lewis had the wisdom (or prudence) to back off Hitler in 1939, in *The Hitler Cult,* while Pound clung to Mussolini and Italy to the bitter end. In 1939 Lewis completely reversed himself, describing Hitler as Gothic, German, Romantic, and of weak intellect. Somewhat maliciously, he associated his old aesthetic enemies—Yeats, Synge, and Joyce (but not Pound)—with Hitler's *volkisch* romanticism (52). Whereas he previously presented Hitler as a necessary evil to set against communism and finance, in 1939 he found him merely vulgar.

Lewis's loyalty to the social and political values of the Western democracies (or his instinct of self-preservation) proved stronger than his elitism, anti-Semitism, and commitment to the cultural values ostensibly threatened by the leveling and internationalist tendencies of communism. Pound's loyalty was to an ideal community that had never existed—and probably would never exist—rather than to any one nation or society. His passionate belief in the possibility of such a community deluded him into thinking that Fascist Italy approximated it, and he had the courage—or folly—to stand by his convictions.

His expatriate status may also have been a factor. Pound had turned his back on his native land and then soured on England. Though his move South from London to Paris and finally to Rapallo was primarily a search for a cheap and congenial environment, Pound describes it retrospectively as a political and spiritual journey in *Jefferson and/or Mussolini:*

> London was in terror of thought. Nothing was being buried. Paris was tired, very tired, but they wanted *table rasé,* they wanted the dead things cleared out even if there were nothing to replace them.
>
> Italy was, on the other hand, full of bounce. I said all of this to a Lombard writer. I said: London is dead, Paris is tired, but here the place is alive. (49)

Pound always believed in his unerring capacity to recognize the genuine and the fine in poetry and the arts and to distinguish it from kitsch and the phony. He thought he could do the same with political leaders and economists. And no doubt his long practice of polemical writing in defense of modernism against the uncomprehending assaults of the philistine public had conditioned him to be impervious to criticism.

It is common to find an affinity between Pound's aesthetics and his politics. Most commentators who do so, such as Fredric Jameson, conclude that the affinity discredits the aesthetic. Vincent Sherry is an exception to this rule. He has an intricate and rather hermetic argument that aestheticizes the politics of Pound—and Lewis as well—in a novel manner. He asks, "May one admire the artistic achievement of Lewis and Pound, then, by detaching it from the social value it discovers so stubbornly in their work?" Since that "social value" is fascistic, the question is of some moment. His answer is: "The question remains urgent but unanswerable, for it summons our full, understandably mixed response to the work of these major modernists—to its sometimes appalling greatness. One may argue that the aesthetic of authority immanent in the work of the Anglo-Americans develops, through the twenties, into the imminent apocalypse of dictatorial fascism" (187). I take this to mean that their work is aesthetically great, but ideologically retrograde—a small emendation of the standard New Critical defense on the grounds of aesthetic autonomy. But there is no reason to suppose that there is any entailment between aesthetic practice and theory on the one hand and political engagement on the other. In any case, the "aesthetic of authority"—the expressive aesthetic to which the modernists undeniably adhered—has a much longer history than does fascism.

Redman cannily argues that Pound persuaded himself of his political insight by the expedient of considering Mussolini as an artist, thereby relieving him of any requirement to be consistent or logical. Of course, if Mussolini had been an artist, then Pound was just the man to recognize his value. As Redman puts it, "Who possibly was in a better position to judge the work of a fellow artist than Pound, one of the preeminent critics of this century?" (118). There is much to be said for this view, though it pretty well abandons the possibility of granting any merit to Pound's political thought.

It is true that Pound was attracted to fascism because it was authoritarian and content-free. Pound thought Mussolini could serve as a bulwark against the perceived venality and ineffectuality of liberal, capitalist democracies, just as Lewis thought Hitler could. But the most important factor of all was that Mussolini, unlike all the other established political figures Pound approached, actually agreed to meet him. Pound seems to have been flattered out of his senses by his one interview with Mussolini. The high importance it had for him is reflected in a letter to W. E. Woodward expressing his lack of enthusiasm for a visit to the United States:

> At the same time I am willing to come IF it wd/ be the least god damn use. I am willing to talk sense to old Prof/ Warren.
> If Muss/ who is more a man than F/D/ [Roosevelt] can take off a half hour to THINK about wot I say to him/ bigod I ain't going to set in anybody's front hall asking permission from anybody's third footman to hang up me cap/. (7 Feb. 1934, "Letters to Woodward" 119)

For Pound to imagine himself a major player on the world stage, as he does in this letter, is a fantastic vanity—one that Mussolini's "favor" fatally reinforced.

From the time of his audience with Mussolini on 30 January 1933 Pound regarded himself as the court poet of the Fascist Era. He subsequently wrote eight letters to Mussolini—the last on 28 October 1943. Most of them enjoin Mussolini to adopt the Social Credit national dividend and Gesellite stamp scrip, but have no effect. One letter bears a bureaucrat's note, which finds Pound's Italian "incomprehensible" and offers the opinion that the author was "mentally unbalanced" (Heymann 320). When the League of Nations imposed sanctions on Italy in response to the invasion of Ethiopia (on 3 October 1935), Pound wrote to Mussolini's secretary, Alessandro Chiavolini, with a preposterous scheme for a new Italian-led League of Nations as a way around the sanctions (Zapponi 50). Again, when Mussolini and Hitler supported Franco in the Spanish Civil War, Pound wrote suggesting that Douglasite economic policies be applied immediately in Spain (Zapponi 51). In December 1936, Pound wrote directly to Mussolini, again suggesting that he adopt Gesell's stamp scrip in lieu of taxation. He received no response to any of these initiatives (Heymann 323–24).

Pound had to confront criticism of Mussolini for his failure to follow Douglasite economic policies from the very beginning of his Fascist period. While writing *Jefferson and/or Mussolini* he was in correspondence with his old Paris friend, William Bird, founder of *Three Mountains Press* and the publisher of *A Draft of Sixteen Cantos* (1925). Bird was an American journalist stationed in Paris. He explained the origin of Three Mountains Press to Robert Knoll:

> I started the Three Mountains Press simply to have a hobby. Most of my friends were golfers, but sports never interested me greatly, whereas ever since my childhood I had had an interest in printing. I discovered on the Isle St. Louis a French journalist, Roger Devigne, who was printing books on a hand press of about the Benj. Franklin vintage. I arranged with Devigne to print English books on his press, after acquiring a full series of Casion type for that purpose. After a short time, however, the adjoining shop fell vacant, and I bought a hand press of my own, also of a model about two centuries old.
>
> Hemingway, who was then a young journalist and whom I had met when we both covered the Genoa conference (1921?) suggested that Ezra Pound, then living at 70 bis r. N. D. des Champs was busy writing a long poem and might be willing to have some of it printed. I went to see Ezra, and after a couple of days reflection he came up with a series of 6 books which he proposed to publish. He said the thing to do was to have a series of books that went together, and not just print things as they came along. Thus Ezra became editor of the Three Mts. Press. (5 May 1956, Bird Manuscripts. The Genoa conference was 10 April to 19 May 1922.)

Encountering financial and personal difficulties, Bird sold his press and fonts to Nancy Cunard in 1925 or 1926, but not before publishing a deluxe edition of *A Draft of Sixteen Cantos.*

Bird was Paris correspondent for the Consolidated Press Association and the *New York Sun.* He was well-informed about current affairs and held quite radical economic views, making him an ideal interlocutor for Pound, as he turned once more to economics. Bird is the unidentified "correspondent" whom Pound cites at the beginning of chapter 23 of *Jefferson and/or Mussolini* commenting on *Mercanti di Cannoni*. In the letter Pound cites (written on 14 December 1932) Bird deplores the deflationary policies pursued by all the national governments of the day, complaining, quite accurately, that they contributed to the severity of the depression. Pound approves of this analysis. However, he complains that in the next letter his correspondent "falls flop into catalogued fallacy, possibly from haste, confusion of office work, etc." (*J/M* 87–88).

That "next letter"—not cited in *Jefferson and/or Mussolini*—was a very long one. It gives a good indication of the developing intransigence of Pound's views and of his inability to respond appropriately to criticism of them:

Don't go high-hatting me about Economics. I was a Technocrat 'way back in 1919 (before they had found that stylish name for it.) Somewhere in my archives is a copy of H. Scott's first manifesto, which was typed in about a dozen copies, none of which ever got into a printer's hands, so far as I know. It was Mont Schuyler (you remember him?) who introduced me into those underground milieux. Delegates came from the I.W.W., the Pennsylvania mining unions, etc., to hear the new gospel, preached in the catacombs of Greenwich Village. . . .

A committee was formed at the request of Tammany to advise that forward-looking body how the revolution might be accomplished by peaceful means. A session was held at the home of Nina Wilcox Putnam which generated more heat than light. Most of the reddest labor leaders including a couple of Roosians finally thought that the most the Legislature could do would be to increase the income tax. Somebody said it should simply mean that big NY corporations would move to N. Jersey. It may surprise you, mon cher Ezra, but it was yr present correspondent who put the discussion to bed with the proposition that since the State exists for the protection of privilege, it could hardly function in the direction of the suppression of the same. An opinion which the same correspt. respectfully maintains to-day.

Subsequently we retired to a nearby coffee-house—some of us—to see if better progress could be made in a smaller and less formal committee. The conclusion was that a non-violent revolution was impossible, but that the State, if it really feared that a violent one was inevitable, might do much to render it less destructive of real values. . . .

That the existing system based on prices is doomed to collapse is easily demonstrated, and in fact [Howard] Scott[, a cofounder of Technocracy,] had then (1919) worked out a chart which indicated that the collapse would come inevitably within 15 years. That would be 1934 at the outside limit. But I understand he has somewhat modified this conclusion because of the fact that he did not then take into consideration sufficiently that the war had provoked a temporary speeding-up of the rhythm of economic phenomena, and that peace would slow down the process. It is also impossible to calculate the resiliency or elasticity of the price system. Things have been done and are being done to maintain it (or the appearance of it) which *a priori* might have been considered impossible. England for ten years has supported an average of 2,000,000 idle men out of state funds. America is creating fantastic 'credits' based on nothing more substantial than carbon monoxide gas, and until some little boy with a very piercing voice shouts "But the King hasn't got any pants on!" there is no reason why this kind of juggling shouldn't continue for some time.

On the other hand the notion that America is in no danger of revolution because we haven't many registered members of the Socialist Party is twaddle. I expect any day to see on the front page of the NY Herald that a mob of 4,000 unemployed have walked into the city hall at Cleveland Ohio and sat down in the mayor's chair. The next day the same thing will happen in Denver, Atlanta, and Bangor, Me. State Militia called to deal with the situation will fraternize instead. And then what? Hmmm. (13 Jan. 1933, Pound Papers)

With Bird's letter, we should be in a position to identify the "catalogued fallacy" into which Pound said he had fallen. Pound's elaboration is not very helpful: "From a discussion of effects which of necessity follow certain causes he falls into a description of what has been, without apparently perceiving the difference in the nature of the two cases" (*J/M* 88). To readers of *Jefferson and/or Mussolini,* who could not have had any idea of the content of Bird's letter, Pound's critique is thoroughly opaque. (Even with Bird's letter, his criticism remains obscure. I take it that he considers American conditions in 1919 irrelevant for Italy in 1933.)

When Bird asked for the second time (22 February 1934) if Mussolini had responded to Pound's points in his "Volitionist Economics" handbill, Pound asserted that he had, while awkwardly admitting that in truth he had not: "YES, the boss did answer my questions under the terms they were asked. Namely that AS my questions would undoubtedly have blown hell out of Europe and precipitated no end of a hell of a perfectly useless rumpus, I was not asking them in the hope of making a mere disturbance, and that they were there to be mentioned pubkly [publicly] IF and when USEFUL" (Pound to Bird, 24 Feb. 1934, Bird Manuscripts). In short, Mussolini did not respond to Pound's questions, but put him off with a flattering—and doubtless insincere—assessment of their importance.

In this same letter, Pound continues to berate Bird in a very abusive and intemperate manner not at all characteristic of their earlier correspondence (this letter was written within a month or two of Pound's very rude

reception of Yeats in Rapallo). His political position is already much hardened from that of only a year earlier and his temper much shorter. The
accommodation with communism proffered in *Jefferson and/or Mussolini*
is no more, elitist sentiments are front and center:

> For all our time/ the sonsofbitches have maintained a nightmare which
> is now as god damn idiotic as having people die of thirst in the attic, be-
> cause some syphilitic kid has turned off the water in the basement. [. . .]
> And the communists are more god damn stupid than any one and all
> revolution and all etc/etc/ comes from the tiresome college grad/ class/
> wot wuz called the lawyer an purrfesshinal class/ the stewd/dent class/
> like you and me and Lenin and the big Bull Mooseolini.

In his response Bird pointed out Pound's willingness to approve whatever Mussolini did or said, in contrast to his promptness to condemn
whatever was said or done in the democracies:

> Question, to be passed on to Rome or anywhere: What difference would
> it make if Keynes DID admit publicly that he was a shit?
> What difference would it make if FDR had brains? . . . Italy you say
> elsewhere is the one country in the world that you yourself couldn't gov-
> ern better than it's governed. Cf. Naples slums, Fiat, tsk tsk. What new
> light has Italy brought on the economic problem? B. M. [Benito Musso-
> lini] has more power and plenty more intelligence than Frank. The re-
> sults are meagre. It must be supposed that the causes are beyond his
> control. . . . Explain to me why BM hasn't instituted the National Divi-
> dend and Stamp Script [*sic*] and I will then tell you why I think it's a waste
> of time to fuss with the idea.
> You focus all your attention on the countries that are least likely to yield
> anything—England, France, U. S. Countries that you confess are in the
> grip of scoundrels and imbeciles, and wouldn't do what was right if they
> knew, and couldn't know because they haven't the brains.
> While right under your feet is a country ruled by one man, wise and
> honest, and you simply say the country is so well run that you have no
> suggestions to make. (28 Feb. 1934, Pound Papers)

This time Pound's response was not intemperate, and they continued to
correspond and debate economics. Pound wearies of it before Bird, and
tries to conclude it with a brush-off early in 1935:

> ALL yr/ damn points have been treated; mostly a dozen times over.
> The difficulty of getting it down ONCE as near foolproof as possible/
> precludes (ef thets the woid) letch to rush it into partial xxxpression in
> private correspondence with semi persiflagical N.A.N.A. (2 Apr. 1935,
> Bird Manuscripts)

The pattern of the correspondence with Bird is repeated again and again: Pound attempts to recruit a correspondent to his program of economic reform; the would-be recruit offers criticism or asks for clarification; Pound repeats himself with added emphasis; when that fails—as it invariably does—he turns abusive or querulous. This is a pattern one would expect of the novice whose hard-bought and only half-understood lessons are questioned or contradicted by a fellow student—and that is just what Pound remains so far as economics are concerned.

Despite Pound's efforts to break off the debate, Bird persisted. On 2 May 1935 he wrote after hearing of Pound's speech of 11 January 1935 that was broadcast to America over shortwave radio, incidentally claiming credit for initiating the idea of shortwave broadcasts from Rome to the United States:

> I heard you made a radio speech to the US in January about the economic triumphs of fascismo. Little did you know probably that you were indebted to me for the opportunity, i.e., it was I, in August, who persuaded the It. Govt. to present these programs to American short-wave listeners. I should be extremely curious to know where the economic superiority of the fascist system lies, as when I was in Rome I sought in vain for any indications of it. As for monetary policy . . . I forbear to proceed. It seems quite apparent that FDR has gone further along the right road in 2 yrs that the other chap [Mussolini] in 13, and under constitutional and legal handicaps that the other one doesn't have to contend with. (Pound Papers)

Just five days later Pound received another troublesome letter from Bird, criticizing Mussolini even more pointedly than before:

> Please understand that I don't yield even to you in my admiration for the boss. He knows exactly what he wants to do and is doing it. Unfortunately he is doing (because he wants to) precisely what all the ignorant bastids [*sic*] and sons of bitches are doing in other countries, out of sheer ignorance and cussedness. If it had happened that the boss really wanted to better the economic condition of the country, there is no doubt whatever that he could have done it, as I can't see where the obstruction would come from. It just happens that for reasons best known to himself he doesn't want to. . . . What discourages me in my correspondence with you is not my own ignorance, which God knows is sufficient, but your bland assumption that smokescreens are still useful, now that infrared photography has been invented. Off with the false whiskers!
>
> I'm sorry I haven't read ALL your writings on economics, it's just been my bad luck that all I *have* happened to see raised more questions than they answered, & when I apply to the author for elucidation he takes two pages to tell me why he hasn't got time to write me a telegram. (Bird Manuscripts)

There are several more letters from Bird in this vein.

From this correspondence alone it is plain that Pound knew perfectly well that Mussolini was not, in fact, following those economic policies Pound so ardently recommended. Bird even pointed out that Roosevelt's New Deal was closer to Douglasite theories than anything Mussolini had done[4] and was achieved under the constraints of a democratic government. None of this made any impression on Pound. When Pound finally responds in July, he lamely accuses Bird of ignorance:

> There is no way out save by MONETARY reform. If you stick down a hole a[nd] neglect the growing mass of elucidation on this subject, you are merely part of the god damn ignorance, which is naturally the ROOT If the shite [*sic*] and murderers ignore the way out, it takes time to educate the unconscious obstructors. You seem to WANT to maintain your ignorance, despite the falling of the leaves.
> Present system merely geared to create interest bearing debt. (22 July [1935], Pound Papers)

This letter taxed Bird's patience enough to elicit a sharp condemnation of Mussolini that pretty well puts an end to the discussion, but does not move Pound:

> Fer gawd's sake, however, comma, don' tell me that the reason why Italy doesn't need Social Credit and National Dividends is that Mussolini has planted more wheat. Suppose I pointed out to you that the U. S. and France, which never have had the blessings of Fascist rule, have always (and still do) maintained a far higher standard of living than Italy. Would you say this meant that there was no need of doing anything about their economic system? And have you ever heard any more bosh uttered by any statesman of any nationality, concerning the currency question, that the Duce has uttered repeatedly? What about that stone monument wherever it is, on which is carved his resolve to maintain the lira on gold ruat coelum ["even though the heavens fall"]? Let's talk sense.
> Fact is that nothing has been done in 12 years of fascism to alter the bases of the capitalist system. I know it, you know it, he knows it. Whether he is INTENDING to do something is another matter. But if so the question What is he waiting for? is still valid. And you, who are so impatient with others (who in most cases haven't the POWER) ought to be asking it. (2 Aug. 1935, Pound Papers)

As we shall see, Bird's exposure of Mussolini's failure to take the advice Pound so liberally offered was repeated over and over again by other correspondents. But Pound refused to criticize Mussolini, while denouncing Britain, France, and the United States for their parallel intransigence. The phenomenon almost defies comprehension. It would seem that since he was convinced that Mussolini was a "factive personality" like Odysseus, Malatesta, Jefferson, and Lenin, Pound did not want to hear any suggestions that his actions were unwise or out of step with Pound's economic principles, even when they came from Douglas himself, as we will see below.

One is driven to the conclusion that a personal trait of stubborn arrogance, coupled with an incapacity for abstract reasoning, contributed more to Pound's political errors and moral failures than any putative propensity of literary modernism for fascism or racism. Despite a bumptious style that made him believe that he was always in front of a parade, Pound always followed and never led, at least in the field of economics. Lewis's canny caricature of Pound's personality accounts for his political behavior better than any purely ideological account. He claims that "the particular stimulation that Pound requires for what he does all comes from without; he is terribly dependent upon people and upon 'atmosphere;' . . . is easily isolated, his native resources nil" and is always "glad to be in the neighbourhood of a big drum." As well as being "a man in love with the past," Lewis saw Pound as an "intellectual eunuch," so susceptible to the ideas of others that he calls him "a little crowd" (*Time* 41, 70).

Though Lewis is engaging in hyperbole, his assessment of Pound has more than a grain of truth. Made as it was in 1927, it is free of apologetic motives and is in fact an attempt to undermine Pound's aesthetic influence and reputation. The claim that Pound was an intellectual sponge, taking up the ideas of others and holding them without any true assimilation, seems to fit the facts. Damaging as it is to his intellectual status, it is less damaging than the judgment that he fully understood what he was doing when he embraced the Axis cause. I do not believe that Pound was either mad or depraved. But he was a bloody-minded fool whose rhetoric became more and more violent as he grew more and more uncertain and confused. Pound's personality was one that could not rest in uncertainty or doubt, and his intellect one uncomfortable with abstractions.

Notes

1. Of course, Pound did not have to face the question of racism in *Jefferson and/ or Mussolini* because it was not yet an aspect of fascism and would not be until the proclamation of "The Manifesto of the Race" on 14 July 1938.

2. Gottfried Feder was a Nazi deputy in the Reichstag in 1931 and the Nazis' economic critic. His critique of capitalism had several points of contact with Douglas's in that he blamed "loan capital" (*Leihkapital*) and "international finance" for the economic difficulties of the 1930s.

Hitler endorsed Feder's economic ideas in *Mein Kampf* (chapter 8). Pound cites the passage in "What Is Money For" (1939), crediting Lewis with discovering it: "Note the paragraph from 'Mein Kampf' magnificently isolated by Wyndham Lewis in his 'Hitler': The struggle against international finance and loan capital has become the most important point in the National Socialist programme: the struggle of the German nation for its independence and freedom" (*Selected Prose* 299). Hitler got rid of Feder in 1936 under pressure from German industrialists.

3. In law, Italy was a parliamentary monarchy with a Grand Council advising the king. Mussolini was overthrown after he convened the Grand Council and it turned on him, petitioning the king, Victor Emmanuel, to replace Mussolini with General Badoglio on 24 July 1943. The council was acting in response to the Allied landing in Sicily and Mussolini's panic sacking of his cabinet. The council met only at Mussolini's instigation, and that had been infrequent since its formation in 1928 (see Clark 238–39). It was not possible for either the council, the king, or parliament to take policy initiatives or any other action independently of Il Duce—short of dismissal. It would be as if impeachment were the only initiative open to the U.S. Congress.

4. Bird is probably thinking of the stimulative policies of the New Deal, including an expansion of the money supply through a increase in the official price of gold. In other respects, the New Deal bore little resemblance to Social Credit.

CHAPTER 5

The Keynesian Revolution
and Social Credit

To appreciate the attraction of an economic analysis as seriously flawed as Social Credit, we must have some understanding of the state of economic opinion in the early years of this century and of the nature of economics itself, a social science marked by consensus more than by unchallengeable demonstration. We have already seen Keynes's caustic assessment of the appeal of orthodox economics as resting on its complexity, counterintuitive conclusions, austerity, internal coherence, and justification of the status quo—all of which counterbalanced its failure to fit real-world events. Joan Robinson, a prominent Keynesian, made the same point (more gently) thirty years later:

> The dominance of equilibrium was excused by the fact that it is excessively complicated to bring into a single model both movements of the whole through time and the detailed interaction of the parts. It was necessary for purely intellectual reasons to choose between a simple dynamic model and an elaborate static one. But it was no accident that the static one was chosen; the soothing harmonies of equilibrium supported *laisser-faire* ideology and the elaboration of the argument kept us all too busy to have any time for dangerous thoughts. (70)

One of the major attributes of Keynesian economics is its attention to "Kuhnian" features of the discipline, that is, to the predispositions that underpin economic theories. Such features of economic theory are as evident in current disagreements within the discipline as they were in

Keynes's or Robinson's day. Robert Heilbroner and William Milberg base their critique of the present state of economic theory on similar grounds, drawing a distinction between "visionary" predispositions and analysis:

> By vision we mean the political hopes and fears, social stereotypes, and value judgments—all unarticulated . . . —that infuse all social thought, not through their illegal entry into an otherwise pristine realm, but as psychological, perhaps existential, necessities. Together vision and analysis form the basis of everything we believe we know, above all in that restricted but extremely important area of knowledge in which we seek to understand, and where possible to change, the terms and conditions of our collective lives. (Heilbroner and Milberg 4)

Though avoiding the Marxist terms *ideology* and *false consciousness,* Heilbroner and Milberg concede the affinity of their position with Marxism (86). Robinson is less guarded and characterizes laissez-faire[1] economics as an ideology.

Heilbroner and Milberg conclude that "the fall of Keynesian theory from its position of unquestioned hegemony . . . is grounded in visionary or ideological considerations" rather than any technical or analytic inadequacy (66). In their judgment "the heretical, and ultimately indigestible aspect of Keynes's work may not have been its emphasis on large-scale malfunction [of the economy], but his ascription of the malfunction [of economies] to social rather than mechanistic causes" (104).

If economic theories and policy prescriptions are a mixture of rational analysis and social objectives, as Keynes, Robinson, and Heilbroner and Milberg claim, economics is a legitimate subject of humane study, and hence of a poet's attention. Unfortunately, a pure heart is a poor substitute for technical competence. Pound, Orage, and Douglas were all woefully undertrained and as a consequence stumbled repeatedly into blunders. In addition they simply did not do the numbers.

By the same token, orthodox equilibrium theory, as a static model, could not take adequate account of the greatly increased dynamism of modern economies as a result of unpredictable and rapid technological change. And neither bourgeois nor Marxist economic thought had liberated itself from an economic model dominated by a class structure in which a mass of relatively impoverished and low-skilled laborers were directed by educated and affluent managerial and governing classes. Existing class structures were justified by the economics of scarcity and buttressed by a moral code that saw prosperity as a reward for virtue or merit and poverty as a punishment for vice or depravity. It is to Pound's credit that he refused to believe in the necessity of such a social structure. Of course he was temperamentally hostile to "bourgeois morality" on bohemian grounds as well. Although he wished to share prosperity equitably with all, he was no democrat, preferring a benevolent tyranny that would leave the citizenry free to pursue their lives unconcerned with issues of governance.

Equilibrium theory rests on two fundamental axioms: that the expansion or contraction of the money supply will affect the price level but not the level of production or employment (quantity theory); and that the economy is self-regulating and will inevitably come into equilibrium at full employment (Say's law). The self-regulating mechanism is a flexible wage rate: wages will fall until all labor on offer is hired, at which point they will tend to rise until labor costs prevent employers from hiring. A further assumption is that the wages cannot fall below "subsistence," by which is meant traditional levels of subsistence, not mere physical survival. This last assumption is the social and political element in the theory. There is no economic reason for wages to have such a floor, but it was recognized that workers would revolt if wages fell below it. In this "classical" or "orthodox" theory an increase in the money supply will raise prices and wages, but will not affect employment or production. And, of course, a decrease in the money supply will similarly lower prices and wages, without any other effects.

The essence of the Keynesian revolution was to undermine these two axioms, most especially the quantity theory view that "money does not matter." He did so in part by demonstrating that money or purchasing power was not automatically and immediately recirculated in the economy. Equilibrium theory depends upon the presumption that rational agents will not hoard, since hoarding foregoes the interest or dividend income that investment will bring. Keynes's demonstration showed that in a modern financial system individuals might hoard—that is, hold cash—since they had no pressing need of greater income. He called this propensity to hoard the "liquidity preference." He also described macroeconomic conditions in which many individuals would become "risk averse" and hold large cash reserves. The Great Depression, which no one had been able to explain, was an instance of such behavior.

It should be remembered that saving accounts, bonds, and other financial instruments do not constitute hoarding, since those funds are reinvested by the bank or the bond issuer. Hoarded resources are those that are withdrawn from the financial and productive system, such as cash reserves held by corporations and individuals in vaults or in demand deposits. The key element of Keynesianism was the role he assigned to the interest rate. The liquidity preference, he argued, "fixes the quantity of money which the public will hold when the rate of interest is given" (168). In other words, the level of saving and investment will respond to fluctuations in the interest rate and that, in turn, will respond to changes in the quantity of money in circulation. His model showed "the rate of interest falling as the quantity of money is increased" (171). Thus, he demonstrated how a modern economy could fail to regain equilibrium over a long period *and also* indicated what measures could be taken to bring it into equilibrium.

A signal virtue of Keynes's argument was that it did not reject the tautology that an increase in the quantity of money must produce an increase in prices (that is, inflation). Instead, he showed that there is a perturbation in the equilibrium caused by the tendency of individuals and corporations to hoard under certain circumstances. They may withhold investment because risks are perceived to be too high at the present or in the expectation of greater rewards from future investment than can be earned from immediate investment or, as was the case during the depression, in the expectation of falling prices. In this way he introduced uncertainty into the economic model and allowed a role for the manipulation of the money supply. He also preserved the logical rigor of equilibrium theory, while showing why it failed to operate in practice as logic and mathematics predicted. Earlier economic heretics had been able only to point to the poor fit between economic theory and the actual performance of economies.

Keynes also showed that wages did not respond uniformly and smoothly to market forces and observed that this perturbation in the formal rigor of economic models caused great suffering: "Except in a socialised community where wage-policy is settled by decree, there is no means of securing uniform wage reductions for every class of labour. The result can only be brought about by a series of gradual irregular changes, justifiable on no criterion of social justice or economic expediency, and probably completed only after wasteful and disastrous struggles, where those in the weakest bargaining position will suffer relatively to the rest" (267). The solution of a "socialised community" is mentioned only as a bogey man; Keynes is far from recommending such a solution. On the contrary, he invokes the socialist solution to impress upon his readers the need to do something to alleviate economic suffering.

Keynes does not deny that the "classical" laissez-faire response to severe unemployment will eventually bring the economy back into equilibrium, but points out that it will be slow and painful. Writing as he was in 1935 when the Western democracies had experienced five years of stubborn and massive unemployment, Keynes's analysis had a ready audience. Though his remedy—the expansion of the money supply—was one that many heretics had recommended, they lacked the theoretical ground that Keynes provided.

Keynes stressed that this remedy would neither disrupt the status quo nor require institutional reform:

> A change in the quantity of money . . . is already within the power of most governments by open-market policy or analogous measures. Having regard to human nature and our institutions, it can only be a foolish person who would prefer a flexible wage policy to a flexible money policy, unless he can point the advantages from the former which are not obtainable from the latter. Moreover, other things being equal, a method which it is comparatively easy to apply should be deemed preferable to a method which is probably so difficult as to be impracticable. (267–68)

A "flexible wage policy" means allowing wages to fall. Keynes points out that in addition to its social effects, falling wages increase "proportionately the burden of debt," whereas a "flexible money supply . . . whilst leaving the wage-unit unchanged has the opposite effect" (268). Falling wages are achieved by what we now call a "tight money policy," or high interest rates, which also causes deflation and hence a heavier burden of debt. The alternative—an easy money policy—requires low interest rates and is typically accompanied by inflation, and hence a partial evaporation of debt.

This, in a nutshell, is what has become known as Keynesian economic policy. In times of unemployment the government increases the money supply so as to stimulate economic activity. Two methods are used: "open market policy," or the purchase of securities, and the lowering of central bank interest rates. The issuance of more bills and coins is also possible, but it is of little importance since they make up such a small portion of the currency in circulation. Keynesian policy differs from monetarism in that Keynes recommends an active "management" of the money supply, while the monetarists would maintain a steady growth and leave the rest to the market. But both modern schools of economic thought agree that "money matters," that a change in the quantity of money will affect the level of economic activity. Both schools remain laissez-faire to the extent that neither recommends any regulation of wages or prices—the method adopted by both fascist and socialist countries and recommended by Douglas and Pound.

Since Keynes's prescriptions flew in the face of quantity theory as it was then understood, it was perceived as heretical and erroneous. Some such modification as Keynes's was nearly inevitable since, as Roy Green points out, equilibrium theory depends upon "the assumption of a fixed level of output" (1). Such an assumption applied reasonably well to the agricultural and staple economies of the eighteenth century, but is woefully inapposite for industrial, manufacturing economies characterized by a relentless and unpredictable increase in both level of output and productivity. Social Crediters—and Pound—stressed this point.

Another important component of Keynes's position is the role he assigns to the balance of trade. He pointed out that most economists were free traders, assuming that international trade, like domestic economies, was self-regulating, but most political leaders also held to the old mercantilist view and pursued policies designed to produce a trade surplus. Green describes this situation as follows:

> Mercantilism was the dominant system of economic policy and ideas in the sixteenth and seventeenth centuries. The wealth of a nation, according to the underlying principle, comprised only its money, i.e., gold and silver. The principle was formulated in two stages. The first has come to be known as "bullionism." This constituted the "pre-history" of mercantilism and expressed the principle in its most superficial guise. Here wealth was objectively located in the *physical substance of money*. The second stage of mercantilism still accepted that wealth consisted solely of money but found its source in the *subjective activity of labor* which produced things exchangeable for money, rather than in the material object. (26; his emphasis)

It is the second stage of mercantilism that Keynes had in mind when he broke rank with orthodoxy and partially endorsed mercantilist objectives:

> a favourable balance [of trade], provided it is not too large, will prove extremely stimulating whilst an unfavourable balance may soon produce a state of persistent depression. . . . Thus, the weight of my criticism is directed against the inadequacy of the *theoretical* foundations of the *laissez-faire* doctrine upon which I was brought up and which for many years I taught;—against the notion that the rate of interest and the volume of investment are self-adjusting at the optimum level [Say's law], so that preoccupation with the balance of trade is a waste of time. For we, the faculty of economists, prove to have been guilty of presumptuous error in treating as a puerile obsession what for centuries has been a prime object of practical statecraft. (338–39)

Keynes's followers credit him with instituting a Kuhnian paradigm shift within economics, and the hostility with which it was received tends to support their view. Hyman P. Minsky accepts this assessment of the Keynesian revolution in *John Maynard Keynes*, but argues that the revolution was aborted, maintaining that self-proclaimed Keynesian advisers "violated both the spirit and the substance" of *The General Theory* (161). Even in its bowdlerized form, Keynesian economics destroyed the mathematical certainty of orthodox economics and replaced it with an uncertain assessment of the probable behavior of economic agents in response to events and the policy decisions of governments. Since Keynes it has been the role of governments to manage or manipulate this uncertainty, and to that extent it forced a departure from the pure laissez-faire policies that had dominated the field since Adam Smith.

The revolutionary nature of Keynesian economics is corroborated by its institutional history. Heilbroner and Milberg maintain that Keynes's analysis was modified in the course of being absorbed as orthodox economic doctrine by setting aside the uncertainty found in such concepts as *liquidity preference, propensity to consume,* and other behavioral imponderables in the saver, investor, and consumer. J. R. Hicks very quickly began the accommodation of Keynes to orthodoxy with the IS/LM diagram (I = investment, S = savings, L is a function of income, and M = money). This formula, published scarcely a year after Keynes's *General Theory,* suppressed uncertainty. Still another accommodation was achieved by Paul A. Samuelson, whose 1948 textbook, *Economics,* divided the discipline into micro (Marshallian or classical) and macro (Keynesian) economics (Heilbroner and Milberg 40–42). To this day North American economics departments teach Keynesian and Marshallian economics as separate subjects. In short, the old scarcity economics of Smith and Ricardo has survived intact within the discipline of economics alongside the Keynesian account of underconsumption.

Whether Keynes's contribution to economics deserves to be put alongside the Copernican revolution in physics upon which Kuhn built his model of the paradigm shift is not an issue this study can address. However, it was so received in the immediate postwar period. The persistence of the bifurcation introduced by Samuelson also suggests that the Keynesian revolution meets the Kuhnian criterion of incommensurability (see Kuhn chap. 6). Equally important for our story is the fact that Keynesian economics was quickly domesticated by academic economists:

> by the early post–World War years a true classical situation had appeared. Keynes's "general" theory had become accepted by economists in a way that must have more than fulfilled its author's hopes, although at the expense of a considerable weakening of its originality and power. . . . The disruptive, uncertainty-centred model of the *General Theory* was converted into a pastiche of ideas, not so much blended as permitted to co-exist, with their mutual contradictions and inconsistencies allowed to go unresolved. (Heilbroner and Milberg 44–45)

By the end of the twentieth century the Keynesian hegemony was seriously challenged, but not entirely displaced. The cause of the rise into and fall from grace of Keynesianism is not, in Heilbroner's and Milberg's view, due to inadequacies in the theory, so much as to the ongoing struggle of sectors of society in the face of changing circumstances: "the Keynesian classical situation . . . was based on a vision whose central message was not so much the endemic dysfunctionality of the capitalist order—that has an ancestry dating at least to Marx and before him to Malthus—but the enduring conclusion that the use of government powers of demand management would be the only remedy capable of setting the disorder to right. This may have been a distasteful message for capitalism, but it was clearly not one that could be ignored" (115). Put bluntly, Keynesian economics maintained the basic structure of capitalist economies and economics by permitting some government interference, but much less than was recommended by Marx and other socialists. The heretics who inform Pound's economics, in contrast, wished—somewhat inconsistently—to retain laissez-faire, that is, to restrict the government to a passive role in the economy. Proudhon, Douglas, Gesell, and Kitson all located the cause of economic malaise in the monetary and financial system, especially in the role of the banks. The Keynesian revolution, by contrast, left the banks and other financial institutions untouched, hence Pound's continued hostility toward Keynes.

The decline of Keynesianism since 1970 reminds us that economics is a shifting and contentious social science. Even within capitalist economics, monetarists and Keynesians regard one another with suspicion and offer conflicting policy advice. There was much greater unanimity in 1919 when Douglas first promulgated his economic theories. In the penultimate chapter of *The General Theory*, Keynes provides an overview of economic heretics who had theorized a "deficiency in aggregate demand." He places Bernard Mandeville (for *The Fable of the Bees*), Thomas Malthus, J. A. Hobson, Silvio Gesell, and Major C. H. Douglas in this category. Others who would qualify equally well—notably Simonde de Sismondi (*Nouveaux principes d'economie politique*, 1819), Pierre Proudhon, Arthur Kitson, and J. A. Hobson—do not get a mention.

Keynes begins his discussion with Silvio Gesell, whose *Natural Economic Order* (1916) was brought to his attention in the postwar years. However, he confesses that at first, "like other academic economists, I treated his profoundly original strivings as being no better than those of a crank." Later he paid Gesell's views tribute because "their significance only became apparent after I had reached my own conclusions in my own way" (353). Though Gesell "has constructed only half a theory of the rate of interest" (356), Keynes concedes that "the idea behind" Gesell's principal policy recommendation, stamp scrip, "is sound" (357). We will return to Gesell later, for in 1933 Pound adopted Gesell's stamp scrip money as a permanent component of his economic tool kit. He learned of it, not from Gesell's book, but from the issue of stamp scrip in the Austrian village of Wörgl (1931 to 1933).

Common to all underconsumptionist theories is the belief that purchasing power can be insufficient to purchase available goods and services. The causes are various: it lies idle (hoarding), it is co-opted by interest charges (Douglas's A + B theorem), or it is exported (Hobson's view). Malthus was the first economist to articulate an underconsumptionist view in the postmercantilist period. He stood alone against the equilibrium theorists—Smith, Ricardo, and Say—in his belief that expenditure or consumption could be as beneficial to the economy and the state as saving.

Keynes regarded Malthus's loss of the argument as a disaster and cites a letter from Malthus to Ricardo (6 July 1821) in *The General Theory* as an anticipation of his own position: "The question is whether this stagnation of capital, and subsequent stagnation in the demand for labour arising from increased production without an adequate proportion of unproductive consumption on the part of the landlords and capitalists, could take place without prejudice to the country" (363). Malthus contended that it would be wise to encourage consumption even at the cost of a diminution of savings and investments. Ricardo took the opposite tack, arguing that only investment in capital goods could create wealth, and hence counseled parsimony as the engine of prosperity. Ricardo's view carried the day.

Keynes was acutely conscious that he was attempting in 1936 what Malthus had failed to achieve in 1798 with his *Essay on the Principle of Population*. He went so far as to declare that "to dig holes in the ground, paid for out of savings, will increase, not only employment, but the real national dividend of useful goods and services." But he quickly adds a moderate qualification: "It is not reasonable, however, that a sensible community should be content to remain dependent on such fortuitous and often wasteful mitigations when once we understand the influences upon which effective demand depends" (Keynes 220).

Though he saw that a modern industrial economy could not rely upon the magnanimous expenditure of the wealthy on luxuries and the arts, Keynes's theory does legitimate such expenditures. Economic support of poets, composers, sculptors, and painters distributes purchasing power without creating a corresponding increase in consumables. Artists not only produce works of beauty but also absorb excess production. Keynes lists mansions, tombs, cathedrals, monasteries, and embassies as useful diversions of "wealth toward assets which will in fact yield no economic fruits whatever, [but which] will increase economic well-being" (220). Pound ought to have been attracted by this observation, for he praises the same aspect of Douglas's economics: "C. H. Douglas is the first economist to include creative art and writing in an economic scheme, and the first to give the painter or sculptor or poet a definite reason for being interested in economics; namely, that a better economic system would release more energy for invention and design" ("Murder by Capital: 1933" in *Impact* 90). But despite Keynes's rehabilitation of underconsumptionist theories, Pound never has a good word to say for him.

Pound's attitude toward Keynes was established in the twenties, but does not seems to have been based on much acquaintance with his writing.[2] In "The Revolt of Intelligence" (18 March 1920) he lumps Keynes together with Pigou and attacks the latter for his belief that the depression of 1920 in the United Kingdom was the result of money being too cheap (Pigou had been a member of the now notorious Cunliffe Committee of 1918–19, which recommended Britain's return to the gold standard at deflationary levels). Just two weeks later in "Probari Ratio" Pound slams Keynes's *The Economic Consequences of the Peace* (1919), which warned that the war reparations levied against Germany were excessive and would be counterproductive. Nearly twenty years later, in *The ABC of Economics* (1939), he acknowledges Keynes's change of view—"Keynes may have found it out by now; he was incapable of understanding it in 1920"—and calls for Keynes to make a public acknowledgement of the value of Douglas's ideas, apparently in ignorance of the heavily qualified tribute paid to him in *The General Theory* (*Selected Prose* 262).

At the time of the publication of *The General Theory* Pound wrote to Christopher Hollis: "That scamp Keynes has caved in. I introduced him to Doug/ years ago. Fack also comments on K's taking 15 years to admit plain truth of Gesell. I wonder if Butch[art]'s vol. Was the last NAIL. Swindle damn well up. U P UP, when the tradition staked out and printed" (20 Mar. 1936, Pound Papers; Montgomery Butchart is a Social Crediter and the author of *Money*, a compilation of monetary crimes throughout history).

He also commented on *The General Theory* in a March 1936 letter to Douglas in which he attempts to get Douglas to admit some virtue in Gesellism. Oddly he makes no mention of Keynes's less than flattering comment about Douglas:

> Yaas/ yass/ any kind of Gessellism Keynes wd/ take up (after FIFTEEN years being told by Fack etc.) Wd/ be trype.
> However/ do you (for private use) see flaw in my argument that Gesell was PARTIAL, not wrong. [. . .] A recognition of FACT and reality in that some goods are perishable. Dividend IN stamp scrip, and a proportion between S/S/ [stamp scrip] and fixed money would solve a great DEAL.

S/S? Can be understood by simple people. Use of it wd/ naturally lead to understanding of Doug/ite book keeping.

But I agree with yr/ swat at Keynes, Gettin results, something that happens in given day or month has relation to what people can be purrsuaded to do.

Also would bust bank monopoly, any direct issue of money by state or industrial company is a swat at banks corner in money. (Pound Papers)

Douglas's reply on 3 April is a curt dismissal of Gesell's stamp scrip money as inflationary.

He was less generous to Keynes in his correspondence with the Gesellites Hugo Fack, the American publisher of Gesell, and E. S. Woodward. Both men were friendly to Keynes's *General Theory,* regarding it as a first step toward their own position. Woodward scolded Pound (in a letter of 10 May 1937) for his low estimate of Keynes and predicted (inaccurately) that Pound would change his mind, adding that the prominent guild socialist G. D. H. Cole thought *The General Theory* to be the greatest book on economics of the century.

Fack was equally impressed by Keynes's change of heart and repeatedly enjoined Pound to give up his hostility to him. He compared Keynes favorably to Irving Fisher in a letter of 26 February 1937, stressing that it took great courage for Keynes to admit that his earlier views had been in error. Pound's response to Fack is far more hostile than his response to Hollis had been:

I am not going to send you money to encourage your ignorance / OR to pay for boosting Keynes, who is just as greasy though slightly softer a shit as and than Lippman.

Keynes is a servant of mammon. He admits a little truth because Cambridge is ON, and he cd. no longer go on lying and protecting Monty Norman, without getting caught out by his little pooplick [public?]. There comes a point when a crook takes cover. Tells a little truth in order to gain credence for his version of the story. (1937, Pound Papers)

Apparently Pound did recognize some degree of compatibility between Keynesianism and Social Credit, but his hostility toward Keynes prevented him from celebrating it. In the end Pound broke off the correspondence largely because of Fack's sympathy for Keynes. When Fack sent Pound some Gesellite material asking him to distribute it in January 1941, he refused to do so because Fack had cited Keynes favorably: "Everyone now knows Gesell's name. But serious men like Por, seeing YOU quote Keynes, think you are an ass or a hayseed" (10 Feb. [1940], Pound Papers).

Of course, Pound was under no obligation to accept the judgment of

Woodward and Fack, but it appears that his hostility to Keynes was more personal than technical or ideological. He keeps stressing that he has met Keynes and knows him to be a despicable individual.[3] His inability to accept Keynesianism is in strong contrast to his early enthusiasm for the New Deal, his continued enthusiasm for Mussolini, his friendly relations with Gesellites, and his flirtation with the Catholic reformers, all of which conflicted with Social Credit economic theory and policy. Pound was willing to overlook these disagreements in the interest of economic reform, but he had no such tolerance for Keynes, even though he represented the best hope for economic reform. Indeed, Keynesianism did bring about considerable reform along lines compatible with Social Credit. But Pound and Douglas would have nothing to do with him or his ideas. As late as 1951 when Olivia Rossetti Agresti suggested that Keynes held views of which Pound might approve, he denounced Keynes, cast aspersions on his motivation, and expressed doubt that he had truly changed his views (Pound to Olivia Rossetti Agresti, 3 May 1951, Pound Papers).

Despite a significant degree of compatibility between Keynesianism and Social Credit, there is still substantial disagreement between them. Douglas addressed the problem of insufficient purchasing power by the direct expansion of it through the national dividend. These payments to individuals would, in Douglas's view, make up the shortfall in purchasing power shown to exist by the A + B theorem. Keynes dismissed the A + B theorem as "mystification" and recommended expansion of the money supply through the sale by the central bank of treasury bonds to private banks and other financial institutions. Because the state paid interest on these notes Douglas and Pound regarded this practice as iniquitous and usurious. They insisted—quite accurately—that the state has the power and right to issue currency directly, thus avoiding paying interest to the banks on credit or fiat money.

Their outrage was based on the knowledge that banks buy the treasury bills with credit they give themselves with a stroke of the pen. Believing that the interest charged by the banks created the shortfall in purchasing power shown by the A + B theorem—though he was certainly wrong on this point—Douglas wanted all credit to be extended by the state directly to individuals through the mechanism of the national dividend, thus circumventing the banks.

Douglas targeted the privilege of banks to extend credit in his very first book: "it must be perfectly obvious to anyone who seriously considers the matter that the State should lend, not borrow, and that in this respect, as in others, the Capitalist usurps the function of the State" (*Economic Democracy* 124). Pound repeats this central insight on many occasions. The fol-

lowing from his second *Esquire* article, "Mug's Game?" is a reasonably suc-
cinct instance. He compares banking to banditry and drug trafficking: "As
long as the state or the people is willing to *hire* its own credit *from* banks
and gamesters to whom the politicians have given it free gratis for the
taking, crime (such as banditry, dope smugglings) is a mug's game" (*Ezra
Pound's Poetry and Prose* 7:243). Pound and Douglas believed that Keynesianism did nothing to redress this "crime." They were not quite correct
on this point, however.

Keynes certainly did not target banks as criminal usurpers of a public
good, but he did predict that interest rates would fall to nearly zero in a
properly managed economy: "the rate of interest is likely to fall steadily,
if it should be practicable to maintain conditions of more or less continuous full employment—unless, indeed, there is an excessive change in the
aggregate propensity to consume (including the State)" (375). We know
from postwar experience that an "excessive change in the aggregate propensity to consume"—both of individuals and of the state—is an apparently inescapable consequence of full employment and one that appears
to lead to "stagflation." The stagflation of the seventies has been used
unfairly by monetarists and other conservatives to discredit Keynesianism.
In point of fact, he foresaw the possibility of stagflation and proposed
mechanisms to avoid it.

One of the last public acts of Orage was a speech broadcast on the BBC
in the autumn of 1934. It was one of a series hosted by Graham Hutton
and published in 1935 as *The Burden of Plenty*. This series presents a wonderful snapshot of the range of economic opinion of the day and reveals
Orage as very much out of his depth in the company of the other contributors, which included Keynes. Keynes declined to have his contribution
published on the feeble grounds that talks ought not to be published.
Hutton's summary of it reveals that it contained the essence of *The General Theory*, deploying the "orthodox/heretic" dichotomy and aligning
himself with the heretics. He introduced the theory of "over-saving" and
recommended lower interest rates to encourage investment. No doubt
Keynes withheld his talk so as not to anticipate his book, which must have
been well advanced at the time of the series.

In addition to Keynes and Orage, other contributors who seriously
questioned the orthodox prescriptions for economic recovery were the
underconsumptionist J. A. Hobson, the Labour politicians Hugh Dalton
and Barbara Wootton, and the civil servant Arthur Salter. Representing
orthodox opinion and the gold standard were Lionel Robbins of the London School of Economics, the banker R. H. Brand, and H. D. Henderson.
The Labour representatives recommended central planning as the key to

a solution. But Keynes, Hobson, and Salter all offered some version of an underconsumptionist analysis, with Hobson alone employing the term. Orage's talk was in the form of a parable illustrating the A + B theorem and stands out as amateurish and opaque beside the other contributions.

Amazingly, I have found only one reference to this series in Pound's correspondence with Orage, and that is in a postscript: "The BBC have asked me to give a talk in a series—Keynes, Salter, etc. all in. Have accepted for Nov. 5" (21 Aug. 1934, Pound Papers). There is no further mention of the series by either man. Orage died on 16 November, just eleven days after his talk, but it seems likely that the topic would have come up between August and November. We know that Pound heard Orage's talk, for he describes listening to it in his memoir of Orage, "He Pulled His Weight," and it is hard to believe that he did not listen to at least some of the others. But if he did, they made little impression on him. One possible explanation of Pound's neglect of this series is that he was busy pursuing Gesellism at the time.

It happens that one of the orthodox contributors, Lionel Robbins, had himself been an admirer of Orage in his youth. He had fallen under Orage's spell in the last years of the first war when he was a twenty-year-old medically discharged infantry lieutenant. He had first been attracted by guild socialism as represented in the pages of the *New Age*. The principal figures in guild socialism—essentially a British syndicalist movement—were S. G. Hobson and G. D. H. Cole. At the time Robbins saw it as a way of resolving economic problems without social dislocation: "A marriage between the state socialism of the Fabians and the organization of the trade unions would build on existing conditions, thus providing at once continuity of ownership, freedom for the producers and the abolition of the institutions of the unjust and inefficient capitalist system" (Robbins 58). On this assessment one would have expected Pound to have been interested in guild socialism, but he was not. Though the *New Age*'s championing of guild socialism coincided with his own association with the journal, Pound ignored it and evinced an interest in social and economic issues only after Orage adopted Douglas's ideas and launched Social Credit. That shift cost Orage the support of Hobson and Cole. It also had consequences for Robbins, who was impelled to undertake the study of economics to sort out the matter.

Robbins was intrigued by Douglas's scheme, but doubted that it was sound and workable. He puts the matter as follows in his autobiography:

> He [Douglas] had discovered, or thought he had discovered, an absolutely fundamental flaw in the financial system of modern societies, namely that it inevitably distributed as income a volume of money

insufficient to purchase the product of industry at profitable prices; hence a continual tendency to depression and unemployment. To remedy this was clearly the first priority for all social reformers. Once this was done—and the cure involved an alteration in the mode of issuing money, disturbing to no one but reactionary bankers—the natural resiliency and productivity of modern industry would produce a state of affairs in which, acute poverty being a thing of the past, Guild Socialism, worker's control and all such aspirations could be considered at leisure. (66)

If this is how Social Credit appeared to Robbins, it is little wonder that Pound was seduced by it. Robbins confesses that he "had always been deeply impressed by the authoritative tone of Orage's commentaries; and the fact that he recommended this point of view weighed heavily with me" (66).

Pound had written to Robbins on receiving for review his book, *The Great Depression,* shortly before Orage's radio talk. Galbraith characterized *The Great Depression* as "the most famous book on the depression" (*Money* 186–87), though it was completely eclipsed by Keynes's *General Theory,* which appeared just two years after it. Upon receipt of it Pound sent Robbins his "Volitionist Economics" handbill, to which Robbins replied in a long letter of 18 September 1934. In it he mentioned his early enthusiasm for Orage and Douglas and pointed out why their economic ideas were unsound. His letter was extremely cordial, even speculating that a future literary history might record that Robbins had persuaded Pound of his economic errors, thus saving a great poet for posterity. He wrote two cordial letters praising Pound as a poet and inviting him to lunch the next time he was in London.

Pound was not to be charmed. All four of his undated replies are abusive and rude, in contrast to his more careful approach to W. E. Woodward in the previous year. He sent Robbins's first letter to Orage, who was uncharacteristically hurt by it, perhaps feeling the pain of a scorned former mentor: "I'd really like to spit in his face. Unfortunately the contempt of people he regards as mediocrities doesn't get under his skin. Only from somebody he admires could he take a blow to his pride. And as he admires nobody (you as poet, for example, only in an exhibit), he is immune in his self-conceit" (21 Aug. 1934, Pound Papers). Orage forwarded it to Douglas, but there is no record of Douglas's reaction.

In his autobiography Robbins relates that in 1917 he had asked the Labour leader Arthur Greenwood if there was any merit in the Douglas scheme. Though Greenwood "was very willing to say that it was all nonsense," Robbins writes, "the refutation of the A + B theorem . . . was something which was quite beyond him." It was also beyond the young Robbins, who had not yet begun economic studies (66). Greenwood set up a committee of the Labour party to consider the Social Credit scheme. It included the guild socialists G. D. H. Cole and S. G. Hobson as well as the more orthodox Labour economists Sidney Webb and Hugh Dalton and the historian R. H. Tawney. Douglas and Orage were both invited to appear before the committee, but declined, according to Dalton, "on the ground that the committee contained too many Socialist economists" (6).

Forced to rely on published sources, the committee concluded in its 1922 report that Douglas's economic analysis was faulty in several respects. It accepted three criticisms: the importance of the availability of credit and its cost (or interest rates); the need to keep the quantity of currency in balance with the size of the economy; and that the banks' allocation of credit on the criterion of profitability rather than of social utility has a deleterious effect. But the committee did not endorse Douglas's identification of the banks as the source of all economic injustice and held to the socialist view that it was the capitalist system itself, and its reliance on the profit motive, that was the root cause of the maldistribution of wealth and misallocation of resources: "But the [Social Credit] theory is wrong in supposing that the issue of unlimited credit would do anything to destroy attempts by manufacturers to gain high profits by restricted output at high prices when trade conditions are favourable to such a policy. The evil lies not in the banking system alone, but in the whole capitalist organisation of industry and finance, of which this system forms a small part" (Labour Party Committee 9). The committee concluded that Social Credit was "theoretically unsound and unworkable in practice," as well as "out of harmony with the trend of Labour thought and . . . fundamentally opposed to the principles for which the Labour Party stands" (11).

By the time the Labour Committee report came down, Robbins had begun his study of economics as an undergraduate at the London School of Economics. Though he "did not find any direct refutation of the A + B theorem" in his studies, he "did find an intellectual quality and a cogency of argument on a plane quite different from that of any of the works which had had such influence on my thought and action up to then" (Robbins 67).

Robbins's story provides some perspective on Pound's introduction to economics. Only nineteen in 1917, one would expect Robbins to have been more impressionable than the thirty-two-year-old Pound. But instead of swallowing Douglas whole, as Pound did, he sought to educate himself, and in doing so discovered that the quality of economic analysis offered by Douglas and Orage was impressionistic and vague. Pound did read widely in economics, but not until 1931 when the depression and fascism drew him into political and economic speculation and even then did so without any guidance from those more competent than himself. Not surprisingly he proved incapable of sorting out the confusing and contradictory theories and analyses he encountered.

By the time of the 1934 radio series Robbins was stoutly orthodox. His talk presented the argument of *The Great Depression*, blaming the depression on an *abundance* of money and credit, in direct contradiction of the underconsumptionist thesis. Such wrongheadedness tended to confirm Pound's judgment that economists were either fools or in the pay of malign powers. Hobson, Salter, and Keynes all offered analyses much friendlier to Social Credit perceptions, but so far as one can tell from his correspondence and published articles, Pound ignored the entire debate, as did Douglas and Por.

Robbins admits in retrospect that his assessment of the causes of the depression was wrong:

> I had become the slave of theoretical constructions which, if not intrinsically invalid as regards logical consistency, were inappropriate to the total situation which had then developed and which therefore misled my judgment.
>
> I shall always regard . . . my dispute with Keynes as the greatest mistake of my professional career, and the book, *The Great Depression*, which I subsequently wrote, partly in justification of this attitude, as something which I would willingly see forgotten. . . . It will always be a matter of deep regret to me that although I was acting in good faith and with a strong sense of social obligation, I should have so opposed policies which might have mitigated the economic distress of those days. (153–56)

Robbins's mea culpa, like that of Pigou mentioned earlier, underscores the difficulty of seeing clearly during those turbulent years.

Pound never admitted any error in his economic analysis, convinced as he was that he could see clearly where others floundered in error. In his 1934 letters to Robbins, he accuses this amiable gentleman of stupidity, venality, ignorance, and cowardice and rejects all of Robbins's arguments out of hand. Those arguments, it is true, rested primarily on equilibrium theory, which Keynes was soon to revise. But Douglas, Orage, and Pound also accepted equilibrium theory, though they denied (inconsistently) that expansion of the money supply would merely raise prices. The incoherence of Douglas's position was glaringly evident in his testimony before the Macmillan Committee on Finance and Industry on 1 May 1930, more than four years before the radio debate. Keynes was a member of this committee, and his cross-examination of Douglas no doubt intensified the latter's dislike of him.

The full transcript of the exchange between Douglas and the committee was published by W. R. Hiskett in *Social Credits or Socialism* (1935).[4] In contrast to the Labour Committee of 1922, this time Douglas agreed to make a submission and to answer questions about it. Keynes questioned him quite sharply on the A + B theorem (56–61), attempting to get Douglas to see that the A expenditures on capital costs, raw materials, and interest must all reappear in the B payments of wages, salaries, and dividends. Though he could not get Douglas to admit it, Keynes's questioning did demonstrate the incoherence of the theorem and left Douglas somewhat befuddled. Keynes ended his cross-examination with the query: "Do you mean that the receipts of capital are greater than the amount it pays out in dividends?" To which Douglas replied, "Yes; that is an obvious statement of fact; the accounts of any company will show that" (61).

Keynes's question contains the nub of the principle of retained earnings that he deploys in *The General Theory* as part of his account of the "stickiness" in the flow of savings into investment. However, Keynes locates the shortfall in investment, whereas Douglas locates it in consumption—a crucial difference, and one that makes Keynesianism still part of economic orthodoxy. Another committee member, Professor Gregory, summarized Douglas's claim (which he disbelieved) in a question that anticipates Keynes's own later view: "Is it that there always is a tendency for the quantity of purchasing power to lag behind the volume of output?" To which Douglas replied, "That is what I am trying to prove" (67). Gregory then goes on to challenge Douglas on the grounds that his scheme would undermine the gold standard, a consequence that Douglas does not fear.

It is plausible to suppose that Keynes's participation in the cross-examination of Douglas in 1931 contributed to his own developing theories. Certainly Douglas believed that Keynes had stolen some of his ideas in *The General Theory*. But instead of feeling aggrieved for not receiving sufficient credit, Douglas completely disassociated himself from Keynesian policies, denouncing them as inflationary. This may have been his genuine opinion, though it is hard to see how his own scheme could avoid running the same risk. The gold standard man, Gregory, submitted him to a grilling on this point, asking him several times what he would choose if he could get full productive capacity only at the price of inflation. Douglas stubbornly refused to give an answer (73–74).

Pound read the Hiskett volume and commented on it in a letter to Douglas of 13 June 1935 (Pound Papers). Oddly, he makes no mention of Keynes at all, but complains of the line of questioning that Gregory took and also of Hiskett's summary comments: "Two prize specimens of MIND have arisen. One is Gugg Greg/ [Gregory] of the Lunnon School of Economics. He, as they call it REFUTES Maj. Douglas by leaving out Time. I mean, as it were Doug sez: a automobile movin at 65 miles per hour will git from Noo York to Phila. Quicker than one movin at 33 and 2/3rds miles per hour. Oh NO, sed Prof. Gergory [*sic*] alias whassis name, a ortymobile goin at 33 and 2/3rds miles per hour will travel JUST AS FAR in going from Noo York to Philadelphia as one going several miles faster."

I have Hiskett's text before me, but Pound's riposte is so tangential, I cannot determine which of Gregory's two substantial interventions he has in mind. I suspect it is the first one, because it involves an automobile. Gregory pressed Douglas on the scheme he had outlined earlier (45–46) to give the purchaser of a £100 automobile a voucher for £25 that could be deposited or cashed at a bank and that the bank could have redeemed by the British Treasury. When asked (by McKenna) where the "Treasury gets its credit from," he replied, "The Bank of England at the present time supples the Treasury on Ways and Means Account with money out of the credit of the country. That is simply the creation of fresh money. That is the case I think" (47). McKenna asked if the Treasury could translate the liability into currency notes, and Douglas replied, "If the bank so desired." This exchange touches the core of Social Credit, that is, the policy of extending treasury fiat money directly to consumers instead of indirectly through the sale of treasury bills to banks. But Douglas was unwilling— or unable—to articulate this policy to the committee except in the form of anecdote and, more damagingly, was incapable of defending it.

The committee pursued Douglas, pointing out, as any orthodox econo- mist of the day would, that his scheme would be inflationary. Douglas merely denied that consequence without explanation. When asked how he could "prevent prices from rising," he replied, "I cannot see, as a mat- ter of fact, how it can possibly cause prices to rise, again as a matter of mechanism, by this process" (54). Pursued on this point, he just repeated his denial that it would be inflationary.

Eventually Gregory intervened, attempting to find out how the £25 credit would be canceled: "How do you get it back? You get it from the consumer, you pay it into the bank, who pay it into the Treasury, who get additional credit from some source, but you never do get that back?" Douglas seems to have become confused and refused to give a direct an- swer, even though he had already given the appropriate explanation to McKenna. The Social Credit view was that the £25 per transaction repre- sented an addition to the total money supply of the nation. It would be "redeemed" by the anticipated increase in the nation's productive capac- ity, that is to say, the total supply of money and the total supply of goods and services on offer would come back into equilibrium, since *both* in- creased. The increase of purchasing power would prompt a corresponding growth in production. In fact, this is pretty much the way the money supply is managed today.

But instead of clarifying his earlier response, Douglas weakly offered to prepare a detailed report at some future date and gave a very general observation: "the point that I want to hammer home is that it is inconceivable that you cannot get a mechanism which will enable you to equate purchasing power to the capacity to deliver" (55). Douglas's testimony reveals with startling clarity that he had no detailed understanding of how national economies functioned and no clear idea of how his particular insights could be implemented. That he should be so uncertain and vague in 1930, more than decade after he first articulated his ideas, is damning indeed. Pound's defense in the letter to Douglas is less evasive, but is far from perspicuous. His point seems to be the same as Joan Robinson's—that orthodox economics abstracts away from dynamic and temporal considerations. But I cannot see the pertinence of this observation to Gregory's queries.

Douglas's testimony before the Macmillan Committee highlighted his limitations as an economist even more glaringly than Orage's radio talk highlighted his. It is little wonder that Pound could not maintain a straight course in economics with such guides. Left to his own devices, he might well have done better, since he was clearly less hidebound and touchy than they. Their failure to accept Keynesianism as at least halfway toward their own vision of an industrial paradise is partly attributable to their inability to understand his argument. But in the end their intransigence probably has more to do with sociological and psychological factors than with economic theory. Keynesianism was designed to "fix" the malfunctioning capitalist system and to rescue the status quo. Social Crediters also wanted to fix the capitalist system, but as outsiders, they wanted to overturn the status quo, to replace the incumbent political and economic elites with themselves or their candidates.

Keynes was a prominent member of the social and academic elite. Social Crediters were all outsiders on both counts, though they thought of themselves as an elite avant-garde. In this respect—but in no other— Pound is a typical Social Crediter. He manifestly regarded himself as a member of an elite avant-garde whose destiny was to displace a sclerotic *derrière garde*. By the 1930s the Social Credit movement had matured—or perhaps one should say, decayed—from an association of like-minded reformers into a fringe political movement jealously guarding its small bit of turf from competing reformers—whether Gesellites, Technocrats, Fascists, or Keynesians—even though their turf was mostly crab grass.

Pound, in contrast to mainstream Social Crediters, remained a fire-breathing radical reformer willing to ally himself with anyone opposed to the status quo. At least he was until 1936, when his position hardened. His fascist-style commitment to a state of permanent revolution was accompanied by a principled eclecticism that deliberately sought out disparate individuals, groups, and ideas in the hope that it would all eventually come together like the rose in the steel dust. Unfortunately it just left him sailing after knowledge without rudder or keel, at the mercy of every shift in the wind.

E. S. Woodward, himself a fringe actor on the Canadian political scene, saw this feature of intellectual vagrancy in Pound and describes it in a letter to Hugo Fack. He finds Pound very odd—sulky, bad tempered, and bad mannered. But he also thinks him brilliant, sincere in his devotion to economic reform, and a hard worker. He acknowledges that Pound reads omnivorously in economics and writes tirelessly, but complains that he thinks too little and that his letter makes no sense. In Woodward's opinion Pound understands neither Gesell nor Douglas, and I cannot disagree (Woodward to Hugo Fack, 9 Nov. 1937, Pound Papers).

For most of the heretics, as well as for Keynes, the key to the business cycle was the management of the money supply, while orthodox economists held that money did not matter. Social Crediters are commonly derided as "funny money" folks, implying that their ideas about money are absurd. But even though the A + B theorem is certainly wrong and the national dividend as envisaged by Douglas is certainly unworkable, the Social Credit understanding of the nature of money and its role in the economy was fundamentally sound. To substantiate this claim, it will be necessary to make an excursion into the tangled and mysterious field of central banking, where Pound got hopelessly lost.

Gesellites, Douglasites, Fabians, Marxists, and orthodox economists agreed on very little, but all conceded that the conduct of the banking industry was pivotal for the prosperity of a nation and the level of international trade. In the thirties practically everyone looked to the banks as either the cause of or the solution to the problem. Agreement, however, stopped there. Robbins thought the slump was caused by the excessive cheapness of money or credit, while Keynes, Douglas, and the Gesellites thought the reverse. There is not much more agreement on this matter today, when Keynesians advise reflation and low interest rates and conservatives advise deflation and high interest rates. However, today everyone agrees that money matters—which is to say that the old quantity theory is dead.

Banks and interest rates were the special preoccupation of Social Credit. The morality of bank profits earned through the banks' privilege of extending credit remains an issue debated in the Sunday supplements today. This is not the place to decide that issue, but it should be recognized that the Social Credit targeting of banks was not entirely idiosyncratic. As well as returns from interest on mortgages and commercial paper, banks also earn interest on government paper, a very nearly zero-risk endeavor. Pound and Douglas thought this practice iniquitous, but it continues in all capitalist countries to this day. Money supplies are expanded through government debt, not by the direct issue of currency or credit by the government to individuals and corporations. One justification for this practice frequently cited is that it imposes some "discipline" on the state.

Historically speaking this practice is a carryover from the days when gold was money and bank notes and government currency were merely certificates for gold. That is why many currencies bore the inscription, "Will pay to the bearer on demand . . ." Originally gold (or at some times and places, silver) is what would have been paid. None of the major currencies is bottomed on gold or any other commodity any longer. They are all "fiat money," that is, paper money or money of account whose value rests on the confidence that it is negotiable for goods and services or for other currencies (see Friedman 341). Negotiability is also the true basis for the value of the precious metals, but the superstition persists that they are "real" money and are intrinsically valuable. It is true that the rarity and difficulty of production of the precious metals means that their supply cannot be expanded at will and without cost, as can be done with money of account, and are therefore less susceptible to manipulation. The great defect of the precious metals, however, is that they cannot supply the needs of modern economies for an ever-expanding supply of currency. Their virtue—inelasticity—is the Achilles heel that has led all nations to abandon them.

Whatever the merits of a system that permits private banks to charge governments interest on credit they create with the stroke of a pen, it is important to recognize that Douglas and Pound were not entirely mistaken on this point, though they exaggerated its importance in the economy. Banks of discount cannot create credit without limit, and there are risks, as bank failures attest. Nonetheless, they had put their finger on a genuine problem in the organization of the economies of the European nations and their former colonies.

When Pound was radicalized by Douglas and Orage most central banks were private institutions that retained the profits of issuing currency, known as seigniorage. Today most industrial nations have central banks that are either owned by or are branches of the government. That has been true of Britain since 1946 when the Bank of England was nationalized. Canada created the Bank of Canada as a Crown corporation, or government-owned institution, in 1936. France, Germany, Switzerland, and Italy all have government-owned central banks, most created in the 1930s. The United States does not have a central bank, but a legally empowered consortium of private banks called the Federal Reserve. The "Fed" was established in 1914, and except for a significant overhaul by the Roosevelt administration in 1935, has remained essentially the same ever since. Central banks and the Fed operate in much the same manner except that central bank profits accrue directly to the government treasury.

The fifth edition of Harry D. Hutchinson's *Money, Banking, and the United States Economy*, a standard text on banking in the United States, has a table showing that the Federal Reserve banks earned $15,493,000,000 in interest on U.S. securities in 1982 (116). U.S. securities are government paper bought by the private banks of the Fed. The Fed is limited by law in the amount of securities it can purchase directly from the U.S. Treasury and buys most of its government securities on the "open market" from private individuals, dealers, and financial institutions, each of which takes a commission. The profits of the Federal Reserve banks are much larger than they would be if the banks were lending their own money, as Hutchinson explains: "You too could show billions in profits if you had the powers of the Federal Reserve banks. Almost all their revenue was interest on their $100–plus billion portfolio of US securities. These securities—accumulated over the years through open-market purchases by the System—are acquired almost without cost because they, as the nations' ultimate monetary authority, possess the power to simply *create* whatever money is needed to buy them" (107). However, the Fed returned all but $157,000,000 of its enormous profits to the Treasury. Thus the Social Crediters' complaint that the state pays interest on monies it borrows, but could just as well have created itself, no longer applies. However, the complaint was justified when they made it, as Hutchinson points out: "Federal Reserve bank profits have regularly been so embarrassingly large that it was necessary to find a technicality in the law to authorize their return to the Treasury." This return of interest income to the Treasury means that "the portion of the national debt owned by the Federal Reserve System is virtually costless" (107n5).

According to Hutchinson's figures, the Federal Reserve banks paid themselves $79,000,000 in dividends from the profits on U.S. securities in 1982. This return is only .079 percent on the $100 billion portfolio, but it is very easy money, since that portfolio was created ex nihilo and is guaranteed by the state (the Fed also retained about $80 million as a "capital surplus"). And the brokers who buy government securities and then sell them to the Fed all take a commission. And, of course, those individuals and institutions that retain the government securities do not return the interest they collect on them to the Treasury as the Federal Reserve banks do.

Today, then, the situation is not as scandalous as it was in the twenties and thirties. Nonetheless, the sale and purchase of government securities is still a very large trade, and one in which considerable profits are earned, well beyond the modest profits retained by the Fed. If Douglas, Pound, or Kitson were still alive, they would no doubt condemn the current system as well, pointing out that none of these banks, brokers, or other financial institutions is required. In Douglas's analysis the government could issue currency directly without any cost to itself beyond minor administrative expenses—and, of course, without any profit to third parties. (Kitson's solution was more radical. He would permit any business to issue currency against its own security.)

Reform of the American Federal Reserve System interested Pound from as early as March 1931. He wrote to Senator Bronson Cutting in that month about President Hoover's nomination of Eugene Isaac Meyer for governor of the Fed. Pound suggested several changes in the selection and structure of the Federal Reserve Board with a view "to democratize the credit control," though he does not recommend that the Fed be abolished or even nationalized (Walkiewicz and Witemeyer 54–55). Nonetheless, Cutting (with Congressman Wright Patman of Texas) proposed a bill to nationalize the Federal Reserve System in June 1934. Of course the bill did not pass (Walkiewicz and Witemeyer 101–2). The Roosevelt administration did reform the Fed in 1935, but did not nationalize it.

Another American politician who was willing to attempt nationalization of the Fed was Jerry Voorhis (1901–84), Congressman for the Twelfth District of California from 1936 to 1946, when he was defeated by Richard Milhouse Nixon.[5] As with Cutting, Pound thought that he had found an ally in Voorhis. One of the three epigraphs Pound put at the head of his "Introductory Textbook" (1939)—a remark by John Adams—was quoted by Voorhis in a speech in the House of Representatives on 6 June 1938: "All the perplexities, confusion, and distress in America arise, not from defects in their constitution or confederation, not from want of honor and virtue, so much as from downright ignorance of the nature of coin, credit and circulation" (*Selected Prose* 159–60).

In response to this speech Pound wrote to Voorhis on 9 January 1939, praising his initiative, but complaining that he saw fit "to cite a scoundrel like Keynes." He wrote eight more letters to Voorhis, the last dated letter is 2 April 1940. The letters assume that Voorhis is an ally, which he clearly was not. They are pro-German and openly anti-Semitic, mentioning Willis

A. Overholser's *A Short Review and Analysis of the History of Money in the United States*. He had a copy of Overholser's book sent to Voorhis (letter of 24 Oct. 1939), but there is no indication that Voorhis received it. Pound even asserts in a 13 September letter that Hitler is a better friend of the common man in England than Churchill and his cabinet. He encourages Voorhis to try to keep the United States out of the war.

Voorhis sent only one reply, a brief note dated 2 May 1940 in which he thanks Pound for his approval of bill H.R. 8080 and mentions that he had a talk with George Tinkham, who spoke highly of Pound (Pound met both men during his 1939 visit to Washington, but it is not clear how he was received). In any case, Pound stops mentioning Voorhis. Neither Voorhis himself (in *Confessions of a Congressman*) nor his biographer, Paul Bullock, mentions Pound. Voorhis is unlikely to have warmed to Pound's pro-German, anti-Semitic, and anti-British rhetoric on the evidence of the following statement of his political principles:

> Either he [the political activist] believes concentration of economic or political power is bad or he doesn't. The communist philosophy, like that of the fascists, holds that liberty is utterly unimportant and that concentration of power is necessary and altogether desirable so long as it is concentrated in communist hands. But unless the American progressive or liberal values liberty and unless he opposes with all his strength such concentration of power, he is neither worthy of the name nor will he be able to build a strong, forward-looking political movement in the United States. (Voorhis 62)

A schoolteacher, Voorhis first ran for the California congress in 1933 as an End Poverty in California (EPIC) candidate, that is, an Upton Sinclair Progressive, but he was not elected. He then ran successfully for U.S. Congress in 1936 (Voorhis 17–19). He was recognized as the leading member of the Progressives in Congress. True to their EPIC background, the Progressives sought to increase government spending so as to stimulate employment (Bullock 71–72). In 1937 they managed to get the Fair Labour Standards Act passed, which legislated a minimum wage of twenty-five cents per hour and a forty-hour week (Bullock 78–80). In addition Voorhis was a monetary reformer, having read Irving Fisher, Frederick Soddy, and Frank D. Graham. According to his biographer he also discussed monetary question with bankers, technicians, and fellow legislators (Bullock 90).

Voorhis's special concerns were central banking and the national debt. Like Pound, he was disappointed at Roosevelt's failure to reform the financial and monetary system of the United States. He also believed that "the monetary and fiscal system of the nation" could have been adapted "to the needs of the age of dynamic production in which we live." Much to Voorhis's disgust, instead of expanding the money supply directly, the Roosevelt administration resorted to deficit financing:

> The banks of the country, at first reluctantly, then with a keen eye to riskless earnings, transformed themselves from business enterprises to manufacturers of "checkbook" money for the government of the United Sates. Since the creation of demand deposits on their books was a costless process and since the banks were paid dollar for dollar in interest-bearing United States securities for every dollar they created, this "deficit financing" program had its appeals to the financial powers of the country.
>
> But it was a poor substitute for what might have been done. (Voorhis 84)

Most strikingly, Voorhis echoes Douglas's insistence that "the state should lend, not borrow" and also that the money supply must expand in step with the increasing output of goods and services:

> We might also have come to grips with the fact that, as the productive capacity of the nations increases, so the credit of the nation must expand instead of its debt. But all through the disastrous years of the deflation that followed 1929, all through the period of the New Deal, and even in the face of war, our government compelled itself to borrow into circulation at interest from private banking institutions every dollar of the new money so vitally needed to balance increasing production, to overcome depression and unemployment, to forestall agricultural price declines, and to defeat our foreign foes. (84)

Given these shared opinions and policies, it is hardly surprising that Pound thought he had found an ally in Voorhis. But whereas Pound thought he could do an end run around the political process by directly converting those in power to his views, Voorhis attempted to achieve reform through the political process.

Voorhis did have one opportunity to alter the course of American history through direct influence. After a long effort, he managed to secure a private interview with Roosevelt to present his proposal to nationalize the Federal Reserve banks. Much to his surprise, Roosevelt agreed. Voorhis left the meeting in a state of incredulous euphoria. But he shortly received a phone call from Roosevelt's secretary, General Watson, indicating that the president had had second thoughts and was at that moment consulting with Marriner Eccles. Another call informed him that the president had decided not to buy out the banks after all (Voorhis 175–76). Voorhis does not give the date of this interview, but his biographer places it "sometime in 1940," prior to Eccles's appointment as chairman of the Federal Reserve Board in November 1934 (Bullock 176).

Undaunted—and with the advice of Irving Fisher, Robert Hemphill, and Robert L. Owen—Voorhis introduced a bill in the spring of 1939 to reform the Federal Reserve System and spoke about it on 5 July. Its proposals were similar to the Cutting-Patman proposal of 1934, which also failed: that the government purchase the Federal Reserve banks; that a new board be appointed to be the "direct monetary agent of Congress"; that social welfare expenditures not be funded by borrowing, but by "direct use of the nation's credit"; that a policy of full employment and stable money (1926 levels) be adopted; that banks be required to "maintain dollar-for-dollar reserves against demand deposits"; that government regulations of banks and money be "simplified"; and that guaranty of deposits be extended to savings and time deposits (Voorhis 171–72). All of this was just the sort of reform that Pound was constantly recommending.

Many years later, when writing his memoirs in 1947, Voorhis was still indignant about the gift that the American people had given to the Federal Reserve banks: "The business of the Federal Reserve Banks today consists almost entirely of creating money and lending it at interest to the United States Government. When the Federal Reserve Banks buy government bonds, they buy them with credit created for the purpose—with entries on their books. But the people of America pay interest on those bonds from that time on. This sovereign nation has given to these privately owned banks the power to create its medium of exchange" (174). We have seen that the Fed now returns its interest earnings to the U.S. Treasury, but it was still retaining them in 1947.

Though he never saw the reform of the American banking system he so desired, he did not give up the fight. He tried to force the Roosevelt administration to finance the war effort with interest-free government paper, but met with no success:

> When a bill was presented to the House providing for direct borrowing by the Treasury from the Federal Reserve Banks, I offered an amendment which would have required that any such loans be at a zero interest rate. . . .
> My amendment was not adopted. And the Federal Reserve Banks, with a total capitalization of only $156,000,000, "bought" from the United States Treasury some $20,000,000,000 of interest-bearing certificates of the people's debt during the war. How could they? Simply because Congress had given to the Federal Reserve Banks the power to create money. (179).

But, however frustrated Voorhis may have been at his failure to bring about a reform he believed to be just, he did not conclude, as Pound and Douglas did, that his failure was caused by the opposition of malign and surreptitious forces. Pound's indignation that the profits earned by the Federal Reserve banks did not accrue to the benefit of the citizens of the United States was justified. But he magnified the impact of the injustice out of all proportion and succumbed to the temptation to demonize those who disagreed with him. With the exception of Douglas and Kitson, none of his collaborators fell into that error.

Notes

1. It is a trivial matter, but there does not seem to be any agreement on this French term. Some writers, such as Robinson, use the infinitive (*laisser*), while others, such as Keynes, use the imperative (*laissez*). The term originates in the response that the Flemish merchants gave to Jean Baptiste Colbert (1619–83), Louis XIV's chief minister, when he asked how he could improve their trade. Their response was "*Laissez le faire,*" that is, "Leave it alone." If we are to be faithful to its historical origin, then, we should use the imperative, and that is what I do.

2. In a letter to Christopher Hollis (7 September 1936, Pound Papers) Pound claims to have introduced Keynes to Douglas "about 1920." Presumably this was on the same occasion that is memorialized in canto 22, where Keynes is disguised as "Mr. Bukos." I have been unable to locate any further information about this meeting.

3. Though I have not found anything to corroborate it, I suspect that Pound's hostility to Keynes may have been motivated by his homophobia. Keynes was an open homosexual in a time when there was little tolerance for homosexuality.

4. Pound had read the report earlier, for he told Cutting in a letter of 11 February 1932 that "The Macmillan Report (of stuff.) I only read it a few weeks ago because I supposed it wd. Be BUNK, and it was" (Walkiewicz and Witemeyer 72).

5. Earle Davis is alone amongst writers on Pound to discuss Voorhis and gives a sympathetic portrait of him in *Vision Fugitive* (194–96).

CHAPTER 6

The ABC of Economics
and the New Deal

From 1931 Pound devoted enormous amounts of time and energy to the promulgation of the "new economics" of Douglas, to which he added a number of other components, notably the stamp scrip of Gesell. He pursued this task with single-minded and selfless devotion, believing that the security, prosperity, and well-being of the world could be achieved only if the new economic theories gained general acceptance. He told W. H. D. Rouse in a letter of 30 December 1934: "I have been for two years in a boil of fury with the dominant usury that impedes every human act, that keeps good books out of print, and pejorates everything" (Paige 349). His economic evangelism was carried forward at the expense of his poetry. It absorbed vast quantities of his time and energy and, as Massimo Bacigalupo and Michael Bernstein have shown, very nearly turned *The Cantos* into a political tract.

By placing under close scrutiny specific exchanges between Pound and interlocutors whom he sought to convert to Social Credit, the eclectic and fundamentally incoherent nature of his economic doctrine will become apparent, as will his inability to persuade others to his views. He emerges as someone exceptionally open to new ideas and new perceptions, but singularly inept at modifying them in the light of one another. This trait made his efforts to educate the world through his journalistic activities even more difficult than it intrinsically was, given that the ideas he wished to promulgate were often at loggerheads. Gesell and Douglas offered mutually incompatible economic analyses, as both Douglas and Orage told him repeatedly, and neither conformed to Mussolini's fiscal policies. Yet Pound insisted on clinging to all three at once.

Pound's willingness to mix disparate ideas without providing any embracing framework is widely regarded as a great strength of his poetry. It certainly helped him in his role as a discoverer, promoter, and mentor of literary talent. Eliot and Joyce are his most celebrated discoveries, but he did the same and more for literally scores of writers throughout his career, rarely turning down a request for advice from *les jeunes,* as he called those who sought his advice and encouragement. But a tolerance for conflicting ideas and modes did not serve his role as an economic guru well.

His success as a discoverer and promoter of literary talent encouraged him to believe that he could do the same for economic and political talent, as evidenced by the following comment in a letter to Odon Por: "do as I do, catch the bright lads ONE AT A time and break it to them gentle// it takes a LONG time/ but the buggars finally know that Joyce and Lw// W. Lewis are better than D. H. Lawrence and Huxley. and I spose econ/ light will infiltrate at about the same snail's pace" ([autumn 1938], Pound Papers).

Pound's patience, consideration, generosity, and diplomacy in exchanges with other poets—peers and neophytes alike—is in stark contrast with his impatience, shrillness, impetuosity, and abusiveness in exchanges with peers and superiors in economics. Even his public pronouncements contrast, though not so sharply. *ABC of Reading* is disjointed and cryptically heuristic where one might expect clear, progressive exposition and exemplification in a work so titled. But one is accustomed to granting genius such license. Pound even incorporates an anecdote about Louis Agassiz, a biology student, and a fish to justify a heuristic technique that is rather like a koan. The student is obliged to come to understanding without direct instruction on the grounds that true understanding involves what (after Thomas Kuhn) we have come to call a "paradigm shift."[1] The revelation must come all at once, as in a satori, or not at all. As we have seen, Pound registers his own conversion to Social Credit as just such a satori in canto 39. Unhappily, no one exposed to Pound's instruction in economics has reported a similar revelation.

The opening page of *The ABC of Economics* (1933) is doubtless intended to be a clear statement of fundamentals, but instead it badgers the reader. The "preliminary clearance of the ground" begins with a kind of accusation: "I beg the reader not to seek implications. When I express a belief I will say so. When I am trying to prove something, I will say so. At the start I am attempting merely to get the reader to distinguish between certain things, for the sake of his own mental clarity, before he attempts to solve anything." These are the words of someone very much on the defensive. When he comes to "clear the ground," his definitions of *property* and *capital* are quite opaque. He tells us that *capital* "implies a sort of claim on others, a sort of right to make others work. Property does not." He goes on to explain that his "bust by Gaudier" is his property, but his "bond of the X and Y railroad is capital." The difference, he explains, is that the second yields income, while the former does not: "Somebody is supposed to earn at least 60 dollars a year and pay it to me because I own such a bond" (*Selected Prose* 232).

The distinction is important to him because he wants to preserve private property while attacking what he understands to be capital, but it makes no sense as economics. The bust by Gaudier does not bear interest but it has certainly accrued capital gains, while his railroad bonds have the same cash value (in a currency much reduced in value) at maturity as they did when bought. His notion that only interest-bearing paper is capital is just wrong. In addition he leaves shares out of account, not to mention direct ownership of an enterprise by its operator.

The point is not that Pound was incompetent in economics—though he was—but that he was incompetent as a teacher and propagandist of economic theory. Indeed, the lack of accuracy and perspicuity in his introductory definition scarcely matters, because it is not relevant to the following exposition and argument, which focus on the important, and surely correct, Social credit insight that modern technology has rendered scarcity economics obsolete:

> Sane engineers and wise men tell us that the question of production is solved. The world's producing plant can produce everything the world needs.
> There is not the faintest reason to doubt this. (234)

More than sixty years later this perception is still not widely accepted as true, though it certainly is true for the industrialized world. Despite our immense productive capacity, poverty, undernourishment, poor housing, treatable disease, and public debt persist. Pound's moral outrage at this situation was entirely justified. Alas, moral outrage is no substitute for understanding.

In 1933 it was still received opinion that the business cycle of boom and bust was caused by "overproduction." Even Franklin Delano Roosevelt so identified the problem in an early speech: "Our recent experiences with speculation have distorted the perspective of many minds. . . . What had been lacking was the kind of planning which would prevent and not stimulate overproduction. . . . It is natural that the scrapping of industries, and even institutions which seemed the bulwarks of our strength, bewildered even those who had heretofore been able to find in past history practical suggestions for present action" (9–10). No doubt it was speeches such as this that led Pound to his early negative assessment of Roosevelt, reflected in a letter to the Paris edition of the *Chicago Tribune:* "F. Roosevelt's speeches show absolute and blank ignorance of economics, and something near economic imbecility, i.e. incapacity to think about such subjects at all" ("Pounding Away" in *Ezra Pound's Poetry and Prose* 5:379).

Pound and Social Crediters were not bewildered, but outraged. They knew that the problem was underconsumption, not overproduction. Pound makes the point repeatedly in *The ABC of Economics:* "Probably the only economic problem needing emergency solution in our time is the problem of distribution. There are enough goods, there is superabundant capacity to produce goods in superabundance. Why should anyone starve?" (234). The solution he offers is to shorten the working day to five hours. While this would spread work and wages more widely, it was not at all in accord with Social Credit or Gesellite policy: "I admit it is not the whole answer; but it would go a long way to keep credit distributed among a great part of the population (of any country whatsoever), and thereby to keep goods, necessities, luxuries, comforts, distributed and in circulation" (236). This is a reasonable and humane suggestion and would no doubt have gone some way to alleviate suffering during the depression, but it fails to address the problem of inadequate purchasing power. Pound neglects to make the crucial suggestion that the hourly wage be increased so that the workers received the same—or nearly the same—wage for five hours as they had received for the standard eight or nine hours. Only an increase in the aggregate wage package would address the problem of underconsumption.

The Douglas plan was to expand the money supply through a direct distribution of money to individual consumers, either by the national dividend or by direct rebates on purchases. Pound's shortened work day does not address underconsumption at all. All it could possibly achieve would be a broader distribution of inadequate purchasing power—a socially redeeming feature to be sure, but not a solution of the underlying problem of inadequate aggregate purchasing power.

His exposition in *The ABC of Economics* soon begins to wander all over the map. In one paragraph he sings the virtues of small, neighborhood stores and shops over larger and fewer ones, and in the next paragraph of his grandfather's factive personality (239). At this point he notices that he is wandering and attempts to justify it by an appeal to the "ideogrammic method": "Very well, I am not proceeding according to Aristotelian logic but according to the ideogrammic method of first heaping together the necessary components of thought" (239). But this characterization of the ideogrammic method is a travesty of what we find in *The Chinese Written Character as a Medium for Poetry:* "Chinese notation is something much more than arbitrary symbols. It is based upon a vivid shorthand picture of the operations of nature" (Fenollosa 8).

Several pages later, he turns to the question of currency, which he defines idiosyncratically as "the certificate of work done" (240). In the context of the discussion of money, he now reveals that the pay packet for four hours could be maintained at the same level as for eight hours. As if the misplacement of this observation was not confusing enough, he praises leisure as opposed to wealth, when the point he should be highlighting is the need to expand purchasing power.

To compound the confusion, he goes on to suggest that workers might be willing to take a reduction in wages in exchange for increased leisure time and security of employment. While this observation is no doubt true, and is in fact being acted upon in the nineties, Pound has completely forgotten the central issue—underconsumption. He does observe (finally applying a Social Credit insight) that no reduction in pay packet would be necessary because the "wage" is measured in currency, and that can be expanded at will: "There are various credit schemes which could take care of the problem of leaving the figure 10 on the bit of paper, even though the day's work were cut in half" (241).

Pound's exposition can leave the casual reader only befuddled. The Social Credit analysis shows that purchasing power *must* be increased because there is a structural incapacity of modern industrial economies to consume their entire production. But Pound argues for a reduction in the day's hours of work so as to create more leisure and adds, almost as an aside, that individual wages could be maintained if it were so desired. But on an underconsumptionist analysis the increase in aggregate purchasing power is the sine qua non of economic reform. Pound's proposed reduction in hours of work would achieve that increase *only* if the larger number of workers received a larger aggregate wage than before the reduction in hours. The fact that Pound's proposal is not in conformity with Social Credit policy is another minor difficulty.

On economic questions Pound had some of the attributes of a crank, such as his failure to present a reasoned and coherent argument and his impatience with those who resisted conclusions put forward without adequate explanation. On the other hand, he was unlike a crank in his openness to new ideas and perceptions. Unfortunately, the new ideas, perceptions, and projects were commonly adopted without abandoning old ones, even in cases where they were clearly incompatible or even contradictory. Social Credit and fascism may have been compatible, but Social Credit and Gesellism were not.

Pound has provided us with a characterization of crankish thought that we can fairly apply to him:

> The loss of a sense of measure is unlucky. The component of error in an idea shows in its working out.
>
> And before that demonstration occurs an idea does not go into action, this is because of some inherent defect in the idea (vide the whole story of cranks from the dawn of all human records). . . .
>
> The thinking man does not insist on conserving the first plan of an engine or an invention. Cranks do. Cf. The general incompetence of economic theorists. (*Guide* 188–89)

His target in these remarks was his Social Credit colleagues who were unresponsive to his Gesellite heresies. Although Pound was certainly not guilty of the closed-mindedness with which he charges his Social Credit colleagues, he does cling obstinately to old ideas even as he adopts new, incompatible ones.

Pound's intelligence does not seem to have been well adapted to the task he set himself. He confessed—or boasted—to Arthur Kitson that he was uncomfortable with abstractions: "BUT I am all agin' abstraction. Got to begin somewhere. I got a poetic I.E. concrete mind. Prefer something one cd/ shoot to a nebulous and anonymous ambience" (30 Nov. 1933, Pound Papers).

Economics cannot be understood by piling up "concretes" or "gists and piths," however perceptive and well-intentioned the compiler. Yet that is exactly what Pound tried to do. He took this and that from here and there and piled it all together. When anyone complained that it did not hold together, he turned away, repeated himself more loudly, or became abusive. I believe that the most important single factor in his tumble into extremism was his frustration at his own inability to "make it all cohere," to cite his own palinode from canto 116: "And I am not a demigod, / I cannot make it cohere" (816).

Pound's attempt to recruit the American historian W. E. Woodward for the economic reform movement displays these internal tensions—as well as external ones—in high relief. He first wrote to Woodward in January 1933 after reading his *George Washington: The Image and the Man*. Soon after establishing contact, he sent Woodward the still unpublished *Jefferson and/ or Mussolini*. Woodward read it, and despite rejecting most of Pound's views, recommended it to Liveright, who published it in 1935. Having got

Woodward's ear, Pound bombarded him with Social Credit and Gesellite literature, amongst which was a typed manifesto.

The manifesto is a good summary of what Pound thought could and should be done and that he hoped Roosevelt would do, if elected. After a brief preamble he lists four points that combine three Social Credit policies—a national dividend, the abolition of taxes, and administered prices—with Gesell's stamp scrip:

I. The value of the country be assumed sufficient to pay at once
   5 dollars per week, dividend to every adult
   3 dollars per week per first child
   2 dollars per week for second child.
nothing for any more children.
(The real value of the nation is vastly greater, but so long as the initial trial estimate does not exceed the real value, it doesn't matter whether we start by assuming say 12% or 20% or any other % of that value.)
2. All government payments to be made in stamp scrip. Stamp to value of 1% to be affixed monthly.
3. All taxes to be radically cut, say 50% to start with, & being gradually eliminated altogether.
4. Prices to be FIXED temporarily where they now are, and gradually to be reduced as per CH. Douglas's computation system. (enclosure in letter to Woodward, 4 Mar. 1934, Pound Letters)

The first, third, and fourth proposals conform to Social Credit policy. They are designed to guarantee that the nation consume its entire production on a year-by-year basis so that there would be no surpluses that had to be exported or wasted in armaments.

The national dividend, accompanied by administered prices, would ensure that everyone received a share (somewhat above subsistence) of the national wealth whether they worked or not. But it is not at all clear what role Gesell's stamp scrip (proposal number 2) would play in the Douglas system. As a bearer of negative interest it is designed to eliminate hoarding, and as a self-liquidating currency, it permits an expansion of the money supply without exerting inflationary pressure. But the national dividend fulfills the first function in the Douglas scheme, and regulated prices fulfill the second. As far as hoarding is concerned, Douglas did not think it would be a problem since, except for a prudent reserve, he expected the nation to consume its product entirely each year. There can be no hoarding if there is no surplus. Moreover, when everyone is guaranteed a sufficiency, and the expectation of reward through speculation is removed, what would be the motive for hoarding?

Pound attempts to explain the rationale behind these proposals in typically combative notes:

Notes: The abolition of taxes follows Douglas's dividend. It also follows stamp scrip.

(This latter is RECOGNIZED TO BE SOUND, by men in high position. Just as one receives personal assurance that the President UNDERSTANDS that the WHOLE people must be able to BUY what the WHOLE people produce [. . .] though to date the President has not yet publicly said so.)

Roosevelt did come close to saying so in his inaugural address of 4 March 1933, which contrasts strongly with the earlier speech on the evils of overproduction:

> Our distress comes from no failure of substance. We are stricken by no plague of locusts. Compared with the perils which our forefathers conquered because they believed and were not afraid, we have still much to be thankful for. Nature still offers her bounty, and human efforts have multiplied it. Plenty is at our doorstep, but a generous use of it languishes in the very sight of the supply.
>
> Primarily, this is because the rulers of the exchange of mankind's goods have failed through their own stubbornness and their own incompetence, have admitted their failure and have abdicated. Practices of the unscrupulous money changers stand indicted in the court of public opinion, rejected by the hearts and minds of men. (262–63)

On such evidence it is not surprising that Pound thought he could convert Roosevelt to Social Credit. Of course, Roosevelt left the banks pretty much alone, even rejecting the less radical advice that Irving Fisher offered him. The New Deal did escape the paralysis of strict quantity theory and did expand the money supply, but it did so through the purchase of securities by the Federal Reserve banks on the open market. Roosevelt did not give transfers directly to individuals on the model of Douglas's national dividend except as emergency relief. The best Roosevelt could manage in that direction was public works—something Mussolini had been doing for some time.

Pound's inconsistency is apparent in the hostility he expresses toward payments to the unemployed. His objection is grounded on moral, not economic considerations, since relief payments would help—however meagerly—to make good the shortage of purchasing power: "As for the British Dole and American 'relief' DAMN both of them. They degrade the recipient. The man who wants the dole is no good. The man who don't want it is insulted if forced to receive it. It is opium in that it is not necessary, and can only be approved by the recipient's being deceived into belief that it is the only means of relief." This expression of a healthy respect for the work ethic is rather surprising from a man who never held a regular job. It is totally out of keeping with the Social Credit perception, which Pound fully endorsed, that there is not enough work to go around in a modern industrial society. And it is in contradiction of the praise of leisure in *The ABC of Economics*. Moreover, Douglas's national dividend is not different in any fundamental respect from other transfers to individuals, such as relief or unemployment insurance, except that it would be clearly identified as an entitlement for everyone rather than a humiliating gift to economic casualties.

To add to the reader's confusion, the manifesto concludes by challenging Roosevelt to adopt the national dividend on the grounds that it is in accord with his analysis of the difficulty and with his objective of restoring prosperity:

> After Roosevelt's speech on March 4th [the inaugural address of 4 March 1933 cited above] the issue is clear, and I shd. think, unavoidable: Why shouldn't the increase in purchasing power (which Roosevelt demands, and admits to be necessary) be distributed per capita to the citizens, instead of being "allocated" by special favour to banks or to groups of "employers"?
>
> The enormous source of the government's credit lies in the nation's real profits, that is, the excess of what it produces (or can produce) over what it consumes.
>
> This is the meaning of "Economic Democracy" [a Douglas book title].
> IS THAT CLEAR?
> Does anyone dare stand up and answer it?

We have seen that many did stand up with answers to these claims, without disturbing the conviction of Douglas and Orage that they saw clearly where others were confused or dishonest. But there is no hint in the manifesto of a political agenda; no suggestion that the United States should turn fascist. And there is little if any innuendo suggesting bad faith on Roosevelt's part. Pound's motivation still appears to be humanitarian, not partisan. A few years later, that will have changed, as the world slipped into military confrontation and war. And even though his recommendations mix methodologies, they are not so different in principle from the suggestions for "reflation" or expansion of the money supply that Irving Fisher made in *Stable Money* and in *Stamp Scrip* and which became standard practice in the wake of Keynes. But, as we shall see, they were significantly different in detail.

As a member of Roosevelt's Business Advisory Committee, Woodward was in a position to exert some influence. However, he was orthodox in economics and therefore unlikely to endorse any underconsumptionist analysis. In any event, Woodward rejected every aspect of Pound's analysis and sent him a devastating critique of the Douglas scheme in a letter of 25 May 1934, which he wrote after attending a lecture Douglas gave during his American visit.

Obviously a fair-minded man, Woodward reread Douglas's 1924 book, *Social Credit*, to see if there was anything in it, even though he was singularly unimpressed by Douglas's speech: "I have just read his book again, and 204 pages out of 212 are devoted to sophomoric essays on the money system, production and consumption, etc. etc." He was particularly dismissive of the idea of a national dividend: "In the United States there are about sixty million adults. Suppose you paid a national dividend to each of them of $10 a month; that would mean $600,000,000 the first month, and so on, and so on. By the end of the year you would have prices sky high because of inflation. I know that Douglas says prices would not rise, as they would be controlled, but you can just bet one hundred to one that they would rise. With that universal and unrestrained inflation the dollar would not be worth ten cents at the end of two years" (Pound Letters). Note that Woodward reduced Pound's dividend of $5 per week by about half and did not include any amount for the per child allowance Pound had proposed. Tellingly, Pound said nothing about the details of Woodward's calculation, whose results would have been far worse if he had used Pound's figures.

The total annual wage package in the United States was $2.7 billion in 1926. By 1932 it had fallen to $903 *million,* that is, from better than $400 per adult per annum to about $150 (Frederick 251). Woodward's $600 million per month would have raised aggregate annual income by $7.2 *billion,* an increase almost three times as large as the aggregate income in 1926. Obviously such an increase would have been wildly excessive. Pound's recommendation was still more so. He wanted to give every adult $5 per *week* plus $3 for the first child and $2 for the second. If Woodward's estimate of 60 million adult Americans is accepted, and we assume an average of only 0.25 children per adult, the annual sum would be $17.5 billion. Such a sum would have *raised* aggregate income by more than seven *times* the total of 1926. Clearly Pound's scheme was ill-considered, to say the least.

The general point—that the depression persisted because of an aggregate shortage of purchasing power—was valid, but Pound, Douglas, and Orage had no idea how to move from the general point to practical policy prescriptions. Douglas was too arrogant and muddle-headed to work out the details. Pound and Orage were apparently innumerate. In any case, none of them advanced the cause of economic reform by pressing for absurd remedies.

Woodward had sent up a question at Douglas's lecture, asking how he would put his plan into action, but Douglas, as always, just evaded the question: "Then he started to talk about steam engines, and reminded me very much of Howard Scott [a cofounder of Technocracy], who will begin to talk about Technocracy and wind up with reducing diets."[2] Later in the letter, he concedes that the scheme Douglas presented—a national dividend, the abolition of taxes, and administered prices—could work, but notes that it would be incompatible with a capitalist, free enterprise system: "It seems to me that Major Douglas's Social Credit plan could be carried out only in connection with the national ownership of land, buildings, factories, farms, stores, and so on. Then it would be easy enough to work it—also easy enough to keep down inflation, because when paper money would be issued under those conditions it would be spent with some Government concern and would be called into the Treasury and destroyed."

Woodward's contention that Social Credit required the nationalization of all industry and commerce is a fatal objection for Social Crediters, who thought of themselves as free enterprisers. Douglas initially believed that if the state took over all banking functions and issued dividends (which otherwise would have been bank profits) no other changes would be necessary. Criticism had driven him to abandon his laissez-faire inclinations and to add price controls to his scheme, but if nationalization was necessary, nothing would be left of Social Credit to distinguish it from socialism. Of course, Woodward knew that. Pound's response to this criticism— if he made one—has not survived.

Woodward failed to find anything to admire in Douglas's attempt to show how Social Credit would work if applied to Scotland: "Well, it doesn't show anything of the kind. Within the last hour I have read it four or five times and I must say it is an absurd, muddled statement. I don't believe that there is a person living who can make sense of it. In one part of it[,] it would seem that the plan is based on taking over all industrial undertakings, but on the next page he says that it will be clearly understood there would be no interference with existing ownership." Pound's response is not very robust; he dissociates himself from Douglas, implying that Douglas's errors are mere matters of expression or detail, and that in any case, he (Pound) is laboring to correct them:

> If Doug flops it is all the more reason we shouldn't.
> Seems to me it wd/ be damn waste of time treating Doug's first tongue-tied attempt to get out of engineering into book writing, as if it were a sort of Koran and me a hidjibidji expounding the arcane meaning of what he was possibly trying to say.
> JOB is to find the RIGHT idea, and its clearest possible formulation. [. . .] I am fighting with Orage and Douglas the whole time ANYhow. I am very glad to have yr/ letter which I shall use in attempt to shake 'em into greater clarity of statement. (5 June 1934, Pound Letters)

True to his word, Pound forwarded Woodward's criticisms to Douglas by way of Orage, prefacing it with the comment, "Here is a letter from possibly the most important man I have smoked up into an interest in Doug./" After noting that Woodward left the Douglas policy of fixed prices out of account, he admits,

> BUT that don't affect the facts A/ that Soc/ Cr/ is NOT YET verbally formulated in satisfactory, or nearly-enough fool-proof manner.
> Plus B. the republication of Doug's early work UNREVISED or insufficiently revised, makes for muddle and incomprehension.
> C. the ipse dixit/ etc. aint enough.
> D. the more damblasting of everybody who dont agree on sight, dont help matters.
> You onnerstand this is important because W/ is the NEAREST WE HAVE GOT TO Roosevelt up to date. ([June 1934], Pound Papers)

But it did not have the desired effect. He was unable to "shake them into greater clarity of expression."

Orage's reply was evasive and general, and he scolded Pound mildly for the weakness of his faith in Social Credit:

> Obviously W. E. W. must be replied to. Douglas is away at present, but I'll give him the letter on his return. I could, however, anticipate his reply: "there aint no *bridge* in the abstract; but specify where & what you want it for, & I'll design you one on S. C. principles." Douglas has not THE PLAN, & cannot have one; even his Scottish Scheme is only exemplary. W. E. W.'s other points are not so serious [?] either & I'm surprised by your agreement with certain of them. However, I'll see what Douglas has to say. (Orage to Pound, 8 June 1934, Pound Papers. Orage's letters are handwritten; I am not certain of some words.)

Douglas replied a few days later, on 13 June 1934. As in the case of his evidence before the Macmillan Committee, he was evasive and defensive. Rather magisterially, he said that he had never heard of Woodward and added petulantly, if Woodward "thinks very poorly of my intelligence, I think even less of his." Beyond that he refused to respond, claiming that he had already expressed himself with clarity. Pound was disappointed, asking in the margin of Douglas's letter, "Is our deah ole military friend gettin a swelled head or wot?" (Pound Papers).

Pound did not give up immediately. He wrote back, detailing Woodward's bona fides and scolding Douglas for his pomposity:

> It is no use your trying to high hat everyone. You have delayed things long enough. And alienated plenty of people who were of good will and who had, by comparison with the multitude, a fair first years education in econ/. [. . .]

How the hell you expect to GET into touch with people who ARE near
the centers of administrative power if you must high hat those who are
well disposed I dunno. ([June 1934], Pound Papers)

This brought no response. Orage—though as defensive as Douglas—did
concur with Pound's estimate of Douglas's pompous inflexibility: "Though
I didn't like W. E. W.'S attitude to Douglas (he wouldn't have adopted it
to Keynes or Stamp or any such orthodox shit), I'm glad you wrote as you
did to Douglas. Truth to tell, I'm nervous about Douglas's ability to carry
corn, having seen several alarming signs of swelled head. This is *one* of the
reasons I'm not identifying the N. E. W. too explicitly with the movement"
(18 June 1934, Pound Papers).

Abandoned by his mentors, Pound did the best he could, circulating
his own response to Woodward's critique in letters to Senators William
Borah and Cutting, hoping for some help:

> I have just had a seven page letter from W.E. Woodward complaining that
> Douglas (C. H.) Didn't answer his question ETC.
> The whole of W. E. W.'s muddle arising from his not having grasped the
> possibility of a FIXED price, let alone of "compensated or adjusted or
> just" price.
> If a man as intelligent as Woodward, as near to the works, hasn't SEEN
> that yet, there must be "countless millions" needing primary instruction.
> (7 June 1934, Walkiewicz and Witemeyer 133)

(Notice that Pound's echoic mind has picked up the epithet *muddle* that
Woodward applied to Douglas. He repeats it in several places immediately
afterward.)

It is certainly true that if prices remained fixed, an increase in the money
supply would not cause inflation, but that is a mere tautology. Experience
shows that in a market economy, administered prices cause a decline in
the supply of goods on offer and/or a black market at unregulated prices.
In short, as Woodward pointed out, price fixing by the state is incompatible with the free market economy that Social Credit was supposed to rescue from the socialist "servile state." It is certainly possible in principle to
increase consumption and production by an increase in the money supply without raising prices, but postwar experience has shown that it is not
so easy in practice. Though loath to admit that inflation would be a problem, Douglas was sufficiently moved by criticisms to adopt the impracti-
cal policy of price controls—and Pound followed him, invoking the
Canonists' "just price."

Douglas's failure to answer Woodward's criticisms is yet another indication of his incompetence. Pound was prepared to revise his views if

Douglas and Orage would help him, but they were intransigent in the face of Woodward's criticism. Pound was forced to choose between his long-time allies and their critics on trust and loyalty rather than reasoned argument. Pound stuck to Social Credit, though he continued to take economic wisdom where he could find it without regard to its Douglasite orthodoxy. One of those non-Douglasite enthusiasms was for Silvio Gesell. Just a month before this exchange with Woodward, he had tried to interest Orage and Douglas in Gesell, but was rebuffed, as he was when he tried to push Mussolini on them. One might have expected Pound to have severed his ties with Social Credit, given these bones of contention. But he did not—not even after Orage's sudden death on 6 November 1935.

Pound's failure to dump Social Credit was surely based on his belief that its economic analysis was correct. No other explanation accounts for his clinging to it in the face of Douglas's contempt, Orage's discouragement, and Mussolini's total indifference to it. The fact that his belief in Social Credit was proof against discouragement and devastating detailed criticism forces the conclusion that he was out of his depth. He simply could not make rational judgments about the practicality, wisdom, or theoretical coherence of the policies and principles he espoused. This failure is not a shameful one. I hope to have shown that confusion and blind adherence to erroneous theories and policies was the order of the day in the field of economics. Pound saw clearly—and correctly—that others were confused. Unfortunately, he could not see—or could not admit—his own confusion or the error of his mentors.

The exchange between Pound, Woodward, Douglas, and Orage demonstrates that Pound's economic evangelism in the early to midthirties was not driven by a commitment to fascism or even to Social Credit. He was open to criticism, willing to adapt his views in the face of new ideas or information, and willing to adopt any scheme he thought might improve general welfare. Instead of an inflexible credit crank, he emerges as someone attempting to broker an agreement between disparate economic reformers in the hopes of persuading those in power to repair technical inefficiencies in the economies of Western nations. The particular political system was a matter of little moment to him, for the economic reform would be to the benefit of everyone and would be equally effective under any regime or ideology. Thus Pound could believe that Roosevelt and Mussolini were on the same track, so long as they both took steps to stimulate consumption. It mattered little to him that Mussolini was a dictator and Roosevelt a democrat.

It was in this spirit that he praised Jefferson, Lincoln, and Mussolini in *Jefferson and/or Mussolini*. As he told Douglas in the scolding letter cited above, "State of W's muddle is of less importance, than FINDING verbal formulations sufficiently CLEAR to penetrate the minds of active men." Pound truly believed that if only he could make his ideas clear, all right-thinking men and women would promptly accept them. It is difficult to imagine an adult holding such an absurd view, but Pound certainly did. Such naiveté is rather charming in a poet, but it left him with only two ways of accounting for his failure to persuade others: either his ideas were muddled or his audience was badly motivated.

From 1931 to 1935, he was inclined to the former hypothesis and labored to clarify his understanding of economics. But he only sunk further and further into contradiction, confusion, and incoherence. Unable to admit his own confusion, which others made manifest to him, he grew more and more shrill. At the same time, international tensions rose, making it necessary to choose sides. The coincidence of these two developments proved too much for him. After truly heroic efforts, he abandoned forever the first hypothesis and adopted the second, moving the fault from himself to others and at the same time shifting the question from one of truth or error to one of good or evil.

That shift was already beginning to take place in 1934. Woodward noticed, and was offended by, Douglas's anti-Semitism—a failing in him that Pound had ignored:

> I notice that on page 29 of "Social Credit" he goes out of his way to attack the Jews. What he says on that page would be sufficient to kill his Social Credit scheme in the United States. What have the Jews got to do with it? Everybody of intelligence in this country is bored to death by the argument that the Jews have a mysterious control over money and finance. We know better; we know they haven't. Besides, in a serious economic work questions of race or religion are a little extraneous. (Woodward to Pound, 25 May 1934, Pound Letters)

Pound did not respond to this remark in the next letter, but he returned to it in a letter of 20 June: "note re/ jews. I don't care a damn WHOSE. Everybody in Europe with ANY knowledge is convinced that there IS a continual drive toward war/ worked by international finance banks and gun sellers/ The only difference in view is re/ AGAINST WHOM. some say against Russia; some against Germany" (Pound Papers). This is one of the earliest references Pound makes to a conspiracy, whether Jewish or not. Even though Douglas was openly anti-Semitic from the beginning, Pound had previously ignored that aspect of his mentor's views.

In the letter of 25 May, Woodward predicts that Social Credit will be a dead issue in the United States within a year, as Technocracy already was, and in closing, responds to Pound's insinuation that its failure to catch on could be attributed to the implacable opposition of a conspiracy of bankers or Jews: "In your last letter you say, 'Have you any idea of the mental or financial obstacle that prevents discussion of scrip and dividend?' Why, yes; I can tell it to you in one sentence. There is nothing at all to talk about. There is no proposition of any kind made. Even Major Douglas himself says he will leave it to us to formulate a plan. That being the case, all that Major Douglas has to deliver is a lot of generalized talk about the function of money." Although somewhat too sweeping, this is, I think, a fair criticism of Douglas and Social Credit, and one that Keynes also makes just two years later in *The General Theory*. Noting that "the strength of Major Douglas's advocacy has, of course, largely depended on orthodoxy having no valid reply to much of his destructive criticism," Keynes adds: "On the other hand, the detail of his diagnosis . . . includes much mere mystification" (370–71).

Like so many other of Pound's efforts to convert correspondents to his views, the Woodward escapade ended in disaster. But Pound proved to be immune to rejection. As we have seen, the devastating criticism of William Bird and of Wyndham Lewis sometimes moved him to anger, but never to revision or modification of his views. The same was true of the perennial criticism he received from his old friend William Carlos Williams and even from fellow Social Crediters. Douglas, Orage, and Por all castigated him for obscurity, inconsistency, or simple confusion, but none of this criticism could deflect him from the course he had set himself.

An exchange with Por six years after the one with Woodward illustrates even more emphatically Pound's inability to adjust his exposition so as to reach an audience. Por was a Social Crediter and admirer of Mussolini, but not, according to the biographical sketch he sent Pound, a Fascist: "Hungarian. Syndicalist. Guild Socialist. NOT fascist. Free lance. Now, also Director Rome Office of Istituto per gli Studi di Politica Internazionale (Milan) like that of Foreign Affairs in London, which publishes, reviews books, and arranges lectures, Independent Institute" (28 Mar. 1935, Pound Papers). Though "not a Fascist," Por had rushed into print with *Fascism* on Mussolini's rise to power in 1922. He portrayed fascism, accurately enough, as an empty vessel: "Fascism, we repeat, although it has theories is not a system; this is one of the reasons of its success. Theories arise out of acts and not acts out of theories, and Fascism moulds itself, day by day, by means of daily action and experience" (170).[3]

No doubt this assessment encouraged Por to believe that he could capture fascism for his own economic program. He launched a campaign in hopes of bringing that about, recruiting Pound to the cause in 1934. They became a two-man propaganda machine for Social Credit reform within fascism.[4] Despite their continued cooperation, Por repeatedly felt obliged to complain of Pound's obscurity, begging him to be clearer. He sensibly argued that if *he* could not understand what Pound was getting at, their target audience would have no hope.

Though Pound did not ignore Por's comments, he proved quite unable to make an appropriate adjustment. One instance is particularly revealing. Por wrote to Pound passing on a complaint from Camillo Pellizzi, a professor of Italian at the University of London: "Pellizi [*sic*] says he cant do anything with the dope you sent him. Write [illegible] a clear article people can understand—without consulting an Enciclopedia [*sic*]" (2 June 1940, Pound Papers).

Pound was incensed:

Nuts/ you ass!! Pel/ asks me to write down my IDEAS.
I send a syllabus or catalogue, and ask which PART of the subject he thinks can be useful.
A clear article "people" can understand!! WHAT people? I am not a kindergarten department.
A "CULTURA" is made up of various elements. A curriculum is ordinarily DIVIDED into various subjects. BUT in a CULTURE these subjects have some relation to each other, in fact they all emerge from a basic philosophy; which causes modifications, or rather the life pushed out the dead parts or the decayed precedent condition. Of course IF the universities are NOT expected to change their bunk, it merely means that they, and the schools are NOT OF the present culture. (4 June 1940, Pound Papers)

This last remark exemplifies the inflexibility of Pound's holistic or ideogrammatic approach to instruction: those who fail to agree with him can only be dismissed as "NOT OF the present culture," that is, as those who disagree with him.

Pound believed that he was misunderstood because he was so far ahead of everyone else. Of course, this posture was almost canonical amongst aesthetic modernists whenever their avant-garde artworks were misunderstood. Such a posture may well be useful in art, where there is no question of a correct way of doing things, but in a practical field such as economics, it is more important to be correct than to be different.

Another difficulty that Pound made for himself arises from his commitment to the "ideogrammic method," which is based on an epistemology that supposes knowledge arises effortlessly or not at all. Since such an epistemology leaves no place for articulation and argumentation, Pound had no recourse when misunderstood other than to repeat with emphasis what he had already written. It is this predicament that informs his complaint: "No mutt understands ANYTHING till he has been told it ten times in SIX different forms" (12 July [1940], Pound Papers). He always imagines that the failure is in his readers, not himself. Optimist that he was, despite repeated failures, he remains confident that once his readers have reinvented themselves along his lines, they will understand.

To put it another way, Pound believes that things can only be understood entire, as opposed to piecemeal or one-thing-at-a-time. He adopted Frobenius's term, *paideuma,* as a label for an unanalyzable set of beliefs, attitudes, and practices that make up a culture. His own new *paideuma*—Social Credit economics, a modernist aesthetic, and fascist politics—had to be swallowed whole or not at all. He commonly attributed the failure of his interlocutors to embrace his *paideuma* to insufficient exposure to the whole package or, when that explanation wore thin, to stupidity, venality, or malice.

He seems to have been incapable of seeing how disjointed and cryptic his prose frequently appeared to others. When Por asked him to revise a piece he had written so as to make it clearer, he exploded:

> WOT, my deah Odon, I NEVER seem able to get into YOUR damnblock IS that I have NO bloody means of knowing WHAT the hell you or other readers consider OBscure. [. . .]
> It all looks simple to me and if some blighter dont know that cat spells CAT, or dog DOG
> How am I to tell WHICH words of three letters are incomprehensible. You appear to understand PARTS of my writing, but how the kesl [*sic*] can I tell WHICH parts, if no one ever picks out a particular part and asks: what thehelldoyou mean? (23 July 1940, Pound Papers)

Of course, it is not unusual for exceptionally able people to be blocked when attempting to explain to less gifted interlocutors concepts that seem transparent to them. But even though pedagogical success can never be guaranteed, resourceful teachers will vary techniques and approaches in an effort to get their message across. Pound was singularly lacking in such pedagogical skills, although passionately devoted to the instruction of others. When not understood he could only shout, bluster, repeat, wax sarcastic, and rhetorically throw up his hands in exasperation and despair at the thickheadedness of his interlocutors—or denounce them for acting in bad faith.

Pound's refusal to engage in debate or discussion is compatible with the anti-intellectual tendencies of fascism and Nazism, but Pound was not anti-intellectual and thought of himself as supremely rational. Certainly he did not dismiss argument and discussion in favor of appeals to the heart and the blood, as anti-intellectuals (like Mussolini) typically do, but he does share some of the attributes of antirationalists.

Antirationalists distrust argument on the grounds that it falsifies the originary unity of those entities it purports to discuss by analyzing or dissecting them. Wordsworth typified this organic or holistic position in the phrase "we murder to dissect." Pound is antirationalist in this sense. His frequent celebrations of reason and rationality are perfectly sincere, but his rationality must be understood as Platonic (that is, holistic), rather than Aristotelian or Cartesian (that is, analytic). In such a view, understanding comes unbidden and effortlessly or not at all. And if understanding is not achieved after due exposure, then the fault is not in the presentation or the presenter, but in the inadequacy of the student. This is precisely the stand Pound takes in the letter to Por and in many other places.

Perhaps the most trenchant criticism of this tendency in Pound comes from the pen of George Santayana, whom Pound met through Daniel Cory, Santayana's disciple and secretary. Cory had spent a few weeks' holiday in Rapallo in 1937, and Pound began to cultivate Santayana through Cory. Pound attempted to bring Santayana around to his view of things, sending him a copy of Ernest Fenollosa's *The Chinese Written Character as a Medium for Poetry* (McCormick 400–403), which encapsulates the "ideogrammic method." Fenollosa claims that knowledge arises "actively" from the juxtaposition of particulars, rather than in the Aristotelian or analytic method in which to know *means* to bring a particular under a general, as in the judgment "This object is an APPLE." The ideogrammaticist, in contrast, would merely place a bunch of apples together, confident that the observer would intuit the concept *apple*. The concept is thus thought to be immanent in the apples, and not imposed by the observer in a Cartesian manner.

After perusing the Fenollosa essay, Santayana wrote a trenchant criticism of this "philosophy":

> Dear E.P.
> This mustn't go on for ever, but I have a word to say, in the direction of fathoming your potential philosophy.
> When is a thing not static? When it jumps or when it makes you jump? Evidently the latter in the case of Chinese ideograms, you being your thoughts.
> And these jumps are to particulars, not regressive to general terms. Classifications are not poetry. I grant that, but think that classifications may be important practically; e.g., poisons: how much? what number? . . .
> When you ask for jumps to other particulars, you don't mean (I sup-

pose) *any* other particulars, although your tendency to jump is so irresistible that the bond between the particulars jumped to is not always apparent. It is a mental grab-bag. A *latent* classification or a *latent* genetic connection would seem to be required, if utter miscellaneousness is to be avoided. (20 Jan. 1940, qtd. in McCormick 403–4)

The Fenollosa doctrine is not unlike Heidegger's notion that nature "reveals" itself. It is a mildly mystical and overtly immanentist doctrine, and as such is immune to Santayana's rational strictures. The relevant passage in *Chinese Written Character* is the following:

> The whole delicate substance of speech is built upon substrata of metaphor. Abstract terms, pressed by etymology, reveal their ancient roots still embedded in direct action. But the primitive metaphors do not spring from arbitrary *subjective* processes. They are possible only because they follow objective lines of relations in nature herself. Relations are more real and more important than the things which they relate. The forces which produce the branch-angles of an oak lay potent in the acorn. . . . Nature furnishes her own clues. Had the world not been full of homologies, sympathies, and identities, thought would have been starved and language chained to the obvious. There would have been no bridge whereby to cross from the minor truth of the seen to the major truth of the unseen. (Fenollosa 22–23)

Such an epistemology puts a tremendous stress upon self-evidence and virtually excludes any recourse to reasoned argument. Within it disagreement can arise only from the blindness—whether willful or involuntary—of one party. And new knowledge can be gained only through revelation, insight, or intuition. Hence one can teach only as a guru or Zen master, providing the student with koans that produce either blank incomprehension or a satori. Pound's economic evangelism falls between the technique of the remote, laconic guru and the passionate, voluble persuader. The in-between position combines opacity with passion, producing—alas—more heat than light.

Notes

1. Agassiz, the famous Harvard biologist, gave a graduate student a sunfish to describe. Agassiz repeatedly rejected the proffered descriptions "until at the end of three weeks the fish was in an advanced state of decomposition, but the student knew something about it" (*ABC of Reading* 17–18).

2. No doubt a reference to Scott's infamous speech at the Hotel Pierre on 13 January 1933, broadcast on national radio, which led to the end of Technocracy.

3. Mussolini himself had written: "All doctrines aim at directing the activities

of men towards a given objective; but these activities in their turn react on the doctrine, modifying and adjusting it to new needs, or outstripping it. A doctrine must therefore be a vital act and not a verbal display. Hence the pragmatic strain in Fascism, its will to power, its will to live, its attitude toward violence, and its value" (26).

4. Earle Davis (156–60) and Tim Redman (160) both think that Por led Pound to imagine that Mussolini's fascism and Social Credit were compatible, but they can hardly be correct on this point, for it is Pound who lists the points of agreement at the beginning of the correspondence, not Por. Moreover, their contact was *after* Pound had written *Jefferson and/or Mussolini.*

CHAPTER 7

Modernism, Postmodernism, and Fascism

Although the specter of postmodernism was raised in the previous discussion of Pound's pedagogical technique, the topic deserves greater attention because literary modernism is being reassessed in the light of postmodern criteria. This reassessment has made it increasingly apparent that literary modernism has long been misconstrued as the fulfillment—or the latest development—of liberal humanism or the Enlightenment (see Perkins; Longenbach *Modernist Poetics;* and Lindberg; contrast Galison; Harrison; Kazin; and Perl). Such a view of modernism was to its credit in the forties and fifties when liberal humanism was the "ideology" of choice, but that is no longer the case.

A liberal thought of herself as skeptical and relativistic; a relativist in that she tolerated all views and opinions, including those she thought erroneous, and skeptical in that she thought the truth could not be known but only approximated. But the postmodern perception of liberalism is quite different and Nietzschean in inspiration. It sees modernism as committed to absolutism in science, patriarchy in politics, logocentrism in philosophy, and aesthetic autonomy in literature. Postmodernism, looking to Nietzsche and Heidegger, regards itself as *truly* skeptical and relativistic, dismissing modernist claims to relativism as no more than protective coloring.

The contrasting "inside" and "outside" (or "hindsight") views of modernism are perhaps not entirely incompatible, but they are surely incommensurable. The precise character of the shift in sensibility between the older "inside" view and the current "outside" view is masked by a shared vocabulary—*liberal, relative, skeptical, rational*—while an unnoticed and unexpected continuity is occluded by a cloud of neologisms—*logocentrism, decenter, différance, episteme.*

Quite apart from the inaccuracies of postmodern polemical travesties of modernism, one needs to consider an alternative understanding that emphasizes the visionary, mythical, and even mystical sides. Such accounts are found early—in Edmund O. Wilson's *Axel's Castle*—and late—in James Longenbach's account of the "skeptical visionaries" whose thought he tells us informs High Modernism. The "danger" of such an alternative view is that if modernism is no longer thought to be skeptical and relativistic, it is liable to be judged to be credulous and absolutist or at least dogmatic—to be, in short, right-wing, fundamentalist, and retrograde. Just such a conclusion has long been endorsed by the New York intellectuals in their opposition to Pound's Bollingen Prize and in their suspicion of Eliot's conservative social criticism (see Jumonville). Their assault on modernism has been maintained by Alfred Kazin, who also characterizes modernism as fascist.

The vogue of Nietzschean skepticism and relativism amongst North American literary scholars is no doubt partly due to a tacit axiom of the avant-garde, that credulity and dogmatism are the marks (respectively) of the peasantry and the bourgeoisie. Romanticism, which might be thought of as the "Counter-Enlightenment," chose the credulity of the child, the savage, and the peasant over the dogmatic intolerance of the bourgeoisie and the sophisticated skepticism of the savant. Modernism opposed its own "realism"—typified by constitutive works such as *Ulysses* and *The Waste Land*—to Romantic credulity. It transgressed the prohibitions imposed by bourgeois social mores in the name of truth telling and retained the Romantic fear and loathing of bourgeois dogmatism and intolerance—a feature ignored or denied by postmodern critiques of modernism.

Since modernist literary criticism (often imprecisely equated with New Criticism) was publicly committed to truth telling, it had to hold at bay the "errors" of Romantic fantasy and bourgeois kitsch. Eliot's poetry was perceived to have spectacularly escaped these errors, making him a hero of modernism. However, he soon appalled his modernist admirers by his "lapse" into Anglican credulity and providential hope. Similarly, any lapse of literary texts into paraphrasable plain sense was perceived by modernists as a failure of relativism, whose hermeneutic face was ambiguity, tension, undecidability, polyvalency, and the like.

If modernism is relativistic and modernist art is polyvalent, it is clear that there are strong affinities and continuities between modernism and postmodernism. Such affinities would oblige postmodernism to attempt

to isolate itself from the modern, just as modernism had labored to isolate itself from the aestheticism that preceded it and from Romanticism
(Longenbach *Stone Cottage;* Surette *Birth*). Academic defenders of modernism vigorously resist any allegations of its continuity with Romanticism
partly because Romanticism stands synecdochically in many people's
minds for the cultural disease that brought us fascism and Nazism.[1] Hitler's
rallies—staged by Albert Speer with Wagnerian grandeur—remain powerful icons of Nazi style—tacitly considered a causal factor in the brutality and bellicosity of totalitarianism.

The argument that bad ideas produce bad art has long troubled the
ideologue. Marxist literary criticism legitimates the praise or censure of
literature on grounds of the acceptability of its content. Postmodernism
has broadened this principle to exclude such politically incorrect content
as sexism, homophobia, Eurocentrism, logocentrism, phallocentrism, and
so forth, a practice directly contrary to modernist practice, which permitted all topics and all opinions on the grounds that the function of artworks
is to reveal "reality" to us in all its uncompromising raggedness, irony, and
conflict. It is precisely this aesthetic license that makes Pound such a problem for modernist principles. His fascism and anti-Semitism are intolerable in the face of the Nazis' "Final Solution," yet modernist principles do
not permit their exclusion.

Aesthetic modernism, of course, is not without criteria by which to exclude artworks from the canon. It requires that all approved artworks hold
disparate and conflicting elements in some sort of formal tension. It holds
that the great artworks bring this dynamic conflict to a resolution. Pound's
Cantos easily meets the first criterion, but has a problem with the resolution. Postmodernism has discarded the second criterion and distrusts
those artworks that lead to harmonious resolution, denouncing them as
false, misleading, idealistic, romantic, and naive. Pound's *Cantos* is thus
just the sort of work that postmodernism should approve, since it successfully evades closure while containing as heteroclite a collection of disparate and conflicting elements as one could wish. Unfortunately for Pound's
reputation, postmodernism is militantly opposed to liberalism as well as
to fascism and Nazism. For all these reasons, the Pound controversy has
become very different from what it was in the aftermath of the Bollingen
Prize of 1949; it is still largely waged on aesthetic grounds, however, since
a defense on historical or biographical grounds is no longer possible.[2]

Today the issue of modernist affinities with fascism has become far more
complicated and tendentious. There are few who cling to the principle
of aesthetic autonomy and insist that works of art, and therefore artists,
are above the melee. However, the old Romantic principle that artworks

are organic entities still seems to be tacitly endorsed by most critics, leading to the condemnation of Pound, of *The Cantos,* and even of modernism as a whole. Organicism entails the presupposition that any diseased element in a work of art will inevitably infect the whole. Others take the contrary epidemiological view and argue that a fundamentally healthy organism can produce antibodies that will eliminate the infection. The favorite antibodies in Pound's case are aesthetic autonomy, relativism, skepticism, and humanism.

The fact that modernism, Marxism, fascism, and postmodernism all share a historicist analysis of culture and politics of a Hegelian and Nietzschean provenance is perhaps more to the point. The scandal over the Nazi sympathies of Paul de Man and Martin Heidegger, two postmodern avatars, illustrates the degree to which postmodernism itself shares a provenance with Nazism (see Culler; Sheehan; and Farias). In contrast to the covert Nazism of Heidegger and de Man, the Marxism of Foucault and Derrida has always been explicit and up front. Somewhat surprisingly, these Marxists, like Sartre before them, have adopted Heidegger's philosophy as their guide and beacon despite his association with Nazism (see Farias; and Ott).

Although Pound scholars no longer deny the fascist component of *The Cantos,* Pound scholarship still has not come to terms with this distressing feature of the poem. *The Cantos* is fascist in the straightforward sense that—from *Eleven New Cantos* (1934) to the last fragments—it celebrates the new era of Mussolini's fascism. But, more damagingly, it also embodies totalitarian political, economic, and cultural principles. The particular cultural principal I want to examine here is "historicism," the view that historical events follow either some discoverable principles or some discoverable pattern. Both Nazism and Marxism are historicist ideologies— Marxism taking the first view, and Nazism the second.

Since the term *historicism* has recently taken on a polemical role in literary criticism, some preliminary discussion of my understanding of it would be prudent. In the first place, it should be clear that a "historicist" account of the past is not equivalent to a "historical" one. Many current discussions treat the two terms as synonymous, but to do so is to seed confusion.

Historicism has a double provenance. Karl R. Popper applied it in *The Poverty of Historicism* (1957) to any belief that historical events or processes are governed by laws. His particular target was Marxist historiography, but he was also critical of the claim of the social sciences to scientific status. Long before Popper, the German hermeneutic thinkers Friedrich Schleiermacher and Wilhelm Dilthey employed it to mean what I call "epochalism," that is, the belief that cultures (and their expression in historical events) are comprehensible only from within. People sometimes call this "old historicism." A recent and, in my view, careless use of the term applies it to a belief that a phenomenon can be better understood with knowledge of its genesis, sometimes called the "genetic fallacy." But the belief that knowledge of the genesis of an idea, person, or institution can contribute to an understanding is just a belief in the pertinence of historical information and should not be called "historicism." Obviously this last view is one to which I subscribe.

Hayden White (in *Topics of Discourse: Essays in Cultural Criticism*) and Frank Lentricchia (in *After the New Criticism*) were among the first literary critics to adopt "metahistory" and historicism, respectively, as appropriate ways of conducting literary studies. Lentricchia's historicism derives from Foucault's reflexive model of historical explanation, which is designed to avoid all three of the traditional causal explanations: etiological, formal (or institutional, in the case of history), and teleological. Lentricchia denied the pertinence both of period borders and of the continuity they push against: "These are conceptions of a 'history,'" he writes, "which would generate itself as a unity and a totality while resisting forces of heterogeneity, contradiction, fragmentation, and difference: a 'history', in short, which would deny 'histories'" (xiv).

White's position is even more resolutely reflexive. He postulates the notion that all historical accounts derive from a "metahistory," or "master narrative," that dictates the details of the historical account or narrative and identifies "four principal modes of historical consciousness": metaphor, synecdoche, metonymy, and irony. He continues: "Each of these modes of consciousness provides the basis for a distinctive linguistic protocol by which to prefigure the historical field and on the basis of which specific strategies of historical interpretation can be employed for 'explaining' it. . . . In short it is my view that the dominant tropological mode and its attendant linguistic protocol comprise the irreducibly 'metahistorical' basis of every historical work" (xi). My use of the term *metahistory* is divergent from White's. For me a metahistorical account of the past is not just one that appeals to some one or two explanatory principles, but one that claims to universal validity for all human history. Thus my metahistorians would be people like Artur de Gobineau, Houston Chamberlain, Oswald Spengler, Paul de Lagarde, and Arnold Toynbee. White, by contrast, would class all efforts to present a coherent and rational account of the past as metahistorical.

New historicism and White's metahistory alike advance a relativistic and reflexive view of historical writing in which the past generates an indefinite number of stories or narratives, none of which with any authority or privilege over the others. Historiography based on either presupposition is more interested in demonstrating the hegemonic tendencies of traditional narratives, which seek to generate accounts of the past more authentic, accurate, and true than competing ones. This present study is an exercise in history of that old-fashioned nature.

I use *historicism* in Popper's sense—to designate the belief that historical events conform to laws or patterns—and *metahistoricism* in the more traditional sense (employed by George Mosse in his introduction to Houston Chamberlain's *Foundations of the Nineteenth Century*)—to designate historical accounts in which such laws or patterns are applied. Marxism and Nazism are both historicist in Popper's sense. *Mein Kampf*, for example, though primarily a memoir, is clearly metahistorical in inspiration. New historicist accounts, of course, are not metahistorical in my sense, for new historicism denies the possibility of any canonical historical account. New historical writing instead exposes the causal role of ideology in the production of either standard or metahistorical narratives.

Postmodernist interest in Pound's *Cantos* focuses on the work's cultural historicism and mythopoetic spirituality. New Critical interest, in contrast, had focused on its rhetorical intricacy and verbal felicity. All of these features of the poem—cultural history, mythopoeia, and style—reflect the ambience of the speculative occult briefly examined above. As we have seen, Pound was motivated to attempt an epic poem in the midst of the tangled, violent, and confused first half of the twentieth century by the occult belief that the world was on the verge of a new age. As it has turned out, *The Cantos* is rather more a *symptom* of that period than the transcendent analysis of it that Pound wished it—and that some of his admirers believe it—to be.

Pound described *The Cantos* as a "record of struggle" in *Guide to Kulchur*. If we were to judge the outcome of the struggle, we would have to declare Pound the loser by a unanimous decision and "the march of events" the winner. But having conceded the fascist and visionary character of *The Cantos*, it remains true that current discussions of the fascist tendencies of modernism too often fail to give the terms *fascism* and *modernism* any clearly delimited sense. Some observers equate fascism and Nazism with anti-Semitism, others with capitalism, and still others with totalitarianism.

While it is true that *The Cantos* is visionary and fascist, it does not follow that all anti-Semites, capitalists, and totalitarians are either Fascists or Nazis. The holistic mode of thought that deconstruction has made fashionable encourages investigators to conclude that one shared belief licenses an attribution of equivalence. Such carelessness permits the standard postmodern (and sub-Heideggerean) equation of empiricism, Christianity, liberalism, and Platonism with "logocentrism" or "onto-theology." It is true that all four "ideologies" share the belief that objects of knowledge do exist and that propositions about them can be true or false. But empiricists, Christians, and Platonists regard one another's dogmas as mutually incompatible, and liberals reject all three as dogmatic—which strongly suggests that these belief systems are not equivalent to one another.

So many years later, it is difficult to have a very clear sense of what fascism and Nazism looked like in the twenties and thirties. *Metapolitics: The Roots of the Nazi Mind*, a now much-neglected study by Peter Viereck, is very helpful in this regard.[3] Drawing on Alfred Rosenberg's proto-Nazi historicist fantasy, *Der Mythus des 20 Jahrhunderts*, Viereck traces the central ideas of Nazism to Wagner: the life force of the *Volk*, the Führer concept, and purification of the race soul (Viereck 252). He points out that Alfred Rosenberg and Dietrich Eckart introduced Hitler to Wagner's widow, Cosima, and to Wagner's English son-in-law, Houston Chamberlain, in Bayreuth in 1923. Chamberlain immediately hailed Hitler as Germany's savior (252, 148), and, like Rosenberg and Eckart, remained a good Nazi to the end.

The connections between the German Wagnerians and the Nazis are not just shared tastes and values, but are also historical and circumstantial—much like Pound's connections with Italian fascism. Rosenberg, Eckart, Lagarde, and Chamberlain were the principal "theorists" behind Nazi racist metahistory. Chamberlain explained the course of history through a Gobineau-like theory of Nordic or Aryan superiority in *Foundations of the Nineteenth Century* (German 1899, English 1910). Lagarde, in articles published in the 1880s, reinterpreted the Bible so as to reveal that "the Jews are the arch-fiends of history," and Christianity the "curse of the nordic super-race" (Viereck 169).

The Wagnerian mysticism and creative histories of oppression and skullduggery that Viereck identifies as the fountainhead of Nazism bear very close affinities to the occult and Masonic histories of underground oppressed cults and societies to which Pound was much attracted throughout his career (see Surette *Light, Birth;* and Casillo esp. 95–105). The intellectual ambience in which Pound's Kensington mentors—Yeats, G. R. S. Mead, and Orage—participated was just as Nietzschean and historicist as that in which Eckart, Rudolf Hess, Rosenberg, and Hitler moved and was contemporaneous with it (see Thatcher; Casillo; and Surette *Birth*).

Despite real and broad differences, the proto-Nazis, Nazis, modernists, and postmodernists all assume that historical events are the consequences of immanent or transcendent forces. The metahistoricists among them think historical events are caused by universal forces, whether racial

(Langbehn and Chamberlain), cyclical (Spengler and Yeats), or metaphysical (Hegel and Heidegger). The historicists among them think that
events are caused by ideas: Marx's ideologies, Viereck's "German ideas,"
Foucault's epistemes, or Derrida's *différance*. Thus Viereck believes that
Germanism caused Nazi brutalities; deconstructionists that logical argument or "logocentrism" caused capitalism, that "Eurocentrism" caused
imperialism, and that "phallocentrism" caused patriarchy.

Correlatively, the cure for these maladies is to administer better or "correct" ideas. Viereck prescribes "Mediterranean" ideas as the medicine that
will cure Nazism: liberty, Christian charity, and respect for law. Of these,
liberty is the only one that postmodernism would endorse. The bad ideas
that Viereck thinks caused Nazism are belief in the blood or the *Volk* and
the *Führer Prinzip*, that is, a belief in the Man of Destiny who is above both
law and morality (179). He explains that some of the proto-Nazis he discusses were saved from the error of Nazism by what he calls a "western conversion," that is, an adoption of the values of Mediterranean civilization:

> The western conversion of Langbehn, Nietzsche, Georg, Spengler, and
> the rest, if it is to be a really workable solution of the German problem,
> does not mean the repudiations of all Germanism. It means the union,
> mutually fruitful, of the best in Germanism, and in universal Christian-
> ity, the co-operative union of the two conflicting souls in one breast. The
> key to this solution is that these tension-torn Northmen found peace and
> truth and harmony at last only when their minds wandered southward
> to the Mediterranean-Latin-French civilization, which lured and charmed
> them. (184)

Viereck's contrast of bright, southern Mediterranean clarity with dark,
northern forest vagueness has obvious affinities with—and is perhaps in-
debted to—Eliot's similarly conservative cultural theories. In any case, it
is a culture-theory and a historicist account of events and therefore belongs to the same class of explanation as those offered by modernism and
postmodernism.

The metahistorical assumption that race, Spirit, or Providence determines historical events does not allow historical agents any choice. The
historicist's assignment of a causal role to ideas, however, does permit
historical agents to make choices, for ideas, unlike transcendent or immanent forces, can be adopted or rejected. Hence the historicist explains
historical events by the changing hegemony of philosophies, religions, or
even styles. More importantly she can hope to influence future events by
her own intervention.

Given this understanding of historicism, it is clear that Pound's *Cantos*
is a historicist epic, rather than a metahistorical one. It represents a pro-

grammatic effort to discover and articulate those good ideas that will bring about the New Era—which for Pound turned out to be the *Era Fascista*. *The Cantos* is not innocent of a "romantic" nostalgia for the past, but the poem is designed to *recover* only those fragments of the past suitable for use in an eagerly anticipated future. Pound's project is not, then, contrary to that of Nietzsche, Heidegger, or Derrida. All four reject the present and immediate past as corrupt, degenerate, or misguided and seek to replace (or supplement) it with a future characterized as the rebirth of a remote past. However, Pound's "naive" Enlightenment (or "Mediterranean") optimism about the future contrasts sharply with the pessimistic, and even eschatological, forward glance of the Germans and of Derrida.

In *The Birth of Tragedy* Nietzsche identified the fall from grace with the triumph of the Socratic pursuit of truth over the possession of wisdom and argued that the musical drama of Wagner would restore that grace in Germany:

> If . . . we have rightly associated the disappearance of the Dionysian spirit with a most striking . . . degeneration of the Hellenic man—what hopes must revive in us when the most certain auspices guarantee *the reverse process, the gradual awakening of the Dionysian spirit* in our modern world! . . . Out of the Dionysian root of the German spirit a power has arisen which, having nothing in common with the primitive conditions of Socratic culture, can neither be explained nor excused by it, but which is rather felt by this culture as something terribly inexplicable and overwhelmingly hostile—*German music* as we must understand it, particularly in its vast solar orbit from Bach to Beethoven, from Beethoven to Wagner. (*The Birth of Tragedy* sec. 19, p. 119)

Heidegger followed Nietzsche on this point and hoped for the return of the golden age in a Teutonic rapture.

He expressed this hope in his 1935 address to the undergraduates of Freiburg, telling them that "the destiny of the earth is being decided in Europe—while our own [Germans'] historic being-there proves to be the centre for Europe itself" (*Metaphysics* 42). Like Nietzsche, Heidegger discarded the present in favor of a mystical enfolding of the past into the future: "for us history is not synonymous with the past; for the past is precisely what is no longer happening. And much less is history the merely contemporary, which never happens but merely 'passes,' comes and goes by. History as happening is an acting and being acted upon which pass through the *present*, which are determined from out of the future, and which take over the past. It is precisely the present that vanishes in happening" (44). Though very different in argument, Heidegger's view of the flow of history is not unlike Mussolini's "*anti-storico*" posture in that both privilege an imagined and glorious future over the past *and* the present. For him the present is just a way station to the future, and as inessential as the past.

Derrida is more ambivalent (and more Nietzschean), denouncing all post-Socratic history up to himself. Like Heidegger, he denigrates the present as "a region (let us say, provisionally, a region of historicity) where the category of choice seems particularly trivial." Again, like Heidegger, he regards the future as the determinant of historical events, but for him, as for Yeats, it is monstrous. We are, he thinks, "faced by the as yet unnameable . . . in the offing . . . in the formless, mute, infant, and terrifying form of monstrosity" (*Writing* 292). All of these men (Nietzsche, Pound, Heidegger, and Derrida) were persuaded that they had been born at the end of an era. And they all return restlessly to the topos of the future. Nietzsche's titles attest to a similar obsession with the future—*Beyond Good and Evil* and *Twilight of the Idols*—as well as with beginnings—*The Birth of Tragedy, On the Genealogy of Morals* (even these backward-looking books in fact announce the advent of a new era).

Heidegger and Pound seem to have believed that the past could be recovered through the magical power of words, thereby redeeming history. To this extent they remained faithful to Enlightenment optimism, in contrast to Nietzsche, Derrida, and Yeats. It is somewhat ironic that Pound was almost alone amongst historicists and metahistorians in believing that the catastrophe could be avoided by the power of words. It was surely such a belief that motivated his economic evangelism, as well as his epic ambition. In contrast, most historicists of this century are more Joachite in their expectations. Marx, Lenin, Spengler, Yeats, Mussolini, and Hitler all adopted the cataclysmic view that Nietzsche had been among the earliest to articulate (in *Thus Spake Zarathustra*). Yeats followed Nietzsche in this respect in *A Vision,* and his apocalyptic poems, particularly "A Second Coming," "Prayer for My Daughter," and "Lapis Lazuli" (see Surette "Yeats").

Though *The Cantos* is historicist, it is not pessimistic and eschatological like Yeats's "Second Coming," Lawrence's *Women in Love,* and Eliot's *Waste Land.* Nor does it express a metahistorical view such as the racist theories of Rosenberg, Chamberlain, Gobineau, and the Nazi party, nor yet the cyclical theories of Spengler and Yeats. *The Cantos* is not based on the assumption that historical events are caused by some immanent or transcendent power, nor that they instantiate some overarching historical pattern. On the contrary it is grounded on the assumption that history is determined by individuals, and that individual behavior is rational. Hence the way to have some impact on the course of events is to persuade individuals of the truth and disabuse them of error and falsehood. It is not too much to say that *The Cantos* represents a Quixotic attempt to determine the future by promulgating the truth and denouncing falsehood and error. Alas, Pound put his "truth" and "good ideas" at the service of Mussolini and Hitler, who were committed to falsehood and error.

It may be that Pound was just mistaken about Mussolini and Hitler. That is, it may be that Pound's "truth" has nothing in common with the errors and falsehoods of fascism and Nazism and he was simply blind in thinking that they agreed with him. Unfortunately, as we have seen, it is not possible to seal off Pound's *paideuma* from fascism and Nazism, for he incorporated elements of those ideologies in it.

Since *The Cantos* did not prevent the catastrophe of World War II, as the work was designed to do, we are entitled (on historicist grounds) to conclude that the putatively good ideas in *The Cantos* were in truth bad ideas. Viewed from a Heideggerean angle, we can conclude that fascism and Nazism were not the wave of the future since they failed the test of history: the Fascist Era and the Third Reich were brief, as well as brutal and inglorious. Of course, if we abandon historicism, we are entitled to reject fascism and Nazism on rational grounds because they held a false conspiracy view of historical events and a false racial theory and on moral grounds because their adherents committed evil actions. Rational and moral grounds are the ones examined in this study.

Unhappily, Pound did not take such a view. He came to believe that the "good ideas" of Social Credit were blocked by a conspiracy of Jewish bankers who controlled world events. Such a conspiracy theory is not historicism, but paranoia. However, the paranoia is arguably the result of Pound's adherence to the historicist assumption that events are caused by ideas. If good ideas do not prevail, it must be because they are opposed by bad ideas.

Pound's adherence to the Crocean notion of "ideas in action" is certainly in conformity with fascism. It is found in Mussolini's encyclopedia article, "The Doctrine of Fascism": "Like all sound political conceptions, *Fascism is action and it is thought; action in which doctrine is immanent,* and doctrine arising from a given system of historical forces in which it is inserted, and working on them from within. It has therefore a form correlated to contingencies of time and space; but it has also an ideal content which makes it an expression of truth in the higher region of the history of thought" (7; my emphasis). It is doubtful that Mussolini cared more about this particular doctrine than he did about any other he expressed, but the notion that ideas are immanent in action is fundamental to Pound's worldview. It underpins his belief that one can judge an era from the thickness of the line in painting or from the rhythm of its verse. Art is just that form of action in which the idea is most perfectly instantiated in the action, since it is not encumbered by as many accidents or contingencies as other forms of action.

But Mussolini's "aestheticization" of politics as action was not his only attraction for Pound, whose historical optimism also put him in step with Mussolini and his futurist booster F. T. Marinetti and out of step with the eschatological pessimism of his friends Yeats, D. H. Lawrence, and Eliot. Despite some efforts to render it optimistic (for example, Longenbach "Matthew Arnold"), *The Waste Land* unmistakably reflects the bleak sense of an ending characteristic of Spengler and the metahistoricists. When Eliot turned from dissolution and degeneration to a more optimistic and Christian providential view of historical process, the poem's admiring audience much resented it.

Even the jovial James Joyce's work is imbued with metahistorical fatalism, if not pessimism. He facetiously models his universal history, *Finnegans Wake,* on Vico's metahistorical theories. The earlier and more accessible *Ulysses* copiously—albeit mockingly—reflects the cyclical metahistoricism that animated the work of Yeats and Spengler. And, of course, Yeats's *A Vision* is a hard-core metahistorical work drawing on Madame Blavatsky's *Secret Doctrine,* the *Birth of Tragedy,* and *Zarathustra* in roughly equal parts. (In the context of so many discoverers of historical pattern, it is difficult to avoid observing that *Women in Love, The Waste Land, A Draft of Thirty Cantos, Ulysses, A Vision,* Spengler's *Decline and Fall of the West,* and Heidegger's *Being and Time* all appeared within a ten-year span and—with the exception of Yeats—all of the authors were born within a decade of one another.)

So far as I am aware, the metahistoricism of Joyce's vision in all three of his major novels has been little remarked upon. *Finnegans Wake,* in particular, both mocks and instantiates the linguistic fantasies of diffusionist metahistorians such as Gobineau and a host of European racist philologists who imagined an Ur-people (Aryans) speaking an Ur-language (Indo-European). Joyce's polyglot language in the *Wake* can be thought of as a mocking reconstitution of such an Ur-language out of the kaleidoscopic fragments of modern human languages, just as H. C. E. is a mocking reconstitution of the Kabbala's Adam-Kadmon out of the polyglot European.

Pound, in contrast, seeks to *recover* or make new the Ur-language through the incorporation of Greek, Latin, Provençal, Chinese, and Egyptian among other expressions in *The Cantos.* He imagined that he had found the Ur-language preserved in the purity of the iconic images of the

Chinese ideogram. Pound thinks that any genuine poetry is really expressed in the Ur-language of images and only instrumentally in language. In such a view, no language is an adequate instrument of representation—a belief that underlies Pound's tremendous commitment to translation despite a mediocre linguistic aptitude. Heidegger shared this Romantic or Humboldtian view of language, believing that language was "the house of Being" (Heidegger, "Letter on Humanism," *Basic* 193).

Pound is probably the most "Mediterranean" (to use Viereck's term) of all the High Modernists in that he explicitly endorses all three of Viereck's Mediterranean principles: liberty, charity, and respect for law. If behavior is governed by ideology, in Viereck's analysis Pound ought to have been the most resistant to fascism, but it was his pessimistic or sardonic modernist friends who turned away.

Postmodern critiques draw just the opposite conclusion about Pound. Those critiques argue that because Pound is a Mediterranean poet of light, hard definition, and clear lines, he is just the sort of "logocentric" dogmatist who would be drawn to fascism and Nazism. And they certainly have empirical historical evidence on their side so far as Pound is concerned. Nonetheless, we ought not to forget that Chamberlain, Lagarde, Rosenberg, and Hitler were all strongly antipathetic to Viereck's Mediterranean culture—seeing it as the antagonist of Volkisch Teutonic culture—while Mussolini admired it.

Even though Hitler, Mussolini, Chamberlain, Lagarde, Rosenberg, Pound, and Heidegger all articulated or adopted Nazi and Fascist ideology, it is very difficult to demonstrate that they shared a common set of beliefs and goals. A strictly historicist analysis would have to place them in different political camps. At an absurd extreme, it would be coherent for a deconstructionist to argue that Hitler was not a Nazi, despite his position as leader of the party, if it could be demonstrated that he seldom or never expressed *echt* Nazi views.[4]

Modernism and postmodernism, despite their mutual antipathy, share a faith in historicist explanations founded on the organicist view that "cultures" are explicable in terms of their internal relationships without reference to material factors or forces (see Rorty, *Contingency* 11–16). They differ on the factors to which we should pay most attention, but agree that merely contingent historical accident cannot be an important part of any worthy explanation of a culture. The historicist view that a historical event is the product of ideas is usually attached to an organicist view of cultures as coherent and self-contained matrixes of ideas. A corollary of these two views is that cultures determine historical events.

There is, then, a strong continuity from Romantic cultural theory through modernism to postmodernism. All three movements assign to the arts the role of transmitting cultural values from generation to generation. The difference between Shelley's slogan, "artists are the unacknowledged legislators of the world," and Pound's, "artists are the antennae of the race," is only in the metaphors they choose. Richard Rorty's claim that literature is the model for original thinking of any sort and literary criticism for academic discourse is a continuation of Romantic, counter-Enlightenment polemics. His reliance on Harold Bloom and Paul de Man for his information about literary critical practice and history obscures the continuity of their literary posturing with that of Wordsworth, Shelley, Arnold, Eliot, and Frye (see Rorty, *Contingency* chap. 4).

A tacit corollary of this Romantic and modernist view of the function of art is the belief that artists must also be filters separating out kitsch, inaccuracies, and lies. In such a view of the nature of culture and of the function of art, artists cannot be permitted errors, blindness, or stupidities; they must be culture heroes—demigods—and cannot be permitted to fail. Hence, if a flawed artist cannot be made whole by the sapience of the healing critic, she must be expunged from the canon.

The Romantic/modern view of the artist just sketched is an aesthetic version of the Man of Destiny or *Führer Prinzip*, which Viereck thinks produced Hitler and Nazism. If ideas determine actions, one would expect all of the modernists to have been friendly to fascism and Nazism. It is no accident, then, that most have in fact been accused of fascist sympathies—with varying degrees of justification. Using a historicist reading, the only effective prophylactic against fascism would be an alternative ideology such as liberalism or communism.

But in point of fact, Ezra Pound is the only important English or American High Modernist who was incontestably a Fascist supporter. Moreover, none of the fascist regimes was friendly to modernist art—nor, for that matter, were the Bolsheviks. Such a state of affairs is puzzling only from within a historicist theory of human action. If we reject, as I do, the supposition that ideas alone determine actions, there is nothing anomalous in that individuals engage in cooperative action even though they disagree about many or even most philosophical or ideological matters. Certainly ideas may guide and even motivate actions, but it is quite another matter to maintain that they determine them.

The mainstream view within European thought has been that human acts are determined by rational considerations, but that articulated political, economic, and cultural ideas normally play a relatively small role in comparison to immediate pragmatic considerations. Indeed, when they appear to dominate an individual's behavior, we regard that condition as a pathology and label the individual obsessive. This century has seen that view challenged by historical determinist arguments of the sort surveyed as well as by psychoanalytic theories that human behavior is determined by unconscious emotional determinants. Historicist and psychoanalytic accounts of human behavior are mutually contradictory, but commonly appear side by side in postmodern arguments.

Herbert Marcuse, Jacques Lacan, and Jacques Derrida are the most influential blenders of Freudian psychoanalysis and cultural analysis. Freud himself engaged in cultural criticism in such works as *Totem and Taboo,* but maintained a distinction between rational and irrational motivations of human conduct. Derrida is the most interesting of the group in that he denies that distinction and argues that *intellectual* history is best understood in terms of irrational forces. In Derridean analysis ideas do not dominate a culture because of their truth, their utility, or even their institutionalization, but because of what Freud called their "cathexis," that is, an emotional energy that has somehow become attached to them. Foucault's quarrel with Derrida was precisely on this point. Foucault—more Marxist than Freudian—insisted on the primacy of cognitive institutionalization in cultural analysis over the more mysterious Freudian cathexis.

Derrida's argument against the logocentric privileging of presence amounts to asserting that presence was selected because of its universally high cathexis in ethnocentrism. He tells us that his purpose in *Of Grammatology* is "to focus attention on what I shall call *logocentrism;* the metaphysics of phonetic writing (for example the alphabet) which was fundamentally—for enigmatic yet essential reasons that are inaccessible to a simple historical relativism—nothing but the most original and powerful ethnocentrism, in the process of imposing itself upon the world" (3).

But despite Derrida's brilliance, it remains a little awkward to argue that cognitive history is a history of irrational cathexis and at the same time maintain that ideas cause actions. It may be that this incoherence is passed over because of the degree of cathexis that Marxist and Freudian analyses of culture have achieved amongst "enlightened" academics. Although commonly presented in tandem, Marxist and Freudian cultural accounts are not mutually supporting. They are united only by a common antagonist—"positivism" or, less contentiously, rational empiricism. By *rational empiricism* I mean the view that judges ideas as more or less accurate descriptions of the nature of things and that holds that ideas gain acceptance or rejection on the Darwinian grounds that false ideas fall by the wayside and true ones prosper.

At least since the Romantic period, literary and aesthetic theorists have regarded rational empiricism (or "science") as their antagonist and have (unjustly) attributed all the evils of commerce, industry, and war to it. Postmodern critiques of modernism have continued this habit, but do so within literary culture. Postmodernism tends to align aesthetic modernism with the cold war and the military-industrial complex, in spite of the anachronism of the charge (though the chronology fits the rise of New Criticism, which canonized modernist texts). Moreover it flies in the face of the fact that most modernists turned pacifist after the battle of the Somme (24 June–26 November 1916), in which the Allies suffered 617,000 casualties, and the Germans 500,000, all for an advance of a few hundred meters.

Pound and modernism can be saved from themselves only outside the horizon of historicism. If modernism began with the first Imagist anthology of 1912, then it may be thought to have ended when postmodernism was inaugurated in 1960 with John Barth's *Sot-Weed Factor.* It was not so much an ideology as the label for the common cause of a generation of men and women trying to think through the cataclysmic philosophical, scientific, political, military, and social changes through which they lived in those five decades. They tried to think it through in terms of historicist theories founded on an understanding of cultures as coherent entities.

That they shared such understanding with fascism and Nazism tells us little more than that those were the dominant cultural paradigms of the period. Such shared views could not predict and do not explain the loyalties or disloyalties of individual modernists. And it is even less likely that the logocentrism of individual modernists will account for their political and ideological alignments. The expectation that such categorizations might have explanatory power should be understood as a continuation of those historicist tendencies that have a much longer history than the modernist movement in literature.

It is my belief that the only route to an understanding of the present is through the past, for that is all we know. The postmodern belief that past, present, and future can be equally well understood through the instrument of "theory" (a priori principles and analytical procedures) is presented as a rejection of the Romantic hermeneutic tradition to which modernism belongs. But, as we have seen, it can just as legitimately be seen as the fulfillment of Romantic hermeneutic principles. The old historicist view—adhered to by Mussolini and Pound, among others—was that ideas are embodied in actions. The new, postmodern view is more radical. It denies any possibility of discriminating between the abstract (ideas) and the concrete (actions), but nonetheless assigns priority to the abstract, as in Derrida's oft-cited phrase "*there is no outside-of-the-text*" (*Of Grammatology* 158).

Derrida's phrase suggests that the world is the output of sentences, contradicting empiricism's view that sentences are representations of the world. If the world is the product of sentences, then, *a fortiori*, the world is determined by sentences. Though sentences are not equivalent to ideas, once stripped of any capacity of referring to the world they can only be repositories of ideas. The world is thus reduced to a mere chimera or phantasmagoria as in Platonic idealism. I confess to being a reprobate believer in the reality of the world—that is, a transcendental signified—and will now return to the effort to discover the degree to which Pound's *paideuma* can be disentangled from Mussolini's and Hitler's.

Notes

1. Viereck reflects this link in *Metapolitics*. It is probably traceable to Max Nordau's *Degeneration*, a scurrilous attack on Wagner, Nietzsche, Symbolisme, and aestheticism. First published in 1893, it was translated into English in 1895 and went through seven impressions in that year. It was reprinted in 1898 and 1913. Of course, Nordau knew nothing of fascism or Nazism. For a discussion of Nordau's influence see Thatcher 27–28 and Surette *Birth*.

2. John Lauber's 1978 article, "Pound's *Cantos:* A Fascist Epic," was the first attempt to make a judicious assessment of the degree to which fascism is embedded in *The Cantos*. Although the essay is not at all a hostile assault, and without the very damning evidence of the then still-suppressed cantos 72 and 73, Lauber felt compelled to conclude: "The longest and the most diverse of modern poems, the *Cantos* are not to be encapsulated in any formula or subsumed in any single category. One thing, however, both true and important, which can be said about them is they constitute a fascist epic" (21).

Two years after Lauber's essay Massimo Bacigalupo devoted an entire book (*The Formèd Trace*) to the exposure of Pound's fascism and concluded that *The Cantos* is fascist: "In many ways the *Cantos* belong in those shops that sell swastikas and recordings of Mussolini's speeches, for they are, among other things, the sacred poem of the Nazi-Fascist millennium, which mercifully never eventuated" (x). Bacigalupo also implies that *The Cantos*—and modernism generally—is credulous and absolutist as opposed to skeptical and relativistic: "Primitivism and decadence are in fact the headings under which his [Pound's] work is situated, like contemporary art in general, though Pound's is an extreme and strangely fascinating case" (27, 31–32). Although Bacigalupo makes no effort to substantiate or even illustrate this observation, my study *The Birth of Modernism* tends to corroborate it in a general way.

In my study of *The Cantos*—published in 1979, between Lauber's essay and Bacigalupo's book—I admitted Pound's fascism, but largely ignored the fascist elements in *The Cantos*. And even though my interpretation of the poem rested in good part on an analysis of its occult and secret history components, I remained loyal to New Critical tenets of aesthetic autonomy and took the occult materials to be a "metaphorical structure"—an interpretive schema designed to "structure" otherwise heteroclite material (25–26). My initial response to Lauber and Bacigalupo was to reject their accusations as hostile and unmeasured, and in this I think I was typical of those scholars at all sympathetic to Pound.

Another assessment of *The Cantos* of the late 1970s is found in Michael Bernstein's *The Tale of the Tribe* (1980). Bernstein adopts a structuralist posture that isolates the work from the world just as effectively as the doctrine of aesthetic autonomy, which he explicitly rejects as tantamount to the "aestheticization of *The Cantos.*" He (accurately) describes this approach as "one of the most characteristic critical strategies employed by Pound's admirers" (32). But he himself evades "the thematic content of the poem's historical argument" to focus "upon the narrative principles according to which the historical data is presented" (35).

Scholarly consensus is very differently constituted today than it was at the end of the seventies, when New Critical or structuralist "decontextual" dogmas of aesthetic autonomy still prevailed, and news of Nietzsche's resurrection had not yet reached the wide community of literary scholars. In 1980 Bacigalupo felt safe in dismissing Pound's celebration of Dionysus with the remark (which clearly echoes Nordau's *Degeneration*), "This program has little novelty (one need only think of Nietzsche and of his scarcely profound decadent followers)" (35). By contrast, in 1987 Kathryne V. Lindberg expects a sympathetic audience for her rehabilitative study of Pound, *Reading Pound Reading Nietzsche,* in which she discovers a cloud of what she regards as hitherto unsuspected affinities between Pound and Nietzsche.

Robert Casillo's 1988 study, *The Genealogy of Demons,* is the most detailed and damning of all of the studies of fascism and anti-Semitism in *The Cantos.* He provides an excellent survey of scholarly handling of the issue of anti-Semitism and concludes that "anti-Semitism is a characteristic manifestation of Pound's thought and language" (16). For Casillo Pound's cultural, political, and economic views are consequences rather than causes of, or contributing factors to, his anti-Semitism. He denies that *The Cantos* "can be understood in isolation from his anti-Semitism" (17).

Here I corroborate Casillo's view that *The Cantos* is deeply infected with anti-Semitism, but reverse the relation of anti-Semitism to his other views by showing that Pound long ignored, and even explicitly rejected, anti-Semitic and conspiracy theories overtures from his correspondents. Alas, he eventually succumbed to a paranoid belief in a Jewish conspiracy to control the world, but there was nothing inevitable or necessary about that tumble into absurdity and evil. I do not present this finding as exculpatory for Pound or for his epic, but it does place Pound's errors in the context of the historical nexus in which they were formed— when many more worldly souls also went astray.

"I Cease Not to Yowl": Ezra Pound's Letters to Olivia Rossetti Agresti, edited by Demetres Tryphonopoulos and myself, is the most recent and the most unequivocal revelation of Pound's political loyalties. Most of the letters date from the period of Pound's incarceration at St Elizabeths and demonstrate beyond any doubt that Pound was unrepentant about his Fascist sympathies. In the light of this correspondence it is no longer possible to maintain the fiction that either his fascism or his anti-Semitism was an aberration belonging to a brief period.

3. Viereck (classed as a New York intellectual) wrote *Metapolitics* as a Harvard Ph.D. thesis during the rise of Nazism, and it reflects the passions of the period. Interestingly, Pound knew of Viereck and was extremely ill-disposed toward him. Pound wrote to his son-in-law, Boris Barrati: "Just read that Peter Vierick [*sic*] is going to lecture at Univ. of Florence/ warn Pellizzi and EVERYbody that he is one of the vilest bits of meRRda produced in Baruchistan. And treated his own father like a dog. Total nastiness and shd/ be ostracised" (18 Aug. 1954, Pound Letters). Viereck's father was a Nazi and anti-Semite, but the young Viereck's *Metapolitics* is very hostile to fascism and Nazism. "Baruchistan" is one of Pound's mocking epithets for the United States. He regarded Bernard Baruch as the *eminence grise* behind the Roosevelt and Truman administrations.

4. Some of the published defenses of Paul de Man and Martin Heidegger come very close to such an argument. See Culler; and Richard Rorty's review of Farias's *Heidegger and Nazism*, "Taking Philosophy Seriously."

CHAPTER 8

Silvio Gesell and Irving Fisher

Pound refused to give up Social Credit after he had adopted Mussolini, even though both Orage and Douglas insisted that they had little if anything in common. In Pound's public pronouncements on the relation of fascism and economic reform, he does not claim any theoretical agreement, but only that fascism is achieving appropriate results by its own means. For example, he declared in 1934 in *New Democracy:* "Italy is, as a matter of fact, acting with greater economic enlightenment than any other country in the world, and that means she is economically nearer Gesell and Douglas than are any of the other nations. Her dividends are being distributed as better wheat, and better drainage and cheaper railway transport" (*Ezra Pound's Poetry and Prose* 6:147). Pound is well aware that Mussolini's public works—"better wheat, and better drainage and cheaper railway transport"—do not conform at all to Social Credit policy, though he may have believed that they would alleviate the problem of structural underconsumption. His adoption of Gesell's stamp scrip was another deviation from Douglas that exacerbated his problems with his Social Credit collaborators, as well as threatening to put his economic policy prescriptions entirely at cross purposes.

Gesell was a German businessman who made his fortune in Argentina. He retired to Switzerland about 1900, but was forced to return to Argentina in 1907 because his brother, who had been running their business, had died. During the April 1919 Sparticist uprising when the Bavarian government was taken over by a socialist group, Gesell (by then back in

Germany) was made state minister of finance. Though he immediately ordered the printing of stamp scrip, nothing came of it, for the revolutionary government was overthrown after only a few days in office. Gesell was arraigned on a charge of treason. He successfully managed his own defense and was acquitted (Fisher, *Stamp Scrip* 142–43). Though Pound must have read of this incident in Fisher's *Stamp Scrip*—and later in Gesell's *Natural Economic Order*—he never mentions it, not even after his own arrest and arraignment for treason.

Pound first learned of Gesell through the use of stamp scrip money in the Austrian industrial town of Wörgl in 1932. It had been used earlier (in 1930–31) in the small mining community of Schwanenkirchen, Germany, by a man named Hebecker, who managed to keep his mine open with stamp scrip despite the tremendous German inflation of those years. Both experiments were successful, but both were stopped by the authorities (Fisher, *Stamp Scrip* 144–45).

The earliest mention by Pound of the Wörgl experiment that I have found is in "Points," a 1933 review of Roosevelt's *Looking Forward:* "If the gt. wht. farver ["great white father," that is, Roosevelt] can't understand C. H. Douglas, he is referred to the highly successful demonstration of the virtues of negative interest performed by Herr Unterguggenberger in the town of Wörgl and his attention is respectfully called to the sadistic action of the Bank of Austria, the minute they heard the simple villagers were no longer in distress" (*Ezra Pound's Poetry and Prose* 6:62). And he mentions Wörgl again in a 23 August 1933 letter to the Paris edition of the *New York Herald:* "I don't know about Wörgl being the new Mecca. Irving Fisher has treated analogous ideas in a volume which I have not yet received. Both the Wörgl and the C. H. Douglas propositions recognize fundamental fact, the non-static nature of the public's deficiency of purchasing power" (*Ezra Pound's Poetry and Prose* 6:63). Wörgl appears again in a letter of 30 August to the same paper, and he reviewed Fisher's *Stamp Scrip* in Orage's *New English Weekly* in October (*Ezra Pound's Poetry and Prose* 6:86–87).

The review reflects his Douglasite orthodoxy. He lists seven points of weakness in the Gesell scheme:

1. Lacks a national dividend
2. Stamp scrip is only palliative, does not address A + B
3. Lacks any ethical principle
4. Ignores the social dividend, i.e. public ownership of technological and cultural improvements
5. "A community accustomed to no dividends, would probably not refuse to accept them in schwundgeld" (i.e., stamp scrip)

6. Does not propose the abolition of taxes, as Douglas does
7. If the British dole had been paid in stamp scrip, two-thirds of their problems would be solved.

This negative reaction is in contrast to his endorsement of stamp scrip in his prescriptions for economic recovery in "Points" published in August. Indeed, almost from his first learning of it, stamp scrip became a permanent part of his economic tool kit, despite Douglas's and Orage's hostility to it (cf. Redman 100, 128).

When Pound began pushing Gesell on Orage and Douglas, he met stiff resistance. Unfortunately, only a few of Pound's letters to Orage have survived. The first mention of Gesell in the surviving correspondence is a reference in a postcard from Orage: "To Hell with Woergl" (12 June 1933, Pound Papers). Despite this hostility, Orage did publish a much shortened version of Pound's review of Fisher's *Stamp Scrip* in his magazine. There is no further discussion between them of Gesell for nearly a year, when Orage once again dumps on Gesell: "I don't share your enthusiasm for Stamp Scrip; it's an experiment for les autres to advocate & make; & it's not policy to be identified with it. I'm very dubious, too, of the *economic* value of your great M[ussolini]! However, having just seen Odon Por, I'll hold my horses" (14 May 1934, Pound Papers). Apparently Por was not persuasive, for Orage returns to Gesell in a letter of 6 June 1934:

> Damn it all, E. P., *if* you could get S[tamp] S[crip] accepted, you could get S[ocial] C[redit] accepted. S.S. is just as hard to get swallowed,—& why choke on a fragment. I'm hoarse with repeating that the private Monopoly of credit accounts for everything; & until *that* is realized, S. S. or Sterling, or any other damned thing, is just mice playing with the cat unbelled. The *only* question, strategically, is how to convince, persuade, or kick people into *realizing* the *fact;* & since, up to date, the most effective means seems to be Douglas, I run Douglas & Douglas, & Douglas. If anybody thinks he can get more & better attention by talking S. S. or (London Chamber of Commerce) Stabilisation of Foreign Exchange, more power to him—since every one presupposes the same ultimate thing—the resumption of community control over credit. (Pound Papers)

Pound continued to push Gesell on Orage, eliciting another exasperated response: "It just won't do. We've got enough to contend with without hanging Gesell round our necks. If you can't see the difference between an ingenious piece of finesse &, say, National Dividends—well, you're no politician! Gesell bucks the Money Monopoly just the same as we; but for a paltry object. I don't say we *can* bell the cat; but at least if we do, we want a good time for all mice. Douglas is concentrating attention,

& I'm all against dividing it. This is *final,* E. P. I won't Gesell with you" (3 Oct. 1934, Pound Papers).

Pound's experience with Douglas was much the same. He had written in July: "The real trouble about the Woergl scheme is what has happened to the Woergl scheme, which is another way of saying that the problem of reforming the financial system is not how to reform the financial system, but how to strangle the bankers. Any sermons on this text will be appreciated!" (4 July 1933, Pound Papers). Douglas was not to be moved from his single-minded focus on the iniquity of the banks and their alleged conspiracy to suppress economic truth. Pound had not yet succumbed to Douglas's paranoia, still believing in 1933 that a technical solution for the world's economic ills was at hand and only needed to be advertised. Orage was more worldly wise than either, believing that the solution could be applied only through political power—though he too believed that the Wörgl scheme was suppressed because it threatened the interests of the banks, rather than because it was unwise or unworkable.

Pound is not put off by Douglas's frosty put down and returns to the fray, pointing out that Social Credit was not distinguished by political success:

> The damn trouble IZ that ought [*sic*] gang (New Age) 1919 hadn't tuppence worf of POLITICAL ability in the lot. Having a better article to putt forrard we are still a pale inefficient group of foetid intellexshuls, the perfect cartridge and no canon to fire it.
>
> Gesell and Untreguggie have got as far in 2 years as we have in 15[. . . .] That aint vurry flatterin to Orage and the undersigned [. . .] but shucks [. . .] I come in from the EEEEstheetic side of the pyper. (13 Oct. 1933, Pound Papers)

Pound continues to badger Douglas on Gesell and even picks up the pace after Aberhart formed a Social Credit government in Alberta. But Douglas cannot be moved.

Pound had to rely on Fisher's *Stamp Scrip* for his knowledge of Gesell's economic ideas until he got a copy of Gesell's *Natural Economic Order* early in 1935. He would have learned there of many efforts to put stamp scrip money into practice in the United States, though Wörgl is the only one he ever mentions. However, Fisher's study shows that Pound's enthusiasm for stamp scrip was not particularly eccentric. He remarks in the introduction that "the recent spread of the stamp scrip idea throughout this country" was his principal motivation for writing the book and added: "I have recently answered four or five hundred inquiries about it. The letters come from literally every state in the union, and are written by persons, largely in official positions, who have a practical interest in introducing Stamp Scrip in their several towns, cities and states" (1). (One of those letters was from Pound.)

Stamp Scrip is almost a manual for those who wanted to put stamp scrip into practice. Fisher's underlying motivation is very much in line with that of Social Credit—to effect an expansion of purchasing power: "to unleash a force on which the ultimate cure of the depression really depends. I refer to the credit currency of the land which is now so tragically bottled up and has hitherto baffled the most heroic efforts at rescue. It has simply refused to be rescued—refused with an apparently insane perversity" (2). Intended for a general audience, the book begins with accounts of such homely remedies as barter—recommended in some Hollywood films and apparently being applied in real life (3–5). Though Fisher was an economist of high reputation, he was not reluctant to stoop to popular communication. Mark Blaug calls him "one of the greatest and certainly one of the most colourful American economists who ever lived" (ix–x).

Herr Unterguggenberger, the mayor of Wörgl, an industrial town of about forty-three hundred inhabitants, was inspired by the earlier Schwanenkirchen experiment. He introduced stamp scrip in the autumn of 1931 and managed to keep it going until early 1933. It was still in place as Fisher wrote. The scheme worked in the following way. The town issued its own scrip to its citizens at par (through municipal wages and other town disbursements). The holder was required to affix a stamp worth 1 percent of the bill every month. In this way a one shilling bill would cost the holder 12 pfennig per year, a negative interest rate of 12 percent. The town would redeem the scrip at any time at a charge of 2 percent on the remaining value. It used the proceeds to fund necessary town works. All city employees, including the mayor, received half their salaries in scrip. Thirty-two thousand shillings were printed, but that amount proved more than necessary, and only about one-third of it was kept in circulation. The experiment was a complete success (Fisher, *Stamp Scrip* 22–29).

The mayor had printed on the back of the scrip (the stamps were affixed to the front) the following manifesto:

> Slowly circulating money has thrown the world into an unheard-of-crisis, and millions of working people are in terrible need. From the economic viewpoint, the decline of the world has begun with horrible consequences for all. Only a clear recognition of these facts, and decisive action can stop the breakdown of the economic machine, and save mankind from another war, confusion and dissolution.
>
> Men live from the exchange of what they can do. Through slow money circulation this exchange has been crippled to a large extent, and thus

millions of men who are willing to work have lost their right to live in our economic system. The exchange of what we can do must, therefore, be again improved and the right to live be regained for all those who have already been cast out. This purpose, the "Certified Compensation Bills of Wörgl, shall serve.

They alleviate want, give work and bread. (25n)

The manifesto emphasizes a fundamental Gesellite point—that a smaller quantity of currency circulating rapidly will do the same work as a larger quantity circulating more slowly. The rate at which currency changes hands is called the "velocity" of money, and is now universally recognized as a factor determining the level of economic activity for a given quantity of currency. But in 1933, Gesell's idea was still novel and suspect. Indeed, any idea that cast doubt on the popular belief that money possessed a real and stable intrinsic value was regarded as dangerous and ridiculed as "funny money." Few were willing to admit how "funny" in truth money is.

The Wörgl experiment was eventually terminated by an act of the Austrian government, but the damage had been done; the idea spread around the world. The first American to introduce stamp scrip was Charles Zylstra of Hawarden, Iowa (population 3,000). The town issued $300.00 in stamp scrip of $1.00 denominations in October 1932. The stamps were sold at $.03 each and could be bought with scrip. Each transfer required a stamp, but no dates were applied. Once a bill had thirty-six stamps affixed, it could be redeemed for a fresh one. The scheme was still functioning as Fisher wrote. He pointed out that the lack of dates for affixing stamps was an error and that participants in a transaction could collude to omit the stamp (30–31).

In Evanston, Illinois, a merchants' association introduced scrip called an "Eirma" (Evanston Independent Retail Merchants Association). It issued $5,000.00 worth and sold it to members. The motive was to keep shoppers in Evanston and out of the big Chicago stores. Fifty stamps at $0.02 redeemed an Eirma on the Hawarden model. Neither the town administrators nor the banks participated, though the merchants had the town's blessing. The objective of the Evanston merchants was undermined because the Chicago stores accepted Eirmas without a stamp, if their patrons would take it back in change without a stamp. Nonetheless, the scrip stimulated economic exchange. It was still ongoing when Fisher wrote (31–33).

Fisher describes many similar schemes, mostly in the Midwest: Rock Rapids and Albia, Nevada; Pella and Ildora, Iowa; Granite Falls and Jasper, Minnesota; Mangum and Enid, Oklahoma; Russell, Kansas; Lexington, Ne-

braska; Mangum, Oklahoma; Knoxville, Tennessee; and Merced and Ana-
heim, California (33–38). He closes with three variants, the most curious
of which is "speed money," which involved the use of ordinary currency.
Dr. Nordwall of Norden, Germany, placed an advertisement that he would
give the first man to come to his office 10 Reichsmarks on condition that
the money be used to pay a debt. A messenger boy spent the day setting
the same condition for each creditor. He got a receipt for the last one of
the day and was to begin again with him the next day. Fisher says that as
much as 120 Reichsmarks of debt might be canceled in that way, that is,
twelve transactions. The scheme was operating as he wrote (41–42).

Fisher also printed the "Bankhead-Pettengill Bill" in *Stamp Scrip*. Introduced in Congress by Senator John H. Bankhead of Alabama on 17 February 1933, it called for the issue of $1 billion of stamp scrip in $1.00
denominations with space on the backs for fifty-two stamps—one for each
week—costing $.02 each. Over the course of a year a $1.00 bill would
require $1.04 in stamps—a very steep rate of negative interest. It would
be legal tender. In his review Pound remarks that the issue was much too
large, and that $100 million would have been sufficient, but Fisher, who
had a hand in designing the bill, did not think it too large. Of course, the
bill never passed (79–83). The fact that it was introduced at all is an index of the willingness of people at the time to consider radical remedies.
Pound continued to allude to the Bankhead bill for several years, but always rather negatively, as a stop-gap measure inferior to Douglas's national
dividend.

Perhaps because of his loyalty to Douglas, Pound dismissed both Fisher
and Bankhead in a letter to W. E. Woodward in which he mentions Orage's
lack of interest in Gesell:[1]

> Pore ole Fisher is all over the shop/ his last 78 variants are hooey.
> BUT in the first 40 pages of Stamp Scrip book, he is *merely* REPORTING
> FACTS/ the facts re/ an experiment SUCCESSFUL, my god HOW / of
> a trial of Gesell's ideas.—Not any Fisher thought of.—Dare say Fish didn't
> know what he was writing/ and ole Bankhead can't have understood his
> own bill/ evidently/ anyhow he asked for a Billion (a flood) where a
> hundred million or possibly 30 million/ wd have sufficed.
>
> If I had known more of Fisher's I might have been intelligent enough
> to keep his name out of my note on S/Scrip/ BUT damn it all Orage first
> said 'To Hell with Wörgl' when I wrote him about it/ only way I cd/ plant
> the article was to REVIEW the only book in English that treats it. (28 Sept.
> 1933, Pound Papers)

In view of Blaug's estimate of Fisher as "one of the greatest . . . American
economists who ever lived," Pound's hubris is breathtaking.

The purpose of stamp scrip was to discourage hoarding and encourage spending. In Gesell's scheme it would coexist with money of account such as bank deposits, which would not attract negative interest in the form of the stamps. In fact the banks would pay interest on such money in the normal way. Bank deposits, of course, do not represent hoarding but rather an expansion of aggregate purchasing power since the deposits form the basis of bank credit. Currency or gold hoarded in mattresses or vaults, by contrast, represents a net loss to the aggregate purchasing power of the nation. Stamp scrip is designed to discourage hoarding, not saving.

The economic effect of stamp scrip can be compared to the inflation of the seventies and eighties in the North Atlantic community, which inflicted a similar negative interest rate (though less that 12 percent in most years) on all money, both currency and money of account. That inflation certainly had a stimulative effect, but it also caused a rise in prices and in interest rates, eventually discouraging investment. No such destabilization should occur with stamp scrip. With inflation, creditors and prudent savers both suffer, while debtors and free spenders benefit. With stamp scrip the free spender is encouraged, but neither the saver nor the lender is penalized because only cash attracts the negative interest represented by the stamp. (Presumably the poor, who typically do not have bank accounts, would neither suffer nor benefit directly since they must spend their currency as fast as they get it.)

Fisher is characterized by William R. Allen as "the first of the modern 'monetarists,'" by which he means that "his fundamental premise and basis for all other analysis and policy prescription was this: money matters and matters most." Fisher's view, as Allen puts it, was that "the depression has been, and the recovery will be (and, in due course, was) a monetary phenomenon." Fisher—almost alone among economists of the day—maintained that the depression was caused by a decline in the money stock, most particularly of money of account or "check-book money." The cure was to reflate, that is, to increase the stock of money (Allen 563–64).

Fisher did not discard quantity theory, but maintained that it did not hold in all circumstances: "He was quite clear that the feedback from prices to other elements in the equation of exchange, highlighted in his discussion of 'transition periods,' violated the quantity theory, and he was equally clear that the cycle was a regular real world phenomenon. That is why, in expounding and defending the quantity theory, Fisher was usually careful to note that it did not strictly hold during such episodes" (Laidler 78). The Great Depression was just such an episode. Prior to Keynes's *General Theory* Fisher was the only academic economist to recognize that an increase in purchasing power was the appropriate remedy to the depression.

However, Keynes's analysis and prescriptions were quite different from Fisher's and carried the day when published.

Based on what can now be seen as a clumsy application of quantity theory, the Hoover administration attempted to restore prices by curtailing production. Such a policy was "deflationary." Fisher argued that it would only exacerbate the problem—at least in the short-term. He recommended that the price level be restored by "reflation," a term he coined for a deliberate increase in the money supply. He understood that "deflation reduces employment and reflation restores it" (Allen 564). "Reflation" is not just verbally distinct from "inflation." The latter refers to a fall in the value of money, while the former refers to an increase in the supply of money calculated so as to preserve a stable value. Quantity or equilibrium theory denied that it was possible to increase the quantity of money without diluting its value—that is, without raising prices—which was generally thought to be undesirable. However, since everyone agreed that the fall of prices after 1929 was a problem, it is difficult to understand why it was not given a try.[2]

As we have seen, Douglas agreed with mainstream views on this point. He was adamantly opposed to Fisher's solutions, believing that reflation would necessarily produce inflation: "a policy of inflation . . . a policy of increasing issues of money or credit, in such a manner that it can only reach the general public through the medium of costs, and must, therefore be reflected in prices . . . is absolutely and mathematically certain to reduce any financial and economic system to ruins" (*Social Credit* 118). As a stable money man, Fisher would have endorsed Douglas's stress on stable prices. However, his understanding of economics was far more sophisticated than Douglas's or Pound's—neither of them seemed to understand that the national dividend must represent an expansion of the money supply if it were to have the desired effect of increasing aggregate purchasing power.

Fisher's policy advice was in line with the practice followed today on Keynesian grounds, though he used different mechanisms. Since Keynes, central banks expand the money supply by selling treasury bills to commercial banks, thereby increasing bank deposits and hence available credit. Another mechanism is the interest rate, which, if lowered, will bring about an increase in the money supply indirectly, since more borrowers are willing to contract debts at a lower rate. (The journalist's phrase *printing money* is an anachronism, since bills and coins represent a very small proportion of "money" in circulation at any given time. The vast proportion is "money of account," bank deposits, credit card balances, and commercial paper.) But unrevised quantity theory or Say's law still held sway in the early thirties, and no such policies were considered.[3]

Unlike Douglas, Fisher believed that the deflation the North Atlantic community was experiencing in the 1930s was so damaging as to make the risk of inflation worth running. Today he would have the concurrence of all economists on this point. His aim was stable money—neither inflation nor deflation. Bankers and other creditors are not so committed to stable money since deflation enhances the value of the financial instruments they hold, and therefore increases their profits. However, they abhor inflation since it has the opposite effect on financial institutions, eroding the value of their assets—debts.

Fisher, of course, understood that to achieve stable money, aggregate purchasing power must be held in balance with aggregate economic activity, but unlike his economic colleagues, he believed that the balance was dynamic. Hence, in a period of sharp deflation, such as the 1930s, an increase in purchasing power beyond current levels of economic activity would be stimulative. Unfortunately Fisher did not have a theoretical model to explain why this would be so. Keynes provided that model with the principle of "liquidity preference."

Fisher takes brief notice of Social Credit in *Stable Money: A History of the Movement,* noting that "although not directly devoted to the cause of monetary stabilization, the 'Social Credit' movement deserves mention here, because the evils of an unstable money were discussed in many of its publications" (125). But he did not accept the Social Credit contention that the shortfall in purchasing power was a structural defect of capitalist economies or that the banks had illegitimately co-opted the power to extend credit. Instead of seeing bankers as calculating villains, Fisher regarded them as victims of a narrow perspective:

Bankers have always been looked upon as opponents of a stable dollar. By the very selection which makes them bankers, they are conservative. They think in terms of money and find little occasion in their daily business to measure money in terms of commodities. They naturally rebel against being asked to run their business so as to stabilize the price level, instead of so as to make money; and they rebel still more strongly against being directed by law to accomplish such a task, which most of them sincerely believe is beyond their powers. But their opposition is much less now [in 1934] than it was when the stable money movement began. (115)

Fisher's overriding concern was with "the problem of stabilizing the purchasing power of money." He founded the Stable Money Association in 1925 and devoted much of his not inconsiderable energy to the promotion of that goal, pursuing an interest that began "almost as soon as my economic studies began—about 1892. That was at the end of a quarter of a century of deflation which was about to culminate in the 'sound money' campaign of 1896." At that early date Fisher thought he "had discovered that these evils [of unstable money] were largely overcome in business by compensatory adjustments in the rate of interest," and hence he opposed William Jennings Bryan and his silver solution. Although in 1934 he would not have been so opposed, he still thought Bryan's "proposed remedy [of] 'national bimetallism,' at 16 [silver] to 1 [gold], . . . far from good" (374–75).

On his own initiative Fisher began publishing a weekly Index Number of Wholesale Prices in the *New York Times* in January 1923. It was the first weekly index ever published (384), and was a great success. By 1934 it was being published all over the world, including in official government publications. It is the progenitor of contemporary consumer price indexes. He hoped it would dispel the "money illusion":

> The index of the dollar's purchasing power gave to several million people every Monday morning the opportunity to read of the weekly change in the dollar. It was apparently as a result of this that the phrases "the purchasing power of the dollar," "the pre-war dollar," "the dollar of 1913," "the dollar of 1926," and other expressions, implying a consciousness that the dollar changes, came into general use; whereas previously all indexes were thought of as representing price movements of commodities— money being forgotten. (385)

Fisher's index enabled people to see for the first time that the fluctuation in prices was primarily a monetary phenomenon. The prevailing view, even among the economically literate, had been that price fluctuations were the result of actual scarcities or superabundances of goods, services, or labor. Such a view was not wildly inaccurate in largely autarchic agricultural and staple economies, where supplies did fluctuate widely and unpredictably. But in industrial, and increasingly globalized, economies, the supply side was much better insulated against shortages and surpluses. At the same time, stock markets, currency traders, and other international financial institutions introduced extreme volatility into the money supply—as the stock market crash of 1929 dramatically illustrated.

Fisher's view was not the prevailing one in the 1930s. For example, *Time Magazine* reported on 21 July 1930:

> Into this Midwest oven last week went Secretary of Agriculture Arthur Mastick Hyde and Chairman of the Farm Board Alexander Legge to preach the gospel of wheat acreage reduction. Before they left Washington they solemnly warned wheat producers that ahead of them lay seven

lean years with "world wheat prices . . . appreciably lower than in the last seven years." Messrs. Legge and Hyde opened their campaign at Hastings, Neb. The thermometer stood at 100. Declared Chairman Legge: "Reduce the acreage of wheat, without regard to what is done with the land thus released. You can put this land into grass for the benefit of your children. Do anything with it but don't raise wheat on it. . . . If a great majority of producers could act collectively, adjustment in production becomes easy.

Clearly the secretary of agriculture believed that the solution to the problem of low agricultural prices was the restriction of production, and not, as Fisher believed, an increase in purchasing power. Hyde persisted in such a belief in the face of widespread malnourishment, and even starvation, in the American population.

Fisher offered his analysis of the causes of the depression in a letter to Marriner S. Eccles, chairman of the Board of Governors of the Federal Reserve System:

1 This "recession" is very largely monetary. . . .

3 . . . booms and depressions are to some extent unavoidable. But if monetary control were ideally exercised, booms and depressions would be far smaller than they are.

4 Money management, under appropriate legislative authority, could do far more than it has and could control the volume of circulating medium within one percent of whatever standard is set up. . . .

6 We do not need to subscribe to the naive versions of the "quantity theory of money" to admit that the volume of the circulating medium is an important factor in booms and depressions—both as a cause and as an effect. . . .

8 Even if . . . our present recession in business can be attributed chiefly to a recession in velocity rather than volume, or even if the recession be entirely non-monetary, the remedy could still be an increase in volume. (20 Jan. 1938, qtd. in Allen 565)

This advice is almost diametrically opposed to that followed by the secretary of agriculture (though, admittedly, given eight years later).

Fisher's second point, which I omitted from the list, held "the monopoly price of labour . . . largely responsible for unemployment." This seems both harsh and implausible in 1938 when wages had still not recovered to precrash levels. Economists' treatment of labor as just one of the factors of production helps to motivate the hostility toward the discipline amongst moralists and reformers. During the depression economists recommended even the destruction of wheat and other commodities to support prices—and their advice was followed. Since the direct elimination of labor is not tolerable—even to economists—its price (wages) had to be allowed to fall. The spectacle of governments acting to support the price of wheat and other foodstuffs while forcing a fall in wages was surely enough to radicalize any humane observer.

The foolhardiness of the secretary of agriculture's policy prescription is glaringly evident from an item in *Time Magazine* just five months later (12 January 1931): "City dwellers last week were sharply reminded of the Drought when 500 half-starved farmers and their wives raided the food stores of England, Ark. (pop. 2,408). Most of these hungry citizens were white; had been fairly prosperous husbandmen until last year. Their crops had been ruined. Their provisions were gone." Fisher's prescription of falling wages was also implemented in those terrible years, but unemployment stubbornly persisted at whatever price labor was offered.

Most educated people—even most economists and bankers—supposed that price fluctuations were driven by shortages and abundance. They believed that increases or declines in wages and prices were the result of fluctuations in supply and demand, which in turn obeyed economic laws as iron as the laws of nature. According to quantity theory the supply of money and credit was an entirely dependent variable and therefore played no role in determining the level of economic activity.

Fisher hoped to dispel "the money illusion," the belief that money values are stable and only the value of commodities and services change:

> Until recent times, the difficulty of measuring this purchasing power of money over commodities prevented people from recognizing to what extent monetary fluctuations were responsible for a great number of economic and social disorders. "Prices rise," or "prices fall," people would say, when in reality the purchasing power of money had fallen or risen. "Too many goods, overproduction," seemed to be the obvious explanation for low prices; "scarcity of goods, and profiteering," were the reasons advanced for high prices. Yet the trouble was really due to scarcity of money (deflation) or oversupply of money (inflation). . . . The "money illusion" leads people to assume that money is in itself stable, and they consequently look to the goods for the cause of all price fluctuations. (*Stable Money* 2)

As we have seen, such "money illusion" explanations were still being acted upon at the time Fisher wrote.

As is now well understood, the stock market crash of 1929 caused a sudden and precipitate contraction of purchasing power, which then caused cascading contraction of credit. Banks called other loans when their creditors defaulted on loans extended on the security of stocks. In many cases banks failed, and depositors lost their savings. The resultant contraction in purchasing power brought about a precipitate drop in commodity prices, leading to further defaults, particularly on debts of commodity producers whose revenues collapsed (see Galbraith, *Money* 183–92). The cause of the depression was a liquidity crisis, which caused a collapse of purchasing power that in turn led to a rise in the value of money. But—incredible as it seems today—it was perceived as a fall in prices caused by an oversupply of goods. Consequently, efforts were made to restore prices by restricting supply.

The money illusion is still very much with us sixty years later, though we no longer confuse money with precious metals. Such an equation was not exactly a confusion in the twenties and thirties, since all major trading nations were on the gold standard. That meant that the price of gold was held stable with respect to money and rose or fell with respect to all other commodities.

Writing in 1944, Karl Polanyi caustically characterizes the nature and ubiquity of nineteenth-century belief in the gold standard:

> Belief in the gold standard was the faith of the age. With some it was a naïve, with some a critical, with others a satanistic creed implying acceptance in the flesh and rejection in the spirit. Yet the belief itself was the same, namely, that bank notes have value because they represent gold. Whether the gold itself has value for the reason that it embodies labour, as the socialists held, or for the reason that it is useful and scarce, as the orthodox doctrine ran, made for once no difference. The war between heaven and hell ignored the money issue, leaving capitalists and socialists miraculously united. Where Ricardo and Marx were at one, the nineteenth century knew no doubt. (25)

Fisher's stable money campaign was designed to disabuse people of the illusion that a stable price for gold meant stable money. He argued tirelessly that money was stable only when prices for a general basket of goods and services were stable. His view has prevailed. Everyone now accepts the consumer price index (which Fisher invented) as a measure of inflation or deflation, but we have not entirely escaped the money illusion. Most wage and salary earners are comfortable with inflation so long as wages and salaries increase along with the price of goods and services. But the same is not true of deflation—or even of stable prices. Fisher found this to be the case when the United States indexed wages during World War I:

> during the war millions of laborers worked under such [indexed] wage agreements. But they never constituted a major portion of contracts even in the field of wages and were almost invariably dropped when prices fell, because the wage earner objected to a cut in money wages. As long as

the high cost of living was getting higher, the "Index Visible" employees welcomed the swelling contents of their "High Cost of Living" pay envelopes. They thought their wages were increasing, though it was carefully explained to them that their real wages were merely standing still. But as soon as the cost of living fell they resented the "reduction" in wages, and refused to believe that their real wages were not reduced thereby.

Such experiences afford fresh proof of the practical omnipresence of the "money illusion" and of the impracticability of index wages and index bonds as a general solution of the great problem of unstable money. The only general solution must come, not from mending or patching the dollar from the outside, but from truing it up inside. (*Stable Money* 388–89)

It is obvious that Fisher's view is in the ascendancy at the end of the twentieth century. He would entirely approve of the efforts of Atlantic nations to bring their inflation under control, and he would not have been surprised at the reluctance of wage and salary earners—accustomed over the last fifty years to ever-increasing money payments—to acquiesce in fixed wages and salaries. Almost everyone is happier with a rising income even though it fails to keep pace with inflation than with a fixed income in a period of stable money.

Fisher gives Gesell credit in *Stamp Scrip* for being the first to recognize the importance of the "velocity" of money (45), but he does not endorse Gesell's general theory: "I may note here that the only part of Gesell's program which I have endorsed is his stamped currency proposal—and that without accepting his belief that it would lead to the abolition of interest" (141n66). For his part, Pound was careful not to offend Social Credit sensibilities in his review of Gesell's *Natural Economic Order* in Orage's *New English Weekly* on 31 January 1935. He stressed the near contemporaneity of the first books of the two reformers (Gesell's in 1915 and Douglas's in 1918) and a broad range of agreement. He was particularly impressed by Gesell's criticism of Marxism and by his Proudhonian lineage. He claimed rather vaguely that "Douglasites can use it both as guide to human perceptions and as an argument conducive to Douglas" (6:242).

Pound took only two things from Gesell: stamp scrip and the observation that Marx had ignored the issue of money. He remarked in his review: "'Marx finds nothing to criticise in money.' That is a beautiful sentence." He repeats this observation to every one of his economic correspondents in subsequent years. It became a touchstone for him, and no doubt contributed to his abandonment of the earlier posture of accommodation toward Marxism that he had adopted, even though that posture was probably never more than strategic.

Gesell brought out a new edition of *The Natural Economic Order* in 1919, the year of his brief stint as finance minister in Kurt Eisner's socialist government of Bavaria and indictment for treason. It was a dangerous time. Rosa Luxemburg and Karl Liebknecht had been executed in Berlin by Freikorp forces deployed against the Marxist-led Sparticist rebellion of November 1918. But despite his participation in Eisner's government Gesell's economics were explicitly designed as an alternative to Marxist socialism.

In the preface to *The Natural Economic Order* Gesell outlines a position very similar to that in Hilaire Belloc's contemporaneous book, *The Servile State:* "The proposals made in this book bring us to the cross-roads. We are confronted with a new choice and must now make our decision. No people has hitherto had an opportunity of making this choice, but the facts now force us to take action. For economic life cannot continue to develop as it has hitherto developed. We must either repair the defects in the old economic structure or accept communism, community of property. There is no other possibility" (15). Pound does not appear to have given *The Natural Economic Order* a careful reading. He procured a copy of volume 1 from Hugo Fack, who had reissued Philip Pye's English translation of *The Natural Economic Order.* He did not yet have it by 13 November 1934, for he complained in a letter that it had not arrived (Pound to Fack, 13 Nov. 1934, Pound Papers). Fack sent him another copy. He does not mention receiving it, but his review appeared in *New English Weekly* for 31 January 1935. He loaned his copy to Por in March—declaring that he wanted it back (Pound to Por, 20 Mar. 1935, Pound Papers). All of this suggests that he did not put a great deal of time into a study of Gesell's ideas. Certainly he did not fully absorb Gesell's argument, which was much more thorough and coherent than anything Douglas ever published. He did recognize that both men sought to preserve private property and the primacy of the individual and that both were hostile to all forms of collectivism.

Gesell identified himself as a follower of Proudhon. Nine years older than Marx, Proudhon has been largely purged from socialism by the Marxists. His political legacy is anarchism. Gesell lists seven points on which Marx is in error and Proudhon is right. Most of the disagreements hinge on the difference between Proudhon's functional, or institutional, analysis and Marx's materialistic and dialectical one.

The following is a summary of Gesell's criticism of Marxism and adherence to Proudhon's theories. Whereas Marx saw capital as equivalent to material goods, Proudhon saw it is the product of market forces (that is, capital is simply the exchange value of what one controls, whether labor, goods, or ideas—such as patents). Marx ascribed "surplus value" to the unequal power relationship of workers and capitalists. Proudhon saw that imbalance as an artifact of the market (of buying cheap and selling dear) rather than of power relationships. For Marx surplus value was always positive, but Proudhon recognized that it could be negative (that is, it could accrue to labor when the costs of production exceeded the market price). Marx's remedy for the economic ills he identified was political revolution. Proudhon's remedy was to free economic forces from political interference. Marx—like Sorel—believed that strikes and economic crises would eventually lead to revolution. Proudhon—like Douglas and Pound—believed that monetary reform and technological advances would create abundance, thereby destroying capitalism, since it is dependent on scarcity values. Marx believed that the revolutionary crises would lead to a worker's paradise, whereas Proudhon believed that it would lead to suffering and want. Finally, whereas Marx thought private property was the source of power, Proudhon thought it was money, believing private property to be harmless (*Natural Economic Order* 28–29). The last three points are ones with which Douglas would agree.

If we take Gesell's characterization of Marx and Proudhon at face value, we can see that Proudhon's views are closer to current economic thinking than are Marx's. However, Gesell's economic theory was politically conservative like Social Credit and Keynesianism, whereas Proudhon and Marx both recommended radical reform. Pound seems to have recognized Gesell's political and social conservatism, but not the superiority of his analysis and policy remedies to those of Social Credit. All he took from Gesell was stamp scrip, ignoring all the rest, and also ignoring the difficulty that stamp scrip was incompatible with Douglas's national dividend.

Stamp scrip is an important pillar in Gesell's economic structure, for it deprives money of the advantage that Proudhon had shown it to have over goods—that it does not decay and can be stored at negligible cost: "Let us then, make an end of the privileges of money. Nobody, not even savers, speculators, or capitalists, must find money, as a commodity, preferable to the contents of the markets, shops, and warehouses. If money is not to hold sway over goods, it must deteriorate, as they do" (*Natural Economic Order* 33). Pound does not take this point from Gesell. Instead he accepts Fisher's assessment that stamp scrip should be merely an auxiliary currency employed to stimulate consumer demand in times of economic downturn. Oddly, he adheres to Fisher's view at the same time as he dismisses Fisher as unimportant and incompetent.

Nor does Pound pick up Gesell's criticism of interest—a rather startling oversight considering his strong feelings about "usury." I suppose he felt he had nothing to learn from Gesell on this subject since his very first comment on Douglasite economic theory identified usury as the villain in the piece: "the middle ages had sense enough to dislike usury and we have let it become the basis of our alleged civilization" ("A Letter from London" in *Ezra Pound's Poetry and Prose* 11:4).

Following a very different route than Douglas's A + B analysis, Gesell comes to a similar, though more general, conclusion (once again derived from Proudhon): "Usually, therefore, that is, commercially, the present form of money acts as intermediary for the exchange of wares only on condition that it receives a tribute. If the market is a road for the exchange of wares, money is a toll-gate built across the road and opened only upon payment of the toll. The toll, profit, tribute, interest or whatever we choose to call it, is the condition upon which wares are exchanged. No tribute, no exchange" (229). The tribute of which he speaks is interest charges. One would expect Pound to have picked up this colorful construction of the role of interest, but I have not found it anywhere in his poetry or prose—lending credence to the hypothesis that he did not read Gesell with much care.

Pound took only two points from his reading of Fisher and Gesell: the idea of stamp scrip and the perception that Marx had not understood money. All the rest he ignored, including the second volume of *The Natural Economic Order*, which was devoted to a scheme for "free land," which amounted to the nationalization or state ownership of all land. In contrast to the communist system, the state would not itself work the land, but would rent it to individuals and corporations who wished to use it. Fisher and Keynes are also uninterested in this aspect of Gesell. Keynes misleadingly characterized it as "Georgist," alluding to Henry George (1839–1897), an American economic reformer who believed that all government revenue could be raised from taxes on land—quite a different idea than Gesell's. Pound's enthusiasm for Gesell seems to have been based as much on the fact that stamp scrip had actually been put into practice as it was on any full appreciation of Gesell's Proudhonian analysis of economic factors.

True to form, Pound tried to forge an alliance with the Gesellites, attempting to recruit Hugo Fack and E. S. Woodward for his own program of economic reform. Rather surprisingly, Pound's exchange with the Gesellites is a mirror image of his exchange with the Social Crediters. Just as he pushed Gesell on a reluctant Douglas, he pushed Douglas on the reluctant Fack and Woodward. Obviously he was less interested in purity of doctrine than he was in forging alliances, but he proved to be a very poor recruiter.

Hugo Fack was a German immigrant to the United States. In addition to being a longtime Gesellite, he was also a practitioner of alternative medicine and an anti-Semite. Pound first wrote to him on 26 September 1934 to complain of a piece by E. S. Woodward critical of Douglas in Fack's journal, *The Way Out*. Pound then wrote to Woodward himself (in November 1934). He tried to cultivate Woodward because of his Canadian location and thus his proximity to William Aberhart.

His first letter to Woodward (3 November 1934) opens with praise for Father Coughlin and immediately sets out to persuade Woodward that taxes are unnecessary since government expenditures can be paid for with fiat money. He also invites Woodward to contribute something to Orage's *New English Weekly*. Woodward declined (28 March), explaining that he had publicly criticized Social Credit and was on very cool relations with Canadian Social Crediters. Nonetheless he sent Pound six copies of his booklet, *Canada Reconstructed*, which outlines a full Gesellite reform of the Canadian economy. He recommends stamp scrip, which he has relabeled "demurrage money," as well as bank reform and nationalization of land. Pound commented on it in a letter to Por, revealing that his motive is recruitment, not discourse:

> E/S/ Woodward (not [to be] confuse[d] with W.E. Woodward) has sent me six copies of pamph Canada [Reconstructed]; which I am forwarding to you/ good sign that these Gesellites are friendly to me/ BUT I need help with 'em for RESULTS/
> They are STUCK with WORK, and dont get the idea that there IS NOT work, any more like there was/
> also got a lot of old land superstition. If you review the pamph/ you might tickle 'em on that.
> They must recognize dif/ usury and increment of assn/ and must recog/ dividend as JUSTICE, payable from HERITAGE that belongs to no private person/ richezza statale (or commune). ([23 Apr. 1935], Pound Papers)

These disagreements persist in his correspondence with Woodward and Fack, though the land reform issue is not pursued.

To Woodward he complained: "Why this sectarian desire to prove Gesell the ONLY etc/ the analysis is largely the SAME as Douglas'" and adds— quite contrary to the facts as he knows them—"who was I think the first man to recognize Gesell in England. Or at least a very early recogniser, long before Bachi and co/" ([24 Apr. 1935], Pound Papers). If Pound truly thought that Douglas and Gesell were "largely the same," despite the contrary opinion of both Orage and Douglas, Woodward left him in little doubt that they were not.

In a letter of 6 February 1936, Woodward challenged Pound to point out his alleged misunderstanding of Social Credit and went on to detail the points of agreement and disagreement between himself and Fack, on the one hand, and Douglas, on the other. The crucial disagreement is over the role of money. Woodward sticks to the Gesellite belief that depreciating currency is sufficient to guarantee the distribution of all goods and services—rendering the national dividend not only unnecessary, but impossible. And he castigates Pound for his habit of claiming superior competence in lieu of presenting arguments and evidence.

Like Fisher, Woodward excuses bankers of any culpability for the misallocation of resources that he believes prevails. He confesses that he once thought that bankers were responsible for the economic woes of the world, but has come to understand that they too are victims of economic misconceptions and errors. The cause of economic distress in his view is the money mechanism itself—that is, the reliance on precious metals.

Another point of disagreement between them was on whether machine production had made work virtually obsolete. After reading Kimball's *Industrial Economics* in 1931, Pound thought that it had. Woodward disagreed, pointing out in a letter of 4 January 1936 that there would be sufficient work for the foreseeable future since so many millions lacked decent creature comforts. He also opposed the national dividend on the grounds that it would promote idleness. Of course, increased leisure was just what Pound wanted. He responded very negatively to the focus of Woodward and Fack on the virtues of work, even though Pound himself was a tireless worker. His vigorous rejection of the work ethic here contrasts oddly with the hostility toward relief payments he expressed two and a half years earlier in "Points."

Pound outlines his adherence to Douglas's view that the state, rather than society, underwrites currency in a letter to Woodward of 26 December 1936: "Re/ the STATE. Some guildites wd/ agree with you and some fascists. BUT my view is that the state both creates and owns. The statal increment ENTERS the problem; the minute national money (good and solid) gives GREATER faith than goods money like my grandfather's. Everything tending to keep value of money even, to maintain faith in it that is contributed by the state, by honesty of govt. Custom etc. CONFERS title ON the state proportionate to these increases or this INCREMENT" (Pound Papers).

The big event of 1935 for Social Crediters was the September election in Alberta of the Social Credit party under the leadership of William Aberhart. As we have seen, Pound volunteered to go to Alberta to guide the fledgling Social Crediters in Douglas's place. Douglas was invited, but did not go. John Hargrave of the English Green Shirt movement went in his stead in December 1936—without Douglas's blessing. According to

Woodward, Aberhart invited Hargrave to participate in cabinet and committee meetings, but he soon alienated the Aberhart government by his habit of using press conferences to pressure it into adopting his policies. Woodward—who had also been received into Aberhart's confidence—was unimpressed by Hargrave's plan. He believed it "would have failed ignominiously," even though "true to Douglas economics" (Woodward to Pound, 27 Jan. 1937, Pound Papers).

In the same letter Woodward explained why Douglas's national dividend plan would not work. His objections were essentially the same as those of his namesake, W. E. Woodward—that the dividend represented much too large an expansion of the money supply and would cause rampant inflation. Aberhart did attempt to issue dividends in 1937, but the legislation was disallowed by the federal government (Canadian provinces do not have the legal right to issue currency). Despite this setback, Aberhart found a way to issue some stamp scrip, but Albertans would not accept it, and that Gesellite measure failed also.

Pound and Woodward continued to discuss what the Aberhart government had done and ought to have done. Pound stuck to the combination of stamp scrip and a dividend financed by the issue of new money. Douglas had complained that the 1 percent charge on stamp scrip was a tax. Woodward registers the same objection to the issue of new money: "*All new issues of money are taxes which must be paid by the public.* That's a point S/C [Social Credit] overlooks" (Woodward to Pound, 10 May 1937, Pound Papers; Woodward's emphasis). Despite his sincere admiration of Pound's tireless efforts to promote economic reform, Woodward found his arguments to be of dubious merit. He also complained of Pound's tendency to denounce those with whom he disagrees rather than try to answer their objections. He pointed out, quite justifiably, that Social Crediters as a group were inconsistent and vague about numbers. He predicted that Alberta would be the graveyard of Social Credit—a prediction that turned out to be accurate so far as its career as an economic theory is concerned. Although Social Credit survived in Canada as a national party into the 1970s and as a provincial party into the 1980s, it had long abandoned Social Credit economic policy. Pound, in contrast, never abandoned the nostrums of the A + B theorem and the national dividend despite trenchant criticism from a parade of friendly correspondents. Why he clung to Douglas remains rather a mystery to me. It certainly was not because Douglas offered him any support—either moral, practical, or theoretical.

Notes

1. Speaking of Douglas, Pound wrote to Odon Por: "He dont see Gesell, save as something that interferes with his patent rights. (Oh, well, that is a bit too strong.)" (15 Dec. [1937], Pound Papers). And he wrote to W. E. Woodward: "I tried to analyse Fisher's 'Inflation' book, but Orage sez I am giving the blighter TOO much importance, and won't go on after p/ 23. (i.e. he printed first quarter of my commentary)" (28 Nov. 1933, Pound Letters). Pound is referring to his review in *New English Weekly*. Orage told Pound to drop Gesell: "It just won't do. We've got enough to contend with without hanging Gesell round our necks" (3 Oct. 1934 qtd. in Redman 128).

2. So far as Britain is concerned, Lord Arthur Salter, Keynes, and a group of Oxford economists did recommend increased public expenditure, but not until 1937, a year after *The General Theory*. The British Treasury was still adamantly opposed to such a policy in 1937 (Salter 253–54).

3. Current terminology can be confusing. Keynes's name is now identified with the practice of actively *manipulating* the money supply and is opposed to "monetarism," which recommends a passive, steady expansion of the money supply. But this opposition masks the agreement of both modern economic schools that "money matters." In short, neither of them accept the old quantity theory, which held that strict equilibrium could be maintained at optimum levels of economic activity.

The Social Credit and Gesellite criticism of Keynesian policies is that the new money so created represents public debt. Banks buy treasury bills with money they create *ex nihilo,* as they are entitled to do. But the state could just as easily create the new money directly, without incurring any debt to the banks and the attendant interest charges. This point is very difficult for most people to accept. It will come up again.

CHAPTER 9

An Increasing Eclecticism

Pound's exposure to Gesell remained a bone of contention between him and his fellow Social Crediters, introducing still another strain into his economic *paideuma*. At the same time, world events were taking shape in a way he had not anticipated and to which he proved incapable of responding appropriately. By the time of Yeats's visit in the summer of 1934, Pound had identified Britain as the chief villain in the opposition to economic reform, presumably in the belief that Britain was still dominant in world trade and banking. It is difficult to put one's finger on the cause of Pound's intemperate behavior on that occasion. The failure of Social Credit to take hold in Britain was no doubt a factor. But Fascist Italy was then still well received in the democracies, a condition that altered after Italy's invasion of Ethiopia in October 1935.

A great deal happened between the composition of *Jefferson and/or Mussolini* in February 1933 and the forging of the Axis pact between Mussolini and Hitler in October 1936. Pound wrote it just after Hitler was sworn in as chancellor of Germany (30 January 1933) and Franklin Delano Roosevelt was elected president of the United States. Pound took great hope from Roosevelt's election, but ignored Hitler's rise to power. Late in 1935 he was still lumping England, France, Germany, and the United States together as equally benighted: "Germany is most enslaved, France most befuddled, and neither England nor America inspire a hog's worth of respect" ("The Individual in His Milieu" in *Selected Prose* 279). At this time Pound saw Italy as the only ally of his economic reform movement.

No one in 1933 anticipated the turn events were to take, least of all Pound, who believed that Douglas's economic reforms would surely prevail. With the exception of Hitler himself, no one was anticipating a world war, still less the horrors of the Nazi Holocaust. Pound dared to hope in his review of *Looking Forward,* a collection of Roosevelt's speeches, that Roosevelt would enact Social Credit–style policies, since he appeared to understand the problem of underconsumption:

> WHEN the whole 120 (or whatever it is) millions of the population has NOT sufficient purchasing power to buy all (or approximately all) that they, the whole 120 (or whatever it is) millions produce, the jam or constipation will be worse than if this insufficiency only affected a part of the public.
>
> That perception wd. take him [Roosevelt] very quickly to the A plus B theorem or to Douglas economics, if he hasn't *dans son fort intérieure* already arrived there. ("More Economics" in *Ezra Pound's Poetry and Prose* 6:46)

His enthusiasm for Roosevelt's New Deal was reinforced by Mussolini's reception of Roosevelt as a disciple. Given that Pound supposed, albeit erroneously, that Mussolini was moving in directions compatible with Social Credit, he may be forgiven for supposing in 1933 that he was leading the world toward a glorious future of peace and prosperity.

He was still more convinced of this in 1935 when *Jefferson and/or Mussolini* finally got into print. He declared in a new preface that scarcity economics had died on 6 October 1934 (the date of a Mussolini speech in the Piazza del Duomo in Milan). A month later he declared grandly: "At about 4:14 p.m. on the 6th of October Mussolini *buried* scarcity economics. Distributism came in as a declared state policy. All the live schools of economy can now be regarded under the general caption 'distributist'" ("Child's Guide to Economics 1934" in *Ezra Pound's Poetry and Prose* 6:212). But Pound admits in his obituary note for Orage, written at the same time, that Orage did not share his enthusiasm for the Milan speech: "He died exactly one month after the speech to the Milan workers. It was natural that he should not see this in the same light that I do, or rather that he should have estimated it differently, as a victory, certainly, but perhaps not yet fully as the great and final collapse of Scarcity Economics" (*Ezra Pound's Poetry and Prose* 6:214).

Despite these hopeful signs, between 1931 and 1937 Pound was repeatedly confronted with the awkward difficulty that his economic education was leading him into confusion and contradiction. Excited about Gesell because of the Wörgl experiment, he reacted negatively to the exposition of the idea in Fisher's *Stamp Scrip* and was apparently overwhelmed by the large and carefully argued *Natural Economic Order.* As we have seen, his review of it was careless and based on an avowedly incomplete reading. That he was willing to lend "my precious Gesell, which I want back" to Odon Por shortly after he received it suggests either disappointment or impatience (20 Mar. 1935, Pound Papers). All of this indicates that he had little aptitude for abstract economic argument—a trait he had admitted to Kitson about a year earlier: "I am all agin' abstraction. Got to begin somewhere. I got a poetic I.E. concrete mind" (30 Nov. 1933, Pound Papers).

Instead of studying Gesell, he began early in 1935 to work his way through the Latin of Salmasius's *De Modo Usurarum* (1639). Claudius Salmasius (1588–1653) was a seventeenth-century Huguenot moralist who cited St. Ambrose's wonderful curse, "*Captans annonam maledictus in plebe sit,*" which Pound cites in a truncated form in *Guide to Kulchur* (34) and repeats nearly twenty years later in canto 88 (601). He translates it in both places as "Hoggers of harvest, cursed among the people."

I can only guess at Pound's reasons for turning from Gesell to Salmasius at this particular juncture, but it appears he was more comfortable with the Frenchman's strong moral condemnation of economic skullduggery than with Gesell's intricate arguments for land and monetary reform. He describes Salmasius's book in *Guide to Kulchur* as a "history of where such and such tyrant, dupe, idiot, bewigged pustulent Bourbon, bewigged pietist diseased Stuart got his money and how, from Caesar's time . . . to our own" (115). Such concrete details no doubt appealed to Pound's poetic, concrete mind and provided him with material that could go into *The Cantos,* as Gesell's dry prose could not.

Guide to Kulchur represents Pound's effort to express in prose "where he had got to." It was a new and more comprehensive manifesto designed to displace *Jefferson and/or Mussolini.* However, it was written very rapidly— on internal evidence between 2 March and 22 April 1937, though he was correcting proofs as late as January 1938 (Mondolfo and Hurley 79). He received Gesell's book sometime after 13 November 1934 and lent it to Por on 20 March 1935. He began to study Salmasius as early as May 1935, for he comments on it in a *Criterion* article that he had completed by 3 June. Apparently he was still working on Salmasius a year later, for Tim Redman reports that he was being helped with Salmasius's Latin by Manlio Dazzi in early 1936 (172).

Gesell gets five mentions in *Guide to Kulchur*—most of them cursory— and in one of them he is linked to Douglas, Salmasius, and fascism: "The FOUR active domains, or the four expanses of thought that the truly curious reader shd. look into are Gesell, Douglas, the Canonist doctrine of economics [which he found in Salmasius], wherein interest is treated under the general head of just price, AND the actual practice and achievement in the corporate states of our time" (173).

From the point of view of economic theory this is a dog's breakfast. The theory of just price makes sense only if one accepts intrinsic value, but Proudhon, Gesell, Douglas, and all modern economists hold an exchange or market theory of value. Ricardian orthodoxy and Marx adhere to a material theory of value. Marx is silent on the question of just price, but his theory of surplus value implies it. A just price would be the full value of the labor congealed in a commodity. Douglas, it is true, recommended price controls, but they were intended to prevent inflation rather than to institutionalize relative values, which is what the just price must mean. The notion of just price makes sense only within what Fisher called the "money illusion." He pointed out that the suffering and dislocation caused by price fluctuations could be attributed to the instability of money. With stable money, the market would establish "just" prices. Administrative fiat could never accomplish the feat, especially not with unstable money. Pound's endorsement of Salmasius's just price is, then, one more indication of his poor grasp of the economic issues he addresses.

However, the notion of intrinsic value is not an egregious blunder from within Pound's idealistic and aesthetic worldview, which would support a nonmaterialistic theory of intrinsic value. For an idealist like Pound the value of an act or an aesthetic object derives from the intellectual force it embodies, and its effects arise from that force. The Social Credit notion of cultural heritage fit nicely into this aesthetic/expressive theory of value in that it dematerialized value, while retaining a degree of intrinsicality. Of course, its main thrust was to *socialize* value so that cultural property— whether scientific, institutional, or aesthetic—belonged to everyone. Pound seems to have believed that if everyone had a sufficiency of purchasing power, they would choose the beautiful, the true, and the useful, thereby bringing exchange value into line with intrinsic value. For those of us who have seen the consequences of the enormous increase and democratization of consumer purchasing power of the postwar years, such a scenario appears naively optimistic, but it is neither absurd nor incoherent.

The rapidity with which Salmasius displaced Gesell suggests that Pound's economics were motivated by aesthetic and moral considerations rather more than by technical ones. Salmasius receives approving notice even in "The Individual in His Milieu," a *Criterion* article ostensibly devoted to Gesell that Pound badgered Eliot into accepting: "The archaeologist and serendipidist can wander back through Claudius Salmasius and find the known beginnings of usury entangled with those of marine insurance, sea lawyers, the law of Rhodes, the disputed text of Antoninus Pius on the limits of his jurisdiction. . . . Vast mines of anecdote lie still unexploited" (*Selected Prose* 272–73). Pound will exploit this anecdote in *The Cantos* many years later, but in "The Individual in His Milieu" he turns back to Gesell and misrepresents him, claiming that he "declared against its [money] being the sole fabrication free of tax in a world wherein the good life was being with increasing acrimony, taxed and stifled out of existence. He, thereupon, devised a tax on money" (275). But Pound has got it wrong. The justification for "shrinking money" is not that money evades tax, but that it does not suffer spoilage or incur storage costs as commodities do. Pound does get it right later in the article: "Gesell, as merchant and agricultural thinker, was oppressed by the hideously unjust privilege of durable money over and above farm produce and merchandise" (277). This uncertainty manifests Pound's struggle with an increasingly ragged set of inputs.

When he finished *Jefferson and/or Mussolini* in February 1933, Pound believed that he had worked out the solution to the economic and political problems of the modern age. Such a resolution was, in his view, a prerequisite for an epic poet like himself. Roosevelt's election in 1932 only reinforced his belief that Social Credit economics, Jeffersonian elitist democracy, and Fascist governmental structure were compatible and represented the wave of the future. While this may seem fantastic to us, his view was neither bizarre nor unheard of in the early thirties. After all, Mussolini was a syndicated columnist for the United Press from 1927 to 1928 and for the Hearst chain from 1928 to 1936 (Cannistraro and Sullivan 494). His weekly columns trumpeted the virtues of Italian fascism to the American public with considerable—though diminishing—effect.

Like Pound, Mussolini thought Roosevelt's election represented a move by the United States toward fascism (Cannistraro and Sullivan 367). Amadeo Giannini, the Italian-American president of the Bank of America, backed Roosevelt in the belief that he "was prepared to adopt some of Mussolini's economic policies and adapt them to solving America's problems." Philip V. Cannistraro and Brian R. Sullivan note that "Roosevelt's election filled Mussolini with confidence, as if he were sure of a special degree of sympathy and understanding from the new president. Mussolini went so far as to order Margherita [Sarfatti] and Thomas Morgan to create two articles for *Gerarchia* suggesting what steps the new president should take on assuming office. In essence, the articles argued that Roosevelt should open American markets to Italian goods, forgive the Italian war debt, and adopt the Fascist economic system" (403–4). Encouraged by these good omens, Pound redoubled his propaganda efforts.

As time went on Pound ceased to worry about the contradictions and inconsistencies in his economic beliefs, but he never resolved them. "The Individual in His Milieu" shows him struggling with a heteroclite set of insights, observations, and loyalties. He concedes that Douglas has not, after all, resolved all the outstanding problems of economics, because Gesell had shown him that Douglas had not paid enough attention to money: "Economics in our time is where medicine was when professors studied the subject in Aristotle and refused to look at dissecting tables. The history of money is yet to be written. Even the scattered fragments are comprehensible only to men who start clean" (*Selected Prose* 272). Unable to render the economic analyses of Douglas and Gesell compatible, Pound falls back on an assertion of moral equivalence:

> Between Douglas and Gesell there is a contest of justice with justice, neither, of a right, excluding the other's justice.
> Take it at the surface and wrangle over detail and you will get nowhere, or merely into a tangle. Carry it down to its root *in justice* and you find no needful contradiction. (275)

Pound had got *himself* in a tangle, and he was never to get out of it. In addition to Gesell, Douglas, and Mussolini, he invokes Karl Marx, Henry George, E. S. Woodward, Henry Loeb's Technocratic *Chart of Plenty,* and Mark Carleton. The latter was a botanist who developed new wheat strains early in the century. Pound learned of him from Paul de Kruif's *Hunger Fighters,* which he had reviewed in Orage's *New English Weekly* (22 February 1934).

In the review Pound circles restlessly between Gesell, Douglas, and Mussolini, hoping that by maneuvering them into proximity with one another, he will reconcile the differences of which he is painfully aware, but does not know how to resolve. In a gesture that becomes increasingly common, he invokes the ideogrammic method to paper over his difficulties and hints that Ernest Fenollosa has been ignored because of a conspiracy against him: "In another eighty years a few people may begin to see that the present author's insistence on *Ideogrammic* method has not been mere picking daisies. Fenollosa saw the possibilities of a *method.* The effects of his vision were sabotaged right and left, and the small group of men comprising 'the learned world' will some day feel a disgust for Paul Carus[1] in particular" (*Selected Prose* 281).

By the spring of 1935, when he wrote "The Individual in His Milieu," Pound had given up on Roosevelt, whose New Deal policies he contrasts unfavorably with the policy prescriptions of Gesell and Douglas: "In contrast to the idiotic accumulation of debt by Roosevelt, observe that *if* such government expenditure be necessary or advisable, the direct payment of workers, etc., in stamp scrip would in eight years consume itself, and leave the next decade *free* of all debt. The Roosevelt system is either a fraud or a selling of the nation's children into slavery without the ghost of excuse" (*Selected Prose* 280). Roosevelt's New Deal initially sought to restore purchasing power by government expenditures on public works financed by government borrowing—very much what Mussolini and Hitler did at the same time. Of course, Social Crediters, Proudhonians, and Gesellites all condemned such borrowing as unnecessary since they believed the money supply could be expanded directly, without debt.

He had advised Roosevelt to follow the example of Wörgl in a letter to the Paris edition of the *New York Herald:* "Why, for example, should the Government (as representing the nation) insist on renting all the money wanted for 'improvements'? Herr Unterguggenburger has shown that his town could run on a saner system. He issued currency instead of bonds, every month you had to put a two-cent stamp on your dollar bill. That is to say, the individuals using the money, and therefore those having the money at a given date, paid the rent on it" ("Possibilities of Economics" in *Ezra Pound's Poetry and Prose* 6:53). Of course, Pound overlooks the fact that the self-liquidating character of Gesell's stamp scrip amounts to a tax of 2 percent per month (24 percent per year) on all outstanding currency. Such a tax is substantial, but hardly intolerable. Of course, it could be evaded either by disbursing the money quickly as Gesell intended or by avoiding cash altogether.

Pound's quixotic view of the role of the artist in political action is put quite baldly in a piece published in 1927: "The artist, the maker is always too far ahead of any revolution, or reaction, or counter-revolution or counter-reaction for his vote to have an immediate result; and no party program ever contains enough of his program to give him the least satisfaction. The party that follows him wins; and the speed with which they set about it, is the measure of their practical capacity and intelligence. Blessed are they who pick the right artists and makers" ("The State" in *Selected Prose* 214–15). Pound obviously thought of himself as the artist showing the way. But he did not know the way. Instead he was lost in a dark wood, desperately seeking a Virgil to guide him.

The strain on Pound showed in the appalling way he treated Yeats when he sought his advice in 1934. But it would be wrong, I think, to accept Yeats's view that Pound ought to have kept clear of political engagement. Certainly Yeats did not heed that advice himself. Given the economic and political turmoil of the thirties, Pound is to be commended for entering the struggle and putting so much at risk. Alas, his political and moral judgment cannot be similarly commended. Nietzschean detachment, as expressed by Yeats in "The Gyres," however noble, is not admirable on moral grounds:

What matter though numb nightmare ride on top,
And blood and mire the sensitive body stain?
What matter? Heave no sigh, let no tear drop,
A greater, a more gracious time has gone;
For painted forms or boxes of make-up
In ancient tombs I sighed, but not again;
What matter? Out of cavern comes a voice,
And all it knows is that one word "Rejoice!"
                        (Yeats, *Collected Poems* 337)

Instead of rejoicing Pound mostly ranted.

At this point it seems appropriate to review the factors that motivated Pound to enter the arena of practical politics. The decision to do so was taken with *Jefferson and/or Mussolini,* written in the winter of 1932–33. Pound went to great lengths in that work to put Mussolini in the company of Jefferson, a republican democrat, and Lenin, a revolutionary Communist. (The latter joined Pound's pantheon of heroes when he learned about him in conversation with Lincoln Steffens in 1925. See "Ezra Pound" in *Ezra Pound's Poetry and Prose* 5:200.) Although Lenin was later dropped and Jefferson became overshadowed by John Adams and other American presidents, the political posture articulated in *Jefferson and/or Mussolini* is the one Pound maintained for the rest of his life. His political philosophy amounted to the belief that only a wise and benevolent ruler could govern effectively. Such a ruler was an artist writ large. The only issue was to discriminate between those who were wise and benevolent and those who were obtuse and/or malevolent. Of course, it was the role of the artist to make such discriminations.

The consistent—not to say hidebound—nature of Pound's political "philosophy" prompts one to seek the trigger that set him on the course of political activism. One obvious trigger was the worldwide economic crisis following the stock market crash of 1929. I have not found any statement in which Pound attributes his political engagement to the depression, but there are many in which he attributes it to the arrival of Mussolini on the political scene. One may doubt his own testimony, since he showed no interest in Mussolini until after the crash. The depression also seems to have motivated his renewed contact with Douglas in January 1931 after a decade in which there was no communication.

Though he did not endorse Mussolini in the 1927 piece "The State," he was already moving toward the position he took in *Jefferson and/or Mussolini:* "Both Fascio and the Russian revolution are interesting phenomena; beyond which there is the historic perspective." And he is willing to sacrifice democratic liberties in the name of equity and stability: "The capitalist imperialist state must be judged not only in comparison with unrealized utopias, but with past forms of the state; if it will not bear comparison with the feudal order; with the small city states both republican and despotic; either as to its 'social justice' *or* as to its permanent products, art, science, literature, the onus of proof goes against it" (*Selected Prose* 215). Four years later, he was openly endorsing the purportedly benevolent despotism of Stalin and Mussolini:

> When a country is governed by one percent of its population that one percent indubitably form an aristocracy or something to which aristocratical privilege pertains. Possibly no other aristocracy in 1931 has so great a sense of responsibility as the new Russian "party" [the Communists under Stalin, Lenin having died in 1924]. . . .
>
> Both the Communist party in Russia and the Fascist party in Italy are examples of aristocracy, active. They are the best, the pragmatical, the aware, the most thoughtful, the most wilful [I think he means "forceful"] elements in their nations. ("Fungus, Twilight, or Dry Rot" in *Ezra Pound's Poetry and Prose* 5:315, 317)

Here, as in *Jefferson and/or Mussolini*, it is rule by a strong man or a benevolent tyrant that Pound endorses rather than any particular ideology. He is still uncommitted as to Left or Right, but participates in the hostility of both for bourgeois capitalism. In this respect, he fits the profile of Mussolini himself, who began as a socialist and brought many socialists into his Fascist party.

Pound's fence-sitting might have been a polemical strategy rather than true ambivalence, for in the same 1931 article he speaks of the necessity of private property—a Douglasite position: "Perhaps the sole valid surviving justification of private property is that it can (decently organized) eliminate almost all need of or excuse for any bureaucracy whatsoever. By which I mean that the dollar bill is less bother than a meat card with ten signatures and 14 rubber-stamps. However . . . it will need another 14 or 40 years of purgatory to make anyone outside the small elite consider the nature of credit" (315; Pound's ellipsis).

One of the first books Pound read in his self-education program was Dexter Kimball's *Industrial Economics*. He recommends Kimball to Senator Bronson Cutting in a letter of 9 October 1931 (Walkiewicz and Witemeyer 59), and he reviewed it early in the next year under the title, "The Depression Has Just Begun" (*Ezra Pound's Poetry and Prose* 6:335–37). Kimball reinforced Douglas's perception that modern machine production would create abundance. (It was a common view at the time, as the title of Graham Hutton's 1934 BBC series, *The Burden of Plenty*, illustrates.) The main thing Pound took from Kimball was the shortened work week as a convenient means of redistributing industrial abundance. It became a permanent part of his economic tool kit, even though neither Douglas nor Orage was interested in it.

Kimball was a professor of engineering at Cornell University. Writing before the crash, he was optimistic about the future possibilities of industrial societies. Though confident that the problem of scarcity was solved, he lamented that the problem of distribution remained intractable:

> Highly developed tools of production make possible a high average state of mental development and physical comfort; but the realization of this average depends upon national ideals and the social and industrial organization by which the wealth is distributed. Civilization, therefore, presents two great problems; first that of *producing* sufficient wealth to insure proper living conditions and, second, that of *distributing* this wealth in an equitable manner. Considerable progress has been made in solving the first problem but the second still presents many difficulties. This book deals primarily with the problems of production. (9)

Kimball repeats this observation—and the disclaimer—at least three times in the book, suggesting a very real concern with social justice. In other respects his analysis dovetails very nicely with Douglas's, though it is entirely independent of it. The only suggestion he has for improved distribution of the greater wealth is the shortened work week. Pound made Kimball a permanent, though minor, member of his pantheon of economic reformers, mentioning him in his memorial 1935 essay for Orage, "In the Wounds: A. R. Orage," and again in the 1944 essay "An Introduction to the Economic Nature of the United States." Pound was unsuccessful in his efforts to get Douglas and Orage to share his enthusiasm for Kimball, however.

Kimball focuses on the benefits of industrialization rather than the problem of distribution: "The greatest gain in productive ability that the world has ever witnessed came with the introduction of labor-saving machinery. All the *possibilities* for the physical and mental betterment of humanity offered by the most tremendous gain in productive power mankind has ever witnessed were opened up at that time" (9). But he was not an uncritical oracle of a utopian future of marvelous machines like Marinetti and the Futurists. On the contrary, he stresses the necessity for the state to impose a regulatory framework for technology and commerce if social objectives are to be realized:

> The immediate effect of these new methods [in the nineteenth century] was to reduce the workers concerned to a state of pauperism and wretchedness which was relieved only by legislation and other reactive measures and not by anything *inherent* in the new methods. These productive methods have been tremendously improved and added to, steadily, for over 100 years; and what is the net result? Today, the skilled mechanic who

can save a competence is a rarity. Instead of the individual independence which every man should be able to acquire, governmental and other forms of pensions are being talked of. (9)

Kimball's concern for the welfare of the average worker does not lead him to a collectivist solution. Indeed, he criticizes government pensions on grounds that if properly organized the industrial system would distribute wealth equitably on its own. This "right-wing" position is one to which Pound was predisposed, as he was to Kimball's contention that education was the best mechanism for ensuring an equitable distribution of wealth. Indeed, the only mention of Kimball in *The Cantos* (38/187)—a citation of his description of readers furnished by employers to "provide mental entertainment" for cigar makers—reflects his pedagogic concerns.

Pound takes Kimball to be a Technocrat, but I have found nothing to link him with either Howard Scott's Technocracy or Walter Rautenstrauch's Continental Committee on Technocracy. Kimball is self-identified as a follower of Frederick Winslow Taylor, the originator of "Scientific Management," and of time and motion study. William E. Akin mentions him in his study of Technocracy, but as a follower of Taylor, not as a Technocrat (13). He did share the Technocratic belief that machine production made possible an age of plenty, as did Douglas. But Kimball's remedies are much less radical than Douglas's—a shorter working week and improved educational opportunities for the working class.

Pound's willingness to see hostile forces at work surfaces just a year after his review of *Industrial Economics* in a letter to the Paris edition of the *Chicago Tribune*. Having seized on Technocracy, he charges that it has been suppressed by some sort of conspiracy: "I suggest that the technocracy studies have had to proceed under cover for the past fifteen years and that the only reason they have been permitted has been that the experimenters carefully refrained from mentioning the economic conclusions that cd. be drawn from their work" ("Technocracy" in *Ezra Pound's Poetry and Prose* 1:11). It is not clear what prompted this accusation. It may have been nothing more than Pound's antipathy for Nicholas Murray Butler, the president of Columbia University, where Rautenstrauch's Technocratic research was being carried out.

He returns to Technocracy in an April review of *The Secret International, The New and the Old Economics* (by Douglas), and *Mercanti de Cannoni*. The first and last of these works alleged that governments suppressed information and conspired with the armaments industry. Pound eats it up and adds that anyone wanting to understand the conspiracy exposed in *The Secret International* must also know:

1. C.H. Douglas's writings on economics;
2. *L'idea statale* [that is, the Fascist state]
3. technocratic manifestations; *and that* the French and British press have long resisted open discussion of certain facts, and certain ideas (as for example the lack of attention paid to Douglas's writing back in 1920, 1921 etc.) *and that* Scott's first formulations re/ technocracy date from 1919[2] and have never been printed. (*Ezra Pound's Poetry and Prose* 6:32)

Just months after that review, Pound changes tack, asserting in *Jefferson and/or Mussolini* that Technocracy is incompatible with Social Credit: "So far as political economy is concerned the modern world contains the work of Lenin and Henry Ford, of C. H. Douglas and Mussolini, the somewhat confused results of Veblen and the technocrats, this latter, as I have indicated, is confused because it has been in large part surreptitious. Done under or near a subsidy it either has not had any moral force and direction, or the individuals who had any have had to conceal it and profess to be concerned WHOLLY with mechanical problems" (88). Presumably the "subsidy" alludes to the involvement of Walter Rautenstrauch, chairman of Columbia's Department of Industrial Engineering, who undertook studies to calculate the potential of the American economy based on the power capacity of the nation, in accordance with Veblen's and Scott's principles.

The involvement of Columbia University would be enough to taint Technocracy in Pound's mind, because he was unremittingly hostile to its president, Nicholas Murray Butler, also chair of the Carnegie Peace Foundation and co-winner (with Jane Addams) of the 1931 Nobel Peace Prize. Pound had made an unsuccessful proposal to the foundation, and Butler was the butt of his animosity ever after (see "Peace Pathology" in *Ezra Pound's Poetry and Prose* 6:147). His first letter to W. E. Woodward supports this supposition: "I suppose the technocratic experiments were permitted under the aegis of the gas bag [Butler], because mechanical development was supposed to help the exploiters rather than do any good to the pore bloody ole pubk" (28 Jan. 1933, Pound Letters). It is the only instance I have come across of an animosity based on a personal grievance rather than an ideological antipathy. It is all the more remarkable in the light of Butler's admiration of Mussolini and friendship with his longtime mistress, Margherita Sarfatti.

Howard Scott and Technocracy are left out of Pound's pantheon thereafter, though Dexter Kimball is retained, and he continues to count Harold Loeb as a fellow reformer though a Technocrat. In *Guide to Kulchur,* for example, he refers opaquely to the Columbia University research, reduces Technocracy misleadingly to the belief that industrial technology has solved the problem of production, and claims priority on that point for Social Credit:

> And, more recently, all this yatter about technocracy got out from under the lid. Without, apparently, much moral direction . . . my own belief being that all or most of the technocracy results had to be got surreptitiously, in so far as the members of the Columbia University faculty had, in great measure, to conceal the significance of their findings, and stick to the purely material phase. But in 1918 we knew in London that the problem of production was solved, and that the next job was to solve distribution and that this meant a new administration of credit. I don't think there was any ambiguity about that. (48)

Pound's remark that the Columbia Technocrats concealed their findings by sticking "to the purely material phase" is probably an allusion to their silence on the nature of money—the "immaterial" sign of wealth.

Technocracy had two distinct faces and two moments of prominence. On the one hand it was the personal vehicle of Howard Scott, and on the other it was a serious effort to take account of the social, economic, and political consequences of industrialization. The second face was represented by the economist Thorstein Veblen and the Columbia professor of engineering Walter Rautenstrauch. Other notable proponents of Technocracy (as opposed to founders and theoreticians) were the wealthy man of leisure and writer Harold Loeb and the accountant Stuart Chase. The latter's *Tragedy of Waste* was published in 1925, midway between the two periods of prominence for Technocracy. Loeb was the executive director of Rautenstrauch's Continental Committee on Technocracy for a number of years in the 1930s.

Like Douglas, Scott had an obscure past. Both men presented themselves as engineers, though neither had academic credentials. Scott, however, had the instincts of a demagogue, as Douglas manifestly did not. Rautenstrauch organized research groups; Scott organized paramilitary gangs—not unlike Mussolini's Brownshirts—and staged mass rallies. Technocracy is sometimes seen as an American version of fascism, but it never engaged in organized violence and was contemporaneous with overtly fascist movements in the United States (Elsner 211). Henry Elsner Jr.'s characterization of the incompatibility of Technocracy and fascism is instructive in the light of Pound's inability to accommodate his Social Credit inclinations with his admiration for Mussolini's Fascist state. And it might account for his ultimate disaffection with Technocracy:

> The Fascist, typically, is the little guy caught up in an increasingly organized society which threatens his status, power, and income; he would,

if he could, return to the world of small business, the family farm, and private rather than corporate property, with marked income and status differences. But the technocratic future represents the most extreme extrapolation of the very urbanization-industrialization against which the Fascist reacts; it is a completely bureaucratized society, with equalitarian income, universalistic recruitment of elites, and no property rights apart from immediate personal possessions. (209)

The first Technocratic movement was founded by Scott and Thorstein Veblen in New York in 1919 and was called the Technical Alliance. A group of engineers, scientists, and technicians held meetings in Greenwich Village, where Scott was a well-known figure. Veblen had just moved from Chicago to New York to join the editorial staff of Scofield Thayer's journal, *The Dial*. His series of articles in *The Dial* formulated the basic principles of Technocracy. They were collected in 1921 as *The Engineer and the Price System*.

Pound's well-known association with *The Dial* began two years later when Scofield Thayer called on him in Paris in July 1921 (Stock 240). That contact led to the appearance of "Three Cantos" in *The Dial* for August 1921 and to Eliot's *The Waste Land* in the following year. However, there is no indication that Thayer spoke of Technocracy to Pound in 1921 or that Pound read Veblen's articles.

Like Social Credit, Technocracy petered out in the prosperity of the twenties, but was revived in 1932, when Walter Rautenstrauch formed the Continental Committee on Technocracy with Scott. The second time around Technocracy attracted a great deal of attention. *Time Magazine* declared it the "Fad of the Year" for 1932. However, Rautenstrauch became uncomfortable with Scott—who, by all appearances, was dishonest and incompetent—and split with him after Scott's disastrous speech, broadcast on national radio, from New York's Hotel Pierre on 13 January 1933. After his speech "criticism of Technocracy turned to ridicule" (Elsner 11–15). Scott founded a splinter group, Technocracy Inc., which maintains a marginal existence in the United States and Canada to the present time.

In his 1919 articles Veblen had argued that the real revolution of the twentieth century was technological, not social or political. He concluded that

a violent revolution by the oppressed and exploited is neither probable nor, if it occurred, could it succeed. In America, not only would a successful revolution not follow the Russian example, but it would "necessarily also be of a kind which has no close parallel in the history of revolutionary movements. Previous revolutions were military and political, but a twentieth-century American revolution would be industrial, technological."

212 / POUND IN PURGATORY

The material conditions of productive industry dictate strategy, tactics, and personnel. First, the overturn must not be violent or produce social disorganization—the industrial machine is too delicately balanced for that. Second, any revolutionary movement, to be successful, must be able to put into operation a plan for industrial functioning much more efficient than the businesslike reign of "lag leak, and friction." (Elsner 20; he is paraphrasing Veblen from *The Engineers and the Price System*)

Pound seems to have thought Technocracy challenged Social Credit's claim to priority, for he asserted in *Guide to Kulchur* that "in 1918 we knew in London that the problem of production was solved." He implies that Technology was politically naive because it failed to address the "crucial question . . . how and who was to beak down the ring of craft, of fraud, and of iron" (48). Elsner's paraphrase makes it clear that Veblen had considered how to effect a revolution, though he did not share Pound's paranoid belief in a conspiracy "of craft, of fraud, and of iron." Pound's comment reflects William Bird's assessment of the movement in his letter of 13 January 1933 cited in chapter 4 and betrays an ignorance of its actual tenets.

Like Veblen, Pound thought revolution on the Marxist model was both undesirable and unnecessary. But he was not much attracted to the idea of taking power from politicians and giving it to engineers and scientists, preferring Douglas's national dividend and Gesell's stamp scrip. In 1920 he praised Douglas because he was "for a free exercise of the will" and for his capacity to "arouse and rearouse one to a sense of how far we have given up our individual wills in all matters of economics." He quotes with approval Douglas's repetition of Belloc's distributist sentiments: "the danger which at the moment threatens individual liberty far more than any extension of individual enterprise is the Servile State" ("Probari Ratio" 445).

Pound's somewhat inconsistent combination of liberal individualism with the politics of the strong man was by no means rare in the thirties, when so many saw their individual welfare threatened by impersonal and global economic forces. Pound harmonized these incompatible principles through his confidence in the persuasive power of the artist. He seems to have believed that the power of art could transform a dictator like Mussolini into an economic reformer. He did not believe that the democratic masses could be so transformed. Of course, his influence over Mussolini turned out to be a chimera.

Just as Pound began to consolidate Social Credit and fascism in *Jefferson and/or Mussolini*, he was confronted with the rival of Technocracy. Shortly afterward, he learned of stamp scrip through the Wörgl experiment and then had to accommodate Roosevelt's New Deal. Initially Pound was enthusiastic about all three as potential allies in the struggle. However, Douglas and Orage would brook no such eclecticism. Of his economic associates, only Odon Por was similarly eclectic and pragmatic. It was Por who informed Pound of the reissue of Gesell's *Natural Economic Order* (Por to Pound, 22 Mar. 1935, Pound Papers). In the same letter he commented on the new book of the progressive historian Charles Beard, *The Open Door at Home*. Por described it as "influenced by technocratic and soc. credit literature"—though Beard was neither a Technocrat nor a Social Crediter. He was, however, isolationist and recommended autarchy for the United States, as Mussolini did for Italy.

In the next month Pound recommended Harold Loeb's Technocratic "Prosperity Chart" to E. S. Woodward: "Loeb prosperity chart may cover some of this. My personal feeling is that you Gesellites haven't or until recently hadn't given enough weight to facts underlying technocracy. The enormous potential productivity and steadily diminishing need of work" (25 Apr. 1935, Pound Papers). But a month later he dismisses Beard in favor of a new discovery, *The Law of Civilization and Decay* by Brooks Adams: "Yer BEARD is a mere plod/ following Brooks Adams; whom we ALL ought to have read 40 years ago and DID NOT" (26 May [1935], Pound Papers).

By October, Por was seeking a publisher for an Italian edition of Loeb's *Chart of Plenty*. And Loeb visited Pound in Rapallo some time between October and December of that year. They had previously met and played tennis years earlier, presumably in the early twenties when Loeb was in Paris as editor of *Broom*. Pound encouraged Por to give Loeb's *Chart of Plenty* precedence over stamp scrip in his forthcoming article for the Vatican journal *Osservatore Romano*, apparently in the belief that Loeb's Technocracy and Social Credit were indistinguishable: "The Loeb Chart is the first governmental offer toward a CREDIT ACCOUNT as conceived by Douglas. This is MORE important really than stamp scrip FOR THE MOMENT. so make yr/ Osservatore article Ostensibly re/ scrip/ but WHANG IN the solid progress of soc. Credit ideas in U.S.A." (5 Jan. [1936], Pound Papers). In anticipation of the discussion of Pound's anti-Semitism in the next chapter, it is worth noting that at this date Pound was apparently indifferent to the fact that Loeb was Jewish.

Por not only thought that Technocracy and Social Credit were compatible but also found Technocracy's economic analysis superior to Social Credit's. He was particularly impressed by *The Plan of Plenty*, a fifteen-page pamphlet that had come out of the Continental Committee on Technocracy's First Continental Conference held at Bear Lake in Estes Park, Colorado (3–7 July 1933): "I got in the nick of time the *Report* (Official) on the

Plenty Survey—which I use for a basis of the articles—as this report—unlike Loeb's own book—gives very clear outlines of the solution. The report beats Douglas to a frazzle as far as analysis is concerned. Anyway I left an opening for discussion [of] S[ocial] C[redit] & Stamp Scrip" (13 Jan. 1936, Pound Papers). This is the last mention of Loeb or Technocracy in the correspondence between Pound and Por. There is no indication of why they dropped it, but it may have been simply because the movement gradually died out. The latest mention of Technocracy by Pound that I have found is in "How to Save Business," the third and last article he managed to place in *Esquire* in January 1936. In a rather eccentric survey of the economic reform movements of the day, Pound finds T. S. Eliot's "original sin," Technocracy, Upton Sinclair's EPIC movement, and Henry Ford wanting, and recommends Douglas, Gesell, and Mussolini.

Notes

1. Paul Carus (1852–1919) was the German-American editor of *The Monist*, an important philosophical journal based in La Salle, Illinois. Monism was a quasi-religious movement designed to succeed Christianity through an accommodation to other world religions. He was instrumental in organizing the World Council of Religions held in Chicago in 1893. I do not know why Pound singles him out.

2. There are no Scott publications from 1919. Pound may be thinking of the unpublished manifesto of 1919 that William Bird mentioned in his letter of 13 January 1933 cited in chapter 4. Or he may be attributing Thorstein Veblen's 1919 *Dial* articles on Technocracy to Scott.

CHAPTER 10

Arthur Kitson

Jefferson and/or Mussolini was finished, though not yet published, before
Pound heard of the Gesellite experiment in Wörgl and also before he had
read Arthur Kitson's *The Bankers' Conspiracy! Which Started the World Crisis*
(1933). When he did read it he was sufficiently impressed that he immediately wrote to Kitson, suggesting they collaborate (23 November 1933).[1]
He even mentioned Kitson along with Douglas and Gesell in his 19 February 1934 letter to Mussolini (Heymann 318). *The Bankers' Conspiracy* was
a reissue of Kitson's report to the Cunliffe Committee before which he
had appeared in January 1919 (this committee recommended Britain's
return to the gold standard—with disastrous results). He first published
it in 1919 as *A Criticism of the First Interim Report of the Committee on Currency
and Foreign Exchange.*

Kitson remembered Pound from his London years, remarking, "your
name is very familiar to me, and your articles [in the *New Age*] used to give
me a good deal of pleasure and amusement" (5 Dec. 1933, Pound Papers).
Pound's recollection was dimmer: "You are the man whose articles I remember as having been in the old New Age/ yes. But the physical image
I had in mind is someone else. I don't think we met at Orage's subterra-
nean and unpalatable teas in that g/d/ bun shop or upstairs at 38 Cursitor
St." ([9 Dec. 1933], Pound Papers). Kitson had not remembered that
Pound was a poet, guessing that he was "either a musician or musically
inclined" (7 May 1934, Pound Papers).

Pound's correspondence with Kitson follows a rather different pattern than the others we have examined. Kitson was twenty-five years Pound's senior and, more importantly, had been an economic radical for nearly fifty years when Pound first wrote to him. Indeed, Kitson regarded himself as an unacknowledged precursor of Douglas and Social Credit—and with good reason. He provided Pound with a perspective on Douglas and Social Credit that exposed their shortcomings from an alternative heretical position. William Bird and W. E. Woodward revealed their shortcomings from a more or less orthodox perspective, and E. S. Woodward from a Gesellite perspective. Kitson's complaint was different. He accused Douglas of deceitfully hiding his debt to Kitson's first book, *A Scientific Solution of the Money Question* (1895), and furthermore considered Douglas's economic analysis to be erroneous. Another difference is that Kitson was quite keen on Mussolini and Hitler—especially the latter's anti-Semitism—whereas Bird and the two Woodwards agreed with Orage and Douglas in dismissing Mussolini's Fascist regime as orthodox in its economic policies.

Like all of Pound's other economic correspondents, Kitson eventually lost patience with Pound, complaining that he could not make sense of Pound's economic arguments. The following is from the last letter Kitson wrote to Pound (no response has survived):

> I see your letters and articles in various papers from time to time. Frankly, I sometimes have great difficulty in comprehending your meaning. It has always been a wonder to me that some of our really great writers have so often written in terms or phraseology requiring an interpreter. For instance, most of Browning is to me utterly unintelligible. It may be that I am unusually thick-headed. All my life I have been engaged in work that necessitated plain writing and speaking so as to make the subjects with which I was dealing understandable to the least intelligent.
>
> Please pardon these few remarks which have been prompted after reading some of your effusions. (6 Aug. 1935, Pound Papers)

The last letter in the file is from Kitson to Pound's father, Homer Pound, dated 10 June 1936, about a year before Kitson died, in his seventy-seventh year. It is impossible to say how the correspondence would have developed if Kitson had lived longer, but for the period that it lasted Pound resisted all of Kitson's overtures to share his anti-Semitic paranoia. If Robert Casillo's belief that Pound's anti-Semitism was deep-rooted in his early upbringing was correct, we would expect Pound to have warmed to Kitson's paranoia, but he did not. Pound's silence on Kitson until after 1938, when he began to denounce the Jewish conspiracy, also suggests that those views developed later than this correspondence of 1933 to 1935. Pound's failure to mention Kitson in *Guide to Kulchur,* even though it was written in 1937, is particularly striking since Pound's list of economic radicals is by no means exclusively Social Credit. It includes Gesell, Fack, and Frederick Soddy (a follower of Kitson who gets five mentions in *Guide to Kulchur*), as well as the Social Crediters—Douglas, Orage, McNair Wilson (author of *Promise to Pay*), Peter Larranaga (a civil engineer and author of *Gold, Glut, and Government*), and Por. The American radio priest Father Coughlin and Vincent Vickers ("a country physician") round out the list (246). The *Guide to Kulchur* list contrasts interestingly with the one in the 1944 Money Pamphlet "America and the Second World War," in which the Social Crediters, the Gesellites, and Coughlin are all omitted in favor of Willis A. Overholser, Por, Brooks Adams, and Kitson (*Impact* 194–95). With the exception of Por, these authors are all conspiracy theorists.

As we will see in the next chapter, Kitson serves as a benchmark for Pound's descent into anti-Semitism. But here I want to consider Kitson's contribution to Pound's economic views. The most important is commodity banking, a Proudhonian idea that Pound first encountered in *The Bankers' Conspiracy*. Although Kitson displays his Proudhonian provenance quite generously, uncharacteristically Pound does not give Kitson credit. When he begins to tout the Monte dei Paschi as a model bank, he permits his readers to suppose that it exhibited Social Credit or Gesellite principles, though he does identify it as a commodity bank in "Social Credit: An Impact" (1935):

> You can issue valid money against any commodity (or against services) up to the amount people want. The commodity must be there; services must be available. . . .
> Two kinds of banks have existed: the Monte dei Paschi[2] and the devils. Banks differ in their intention. Two kinds of bank stand in history: banks built for beneficence, for reconstruction; and banks created to prey on the people. (*Impact* 146–47)

"Impact" reflects Kitson's stress on the importance of trade: "Prosperity comes of exchange; a high standard of living comes of exchange of goods; a monetary system, a banking system which sabotages exchanges, and impedes it, is evil. Its sustainers are enemies of the people" (152). The following lengthy citation from *The Banker's Conspiracy* indicates the degree to which Kitson's indictment of monetary and banking practices of the day conforms to Pound's own preoccupations and prejudices:

> Money is the life-blood of trade and commerce, and unless there is an ample supply to meet the growing demands of trade, enterprise is checked, trade is depressed and the public are unable to secure and to enjoy the abundance of the necessaries and good things of life which inventors and scientists have been able to provide. The eminent Oxford

scientist, Professor Frederick Soddy, states that the Gold Standard monetary system has wrecked a scientific age! Whereas modern science and inventions have harnessed the forces of Nature to man's control, so that an abundance of every form of wealth can be readily provided, the world's bankers have stepped in and placed a barrier between production and consumption. They have not been content to take their share of modern wealth production—great as it has been—but they have refused to allow the masses of mankind to receive theirs, and to participate in the wonderful results. In consequence, millions of pounds worth of products have been destroyed. Corn has been used for fuel. Coffee has been thrown into the sea. Fruit has been allowed to rot. Hundreds of tons of fish have been thrown overboard. In fact, the world's productive capacity has been slackened to a mere fraction of what it could have been, by the refusal of the bankers to furnish the public with enough tickets (which we call money) to enable the producing classes to distribute the wealth produced. (36–37)

Pound echoes Kitson's outrage at the destruction of produce in "Mug's Game?" a piece that he probably wrote in late 1934:

I suggest that instead of burning coffee, plowing fields under, etc. it wd. be more intelligent to issue MONEY AGAINST IT up to the amount people WANT.

Ethics, law, IF the government owns this miscalled "overproduction" up to the point of being able to order its DESTRUCTION, it owns it quite enough to issue orders for its delivery to blokes who can use it. (*Ezra Pound's Poetry and Prose* 6:244)

Since Kitson's importance to the development of Pound's economic, political, and racial views has not been recognized, he has attracted little attention from Pound scholars—or anyone else for that matter. Some details of his biography can be found in the essay "Concerning the Author and His Work" by an anonymous friend bundled together with his 1919 report to the Cunliffe Committee in *The Bankers' Conspiracy*—in addition to a foreword and conclusion by Kitson himself. No doubt the reissue in 1933 was prompted by the Macmillan Committee of 1930–33. Kitson was rather a nasty piece of work by this date, an anti-Semite and enthusiastic supporter of Hitler and the Nazis. As already noted, Pound was neither. Though Keynes did not consider Kitson prominent enough to include him in his rogue's gallery of economic heretics, Fisher does mention him in *Stable Money*. Fisher dismisses Kitson's "free money" proposal as ill-considered, but does give Kitson's report to the Cunliffe Committee a qualified endorsement: "Many of the criticisms made by Mr. Kitson were later sustained by actual developments, and the abandonment of the gold standard by England in 1931 was the final collapse of the theories upon which the Cunliffe Report was based" (278).

Kitson was an inventor and entrepreneur who made a fortune from the "Kitson Light," which he manufactured in plants all over the world prior to World War I. His firm lit the Trans-Siberian Railway as well as the railways of India, Austria, Hungary, Romania, and other countries (9). In addition he constructed many hundreds of miles of telephone lines in the United States. The anonymous "friend's" preface to *The Banker's Conspiracy* lists his accomplishments:

> He purchased the Daimler patents and business in America from the estate of William Steinway of New York, and organized the Daimler Motor Car industry before the name of Ford had been heard of. He erected the first incandescent electric plant in the City of Philadelphia, and in Atlantic City, New Jersey. He assisted Brush in his experiments in electric work, and at one time had charge of the laboratory of the Western Electric Manufacturing Co. in New York. He has received hundreds of patents for his many inventions in all branches of Engineering. (10)

However, by late 1933, Kitson's enterprises had been ruined, and he was an embittered man.

Pound first wrote to him not only because he had received *The Banker's Conspiracy* for review but also because he had heard that Kitson planned to start a journal. Kitson's reply was filled with a long account of the financial disasters he had suffered. He complained of his inability to get compensation for losses he suffered as a result of the war and portrayed himself as a target of discrimination because he had refused to profiteer on munitions works. He indignantly reported that he received £50 in damages, when he had claimed £50,000, and was forced to give up his business in 1926 at a loss of £200,000 (5 Dec. 1933, Pound Papers).

Kitson's economic views were formulated during the period of his commercial success and therefore are not likely to have been motivated by the embitterment he felt at his later economic ruin, which perhaps motivated his anti-Semitism. If he was anti-Semitic when he wrote *A Scientific Solution of the Money Question* (1895), he disguised those sentiments. However, he does accuse bankers of conspiring against common humanity in that work, revealing a tendency to conspiracy theory.

His principal objective in *A Scientific Solution* was to promote Proudhon's idea of commodity banking. However, he also cites both Ruskin and Marx frequently and approvingly. He claims that economists, bankers, and politicians misunderstand the nature of money and fail to appreciate the capabilities of scientific industrial capitalism:

There can be no question that the production of wealth during the past
century has been enormously in excess of any, within a similar period,
that the world has ever known. But with the production of wealth, economics has had comparatively little to do. The growth of production has
been due to invention, discovery, and the physical sciences. It is with the
distribution of wealth the science [of economics] is chiefly employed, and
it is in this particular where it has failed. In each country we find wealth
distributed amongst the so-called three factors [land, capital, and labor],
in rent, interest and wages, according to the laws governing these respec-
tive institutions. We find supply and demand governing the prices of all
commodities, even the factors themselves. Exchange is carried on by the
methods and rules approved by leading economists. Money is regarded
by merchants in the same light as the highest authority on finance regards it, and gold has become—thanks to economists and legislators—
the universal basis for currency. The doctrines of Malthus[3] are found to
work like a charm, and the man for whom capital has no employment
finds no plate set for him at nature's banquet. In our dealings with each
other we have imbibed the supreme principle of political economy—
selfishness, and the three cardinal virtues, abstention, deception and
avarice are universally practised. (27–28)

Kitson's perception that technological advance had abolished scarcity is
exactly the same as Douglas's, Kimball's, and the Technocrats'. His view
that a false theory of economics lies at the root of poverty and economic
hardship is underconsumptionist, whose double provenance in Proudhon
and Ruskin, Kitson acknowledges. Social Credit's provenance, we can now
see, is Kitsonian in important respects, though purged of Proudhon's
commodity banks.

The concluding remarks of *The Bankers' Conspiracy* are similar to those
in Dexter Kimball's *Industrial Economics,* written just before the crash.
Unlike Kimball, Kitson was writing from within the Great Depression, for
which he believed he had a solution:

There is but one remedy for the World Crisis, viz. an increase of the
money supplies—not in the banks—but in the pockets of the people,
enabling them to buy more goods. The present problem is not one of
production as it was a century ago. It is wholly one of consumption—
which depends upon an adequate supply and a proper distribution of
money.

The post-war period, ushered in an entirely new era, unlike any former
period in the world's history; a period in which man's inventive genius
has placed within mankind's reach boundless wealth, sufficient for every inhabitant of this planet to enjoy life without encroaching upon supplies needed by any of his fellows; a period in which Nature's powers have

been harnessed to machinery for furnishing all the necessaries and most of the so-called luxuries of life, thereby releasing man from the original curse. And yet amidst all this abundance, we are inundated with myriads of starving, ragged people all because our officials have not the intelligence to see that the old economic theories have become fallacies, the old monetary and banking systems unworkable, and that just as our productive methods to which we owe this Age of plenty have been revolutionized, so our entire economic system must be reorganized. (102)

Pound naturally warmed to this analysis, which tallied exactly with that of Douglas and Kimball.

The scantiness of Fisher's attention to Kitson in *Stable Money* may have had something to do with the tone of Kitson's letters. In a letter of 2 February 1934 Kitson told Pound that Hans R. L. Cohrssen (Fisher's coauthor) had recently asked him for copies of all his books to assist him with a book he was writing on the Fisher stabilization scheme, which Kitson had long ago condemned as silly. Though Kitson complied with the request, he told Pound that Fisher was "kept"—like all other academic economists—and that both Fisher and Keynes wrote what they knew to be false to keep their academic positions (5 Dec. 1933, Pound Papers). Pound displays exactly the same sort of paranoid distrust of academic economists in his polemical writing.

Kitson's claim that Douglas stole much from him is supported by the record. The A + B theorem can be found in *A Scientific Solution*, though not so labeled:

Orthodox economics recognizes three factors in production: labour, land, and capital; and their produce, wealth, is distributed not solely among these, but among other factors which social laws and customs have hitherto regarded as necessary participators in every economic system of distribution. . . . *By distributing wealth as rent and interest, a large proportion of produce is constantly dissipated; consumed without any equivalent being returned.* All that is not devoted to maintaining the three factors, all that does not go to improve labour, land and capital, is wastefully employed, is utilized unproductively, and no true science of economics can possibly countenance such a system, for it tends to the dissipation instead of the conservation of wealth.

Our present system actually taxes itself for its own existence. Thus capital demands interest for allowing itself to perform its natural function in the process of reproduction; likewise rent is demanded when land performs its natural function in production, and these burdens are thrown upon the other original factor, labour. Hence labour is actually punished for performing its duties, for maintaining life and producing happiness. (74–75; my emphasis)

Kitson told Pound that Douglas had concealed his substantial intellectual debt to him:

> I think it was in the year 1919 that Douglas was first heard of. He came to see me in the year 1920 and told me he had taken up the subject of Social Credit through reading my books and articles. I asked him how he came to misrepresent me in his first book so completely that he classified me with Oswald Stoll—who was a prominent advocate of the Gold Standard. Douglas declared he had made an error in this, but promised to rectify it in this next work. His rectification consisted in deleting the entire paragraph and ignoring my work and existence. Although he thanked me for having so generously put his name forward in my "TIMES" articles in 1920, and stated I had "restored his faith in human nature," his gratitude was shown in his refusing to mention me or my books in all his writings. (5 Dec. 1933, Pound Papers)

However, Douglas's national dividend is a very different remedy than Kitson's commodity banking or "free money"—and also less sensible.

Kitson's "free money" is equivalent to Proudhon's idea of "Mutual Banking." In Kitson's scheme firms would issue currency founded on the commodities they produce or the merchandise they sell:

> This system is a co-operative plan by which the members of a community organize themselves into a Mutual Banking Company, the business of which consists in issuing notes, or paper money upon goods which are pledged for its redemption. Every member of the company, providing he has acceptable goods and desires to monetize them agrees to accept its notes in payment for services and commodities. No regular rate of interest for borrowed money is exacted, but a charge just sufficient to defray the running expenses of the bank. In other words, there is no bank stock and therefore there are no dividends. (365–66)

Kitson believed that "free money" would have two desirable consequences. It would eliminate interest charges—reducing the cost of credit to the administrative costs of the lender—and it would ensure that a dynamic balance was maintained between productive capacity and purchasing power. Unlike Douglas, Kitson did not fear inflation, for as a true underconsumptionist, he rejected quantity theory as obviously at odds with the observable behavior of economies. Moreover, since there would be no "legal tender," no one would be obliged to accept any of the monies in circulation. "Inflated" currencies would simply not be accepted.

Pound scholiasts have not noticed that the Monte dei Paschi celebrated in cantos 42 to 44 is presented as a Proudhonian "mutual bank," nor that the commodity money of Thaddeus Pound, Pound's grandfather, is

Kitsonian rather than Douglasite or Gesellite. The issues of the Monte dei Paschi were grounded on the agricultural production of land owned by the corporation of Siena. In an *Esquire* article of 1935, Pound explains that "the credit of the Monte dei Paschi was based in the last analysis on the abundance of nature. It paid 5% on its shares, and lent at 5 1/2%. The overhead and administration charges were kept to a minimum and the profits above that went to public utility (hospitals and the like)" ("Mug's Game?" in *Ezra Pound's Poetry and Prose* 6:244).

In the same article, he tells the story of the commodity money issued by his grandfather: "Sixty-three years ago when the New York banks weren't helping Wisconsin, my grandfather issued his own money, with the inscription 'the Union Lumbering Co. of Chippewa Falls, Wisconsin will pay bearer in lumber or merchandise.' The money was good. It worked. It was never repudiated. Men cut down trees and got fed" (*Ezra Pound's Poetry and Prose* 6:243). Another article, also published in February, "Banking Beneficence and . . . ," makes the same observations, supporting my view that his reading of Kitson provoked his interest in commodity banking.[4]

Pound presumably knew of Thaddeus's commodity money from his childhood. The mention of it in "Indiscretions" (1920) does not assign it the importance it takes on after he has read Kitson: "Thadeus [*sic*] ascended into lumbering; had, that is, a store from which he ministered to the material needs of Scandinavians employed by him to thin out virgin forests of Wisconsin. Companies of this sort paid all or part of their wages in token coinage good only in the company's 'store'" (*Pavannes* 12). If anything, this account suggests exploitation more than economic innovation. The practice of paying wages in company tokens was common— and frequently exploitative—in the United States, as one of Pound's biographers has noted (Wilhelm, *American Roots* 20).

Pound does not mention his grandfather's program again until after his contact with Kitson, shortly after which he sent Mussolini one of his grandfather's Chippewa Falls certificates (25 May 1934, Heymann 321). Thereafter it was a leitmotif in his economic journalism. By his own account, he was unaware of his grandfather's interest in economic reform until 1928: "It was only when my father brought some old newspaper clippings to Rapallo in 1928 that I discovered that T. C. P. [Thaddeus C. Pound] had already in 1878 been writing about, or urging among his fellow Congressmen, the same essentials of monetary and statal economics that I am writing about today" ("A Visiting Card" in *Impact* 65).

Despite Pound's enthusiasm, neither the Chippewa Falls Lumbering Company certificates nor the Monte dei Paschi quite conforms to the model of a Proudhonian commodity or mutual bank. The latter would accept commodities from producers and issue credit or currency to the value of the merchandise. A fisherman would "deposit" fish and purchase whatever he needed with the credit he received. The "credit" would not be a loan, but receipts for goods delivered. In this way, there would always be an exact balance between goods on offer and purchasing power. Credit, in the sense of an advance, could be extended without interest charges and covered by the asynchronous nature of the supply and demand for various commodities according to seasonal variations and the like. Pound seems to have been ignorant of these niceties and adopted only the notion that currency and credit could be bottomed on commodities. The Monte dei Paschi, for example, charged 5 percent on loans, like any bank of discount.[5]

For some reason Pound disguised the provenance of the commodity money idea. Readers of "Mug's Game?" are left with the impression that Thaddeus Pound's commodity money and the Monte dei Paschi were applications of Gesellite rather than Proudhonian and Kitsonian principles, since only Gesell is mentioned in the article. This concealment of his source is very uncharacteristic of Pound, who is forever recommending authors no one else has heard of. Even when he adds Kitson to his list of authorities in the late thirties, he does not correct this oversight.

In the 1935 essay "Social Credit: An Impact," Gesell, Douglas, and the Monte dei Paschi are also featured without mention of Kitson or Proudhon. This essay surreptitiously reveals the degree to which he has changed course by his criticism of the term *fiat money:*

> Money is a form of agreement; it implies an agreed order. It implies an honesty and an ability.
> "Fiat money" is a poor term; it is camouflage made of half Latin. The old Este mandates were valid. "Give to" or "I promise," or "we promise to give to," is the correct reading of the inscription, whether spelled out or implied. (*Impact* 146)

In "The Depression Has Just Begun," Pound recommended that wages be paid in "fiat money, or 'jetons' such as France has used for small coin ever since the war. In France this money is not issued by the central government but by the chambers of commerce. It has no value outside the country" (*Ezra Pound's Poetry and Prose* 5:336). Pound refers repeatedly to the French "jetons" in his prose and correspondence of this period as an instance of the successful use of fiat money. Social Credit was fully committed to a fiat theory of money, as Pound very well knew. Douglas expressed the principle in a 1920 lecture, "The Mechanism of Consumer Control," quoted in chapter 1: "it is simply childish to say that a country has no money for social betterment, or for any other purpose, when it has the skill, the men and the material and plant to create that betterment. The banks or the Treasury can create the money in five minutes, and are doing it every day, and have been doing it for centuries" (78). For Douglas there is no need for any "bottoming" of currency on anything other than the productive capacity of the nation. He was opposed to Kitson's "free money" bottomed on commodities and committed to a state monopoly of both money and banking. In *Credit-Power and Democracy* (also 1920) Douglas explicitly rejects Kitson's scheme. If it were implemented, he says, "we should enter into the manufacturer's paradise and the consumer's purgatory—an era of constantly soaring prices and continuous depreciation of currency" (140).

No doubt because of the antipathy the two men had for one another, Pound did not push Kitson and Proudhon on Douglas and Orage as he did with his other "discoveries." Kitson is also mostly absent from the numerous articles, reviews, and letters that poured from Pound's typewriter. However, he must have been pushing Kitson on Orage, for Orage boasts that he got Kitson into the *New English Weekly* along with Pound's other hobby horses: "See how I think of everything—in due course. Not one of your pts [points] but is in today's issue—including mention of Kitson!" (13 Dec. 1933, Pound Papers). Except for a noncommittal mention in his memorial of Orage in the *New English Weekly,* Pound is silent on Kitson until the radio broadcasts of 1943, in which Kitson is invoked with some frequency. One can only speculate about the motivation for this uncharacteristic reticence. Perhaps it was because he knew of the long-standing hostility between Douglas and Kitson. Kitson's pro-German and anti-Semitic posture may also have given Pound pause prior to 1935. By 1943, when Kitson gets his due from Pound, neither of these factors was in play, since he had by then irretrievably lost his Social Credit allies and had thrown in his lot with the Axis powers, anti-Semitism and all.

There could hardly be two more opposite policies than those of Douglas and Kitson. The former gives enormous economic power to the state, and the latter makes the state a nonplayer in economic management. Kitson is, in this respect, a much purer free enterpriser than Douglas and is faithful to his anarchist provenance in Proudhon. Douglas's plan, as W. E. Woodward noted, could be carried out only in a totalitarian state. The Social Credit idea is to have the state monopolize the issue of credit and currency, thereby eliminating private banks and greatly enhancing the role of the state in the citizen's daily life. Kitson, by contrast, would permit any business or corporation to issue currency, thereby rendering loans or credit—and therefore banks—unnecessary and also much reducing the role of the state in the economy: "I claim that the money problem will be solved as soon as governments cease monopolizing and interfering with the currency. Repeal of all laws prohibiting and restricting the issuing of money, would call into existence numerous systems, competition among which would lead to the survival of the fittest, which is the natural solution of the banking and currency question" (*Scientific Solution* 367).

The Italian Bank Act of 1936, which Pound praises in "The Italian Bank Act" and in "A Civilising Force on the Move: The Bank Reform," nationalized the Italian banks and to that extent is more Douglasite than Kitsonian. But despite Pound's frequent reference to it as an instance of Fascist economic reform, in truth it was neither. Mussolini was forced to nationalize the banks because the system was on the verge of collapse (Clark 265). Though Pound admitted to Douglas that his understanding of the act was imperfect (4 Mar. [1936], Pound Papers), that did not stop him from praising it.

The 1935 essay "Social Credit: An Impact" manifests some discomfort with the discrepancy between commodity money and Social Credit as solutions to economic malaise, first recommending the latter, and then the former:

> You can issue sound money to express the will of the people, which amounts to saying that you can issue it against services wanted. You cannot issue sound money against land, or against anything undeliverable. You cannot issue sound money save against something wanted.
>
> The soundness of money is not limited to its being state money. Countless examples of valid private and valid local money exist. (*Impact* 149)

The list he gives of such private money includes the now ubiquitous, "my grandfather's money issued against 'lumber or merchandise.'" He compounds the confusion by explaining in a note that he is not advocating a return to private money—a recommendation that would be anathema for Social Crediters. But it is difficult to understand what he *is* advocating if it is not private money.

Knowing of the hostility between Kitson and Douglas, Pound confided to Kitson that he too was unable to persuade Douglas and Orage to take fascism seriously:

> For ten years Doug/ and A/R/O/. blind to fascist *economic* direction because it isnt tied to a few ang/sax political gadgets.
> Difference between you and C.H/D[ouglas]/ on p. 2 of yr/ letter possibly due to lack of DEFINITE LANGUAGE.
> Doug/ has spent ten years failing to understand that the public is an-algebraic. (30 Nov. 1933, Pound Papers)

But he was stung when Kitson contradicted Douglas's belief that "currency expansion without the control of prices means merely price-inflation" and attempts to defend Douglas's adherence to quantity theory *and* underconsumption at the same time:

> remove the "merely," or the "means merely" and the sentence is nearer sense.
> Surely currency expansion, *in se,* acting in a non-extant vacuum or world of theory, wd. tend to raise prices?
> I mean if one were only considering those two terms of the equation.
> But to say "it means merely" etc. seems to me (as to you) an error. (30 Nov. 1933)

Pound is mistaken. The fundamental insight of Kitson, Gesell, Fisher, and Keynes is that the total amount of money (including bank credit) in circulation sets a ceiling for economic activity. If an economy expands its provision of goods and services without at the same time expanding its money supply and/or the velocity of money, then prices must fall if the goods and services are to be exchanged. The fall of prices represents a rise in the value of money, and hence will "dampen down" economic activity since loans and other contracts have been entered into in cheaper dollars and must be fulfilled with more expensive ones. It was this phenomenon that produced the boom and bust cycle that the industrialized capitalist countries had experienced throughout the nineteenth century. The monetarists express this insight in the aphorism "money matters." Old quantity theorists, of course, did not believe that money mattered.

Kitson did not reply to Pound's misunderstanding, but in a letter of 2 February 1934, he comments on the same error appearing in a speech by Mussolini, who was reported to have said that he could not see how trade could be improved merely by printing money. Kitson points out that if new money is put in the pockets of people who will spend it, it will certainly stimulate trade. Such "stimulation of consumer demand" is entirely orthodox since the Keynesian revolution, but it was not in 1931. Pound, misled by Orage and Douglas, never understood that the underconsumptionist position they held entailed a rejection of equilibrium theory. They were all blinded by the faulty A + B theorem, which purportedly accounted for disequilibrium by erroneously supposing that interest payments were somehow withdrawn from the economy.

Since by the end of the twentieth century everyone has been socialized to the evils of inflation and public debt, something should be said about the postwar experience of the Atlantic community, which has shown how difficult it is to coordinate the growth of the money supply with growth in economic activity so as to maintain stable prices (or "stable money," as Fisher preferred to say) while maintaining full employment. For the first two postwar decades the Atlantic community suffered steady, though moderate, inflation accompanied by nearly full employment—though there was always an apparently irreducible unemployment rate—and unprecedented prosperity. There was no serious postwar slump as had been experienced after all previous major wars in the industrial age.

But inflation became a serious problem in the seventies and eighties, and the Atlantic community began to experience "stagflation"—significant inflation accompanied by low economic growth. Critics of Keynesianism do not always admit that the inflation of those decades was in part the result of the deliberate policy of Atlantic community governments to "monetize" the shock of the steep and sudden rise in energy prices orchestrated by the OPEC countries.[6] The label *stagflation* masked the orchestration of an enormous transfer of wealth from OECD countries to OPEC countries. At the same time the Atlantic community managed an imperfect recycling of that wealth back to themselves through the sale of assets, armaments, and luxury items to OPEC countries, while cooperatively cushioning the shock by inflating their currencies more or less in concert. At the end of the twentieth century we are in a phase in which the expansion of money is being deliberately curtailed in an effort to restore stability in prices (or—what is the same thing—in monetary values). The result is considerable unemployment in most Atlantic community nations.

The economic problems of the world in the nineties lie outside the scope of this study, but they have once again rendered economics a concern of the ordinary citizen. And Keynesians are now on the defensive in the face of the post-Keynesians, of whom the monetarist Milton Friedman is the most prominent. These days Keynesians are portrayed in the press much as Social Crediters were in the thirties—as dreamers who fail to acknowledge the harsh economic reality that their monetarist opponents wisely respect. Nonetheless, post-Keynesians accept the insights on the stimulative role of growth in the money supply common to Kitson, Gesell, Fisher, and Keynes. They know that "money matters," though they are inclined to preach scarcity and restraint much like their orthodox predecessors.

The point of disagreement between monetarists and Keynesians is primarily over the role of government in management of the economy. Keynesians believe that governments should play an active role in manipulating interest rates and the money supply so as to maintain full employment, while allowing the market to set other prices without government intervention. The monetarists counter that governments are incapable of exercising sufficient wisdom to achieve those goals, and in any case do not possess the necessary tools. Accordingly they recommend that the money supply should be expanded at an invariable rate and that "the market" be allowed to regulate interest rates and prices on that base. In other words, they are laissez-faire like Adam Smith and John Stuart Mill, whereas Keynes was an interventionist—the only feature he shared with the socialists. Like Douglas, Gesell, and Kitson, he believed that his policy prescriptions would save capitalism from the very real threat of socialism. In Keynes's case, the belief appears at this date to have been well-founded.

The Social Crediters and the Marxists were out of step with the movement of economics away from simple equilibrium theory and metallic money, in which Keynes was only the most successful and prominent player (for a discussion of this general tendency see Laidler). All modern economists agree that the value of money is based on a community's willingness to accept it and not on any inherent properties of gold, silver, or any other commodity. This is the very insight that was Douglas's point of departure, but he attempted to combine it with an adherence to simple equilibrium theory, rendering his analysis incoherent.

Marx had taken a different route. He accepted the orthodox position of simple quantity theory and also the Smith-Ricardo labor theory of value, a corollary of which was the intrinsic value of the precious metals as repositories of labor value. Whereas Douglas accounted for the shortfall in purchasing power by assigning it to interest charges, Marx assigned it to the capitalist's appropriation of surplus value as profit. Gesell, Proudhon, and Kitson took a third route and assigned the shortfall to the constraints on money supply caused by adherence to the gold standard and to the control of credit by the bankers. As we have seen, their analysis conforms more closely to current economic wisdom than either Marx's or Douglas's.

Marx and Douglas both assumed an inelastic or fixed money supply, which entailed the consequence that interest charges and/or profits must be appropriated from the wage and salary earners. Douglas believed that this appropriation created a structural shortfall in aggregate demand, rendering a nation unable to purchase its own output of goods and services. Marx was not an underconsumptionist; for him, the capitalist's profits were simply thefts from wage earners. Douglas imagined that interest charges were somehow withdrawn from the economy. He was obviously wrong in this belief, but he had no other way of accounting for underconsumption within equilibrium theory. His national dividend was designed to make good this nonexistent shortfall.

Pound was confronted with just this analysis of the Douglas scheme in his correspondence with the two Woodwards, as with Kitson, Fack, and

Hollis. Although shaken by W. E. Woodward's arguments coming on top of Kitson's, Pound stuck with Orage and Douglas and was unshakable when the same objections were later raised by E. S. Woodward, Fack, and Hollis. He accepted Douglas's belief that the national dividend could be calculated so as to just balance the shortfall in aggregate demand supposedly caused by interest charges, thereby avoiding inflation, even though the numbers proposed by Douglas and Pound himself were grotesquely excessive.

Pound's attempt to convert Kitson to his own eclectic brand of economic reform illustrates the shagginess of this position and his inability to adjust it to meet criticism. In a letter of 13 January 1934 (erroneously dated 1932), he sent Kitson three questions, as a kind of litmus test of economic literacy:

I. What is an auxiliary currency.

II. When money is rented, who shd/ pay the rent, the man who has the money when the rent falls due, or someone who hasn't.

III. What is the effect of every factory and every industry under the present system producing prices faster than it emits the power to buy? (Pound Papers)

The first two questions are Gesellite, though Gesell did not consider stamp scrip to be an auxiliary currency. Pound is following Fisher here. The second question construes Gesell's negative interest on stamp scrip as an interest charge, or rent. Only the holder of the bill is liable for that charge on the date it is due. The third is Douglasite. The phenomenon described is that predicted by the A + B theorem. The answer is "underconsumption," or surpluses of merchandise for sale. Kitson's response was diplomatically evasive, though he did judge the idea of stamp scrip to be "all right" (2 Feb. 1934, Pound Papers). He also suggested that Pound try his questions on Fisher or Keynes. (Oddly, he did not try them on W. E. Woodward, with whom he was corresponding at the same time.)

Pound fares better with his "Volitionist Economics" handbill. Kitson responded to it on 29 September 1934, agreeing with all the statements and adding that he had been preaching these doctrines for forty years. His agreement with the second statement is qualified by the requirement that purchasing power should be distributed only to those in need and not to such high rollers as the Rothschilds and the Rockefellers.

But Pound disagrees in his reply of 2 October 1934. He *would* distribute it to everyone:

Coming back to "all in need"// the number of billionaires is so small in relation to population/ and burocracy such a constant siphylis // HELL !! give the hogs their 100 quid/ it will cost less than bugocrats salaries it

means IMPARTIAL treatment. NEED is NOT a fixed sum ANYway/ a fool
NEEDS more money that I do. does he draw more dividend ??
I need less than an ass who is too stupid to cook.
A good cook NEEDS less than a bad one. (Pound Papers)

Pound's willingness to extend the national dividend even to the wealthy
Jewish Rothschilds contrasts strongly with the animosity that he later displays toward Jews generally and the Rothschilds in particular.

The letter in which Pound told Kitson that he would be mentioned in
a forthcoming canto has not survived, but Kitson thanked him for the
distinction in a letter of 6 August 1935. Kitson does not get a mention until
the Pisan section, however, where he is coupled with James Joyce as a visitor to Rapallo: "But Mr. Joyce requested sample menus from the leading
hotels / and Kitson had tinkered with lights on the Vetta" (canto 77/493).

It was probably the lights incident that Pound had intended to use earlier, for Kitson twice reminisced about it. His firm had installed streetlights
near Rapallo—at Porto Fino Kulm—sometime before 1914, and Kitson
recalls being feted at the grand opening of the illuminated road in a letter of 5 December 1933 and again, more extensively, on 7 May 1934.

Kitson is mentioned again in canto 97 (693):

> Pugno pro patria ["I fight for the nation"]. And
> degradations, depredations, degradations whatsodam
> of emperors, kings and whatsodam,
> Dukes et cetera have since been exceeded,
>   Kitson, Fenton & Tolstoi had observed this.
>   . . . .
> "Window-dressing" as Bryan admitted to Kitson.

The Bryan in question is William Jennings Bryan. Alec Marsh has located
the source for the last line in Jeffrey Mark's *The Modern Idolatry* (251n16).
Though Bryan is quoted as saying "symbol" rather than "window-dressing,"
there can be little doubt but that the following is the passage Pound is
recalling. Mark cites Kitson's testimony before the Macmillan Committee
on 15 May 1930 (the passage is marked in Pound's copy):

> I met Mr. Bryan, the nominee of the Democratic Party for the Presidency
> in 1896. Mr. Bryan came from Nebraska to Philadelphia to see me; we
> had two or three evenings conversation [*sic*]. I put this question to him:
> "Mr. Bryan, do you think that bimetallism is going to solve the economic
> problem?" He said: "No certainly not. Metallism is merely a symbol; the
> real fight is for control of the national credit. If McKinley wins, this country will be governed by the most unscrupulous set of speculators the world
> has ever known. If I win the Government will control its own credit."

So I joined Mr. Bryan. I spoke for him at hundreds of meetings. In fact,
I stumped the State of Pennsylvania on his behalf. (Mark 240)

Pound refers to this exchange—just as cryptically—in his broadcast of 19
June 1943: "Now I repeat to you, I go on repeating to you that when Bryan,
W. J. B. met Mr. Kitson, he said that the silver was ballyhood, to cover a
deeper issue? A more basic issue, namely control of the national credit"
(radio speech 99, Doob 345).

The following remark in "An Introduction to the Economic Nature of
the United States" (1944) indicates that Pound considered the anecdote
to be evidence of duplicity—or at least deceptive prudence—on the part
of Bryan. He has forgotten where he learned of it:

> The "free-silver" movement tried to oppose the interests of the silver
> owners to the gold interests, but did not go to the root. William Jennings
> Bryan headed this movement, and a few oldsters remember it even now.
> Once in a while an idealist plays up to the Silver men, or is started on his
> career by them. A Silverite, privately, will sometimes confess the truth as,
> in fact, Bryan confessed it to Kitson. At the moment I don't remember
> if Kitson published the details of the interview or communicated them
> in a personal letter to the undersigned. Though I have the impression
> that I have seen these details in print. Bryan, knowing that he was con-
> tinuing an honest tradition, or striving to do so, fought vigorously, tak-
> ing advantage of the means that were available to him. (*Selected Prose* 179)

Kitson also reminisced about the Bryan campaign of 1895 in a 10 June
1936 letter to Homer Pound, Ezra's father. The elder Pound was one of
those "few oldsters" who remembered the campaign. However, nothing
in that letter fits Pound's recollection. Kitson does recall Wharton Barker,
a Philadelphia banker, telling him that he had encouraged Bryan to go
to Washington after Bryan's defeat in the election and claim the presidency. Kitson says that Bryan refused for fear of precipitating a civil war.
He also alleges in this letter that McKinley, who won, was guilty of stuffing
ballot boxes.

As we have seen, Pound was largely silent on Kitson until his radio
speeches broadcast after the Badoglio overthrow of Mussolini on 25 July
1943, ten years after he first made contact with him. Kitson appears in the
broadcasts as a conspiracy theorist rather than as an economic reformer.
After speaking about inflation, gold, and war, maintaining that war is orchestrated by those who control money and gold in a 25 March 1943
broadcast, Pound turns to Kitson:

> The late Arthur Kitson spent a good deal of his life trying to educate the
> British and American publics along these lines. It is a pity that the press

of both these ineffable countries did not more potently aid Mr. Kitson. Mr. Kitson believed that process was due to deliberate design of the usurocrats, the financiers who govern and outrage the world by financial, or in plain terms, the usury system, and various methods of monopoly and the control of the currencies of the nations.

Mr. Kitson heaped up a good deal of evidence in support of his theory. No rebuttal of Kitson has been attempted, the enemies of mankind prefer darkness.

There is a considerable library of polemical writin' and a vast mass of official documents which support Mr. Kitson's views. (radio speech 70, Doob 259)

Pound's reticence about Kitson prior to Mussolini's fall and the founding of the Salò Republic in September 1943 is probably due to Social Credit hostility toward him. He may also have been offended by Kitson's overtly anti-Semitic conspiracy theory, but Douglas's views were much the same, and that did not discourage him from identifying himself with Douglas. Whatever the reason, when Pound shares Kitson's racial and conspiracy views, the reticence disappears.

Pound returns to Kitson in the radio speech of 30 March and cites *The Bankers' Conspiracy* on 6 April and once again in a typescript dated 1943 that was not broadcast. He also mentions Kitson in the Italian article "Oro e Lavoro" (1944), translated by John Drummond and published as *Gold and Work* by Peter Owen in 1952, then (with elisions) as "The Enemy Is Ignorance" in Stock's *Impact* (1960). In most of these occurrences, Kitson is linked with Willis A. Overholser, author of *A Short Review and Analysis of the History of Money in the United States.*

By the time of his radio broadcasts Pound was persuaded that World War II was an incident in the struggle against the Zionist plot for world domination: "War is the highest form of sabotage, the most atrocious form of sabotage. Usurers provoke wars to impose monopolies in their own interests, so that they can get the world by the throat" (*Impact* 104). Just after this remark—many versions of which can be found in his journalism of the period—Pound cites the "Hazard Circular" of 1862, a document alleging there was a plot to control American currency at the time of the Civil War. Pound found the document quoted in Overholser on page 45. He follows his citation with a remark—that Stock prudently removed from his reprint of *Gold and Work* in *Impact*—about the assassination of Lincoln, which he found in an anti-Semitic article by William Dudley Pelley, "The Mystery of the Civil War and Lincoln's Death."

According to Tim Redman, Pound summarized two of Kitson's works—*Industrial Depression* and *The Bankers' Conspiracy*—in *La Storia di un Reato,* a twenty-four-page booklet. The translation was done by Olga Rudge, but Redman thinks that Pound "oversaw" it. It was published on 12 May 1944 as the second volume of the Library of Political Culture. *L'America, Roosevelt e la Cause della Guerra Presente* was the first (Redman 252–53). I have not seen *La Storia di un Reato,* but I have read the Kitson books, both of which manifest Kitson's paranoia. The following remark from *Industrial Depression* is typical, except that it does not identify the conspirators as Jews: "The great conflict which has raged during the past sixty years, and still rages, is between private or vested interests on the one hand and public welfare on the other, and unfortunately, for humanity's sake, vested interests have, by means of privately-endowed schools and colleges and the Press, been able to inoculate into the public mind the grossest economic fallacies, whilst many of the hirelings of these interests who fill professorships write and teach doctrines which they know to be economically false" (5).

Kitson certainly contributed to Pound's fall into anti-Semitism, but he was not the initiating agency. I cannot determine if his early reticence about Kitson was caused by Social Credit antipathy for him or by Pound's distaste for Kitson's anti-Semitism and conspiracy theory views. However, it is clear that Pound took from Kitson the Proudhonian notion of commodity money—without acknowledgment—and rejected the conspiracy theory and anti-Semitism. When he does acknowledge Kitson, it is as one who exposes the Zionist plot for world domination.

Pound could not have been unaware of Kitson's anti-Semitism, for Kitson endorses *The Protocols of the Elders of Zion* in *The Bankers' Conspiracy:*

Ample warnings of the debt-slavery which the use of gold as the basis for money inflicts have been sounded from many quarters of late years; but the most effective statement is contained in the 20th Protocol of the Learned Elders of Zion, as translated by the late Victor E. Marsden, formerly correspondent of the *Morning Post.*

"You are aware that the gold standard has been the ruin of the States which adopted it, for it has not been able to satisfy the demands for money, the more so that we have removed gold from circulation as far as possible."

"Economic crises have been produced by us for the Gentiles by no other means than the withdrawal of money from circulation."

Here we have a deliberate admission of what is the policy of the leading international Jewish bankers—a policy which has been carried out in the United States and in France during the last few years.

In Protocol No. 22 occurs the following:

"In our hands is the greatest power of our day—gold." Considering that these Protocols were found in the British Museum eight years before the War, they may be regarded as absolutely prophetic, and are being carried out by the Money-Power in every particular. (40–41)

It is remarkable that Kitson still accepted *The Protocols* as authentic in 1933, for the document had been exposed as a forgery more than ten years earlier in a series of articles by Philip Graves appearing in the *London Times* on 16, 17, and 18 August 1921 (Cohn 71). Graves's articles were accompanied by an editorial recantation of the credence the *Times* had initially accorded *The Protocols* the year before (8 May 1920) in an editorial of astonishing credulity: "What are these 'Protocols'? Are they authentic? If so, what malevolent assembly concocted these plans, and gloated over their exposition? . . . Have we, by straining every fibre of our national body, escaped a 'Pax Germanica' only to fall into a 'Pax Judaica'?" (qtd. in Cohn 71).

Pound is not, in 1933, willing to accept, or even discuss, such views. Kitson wrote to him on 3 December 1933 in this spirit, alleging that *The Week* (a journal edited by Cockburn) was "being run by the Jews." Pound responded in an undated letter (probably of 9 December):

> No, I do NOT believe Cockburn is run by anybody. Started without cash/ was TIMES correspondent in Washington and got tired of BUNK.
>
> I have known him for some years// got a rich uncle from whom he does NOT take money etc... have also met the uncle.
>
> He [the uncle?] came down to Vienna to meet me some years ago. I thought / Bigod here is an exception. I have never met an Eng/man EXCEPT those who come back from the edge of the empire who ever knows a G/D/ thing. Then C's passport happened to fall open on the table, and I read "born in Pekin."
>
> He is a bit hysterical, and old europe in outlook but I imagine he was the first man in Eng/ to print news of Woergl (?? Correct me .. if this is an error.) [. . .]
>
> I think the yarn about jews/ is just the old game of trying to discredit anyone who is inconvenient.// (Pound Papers)

This response displays more anti-English than anti-Jewish prejudice. Despite having been exposed to Douglas's anti-Semitism for many years, Pound was, in 1933, little disposed to see a conspiring Jew behind every bush.

Kitson replied (12 December 1933) that he knew of the Wörgl experiment, having heard of it while attending a conference in Germany. He also praised Hitler and endorsed Nazi anti-Semitic policies, warning Pound that he was wrong to discount "the Jewish menace." And this was after Hitler had assumed dictatorial powers with the passage of the "Enabling Law" (24 March 1933), empowering him to rule by decree. The Nazis had held their first one-party election on 12 November 1933, just a month before Kitson's letter. They garnered 95.2 percent of the vote (Fischer 626–27). Of course, the violent tactics and anti-Semitism of the Nazis were known to everyone at this time, though the Nuremberg Race Laws were not proclaimed until 15 September 1934.

In the light of Kitson's insistence on the Jewish peril, Pound backed off a little: "I didn't mean to deny Hebe-peril. Merely I dont think they happen to be running Cockburn, or that he is particularly runnable" (14–17 Dec. 1933, Pound Papers). We may fault Pound for not taking offense at Kitson's anti-Semitism—as, for example, Woodward did at Douglas's milder anti-Semitism. But at the same time, it is obvious that he has not yet succumbed to the paranoia so apparent in the radio broadcasts and his later journalism.

His lack of interest in the supposition of a Jewish conspiracy was such that Pound made no response at all to *The Protocols*, which Kitson sent with his letter of 2 February 1934. Disappointed at Pound's silence Kitson wrote again on 13 February, asking if he had received the book. But Pound did not reply to this query either and never mentioned *The Protocols* in the surviving correspondence with Kitson—and it does not appear that letters from Pound on this subject are missing.

Pound had written to William Bird just a year earlier (March 1933) mocking Bird's suggestion that there was a Masonic conspiracy. He even picked out *The Protocols* as a prototypical unbelievable fantasy:

> Re/ masons/ yr/ tee/O/ry a bit too like the jew protocols// I find it difficult to bee:leev/ in these GRRREAT minds.
> Obviously ALL visible and whom have been met masons are DUMB.
> But considering the rare natr/ of intelligence of ANY kind, and how little one HAS MET, and how almost never anyone with more than a good half or quarter bean, functioning in ONE or two subjects/
> I find it harrd to beeleeve in the select circle of TITANS, [. . .] and all conducin and converging to ONE GREAT devilry.
> cf/ L/Valli's theories about secret conjurations of troubadours/ secret language of Dante///etc.[7]
> Jheez IF there were six intellectual titans; it WD. leak over somewhere.
> That amount of efficiency wd/ SHO somewhere// instead of which the higher you get the more god damn dumb and unsewn. (Bird Manuscripts)

Pound's sensible skepticism about *The Protocols* in 1933, and his failure to respond to the copy Kitson sent him a year later, are important pieces of evidence in dating Pound's developing anti-Semitism. It suggests that, to whatever degree he may have participated in the widespread bigotry toward Jews of the period, a clear change took place sometime after 1934. His attitude to *The Protocols* had come full circle by 1940 when he wrote to Por: "By way; have you ever read the Protocols; or have you as I was put off by rumour that they were fake/ DAMN dull, hideously written, but complete code, and absolute condensation of history of the U. S. A. for the past 50 years. as Hen Ford and Sideham [*sic*] said/ 'show an amazing knowledge.' Drum/ [John Drummond] has dug up source, in a pamphlet against Napoleon II [*sic*] pubd/ in the 1860s. The russian text a mere summary of the high spots" (11 Apr. 1940, Pound Papers). This remark contrasts sharply with his complete avoidance of Kitson's overtures six years earlier.

Sometime before this letter he had begun to indulge in crude anti-Semitic remarks in his journalism and to distort names so as to make them appear Jewish. Tim Redman (202) cites another letter to Por (1 July 1934) as evidence that Pound discriminates between usurers and Jews and rejects *The Protocols:*

> no use mere caccia al ebrainini. [chasing the little Jews] must chase the ebreiAZZI, the big buggars, Protocols provide for superficial antisemitism as part of plan to confuse the issues.
> Besides the swiss swine (dynasties) in Bunk of FRogs are NOT yidds/.[8]

But Pound does not maintain this distinction, and he was probably trying to mollify Por, who was not at all anti-Semitic and never responds to Pound's overtures on *The Protocols.*

Notes

1. The letter of 23 November has not survived, but Kitson replied on 27 November, thanking him for "your letter of the 23rd," and also thanking him for sending "my book for review to *Today.*" He goes on to doubt that either the *New Age* or the *New English Weekly* will review *The Bankers' Conspiracy.*

2. Pound's source for the Monte dei Paschi is not Kitson, but *Il Monte dei Paschi di Siena e le Aziende in Esso Riunite* (see Terrell 1:170). Cantos 42 and 43 are devoted to the Sienese bank (first published in Eliot's *Criterion* in April 1937).

3. Kitson has in mind Thomas Malthus's *Essay on the Principle of Population,* which concluded that population growth would always outstrip growth in food supply, making famine inevitable. This is the same Malthus that Keynes celebrates as a precursor of his own economic views. But Malthus's underconsumptionist views were expressed in private correspondence with Ricardo and not published until 1930.

4. He also sent W. E. Woodward a postcard (dated 26 February 1934) containing a photograph of a fifty-cent voucher from the Union Lumbering Co., Chippewa Falls, Wisconsin, with the inscription: "Will pay the bearer on demand Fifty Cents in Merchandise or Lumber signed A. E. Pound, secretary."

5. The Monte dei Paschi still thrives as a bank in Italy and has offices overseas. It was founded in 1472 by the city corporation of Siena as a pawn shop on the model of the Franciscan *monti di pietà,* making mostly short-term agricultural loans

on security. It was reorganized in 1624 as Il Monte dei Paschi, at which time it was granted the pasturelands (*paschi*) around the city as a base of income (T. Green 60, 63).

6. *Monetizing* means expanding the money supply, thereby cushioning the shock of the massive transfer of credit from OECD countries to OPEC countries.

Stanley Black cites the statistics: in 1974 the price of oil more than tripled (from U.S. $3 to $11 per barrel). OPEC revenues rose to $70 billion, raising OECD inflation by about two percentage points and amounting to about 2 percent of the OECD's collective GNP. Inflation rose from 5 percent to 14 percent and then fell back to 8 percent. Unemployment rose from 3.5 percent to 5.5 percent in the OECD countries.

In 1979–80 the price rose from $13 to $33, raising OPEC oil revenues to $180 billion, once again about 2 percent of the OECD's collective GNP. Inflation rose from 8 percent to about 13 percent and then fell back to 5 percent. Unemployment rose from 5 percent to 8.5 percent, falling to 8 percent in 1984 (Black 5).

7. For a discussion of Valli's secret history, see Surette "Cavalcanti."

8. Tim Redman cites both of the letters. He takes the former as evidence that Pound first read *The Protocols* in April 1940. He also notes that Pound's copy is unmarked, "showing," he says, "that he did not have a very high regard for the book" (202). He assigns the second letter the date 11 July 1940, though it is undated. Unfortunately for Redman's claim, in the radio speech of 9 March 1943 Pound quotes *The Protocols* with approval.

CHAPTER 11

The Jewish Conspiracy

We have now come to the point where it is possible to date Pound's descent into anti-Semitism and to expose its provenance. I would have preferred to have avoided an extended discussion of this topic because it is almost impossible to comment on it without causing offense. As I have suggested above, commentators tend to take one of two extreme positions: that since Pound was an anti-Semite, he and all his works should be shunned, or that his anti-Semitism was an "aberration" and did not infect his poetry. The first extreme position is adopted in a moderate form by Robert Casillo in *The Genealogy of Demons*. Casillo divides Pound's anti-Semitism into four stages of increasing virulence: first, "suburban prejudice" in 1885–1910; second, one characterized by overtly anti-Semitic remarks, 1910–20; third, an ambivalent but increasingly virulent stage, 1920–40; and finally, biological racism with "an unmistakable resemblance to the Nazi version" after 1940 (4–7).

Unhappily, my research tends to corroborate Casillo's assessment of the last two phases, though I think phase four begins in 1934, not 1940. But I do not accept Casillo's assumption that Pound's progression from mild to virulent racism was inevitable or even predictable. Though Pound's fall into anti-Semitism is undoubtedly related to his economic radicalism, he was an economic radical for nearly twenty years before he became an anti-Semite and conspiracy theorist. He remained in Casillo's "ambivalent" phase until 1934, when a number of factors set him on a course of "research" into the "Jewish problem." He could hardly have escaped Casillo's "ambivalent phase," given that so many of his fellow economic reformers were anti-Semitic, but he might well have resisted a descent into conspiracy theory and outright racism.

It is true, as Casillo argues, that Pound was not well protected from historicist fantasies of plots and conspiracies, but nonetheless he did not succumb to them promptly. And though we must accept Casillo's conclusion that Pound became a full-fledged anti-Semite, I think he is wrong to see Pound's anti-Semitism as biological racism. The evidence overwhelmingly supports the alternative view that his anti-Semitism was motivated by a belief in a Jewish conspiracy.

Douglas, Kitson, and the Nazis all accepted *The Protocols* and believed the Jews to be engaged in economic chicanery and conspiracy. Though Pound was repeatedly exposed to such sentiments at least from 1931, when he recontacted Douglas, he does not repeat them in print until 1936, and he does not endorse them in private correspondence until early 1934. In radio speech 119 he attributes his conversion to conspiracy theory to the reading of Willis A. Overholser's *A Short Review and Analysis of the History of Money in the United States.* But this cannot be accepted at face value because he did not read Overholser until 1938, and his overtly anti-Semitic remarks begin to appear in his correspondence in 1934. Overholser certainly does "expose" a conspiracy to control the American state by bankers, but almost everything in Overholser is also found in Father Coughlin's *Money!* which Pound had read two years earlier. Nor can we attribute his turn to Mussolini's adoption of anti-Semitic policies, for the Italian racial laws were not enacted until July 1938.

It may seem fatuous to be so concerned with the date and provenance of Pound's adoption of such an abhorrent prejudice as anti-Semitism. But they are crucial questions if we are to address the common defense that Pound's anti-Semitism was an "aberration" that did not infect his poetry. An influential example of this apologetics is found in Noel Stock's 1970 biography: "I do not think that he was always right, either in his facts or his ideas, nor does he appear always to have been consistent; but a study of his sayings on the subject during the 1930s shows that he made conscious efforts to be fair, only lapsing occasionally when some item of news or gossip touched off an explosion of anger" (370). Such a defense disregards the evolution of Pound's anti-Semitism. What Stock says is perhaps true of Pound's attitude in the early and mid-1930s, but it is not true after 1940, when "lapses" are replaced by persistent and uncompromising virulence. Stock's position has been largely abandoned by Pound scholars in favor of Burton Hatlen's argument that the provenance of Pound's fascism and anti-Semitism was American populism. But that does not stand up to scrutiny either. To get the story right, we must look at it as a *story*, as a set of events unfolding in time. Since the evidence is that Pound's attitude toward Jews as well as his economic opinions altered over time, as one would expect, it makes sense to look for the causes of those changes in the vicinity of their manifestation, rather than in his early life and opinions. After all Pound was an omnivorous reader and—alas—an intellectual sponge.

It is also inadequate and misleading to describe Pound's position simply as anti-Semitism without distinguishing between simple racism and conspiracy theory. Such a blurring permits apologists to cite passages like the following as evidence that he was not anti-Semitic: "International usury is not entirely Jewish, but the evil done by the Jewish elements in international bleeding is enough to explain hatred of Jewry ten times over. Nevertheless international usury contains more Calvinism, protestant sectarianism, than Judaism. Philosophically, the two forms of this monetary gangrene are pretty much the same" ("Infamy of Taxes" in *Ezra Pound's Poetry and Prose* 7:333). Such disclaimers are the stock-in-trade of anti-Semitic conspiracy theorists. I think Pound is perfectly sincere in what he says, but the concession that some gentiles are involved in the conspiracy offers little solace to European Jews confronted by racial laws, deportation, and gas chambers.

Though Pound's anti-Semitism is not based on racial hatred, in his most virulent phases he adopts the rhetoric of the Nazis' biological racism. However, he had no horror of contact with Jews. He played tennis with Harold Loeb in Paris and welcomed him in Rapallo. He similarly extended hospitality to Louis Zukofsky in Rapallo and accepted his hospitality in New York. He also carried on a long and amiable correspondence with Zukofsky, who told Charles Norman: "I never felt the least trace of anti-Semitism in his presence. Nothing he ever said to me made me feel the embarrassment I always have for the 'Goy' in whom a residue of antagonism to 'Jew' remains" (Norman 363). Pound's friendship with Zukofsky is often cited as evidence that he was not anti-Semitic, but it only demonstrates that he had no personal phobia about Jews, either on racial or cultural grounds. However, Pound scholars have not noticed that it was his Jewish friend Zukofsky who inadvertently set Pound on the fatal course of an investigation of "the Jewish problem."

Pound and Zukofsky began to correspond in 1927. Until May 1934 the correspondence was literary and personal. But sometime before May, Zukofsky had sent Pound the 10 February 1934 issue of *Liberation,* a journal of the Christian party and the Silvershirts of America. It contained "The Mystery of the Civil War and Lincoln's Death," an article by the founder and editor, William Dudley Pelley. Pelley wrote: "According to Bismarck, the awful Civil War in America was fomented by a Jewish Conspiracy, and Abraham Lincoln, the hero and national saint of the United States, was killed by the same Hidden Hand which killed six Romanov czars, ten kings, and scores of ministers only to bleed nations" (Ahearn 159).

Zukofsky had sent Pound the journal as a demonstration of the excesses of anticommunism and anti-Semitism in the United States at that time. But Pound's response was the reverse of what was desired:

> This here bolSHAVik bizniz looks a bit phonier effery day [. . .] and Mr. Pelley's dope about Bizmark sounds all right.
> Wit is this Xtn. [Christian] Economics?
> I spose Mr. Pelley will be annoyed wiff me fer askin if all bankers is jooz? Just like Moike [Mike Gold] iz. [. . .]
> But as light on the American mind, I am deelighted wiff the paper. [. . .]
> Anyhow Pelley is a stout felly. & obv. Onnerstans the murkn mind. (Ahearn 158–59)

With two exceptions, this is the earliest occurrence of overtly anti-Semitic remarks I have found in Pound's correspondence or publications. The exceptions are widely separated. The first is found in the 1912 *New Age* series, "Patria Mia," and the second is in a 1926 letter to Richard Aldington discussed below. The "Patria Mia" remark was removed from the 1950 collection also called *Patria Mia*. It is offensive, but not unusual for the period. He identifies the Jew as an exception to the effect that Frederick Jackson Turner had famously claimed the New World environment has had on the American character, remarking: "The Jew alone can retain his detestable qualities, despite climatic conditions" (*Ezra Pound's Poetry and Prose* 1:78; William Chace first drew attention to this passage; see 7).

It seems reasonable to conclude that Zukofsky unwittingly set Pound on the course of anti-Semitism and conspiracy theory by sending him *Liberation* early in 1934. Pound was so impressed with Pelley's article that he took out a subscription to *Liberation*. From this point on, the "Jewish problem" becomes a frequent topic in his correspondence and journalism.

Zukofsky was a saint in his relationship with Pound and refused to take offense at Pound's remarks, though he did disagree. Pound—with spectacular insensitivity—treated Zukofsky as a useful interlocutor for his "research" on the "Jewish problem." Their relationship was truly remarkable. Nineteen years Pound's junior and the son of Orthodox parents, Zukofsky was himself secularized and a Communist. The correspondence had begun in August 1927, when Zukofsky sent Pound some poems for *Exile,* and continued until March 1940, shortly before communications between Italy and the United States were interrupted by the American declaration of war. Zukofsky wrote Pound again in the 1950s, and after some delay, they once again took up a cordial, though infrequent, correspondence. He had visited Pound in Rapallo in the summer of 1933, and Pound visited him during his 1939 visit to the United States. Pound had received Zukofsky cordially at Rapallo; he dedicated *Guide to Kulchur* to Zukofsky and Basil Bunting; and he warmly accepted Zukofsky's invitation to stay with him in New York should he visit again.

In addition to suggesting that Pound had no personal phobia of Jews, their relationship reveals Pound's extraordinary insensitivity to the sensibilities of others—and also Zukofsky's equally extraordinary tolerance and generosity of spirit. Pound exploits Zukofsky as a friend who can help him in his "research" into the Jewish "problem" because as a Jew, he will have an insider's view of the issue. Since Pound believed the "problem" to be the Jewish conspiracy to impoverish and enslave all non-Jews, it is scarcely credible that he would ask Zukofsky to participate in his investigation of it. Basil Bunting came upon one of Pound's letters to Zukofsky containing anti-Semitic remarks and wrote indignantly to Pound (18 Dec. 1938, Pound Papers), berating him for the stupidity and viciousness of his anti-Semitism and for his insensitivity toward Zukofsky.

In the letter of 10 July 1938 in which he asked Zukofsky's permission to dedicate *Guide to Kulchur* to him (along with Basil Bunting), Pound also asks,

> wotter you know bout Khazars?[1] Bloke has just writ me that "only a small percentage of jews are semites." "Khazars converted between 200 and 1000 de notre ere"
> wot abaht it?
> Neat alibi fer blokes who don't wanna be responsible fer Mike Gold's mentality/ and would eggs/plain a lot.
> Do you pussnly favour being a sem/ or a Tartar? (Ahearn 194–95)

Zukofsky's reply is mild, but firm. He accepts the dedication and then responds to the Khazar business: "But how, why, shd. I know about Khazars, & why shd. they bother you? Are you sure your correspondent ain't kiddin you and doesn't mean the Hebrew word Chazir (= swine)? [. . .] Maybe *Jewish Encyclopaedia* has a convenient article—I remember one on Chinese Jews. But 'pussnly' I don't give a damn whether I'm a Semite or a Tartar" (23 July 1938, Ahearn 195–96).

My claim that Pound's anti-Semitism was based on conspiracy theory rather than race hatred is in no way exculpatory. In his study of anti-

Semitism, Norman Cohn concludes that its core is not racism as is commonly thought, but the belief in a Jewish conspiracy, either because Jews are in the service of the Devil, as those in the Middle Ages tended to believe, or because they are plotting to control the world, as those in the nineteenth and twentieth century tended to believe. Once the distinction between racial, religious, and conspiracy-grounded anti-Semitism is made, defenses based on denials of racial or religious prejudice are rendered impertinent, and Pound's denials that he was anti-Semitic becomes something less than a bare-faced lie—though still a falsehood.

There is evidence that Pound *was* prejudiced against the Jewish religion before he encountered the Pelley "revelation." Pound told Richard Aldington in a 1926 letter that "the root of evil is the monotheistic idea, JEW. JEW and again jew," and condemns Christianity as well, remarking that "Xtianity really jew," lamenting that Christ failed to eradicate Judaism: "Ole J. C. tried to kill it, but all the objectionable features revived, or never died, racial curse too strong for the individual." I take his meaning to be not just that the Jewish people and their religion survived, but that Christianity itself remains Jewish. Though this is an isolated remark and suggests the persistence of a culture and religion he finds unattractive, rather than a conspiracy, it must be admitted that Pound had long been hostile to Christianity, which he regarded as the heir of Judaism.

But it is not clear what sense can be made of Pound's "racial curse," since Hebrew monotheism survived amongst the primarily gentile Christians. Even more oddly he goes on in the letter to speculate that Virgil must have been Jewish because he was monotheistic:

> Apart from Confucius and the Gk. and Latin (excluding that blithering pie-faced monotheist Virgilius Maro, who was probably born in Samaria, or of Nazarenes who had moved up to Mantua six weeks before his mother's miscarriage);
> apart from these things everything is apt to be tainted. I mean these things and the stuff of their lineage. (Pound to Richard Aldington, 4 Mar. 1926, Ezra Pound–Richard Aldington Correspondence)

Bizarre and anti-Semitic as these views are, they are kept out of his poetry and journalism and are rare even in his correspondence at this date. And, of course, they are not linked here—or elsewhere at this time—to either his economic views or a conspiracy to dominate the world.

Pound's antipathy for Judaism is really no greater at this date than his antipathy for Christianity. Moreover, it is motivated by his distaste for Hebrew monotheism rather than by Jewish usuriousness or subversive plotting. Pound's own religious faith was a quasi-Neoplatonic and pagan polytheism or immanentism—worship of "gods in the air" (see Surette *Light* and *Birth*). It is sufficient here to note that although his cultural views supported an anti-Semitic and anti-Christian posture, the chronology will not support the hypothesis that they led to his belief in a conspiracy—and it is that belief which is crucial to his virulent anti-Semitism.

The October 1934 exchange with Kitson over who should receive the national dividend demonstrates that Pound was not committed to a belief in the Jewish conspiracy at that date, even though the exchange took place seven months after Pound had read Pelley's article. However, Pelley's poison was doing its work, for Pound targets Jews two months later in a 1934 Christmas letter to Hugo Fack, another anti-Semite.

As we have seen, Pound first contacted Fack in September 1934 to complain of an article by E. S. Woodward in Fack's journal, *The Way Out*. Always on the lookout for allies, Pound enclosed his "Volitionist Economics" handbill. Fack was equally eager to recruit new people and took the occasion to suggest they work together in the cause of economic reform. Fack was acutely conscious of the conflicts between Gesellism and Social Credit, but hoped to convert Pound, and immediately forwarded a copy of part 2 of *The Natural Economic Order* (the part concerned with money). In a letter of 3 April 1935 he proposed an alliance between Social Crediters and Gesellites, which could bring on board Francis E. Townsend, Coughlin, and Huey Long. Pound agreed; he had already written to Coughlin in February and was also in correspondence with Huey Long, though not with Townsend. Pound and Fack exchanged several letters throughout the balance of the year and continued to correspond until the entry of the United States into the war interrupted mail service with Italy.

In the Christmas letter of 1934, Pound raised the question of Jews— and in a rather remarkable way: "What about JEWS Einstein is a god damn kike/ a goddamn coward. Wont anser my Volitionist 8/ tho' an editor who prints him, said he wd/ ask him to" (Pound Papers). Pound's irritation at the snub from the great physicist would be comical if it were not so offensive. Though Pound later attributes Jewishness to anyone with whom he disagrees, that behavior had not yet become habitual in 1934, nor had his use of racial slurs. He continues on the subject of Jews, asking Fack's opinion about Jewish participation in the abolition of slavery, the American Civil War, and economic reform. All of these interests are new for Pound and are derived from Pelley's article: "Re/ Jews, have never been antisemite, but things do rile me. Is there any trace of jews in abolitionist movement? I doubt it. They were all over the south foreclosing mortgages after 1865. No jews in any ECON refor/ or monetary reform. Only in class war/ exploitable by usurers/ jewish masochism and sadism." Though he is not yet openly speaking of a conspiracy, he is moving in that direction, alleging that the Jews boycotted the abolitionist movement in the United States, exploited the citizens of the South after their defeat, and shunned economic reform. The implication in the last sentence that Marxism (synecdochically invoked as "class war") is Jewish is standard amongst anti-Semites.

Although Pound continues to deny that he is anti-Semitic long after he has obviously succumbed, I am inclined to take his claim in this letter that he has never been anti-Semitic at face value. We have seen the evidence to support that claim. He did not respond in kind to Kitson's anti-Semitic overtures just a year earlier and seems not to have read *The Protocols* that Kitson sent him. But now he goes out of his way to invite Fack to expatiate on Jewish iniquity. This invitation is all the more damning since Pound would have known from the contents of Fack's journal, *The Way Out*, that he was anti-Semitic.

Certainly Fack was not coy about his anti-Semitism in his 9 January 1935 response to Pound's overture. He told Pound that he had belonged to "the anti-Semitic movement" twenty-five years earlier in Germany and had been introduced to Gesell in anti-Semitic circles. He prefaces his description of Jewish conspiratorial activities with the claim that he is free of race hatred, but then expounds standard conspiracy theory stuff, telling Pound that history cannot be understood without knowledge of the activity of the Jews. He also claims that Roosevelt was surrounded by Jews, and even that FDR himself was Jewish. In response to Pound's query about Jewish economic reformers, Fack tells him that Irving Fisher's collaborator, Hans R. L. Cohrssen, was a Jew.

Pound's reply to Fack's letter of 9 January reveals that he had begun actively to seek evidence of a Jewish conspiracy some months before: "J. Drummond, here for some months/ is giving most of his time to jew prob/ / They have made France into a shit heap" (Pound Papers). John Drummond was a young Englishman with whom Pound had been in correspondence since 1932. Their correspondence is almost entirely on literary questions and does not contain any anti-Semitic material at all. Very little is known about Drummond, but it would seem that he played a significant role in Pound's descent into anti-Semitism. The annotated copy of Nesta Webster's anti-Semitic book *World Revolution: The Plot against Civilization* in Pound's library at Brunnenberg belonged to Drummond.

The query in the same letter: "do you know WHERE Bismark [*sic*] wrote that Rotschild [*sic*] started U. S. civil war?" did not come from Drummond's research, but from the Pelley article that Zukofsky had sent him early in 1934. On the evidence of Pound's letter Drummond came to live in Rapallo sometime in 1934. It must have been later than 4 May, for Pound wrote to Drummond on that date (Paige 344). Once in Rapallo Drummond set to work on research into the "Jewish question." But we have no information to indicate whether it was at his own initiative or at Pound's request. The latter seems most likely, because we know from Pound's letter to Zukofsky of 10 February 1934 that he had taken out a subscription to the anti-Semitic journal *Liberation* months before Drummond came to Rapallo. What *is* clear is that Pound turned his attention to the "Jewish question" in the latter half of 1934 and that Drummond was probably acting as his research assistant on that subject.

There can be no doubt but that Drummond and Fack helped to push Pound toward conspiracy theory, but he had already been set on that course by the Pelley article, which he read before he began to correspond with Fack and before Drummond arrived in Rapallo. It was Pound, not Fack, who introduced the subject of Jews in their correspondence. And Pound's relationship with Fack was not such that he would have followed him in a direction he was not already inclined to go. For example, he was not persuaded by Fack's friendliness toward Keynes's *General Theory*. Nor did he accept Fack's criticism of the national dividend or of Douglas's price controls. And he was immune to Fack's lectures on his poor understanding of Gesellite principles—except that they aroused his ire, as did Fack's low opinion of Mussolini. Out of all these disagreements, it seems to have been Fack's sympathy for Keynes that Pound found most unacceptable. About the only thing Pound and Fack did agree on was the need to oppose the Jewish conspiracy to control and fleece the world.

They went on sparring over these disagreements for nearly seven years (1934 to 1941) without either one giving any ground. Pound clung to his understanding of stamp scrip, to Social Credit, and to Mussolini. A 1937 letter to Fack on plans to organize a conference gives a good indication of the prickliness of their relationship:

> What I am working for is a conference whereto I shd/ like you to be invited. BUT there wd. be no use in it for YOU in yr present state of fanaticism and IGNORANCE. The fanaticism is O. K. and your positive Gesellism is O. K.
>
> But you could NOT hold your own in a congress while eaten with superstition and failing to grasp what has been DONE. (22 Oct. 1937, Pound Papers)

The superstition Pound had in mind would seem to have been Fack's belief that Social Credit policies would lead to inflation. He went on to complain that Fack (and E. S. Woodward) was misinformed about fascism and Nazism, especially the recent Italian Bank Act: "I suspect neither you nor Woodward know the RELATION of his last bank balance quirk to the later provisions here. What you MEAN by fascism is something unpleasant but it is a BOGEY / Muss/ has kept Europe out of general war AND Hess and the better lot are now making headway in Germany. NO, this dont mean I want YOU to go nazi [*sic*]. I merely say that things are getting better and that distortion does no good." But Fack did not need much encouragement to "go Nazi." He was enthusiastic about Hitler and German expansionism in his letters to Pound even after the outbreak of war, and Pound responded in kind.

As late as October 1934 Pound's attitude to Hitler is cautious, if not hostile, in contrast to the obvious sympathy for Nazi Germany in the 1937 letter just cited:

> Re/ Germany. If the blighters would make ONE clear statement committing New Germany to honest economics; it wd. help. You and Hutchison both write me about nazi/ virtue/ and after Hitler's coup there was a mass of Italian sympathy/ effaced by the murder of Dolfuss/
> doubtless Comité des forges plotting all over the place/ but german finger in Austria seems clear/ (german agents of Bank of Paris Union, if you like)
> Schacht dont inspire any childlike confidence/
> naturally there is plenty of anti-hun propaganda. Hitler HAD a lot of sympathy after the clean up/ but NO economic declaration has followed, so far as I know. Will they DO anything/ re free economy??? (2 Oct. 1934, Pound Papers)

Pound is, of course, reflecting Italian distrust of the Germans, which was particularly acute after the Nazi-inspired assassination of the Austrian chancellor, Engelbert Dolfuss, the previous April. But he also complains that the policies of Hitler's finance minister, Hjalmar Schacht, are not in keeping with Social Credit prescriptions.

The earliest identification of the Jews as international bandits and conspirators in Pound's published prose that I have found is in the June 1938 article "Infamy of Taxes," more than four years after he read Pelley. He is still a bit shy about his anti-Semitism, lumping Jews with Calvinists and Quakers, even suggesting that the Christian usurers are more dangerous than the Jewish ones: "The Jew is excitable and given to excess. That is the sole reason there are any Aryan governments left on this planet. The Quaker usurer keeps his head. He is cold in the time of crisis, he does not break out into grand opera and rococo gilt furniture. He is more dangerous and deadly than the Jew, and you can't stir up mob violence against him so easily. Both lack the physical courage to risk their own pestilent skins" (*Ezra Pound's Poetry and Prose* 7:333). In the same piece, he refers to Hitler's denunciation of "international usury" in *Mein Kampf* and describes that infamous book as "a work of genius."

Clearly if Pound had held such views in 1933, he would not have reacted to Kitson's anti-Semitism and Bird's conspiracy theory as he did. Some radical change has taken place; neither the Douglasite economic views he had held for twenty years nor the Gesellite views he had held for nearly ten had prompted the change. From early 1933 Pound had corresponded with the anti-Semitic Kitson and organized concerts at Rapallo with the virulently anti-Semitic Gerhart Münch. No doubt these associations helped to draw him into conspiracy theory and race hatred, but their effect was slow and cumulative.

By late 1935 Pound's correspondence had begun to reflect a preoccupation with the "Jewish question." In a letter to Odon Por of August or September 1935 he observes that "so far as I know [there are] no Jewish Social Credit groups," but adds the mollifying remark, "the whole problem is irrelevant to our argument, and there is nothing in Soc. Cr. that wd. cause a segregation of groups according to race." However, he does not drop the matter there, and continues by quoting "a man who has held high office in Palestine." The man said to him "in the Piazza": "No, but antisemitism is something much more ugly than that." Pound explains that he means more dangerous than "ideology and abstract propaganda." We are left to guess what is more dangerous, but are surely expected to understand that it is a conspiracy. Pound continues with an tangential remark on lynching and pogroms: "I have never seen either a lynching or a pogrom but I observe that lynching is directed against an individual usually after a specific crime has been committed and pogroms against a group" (Pound Papers). Pogroms and lynchings, at least from an American perspective, share the feature that in both cases a mob murders individuals selected on the basis of race.

Por appears to have been free of any anti-Semitic sentiments. He tried for several months to get Pound interested in a friend's project to make a documentary movie about Pound. But the friend was a Jew, and Pound ignored Por's overtures. Nonetheless in 1935 Pound muses on racial theories in letters to Por, as he had not previously done. After going on about Jews and pogroms, he concludes, "Before giving my own theories on this subject I shd. greatly like to hear Dr Adler's." Alfred Adler is the psychoanalyst who broke with Freud in 1911 after formulating his own theories of the inferiority complex. Perhaps Pound imagines that some races suffer congenitally from such an ailment.

In addition to Pound's exposure to Pelley and Fack, there were political and military events pushing him toward anti-Semitism. One of them was the Spanish Civil War, which brought about a surge of anti-Semitism in Italy:

> The Communists, the Socialists, and the Liberals had proclaimed the Spanish Civil War to be a crusade against the spread of Fascism. The Nazis explained this all quite simply: Bolsheviks, Marxism, Liberalism, and democracy all were Jewish conspiracies. Mussolini had begun to believe that the most vociferous anti-Fascists in American, Britain, France, and elsewhere were Jews. Mussolini had only a small step to take from concluding that Jews were the enemies of Fascism to the Nazi position that the Jews were the enemies of mankind. (Cannistraro and Sullivan 499)

However, since the Spanish Civil War did not begin until July 1936, Pound was leading, not following, Italian opinion in his move toward anti-Semitism.

Although it does not speak directly to anti-Semitism or racism, Pound's rambling four-part series, "The Atrophy of the Leninists," in the *New English Weekly* (2, 9, 16, and 23 July 1936) announces his definitive break with communism. Until this date, Pound had attempted to broker a common front with Communists, socialists, Social Crediters, and Fascists against the forces of usury. Perhaps it was the Spanish Civil War, which pitted fascism against communism, that finally forced him to surrender this fantasy.

His abandonment of Marxism is an aspect of his fall into anti-Semitism and conspiracy theory. Jewish conspirators are seen to be in cahoots with Marxists in Sergei Nilus's work, which Pound owned and which offered the first publication in English of *The Protocols*.[2]

> Russia was the first victim of what proves to be a movement of an international character. Russia being used as the base of operations. . . .
> With the triumph of the Bolshevist revolution in Russia, a group of internationalists, most of whom were members of the Jewish race, seized the machinery of government and have held it ever since. (*Protocols* 1)

The introduction expresses a paranoia reminiscent of the anticommunist hysteria of the McCarthy era (which also targeted Jews): "The enemy is in our midst. In this country [the United States], as elsewhere, alien agitators who are either Bolshevists themselves or emissaries of the Bolsheviki have wormed their way into some of the loyal labor organizations or put themselves at the head of the Socialists or other radical political parties artificially stimulating social unrest and seeking to turn industrial strikes into political upheavals, leading to revolution and anarchy" (2). Pound had already encountered this kind of paranoia in Kitson, but had resisted it. Here is Kitson in *The Banker's Conspiracy*:

> Unfortunately, the safeguards of public freedom—publicity and the force of public opinion—are rapidly being controlled by the Money-Power. The

press of this country [the UK] is almost entirely in the hands of the banking interests, whilst the Cinema and the Radio are also similarly controlled. It is also known that questions regarding the policy and constitution of the Bank of England which affect the public welfare, are not allowed to be put in the House of Commons, by a recent ruling of the Speaker. (42)

Kitson left his readers in no doubt about who he thought "the banking interests" were:

The most disturbing feature of the present outlook, however, is that the experiences of the past few years have apparently taught our leading politicians and their advisers—the Treasury officials—nothing. We are again being threatened with a revival of the Gold Standard which has been our undoing on many occasions. The question arises: "were these policies recommended and adopted as part of a deliberate conspiracy to enable a group of international bankers to control the world's affairs, as outlined in the Protocols of the learned Elders of Zion? Or are they the result of sheer stupidity and crass ignorance?" (94)

Obviously Kitson thinks the answer to the first question is yes.

In "Gold and Work" (1944), Pound reflects views equivalent to Kitson's, including his identification of virtue with Mussolini and Hitler:

In fact, after the assassination of President Lincoln no serious measures against the usurocracy were attempted until the formation of the Rome-Berlin Axis. Italy's ambition to achieve economic liberty—the liberty of not getting into debt—provoked the unleashing of the ever-accused sanctions. [Pound is referring to the mild sanctions the League of Nations imposed on Italy as a punishment for its invasion of Ethiopia.]

But the great Italian publishing houses, more or less open accomplices of the perfidious Italian press, have not published the works of Brooks Adams and Arthur Kitson in which these facts are given. The press has been perfidious and the great publishing houses have been more or less conscious accomplices according to their capacity. One cannot hope to prevail against bad faith by making known the facts, but one might against ignorance. The publishers have received their information through certain channels; they have taken their tone from *The Times Literary Supplement* and from books distributed through Hachette and W.H. Smith & Son, or approved by the *Nouvelle Revue Française*. (*Selected Prose* 341)

Though Pound had resisted such views in his correspondence with Kitson in 1934, such resistance had disappeared by the time of his endorsement of *The Protocols* in a radio speech broadcast on 20 April 1943:

If or when one mentions the Protocols alleged to be of the Elders of Zion, one is frequently met with the reply: Oh, but they are a forgery.

Certainly they are a forgery, and that is the one proof we have of their authenticity. The Jews have worked with forged documents for the past 24 hundred years, namely ever since they have had any documents whatsoever.

This transparent doublethink contrasts strongly with the contempt for *The Protocols* he expressed in the 1933 letter to Bird. More disturbingly, it is essentially the same argument as Hitler's in *Mein Kampf:*

> The extent to which the whole existence of [the Jewish] people is based on a continual lie, is shown in an incomparable manner in the Protocols of the Elders of Zion, which the Jews hate so tremendously. The *Frankfurter Zeitung* is for ever moaning to the public that they are supposed to be based on a forgery; which is the surest proof that they are genuine. What many Jews do perhaps unconsciously is here consciously exposed. But that is what matters. It is a matter of indifference which Jewish brain produced these revelations. What matters is that they uncover, with really horrifying reliability, the nature and activity of the Jewish people, and expose them in their inner logic and their final aims. But reality provides the best commentary. Whoever examines the historical development of the last hundred years from the standpoint of this book will at once understand why the Jewish press makes such an uproar. For when once this book becomes generally familiar to a people, the Jewish menace can be regarded as already vanquished. (*Mein Kampf,* 11th ed. [Munich, 1942], 337, qtd. in Cohn 182)

By 1944, Pound was spouting the same vitriolic nonsense as Hitler had been since his imprisonment after the Munich beer hall putsch of 8–9 November 1923:

> And no one can qualify as historian of his half century without having examined the Protocols. Alleged, if you like, to have been translated from the Russian, from a manuscript to be consulted in the British Museum, where some such document may or may not exist.
> What we know for certain is that they were published two decades ago. That Lord Sydenham wrote a preface to them. That their content has been traced to another sketch said to have appeared in the eighteen forties. The interest in them does not lie in [the] question of their having been, or NOT been concocted by a legislative assembly of Rabbis, democratically elected, or secretly chosen by the Mysterious Order of Seven Branched Antlers of the Bowling Society of Milwaukee. Their interest lies in the type of mind, or the state of mind of their author. That was their interest for the psychologist the day they first appeared. And for the historian two decades later, when the program contained in them has so crushingly gone into effect up to a point, or down to a squalor. (radio speech 78, 20 Apr. 1943, Doob 283)

These ridiculous and offensive arguments are indistinguishable in style and substance from Hitler's rants. However inflexible and obtuse Pound may have been in his economic speculation, he never sank into such blind stupidity and hatred until he adopted conspiracy theory.

Hermann Rauschning reports a conversation with Hitler in which he scorns the evidence that *The Protocols* is a forgery, much as Pound does:

> "I have read the Protocols of the Elders of Zion—it simply appalled me. The stealthiness of the enemy, and his ubiquity! I saw at once that we must copy it—in our own way, of course. . . . It is in truth the critical battle for the fate of the world."
>
> "Don't you think," I objected, "that you are attributing rather too much importance to the Jews?"
>
> "No, no, no!" exclaimed Hitler. "It is impossible to exaggerate the formidable quality of the Jew as enemy."
>
> "But," I said, "the Protocols are a manifest forgery. . . . It is evident to me that they can't possibly be genuine." "Why not?" grunted Hitler. He did not care two straws, he said, whether the story was historically true. If it was not, its intrinsic truth was all the more convincing to him. (*Hitler Speaks* [London: T. Butterworth, 1939], 235–36, qtd. in Cohn 183)

Both men take the absurd position that even though *The Protocols* is spurious, the conspiracy it falsely documents does exist because events prove it.

The events that allegedly corroborate *The Protocols* are the alignments of World War II, which pitted Germany, Italy, and Japan against Britain, Canada, Australia, France, Russia, and the United States. Here is one expression by Pound of that view:

> Of that understanding, i.e., the understanding between various sets of international yidds. doing business simultaneously from various busnisch addresses located in different world capitals, the [though?] no longer in ALL the world capitals, there has never been any doubt. That is, not for the past 20 years or past 40 years, save in uninformed circles. It is the increasingly well lit nature of the understanding between the Jews who run Russia and the Jews now pullulating in positions of power in London and Washington, that helps the better type of American to understand both Mr. Churchill and Mr. Roosevelt, and the forces that have raised those highly undesirable specimens of inhumanity to the prominence they now enjoy, if enjoy is still the word. . . . In any case the Jewish proposal to make Roosevelt world emperor and to locate the New Jerusalem on the Isthmus of Panama, with NO checks and controls imposed on it, by even the angry Saxons, is an idea which ought to inspire the Countess of Oxford, and Mr. Crowther.[3] (radio speech 69, 21 Mar. 1943, Doob 257–58)

This analysis is much wilder, sillier, and nastier than his earlier belief that munitions manufacturers, bankers, and politicians—especially those of Britain and France—were acting in ways profitable to themselves and inimical to the general interest of humankind. Given the mess the democracies had gotten themselves into during the depression, that earlier view was not patently absurd, though Pound's growing conviction that the root cause was malice rather than economic incompetence and political timidity was surely paranoid. Though Pound's activities and propaganda of the early thirties demonstrate a lack of political perspicacity and a misplaced confidence in his own economic wisdom, prior to 1934 he is free of conspiracy theory, and prior to 1938 there are no anti-Semitic slurs or suggestions of a Jewish conspiracy in his published economic evangelism.

It may be that he was encouraged to publicly express anti-Semitism by Mussolini's passage of racial laws in July 1938 published as "The Manifesto of the Race" in the *Giornale d'Italia* on 14 July 1938. It included ten pseudoscientific propositions on race and declared that Italians were Aryans. Marriage or sexual intercourse between Jews and Aryans was prohibited, and Jews could not employ non-Jews (Cannistraro and Sullivan 511). Mussolini was well aware "that any notion of Italian racial purity was nonsense and that there was no Jewish peril. It was all a matter of politics, to please his new German partners" (Cannistraro and Sullivan 517). It may be that Mussolini's cynical adoption of Nazi racism pushed Pound into extreme and irrational anti-Semitism, but if it did, Pound had been well primed for it by Pelley and perhaps even more by the radio speeches of Coughlin and his book, *Money* which Pound read in 1936.

For some reason, Pound conceals his indebtedness to both Pelley and Coughlin on this score, preferring to attribute his discovery of the Jewish plot to Larranaga, Kitson, and Overholser in a radio speech of 1943 (which may not have been broadcast):

> Pete Larranaga, *Gold Glut and Government*, tells you something. Kitson a bad writer in many ways, piles up obstacles for the reader, possibly *knew* more than any of 'em. Even Woodward does NOT give the clue. He gives some clues but not the debt clue. In course of long desultory readin', the FIRST book I ever struck that would lead the student to an understandin' of the whole historical process in the U.S. was Overholser, in 64 pages, published by Honest Money Founders of Chicago, now I hear; at least they would know where to find it. (radio speech 119, 1943, Doob 406)

So far as I have been able to determine, Pound first read Overholser sometime in 1939, long after his "discovery" of the Jewish plot. He recommended the book to Odon Por in a letter of 31 August 1939 and mentions him in "Introductory Textbook,"[4] citing Lincoln, via Overholser

(*Selected Prose* 160). I have not found any reference to Overholser earlier than this. Wilhelm says that Overholser sent copies of his book to Por and Pound "in the fall of 1938," though he gives no source (Wilhelm, *Ezra Pound* 134). If he is correct, it took each of them nearly a year to get around to reading the book.

On the evidence of the correspondence with Zukofsky on Pelley and exchanges with Fack, Pound's claim that Overholser persuaded him of the Jewish conspiracy cannot be true. Pound may have been simply confused rather than duplicitous on this point. In his radio speech of 30 March 1943 (no. 72), he confused Kitson and Overholser, citing the latter but attributing the citation to Kitson:

> Kitson's *Bankers' Conspiracy* was written to show that extortioner Lloyd's little perception had become the base of a system. A regular practice among Rothschild's and the rest of the bleeders.
>
> The world was to be enslaved according to plan. Slavery consists in having to do uninteresting work, at another's bidding. The modern means of getting a man to work are lack of money, his lack of money, and debt. Mr. Kitson quoted Mr. Lindbergh's quotation of the now famous Hazard circular of 1862:
>
> "It will not do to allow the Greenback, as it is called, to circulate as money for any length of time, as we cannot control that. But we can control the bonds and through them the bank issues." (Doob 266)

In "Gold and Work" Pound says it is Overholser (not Kitson) who cites Lindbergh (*Selected Prose* 339). But he is wrong on both counts—perhaps because he was working on these speeches without access to his library. Overholser does cite the Hazard Circular on page 45, but not as quoted by Lindbergh, and he does mention Lindbergh's speech against the Aldrich bill (53), but not that Lindbergh cited the Hazard Circular.

The Lindbergh in question is Charles A. Lindbergh, the father of the famous aviator. The Aldrich bill, against which he spoke in Congress on 29 April 1913, was a bill to reform American banking laws. Lindbergh prints his speech in full in appendix A of *Banking and Currency and the Money Trust,* which was written in an effort to prevent the proposed banking reforms—reforms he thought iniquitous. Lindbergh *does* quote the Hazard Circular (290–91).

I have not found any evidence that Pound ever saw Lindbergh's book, which was privately printed and achieved scant circulation (Larson 233–34). I think he knew of it only through Overholser. But the Hazard Circular is also quoted in full in Coughlin's *Money!* which Pound did read—*before* he read Overholser. He praised it in a letter to Christopher Hollis of 12 November 1936, two years before he received Overholser's book.

Coughlin also mentions Lindbergh's opposition to the Aldrich bill (92), but he does not say that Lindbergh quoted the Hazard Circular.

Except for the preface to *The Bankers' Conspiracy*—in which neither Lindbergh nor the Hazard Circular is mentioned—all of Kitson's works predate Lindbergh's 1913 speech in Congress, and therefore could not be Pound's source. It is not surprising that Pound conflated Kitson and Overholser, for they present much the same message; it is less clear why he fails to mention Coughlin, whom he could scarcely have forgotten. It is unlikely that Pound had access to *Banking and Currency and the Money Trust* (1913) or Lindbergh's other book, *Why Is Your Country at War and What Happens to You after the War and Related Subjects* (1917), both of which are listed in *Money!* and described as "Out of print. Available in few libraries" (184). I have been unable to find any evidence that he saw them.

The Bankers' Conspiracy purports to expose a Jewish conspiracy for world domination and cites *The Protocols* frequently. Overholser is much more circumspect than Kitson, never mentioning *The Protocols* or Jews. However, any reader disposed to find Jewish plots would not be disappointed by Overholser. Most overtly, he cites the Hazard Circular and a conspiratorial correspondence of 1863 between the Rothschild brothers of London and the New York bank Ikleheimer, Morton, and Vandergould, which accompanied it (43–46). Coughlin cites exactly the same—no doubt apocryphal—correspondence (170–72), which reveals efforts by the Rothschilds to influence the revision of the National Banking Act being undertaken by Congress just after the American Civil War. According to Overholser, the act was revised on 3 June 1864 and 3 March 1865 much in the manner that the bankers wished.

The Hazard Circular was part of this alleged campaign by American and foreign banks to influence legislators and the public. The central issue was "greenbacks," government currency issued to finance the Civil War. In the United States, as in all countries at that time, paper money was not issued by the state, but by banks. State money was specie—gold and silver coins. Only the state issued coins, and only banks issued paper. Greenbacks represented a departure from this practice in that they were issued directly by the state. The New England colonies had experimented with state-issued paper before the Revolution, but the practice was stopped by imperial authorities. Its suppression was one of the grievances that lead to the rebellion. Among the radical aspects of the American Constitution was its provision for state paper. Coughlin, Overholser, and—following them— Pound recurrently insist on this constitutional privilege, which was exercised only once, and briefly, with the greenbacks.

The reason that the United States has never had government paper currency is traceable to Alexander Hamilton's distrust of the state, a distrust reinforced by the collapse in value of the continentals, issued by the colonies to finance the Revolution but not redeemed after 1783. Instead of issuing government paper, Hamilton imitated the British system and created a private bank to issue currency.

The First Bank of the United States was created in 1791 with a twenty-year charter to issue currency. When its charter ran out in 1811, there was a five-year gap between the First and Second Banks, during which several private banks issued currency. The Second Bank was formed in 1816, also with a twenty-year charter. In 1836 the United States reverted once again to multiple banknotes until the National Banking Act of 1862 put the system on a more structured regime. At all times, including the present, American currency has been issued by private banks. The United States is the last major nation whose currency is issued by private banks as opposed to a government bank.

The only two occasions on which the American state issued its own paper were during the Revolution (continentals) and during the Civil War (greenbacks). According to Overholser, on both occasions the banks—both domestic and foreign—conspired to cause these "experiments" to fail, since they allowed the government to meet its obligations when they exceeded revenues without borrowing from the banks. The Hazard Circular was allegedly distributed by European banks among American bankers in 1862 in a successful campaign to discredit the greenbacks. Overholser quotes from it as follows:

> Slavery is likely to be abolished by the war power and chattel slavery abolished. This I and my European friends are in favour of, for slavery is but the owning of labour and carries with it the care of the labourers while the European plan, led on by England, is that capital shall control land by controlling wages.
>
> The great debt that capitalists will see to it is made out of the war, must be used to control the volume of money. To accomplish this the bonds must be used as a banking basis.
>
> We are now waiting for the Secretary of the Treasury to make this recommendation to Congress.
>
> It will not do to allow the greenback, as it is called, to circulate as money any length of time, as we cannot control that. (45)

Neither Overholser nor Coughlin gives a source for the Hazard Circular, nor indeed for any of the other private correspondence each cites. All of this material has the flavor of the forged *Protocols*—an improbably frank admission of bad motives, disregard for public welfare, unrestrained greed, and a claim to surreptitious access to government. By the time of the radio broadcasts, Pound had ceased to express any skepticism about such canards.

Although the beginning of Pound's fall into anti-Semitism can be dated to his reading of Pelley in 1934, his first public expression of it does not occur until 1938—prior to the German invasion of Poland, but coinciding almost exactly with Mussolini's racial laws. "Symposium" manifests anti-Semitism through a disingenuous denial. Earlier than this there had been no need for a denial:

> I am not anti-semite, I am AGAINST the aryio-kike. The aryio-kike is filthiness of whatever racial compost; he has all vices which the anti-semite attributes to the Jew. It is all one to me, whether a man calls himself Vere de Vere or Szarwoodlesy, whether he is *renegado* to Moses or to the canonists. A monopolist is a louse. The monopolists of money are the lowest and largest variety of louse known to man, and no mercy is due to them. They are a filth, their sustainers are filth, and they corrupt everything they get their tentacles on to, from music to the whoring press of the big press owners. ("Symposium—I. Consegna" in *Ezra Pound's Poetry and Prose* 7:337–38)

A less persuasive denial of anti-Semitism is difficult to imagine. In the 1926 letter to Richard Aldington Pound had expressed a cultural anti-Semitism, much like that of the Catholic distributists G. K. Chesterton and Hilaire Belloc, though certainly not derived from them. "Symposium" represents a change from cultural prejudice to conspiracy theory.

Even though I am persuaded that Pound's anti-Semitism was not racially motivated, it is not possible to insulate him from racist views. He had imbibed a general theory of racial divergence from the German anthropologist Leo Frobenius long before he succumbed to conspiracy theory. He first encountered Frobenius's work in 1929 (Redman 84), but his application of the "Frobenian" view of race to political ideology is expressed for the first time in "Race," published in *New English Weekly* in October 1936 (*Ezra Pound's Poetry and Prose* 7:103–4). In it Pound argues that each nationality has a political expression proper to itself: "Communism is Muscovite, Socialism is German and embodies the worst defect of that race, democracy with representation divided in respect to geographic areas is Anglo-American, and the Corporate State is Latin." On these grounds, he judges socialism—allegedly a Slavic and Jewish political mode—to be inappropriate for the United States:

> There was never any talk of decline of parliamentary government until imitations of it were set up in countries whereto it was RACIALLY alien.
> There would be no talk of it now in America, had America not been

flooded first by German and then by Muscovite and Semitic populations. The support of racially alien trends in American politics need NOT give rise to religious furies, pogroms, or discrimination against any man because of religion or colour. (103)

This sort of racial nonsense is new in Pound's discourse at this time. It almost certainly derives from Frobenius, though Pound has adapted it to his own growing conspiracy view of world history.

Frobenius was a rather eccentric Frankfurt amateur anthropologist who enjoyed the patronage and personal financial support of Emperor Wilhelm II, whom he met "for thirty minutes on 16 December, 1912" (Jahn 8). He had no university appointment until he became a professor of ethnology at the University of Frankfurt in 1925, by which time he had already undertaken a half dozen expeditions to Africa as a private scholar. Frobenius was attracted to Nazism and shared some of Pound's methodological idiosyncrasies: "Frobenius did not have the slightest notion of scholarly conscientiousness, but instead possessed fantasy and intuition. Participating in experience, feeling his way into things, and searching for their soul—those were his recipes. And his own propaganda saw to it that they were swallowed by a section of the amazed world as a new scientific method" (Jahn 7).

Pound got the term *paideuma* from Frobenius. However, Janheinz Jahn, who is the closest thing in Germany to a Frobenian anthropologist, considers the idea of *paideuma* to be little better than a fantasy:

This paideuma defies not only human understanding, but also human taming. It is like fate, if not fate itself. It creates structures as it wants to and carries out "pendular movements." Sometime in the most remote past, the pendulum had swung from West to East, and now it was swinging the other way. In the Pacific it created a "highly mythological culture," then on the Asian continent a "highly religious one," then in Central Europe a "highly philosophical one," and finally in Western Europe a "materialistic culture." "In the Eastern Mediterranean it (the soul of culture) culminated in the liberal arts—among which one should also include Greek philosophy—in Rome it expressed itself through the formation of the idea of an imperialist state, in France through a social organization, and in England through the psychology of world economics." The reader who does not "feel along" (*mitfühlen*) but who thinks, realizes with consternation that one can just as easily feel opposite combinations: a highly philosophical Chinese culture, a highly mythological Mediterranean culture, etc. All and nothing can be summarized by such crude cliches. But man (if we disregard the master) is only the being who is *ergriffen*, emotionally gripped, the vehicle of the *paideuma*, which forces his role upon him like a fatality. The only thing that has influence on the paideuma is the environment: "The environment forms the paideuma." And "the paideuma creates races." (Jahn 14)

Like Frobenius, Pound asserts in "Race" that race determines behavior: "But to suppose that a difference of policy is due to a mere ideology or to mere reason, when it has roots in blood, bone and endocrines, is to take a very superficial view of society, humanity and human co-ordinations" (103). And he goes Frobenius one better by endorsing violence as a mode of political action: "The creators of darkness and obfuscators of the press can be damned or shot without any bitterness between one race and another" (103). At the end of the article Pound descends into bathos. Remembering that he is not Latin himself—even though a proponent of "Latin" fascism—he ludicrously attempts to rescue himself from this impasse by asserting that he is nonetheless "Latin to that extent even if I can prove no blood relationship, [as] to be disgusted with imbecility" (104).

Notes

1. I do not know who wrote to Pound about the Khazars. Arthur Koestler's *The Thirteenth Tribe* is perhaps the most accessible discussion of this hypothesis, though D. M. Dunlop's *The History of the Jewish Khazars* is more scholarly.

2. *The Protocols of the Elders of Zion* first became available in English in the translation of a book by Sergei Nilus, *It Is Near, at the Door: Concerning Something People Do Not Wish to Believe and Which Is So Near,* which appeared in 1917 (Cohn 67–68). Nilus printed *The Protocols* in an appendix. It was probably this edition that Kitson sent to Pound, but the version in Pound's library is a later American edition entitled *The Protocols and World Revolution.*

3. Earlier in the speech, Pound recommends that the British sell Australia to the Jews. The speech keys on the Countess of Oxford, who had said on the BBC that she had known "eleven P.M.'s from Gladstone . . . down to the present." Crowther was a writer for *The Economist,* which Pound identifies as "a Rothschild paper."

4. The date of this work is problematic. William Cookson assigns it the date 1938 in *Selected Prose* (159–60). However Gallup gives its first publication as *The Townsman* 2 (Apr. 1939). According to internal evidence it was written after 6 June 1938, for Pound mentions a speech by Jerry Voorhis in the House of Representatives on that date.

CHAPTER 12

From Rome to Washington

The title of this chapter is a little cryptic. The Rome in question is both the capital of Italy from which Pound broadcast his radio speeches and the seat of the Church of Rome, with which Pound attempted to forge an unlikely alliance in the midthirties. Washington, of course, is the capital of the United States, which Pound thought was in the hands of usurious usurpers, whom he imagined he could displace with the help of such figures as W. E. Woodward, Father Charles Coughlin, Huey Long, and Christopher Hollis. Washington is also the site of Pound's postwar incarceration in St. Elizabeths Mental Hospital under indictment for treason. Thus the journey from Rome to Washington is filled with ironies, errors, and a not a little pathos.

I believe that Father Charles Coughlin, known as the "radio priest," was the most important single influence pushing Pound toward conspiracy theory and anti-Semitism. But Coughlin has been entirely overlooked by Pound critics, including myself. Coughlin had begun broadcasting Sunday sermons from his church in Royal Oak, a suburb of Detroit, in 1926, only six years after the beginning of radio broadcasts in the United States. By 1930 "a shortwave hookup carried his voice around the world on station WCAU, Philadelphia" (Warren 34). It is not clear when Pound began listening to Coughlin's broadcasts. He did not have a radio of his own until 30 March 1940 (letter to Ronald Duncan, Paige 441), but he had been listening to shortwave broadcasts for at least five years before that. He praised Coughlin's January 1935 radio speeches in a letter to Por (1

March 1935), and he referred to Coughlin in a 28 March 1935 editorial in Senator Cutting's journal, *New Mexico*, in which he enjoins economic reformers to abandon Roosevelt and the New Deal in favor of Huey Long (the Kingfish) and Coughlin: "More chance of educating Kingfish and Coughlin, than of educating the 'left wing new stealers,' what difference between them and Upton [Sinclair]?" (Walkiewicz and Witemeyer 188). He mentions Coughlin with some frequency in his journalism for the next two years and then stops. Coughlin gets only three mentions in *Guide to Kulchur*—a work begun in March 1937 and in proof by January 1938— and none of the mentions is substantial.

In accordance with his usual practice after reading a book that interested him, Pound wrote to Coughlin in February 1935 after having read *Money!* Given that Coughlin received an enormous quantity of mail— eighty thousand letters in an average week, employing ninety-six clerks to handle it (Warren 34)—it is not surprising that his replies were only "routine letters of acknowledgment" as Redman describes them (162). It is highly unlikely that Coughlin himself read Pound's letters. In any case, Coughlin did not write *Money!* himself. It was ghostwritten for him by Gertrude Coogan, a disciple of Kitson and a virulent anti-Semite. The book sold well. Coughlin showed his character by refusing to share the royalties with Coogan (Warren 143).

Despite Coughlin's indifference, Pound praised him to E. S. Woodward as a "better politician than ANY of us" and told him that "everyone ought to read the four January broadcasts as POLITICAL education" (Mar. 1935, Pound Papers). He boosted Coughlin in several published pieces in 1935 and 1936, often alongside Huey Long (28 March and 17 August 1935 in Senator Cutting's Santa Fe newspaper, *New Mexico;* 11 April 1935 in the *New English Weekly;* and 14 March and 30 May 1936 in the *British-Italian Bulletin*).

After the September 1935 victory of Aberhart's Social Credit party in Alberta Pound wrote to Christopher Hollis attempting to broker an alliance between Aberhart and Coughlin:

> Aberhart probably wasted as premier. CANT just sit down in Alberta and wait for the bastards to attack. If there is a 60 to one chance of sweepin' Canady, AB/ ought to go to it.
> Coughlin born in Canada and he has a radio/ AB/ ought to APPEAL to pop Coughlin,
> sweep of Canada, as you have doubtless already observed wd. keep it NEWS and in fact the "peninsula" or rather dominion is a damn good place to win england. (31 Aug. 1936, Pound Papers)

He made the same suggestion to Coughlin himself: "For God's sake get to a radio and help our Canadian brethren. After the Alberta sweep the Dominion election COULD be swung" (29 Aug. 1935, qtd. in Redman 163).

As it happens, Coughlin did not need prompting to get in touch with Aberhart. They had already met in April 1934, and Aberhart had met Douglas and Coughlin together in Washington in May 1935. Douglas never mentions the meeting in the correspondence, and it seems not to have borne any fruit. Pound did know of it, for he cited the *New Age* report of the meeting in one of his futile letters to Mussolini (1 June 1934, qtd. in Heymann 322). Aberhart and Coughlin met one more time in September 1935, just after Aberhart's election (Warren 100), but Coughlin never did offer Aberhart any public support. Although a fellow Canadian and a pioneer radio preacher like Coughlin—he also began broadcasting in 1926—Aberhart was a Baptist and openly anti-Catholic. Hence it is not surprising that no collaboration ensued between him and Coughlin.

The failure of the Aberhart-Coughlin meeting was certainly not a consequence of any shyness on Coughlin's part about dabbling in politics. He had been an early champion of Roosevelt, speaking in his support at the 1932 Democratic convention that nominated him. His radio talks were almost exclusively on political and economic topics with scarcely any attention to standard homiletic topics. Coughlin grew impatient with Roosevelt's New Deal and formed the National Union for Social Justice in 1935, subsequently forming an alliance with Francis E. Townsend and Gerald L. K. Smith to form the Union party. Smith was a Fundamentalist preacher and the former bodyguard of Huey Long, who was assassinated in September 1935, the same month Aberhart was elected.

Townsend was a physician and founder of a national movement agitating for universal old age pensions, a social benefit that existed only in Germany at that time, having been introduced by Bismarck in the 1880s. The Townsend Plan was to give everyone over sixty a pension of $150 (later $200) a month on condition that the money be spent. The money would be raised by sales taxes. Townsend Clubs sprang up around the United States, and there was even a journal, the *Townsend National Weekly* (Warren 93). The Roosevelt administration eventually introduced Social Security largely in response to the Townsend movement.

Pound refers to the Townsend Plan in several pieces. He is very negative in his *New English Weekly* column "American Notes" written in February 1936 and before his alliance with Coughlin, but praises Townsend a few months later in "The Atrophy of the Leninists," written after Townsend had joined Coughlin and Smith to form the Union party, running William Lemke as presidential candidate in 1936. Coughlin would probably have been the candidate if he had not been ineligible as a Canadian who had migrated to the United States in 1926 at the age of thirty-three.[1] Coughlin nonetheless eclipsed Lemke in the campaign, but to no avail. Despite Coughlin's large radio following, Lemke garnered fewer than a million votes (Warren 93).

In the early years of the New Deal Coughlin was pleased to portray himself as an intimate of the president, and Roosevelt tolerated his pretensions largely because the priest's vigorous anticommunism helped deflect right-wing attacks on the New Deal (Warren 42–45). Though Coughlin was a dyed-in-the-wool anti-Semite from his youth, it was not immediately apparent that his anticommunism was sublimated anti-Semitism. It may have been that his attacks on banks were in fact coded attacks on Jews, but few took them that way, until his anti-Semitism became overt.[2]

Coughlin had revealed his conspiracy-based anti-Semitism in his testimony to the Fish Committee on Un-American Activities in 1930 (later chaired by Martin Dies and then, most infamously, by Joseph McCarthy), alleging that communism originated with Adam Weishaupt, a French Jew, and the eighteenth-century Illuminati. But he kept such inflammatory opinions out of his radio broadcasts in the early thirties.[3] Coughlin's biographer, Donald Warren, tells us that "the priest's private anti-Semitism persisted unmistakably, relentlessly and fanatically throughout his career" (132). In this he provides a clear contrast to Pound, whose private and public statements are devoid of reference to a Jewish conspiracy prior to his reading of Pelley in May 1934.

Prior to 1938, Coughlin attacked Communists, banks, and financiers in his radio sermons and his journal, *Social Justice,* without mentioning Jews—though anti-Semites in his audience no doubt understood that these groups were code for Jews. But *Money!*—published in 1936 under Coughlin's name—is manifestly anti-Semitic. And in 1938 he began to include overt anti-Semitic material in his radio sermons and journal. In *Social Justice* he printed a series on *The Protocols* that repeated the substance of a two-year series Henry Ford had run in the *Dearborn Independent* in the twenties. However, Ford had been persuaded to renounce that series; he publicly apologized for it in 1927. Coughlin's series purported to update *The Protocols* with new research by Casimir Palmer, even though Palmer himself wrote to Coughlin in 1938 to dissuade him from continuing the series and telling him that *The Protocols* was a clumsy forgery. Coughlin stubbornly maintained that the conspiracy existed even if *The Protocols* were a forgery (Warren 149–51)—just as we have seen Hitler and Pound arguing.

In 1935 when Pound began to listen to Coughlin he appeared to be a populist champion of the little man exploited by big business and the banks. Pound undoubtedly saw him as an potential ally in his fight for economic reform, because Coughlin's economic views were very close to his own. He recommended Coughlin to Odon Por in a letter of 1 March 1935 and to Douglas in August 1935. The next year he told Douglas, "COUGHLIN gets better and better/ 2 Feb. and 9 Feb. full of necessary primary INFORMATION, pile driving on which Soc Cr can be built and on which Wall St. cannot stand" (4 Mar. 1936, Pound Papers). However, neither Douglas nor Por expressed any interest in Coughlin. Indeed, Douglas never even mentions that he had met Coughlin with Aberhart in Washington in May 1935.

Pound was on his own in his enthusiasm for Coughlin, defending him in his "American Notes" column in April 1935 against charges of demagoguery and praising his increasing alienation from the New Deal:

> The cry of demagogy against either the Kingfish (Long) or against Father Coughlin don't hold if measured by the ballyhoo of their opponents. No cheaper ballyhoo than that of Johnson, Astor, Moley has ever ramped in America. . . . The Reverend Father with eight million enrolled in his league can very well stand on the defensive. He knows a great many of the facts, and no form of statement can be, in our time, stronger than a simple account of them. (*Ezra Pound's Poetry and Prose* 6:275. Johnson and Moley are probably General Hugh S. Johnson and Raymond Moley, both close confidants of FDR.)

The "facts" Coughlin "knew" at this time were the alleged infamy of the banks and Communist subversion in Mexico and the United States supposedly fueled by recent European immigrants (code for Jews fleeing Nazi persecution). Pound did not attack Jews directly in this article, but he did attack bankers and the Rothschilds and identified communism as a Jewish conspiracy—both new tendencies in his rhetoric. Coughlin constantly attacked banks and Communists in his radio sermons, but he was not yet openly targeting Jews.

It was only after the infamous pogrom of 9–10 November 1938, known as Kristallnacht, that Coughlin became overtly anti-Semitic in his radio broadcasts. As Warren puts it: "From Kristallnacht until the middle of 1942, Coughlin's radio addresses and *Social Justice* articles stressed two themes: that allies England and France had no democracy and no claim for moral superiority over Germany or Italy and that subversive forces within America—Jews in particular—were fomenting a campaign to entangle the United States in a war out of a selfish concern for the plight of Jews in Europe" (Warren 162). These themes are just those stressed by Pound in his radio speeches and his journalism of the late thirties and early forties.

Pound's direct comments on Coughlin do not mention the latter's anticommunism, anti-Semitism, or conspiracy theories, but portray him as an ally in the campaign for economic reform and a crusader for American neutrality in European conflicts, both of which he was. He lobbied successfully against a Roosevelt-sponsored bill of 1934 that would have brought the United States into the World Court at Geneva (Coughlin, *Series* 122–51). Pound agreed, congratulating the Senate for its negative vote in his "American Notes" column in February 1935 (*Ezra Pound's Poetry and Prose* 6:257). And a year later Pound cited a radio speech in which Coughlin supported Italy against the League of Nations sanctions imposed because of the invasion of Ethiopia: "Fifty one of them [nations] ganged up in the League of Nations on one side, against Italy alone on the other side" ("For a Decent Europe" in *Ezra Pound's Poetry and Prose* 7:33). A few months later in his article on the Italian Bank Act, "A Civilising Force on the Move," he once again praises Coughlin's isolationist stance and his economic views.

Pound stops mentioning Coughlin prior to 1938, when Coughlin began to display his anti-Semitism openly, even though, by that time, Pound was openly anti-Semitic himself. I have no better explanation for Pound's later silence on Coughlin than I have for his silence on Kitson. It may be that he disagreed with his economic views, which were no more compatible with Social Credit than were Kitson's.

As it happens, Coughlin's economic views derive indirectly from Kitson by way of Gertrude Coogan. She was the ghostwriter of *Money!* which was published in 1936 as part of the Union party campaign of that year. Warren says that Coughlin got most of his economic information from her. She came to his attention through *The Money Creators* (1935), a Kitsonian analysis of banking and currency. Kitson and his follower, Frederick Soddy, are frequently cited in *Money!* as is Coogan. In addition Coogan was anti-Semitic—described by her own brother as "the most violent and hysterical Jew-hater I have ever known" (Warren 142).

Pound owned a copy of *Money!* and had read at least some of it by October 1936, for he wrote to Wyndham Lewis on 29 October 1936: "Historians and educational apes did NOTHING to dig out real history, visible in quotations now being printed by Butchart, Buck and Coughlin (& Ez. P.)"

(Materer, *Pound/Lewis* 185). He wrote to Christopher Hollis a couple of weeks later: "You, Buck, me and even the back pages of Coughlin's 'Money' have collected several pages that OUGHT to go INTO the educational system" (12 Nov. [1936], Pound Papers). The "real history" of which he speaks is the Jewish conspiracy "exposed" by each of these writers.

The back pages of Coughlin's *Money!* contain the Hazard Circular and the letters from the Rothschilds that are also found in Overholser's *Banking and Currency and the Money Trust*—and a good deal more of the same nature. Coughlin and Coogan trace the conspiracy to the founding of the Bank of England in 1694, a historical turning point also stressed by Hollis in *Two Nations.* Among the documents in the back pages of *Money!* are the passages from John Adams, Abraham Lincoln, the Constitution of the United States, and George Washington that Pound quotes in "Introductory Textbook." In short, much of the anti-Semitic and conspiratorial material he cites in the radio speeches and elsewhere are found in *Money!* But Pound never credits Coughlin, in print or on the radio. Instead he attributes the citations to Kitson, Overholser, and Jerry Voorhis. However, the dates do not fit for Overholser or Voorhis. Pound did not know of them until 1938. And Kitson does not mention the Hazard Circular in anything I have seen. A possible source other than *Money!* is Jeffrey Mark's *The Modern Idolatry* (1934), which Pound owned. Mark prints "an excerpt from a circular issued by the American Banker's Association" in 1877, which is the same text Overholser cites as the Hazard Circular (238–39). This is the same book in which Bryan's remark to Kitson is found. The fact that Pound misattributes that anecdote suggests that Mark's book did not make a great impression on him. It seems plausible, then, to attribute the genesis of Pound's interest in such anti-Semitic texts to the back pages of *Money!*

It is most unusual for Pound to obscure the sources of his information. His motivation in this case is as obscure as it was with Kitson.[4] It is highly unlikely that he just forgot, for he recommended Coughlin to many of his correspondents in 1936 and engaged in an extended discussion of Coughlin with Christopher Hollis in that year.

Pound wrote Hollis after reading his economic history, *Two Nations* (1935). He first wrote in February 1936, when Hollis was teaching at Notre Dame in South Bend, Indiana. Like Coughlin and Coogan, Hollis regarded the foundation of the Bank of England as a watershed in economic history, marking the beginning of financial domination of the political process. The section from Paterson's 1694 charter for the Bank of England cited in canto 46 is found in Hollis's book, but not in Coughlin's or Overholser's:

Said Paterson:

Hath benefit of interest on all
the moneys which it, the bank, creates out of nothing.

(233)

Hollis regarded King William's surrender of the royal prerogative to issue money as a disaster for humankind: "By a strange anomaly private persons were to be permitted to invent that money and put it into circulation in the form of loans. Nor is it any paradox to say that that anomaly is the cause of the greater part of the evils that have since afflicted mankind. Had Charles' experiment succeeded, had it come to be recognized that, when new money was required, it was the business of the King to issue it, the whole history. . . of the world must necessarily have been changed" (19).

Oddly, Pound does not refer to this passage, either in his journalistic notice of Hollis, in his correspondence, or in the radio broadcasts, in which Hollis is mentioned three times, including Hollis's allegation that the Civil War was "wangled": "Read Christopher Hollis on the DEBTS of the South to the City of New York" (radio speech 111, 1941, Doob 388), a revelation he also includes in canto 46:

> Semi private inducement
> Said Mr RothSchild, hell knows which Roth-schild
> 1861, '64 or there sometime, "Very few people
> "Will understand this. Those who do will be occupied
> "Getting profits. The general public will probably not
> "See it's against their interest."

(233)

The citation attributed to Rothschild is found in *Money!* but not in Hollis's work (Carrol F. Terrell gives no source for it in *The Companion to the Cantos of Ezra Pound*). It is from a letter allegedly written by "the Rothschilds" to Messrs. Ikleheimer, Morton and Vandergould, No. 3 Wall St., New York, from London on 25 June 1863. The letter accompanied the infamous Hazard Circular. Coughlin cites it in appendix 5, "Quotations from Prominent Men": "The few who can understand the system," he says, "will either be so interested in its profits, or so dependent on its favours, that there will be no opposition from that class, while on the other hand, the great body of the people, mentally incapable of comprehending the tremendous advantages that capital derives from the system, will bear its burdens without complaint and perhaps without even suspecting that the system is inimical to their interests" (170–71). Pound actually misattributes the remark, for the "he" cited is not a Rothschild, but a "Mr. John Sherman," who, the Rothschilds say, "has written us from a town in Ohio, USA, as to the profits that may be made in the National Banking business under a recent act of your Congress" (170). Overholser prints exactly the same letter on page 45 of *A Short Review and Analysis of the History of Money in the United States,* but Pound did not have a copy of that until 1938, two years after the publication of canto 46, and Jeffrey Mark does not quote these sentences.

Coughlin's *Money!* is cited a second time in canto 46:

> Bismarck
> blamed american civil war on the jews;
> particularly on the Rothschild
>   One of whom remarked to Disraeli
>   that nations were fools to pay rent for their credit.
>   (240–41)

As we have seen, Bismarck's allegation is lifted from William Dudley Pelley's article. The Rothschild reference is from Coughlin and Coogan: "In 1844 Lord Beaconsfield (Benjamin D'Israeli [*sic*]) cited Lionel Rothschild as saying: 'Can anything be more absurd than that a nation should apply to an individual to maintain its credit and, with its credit, its existence as a state, and its comfort as a people'" (169). (Terrell does not identify either of these references.) Obviously Coughlin's *Money!* made a big impression on Pound, finishing the job that Pelley's article had begun in 1934.

Another indication that Coughlin's book played a crucial role in pushing Pound over the edge into anti-Semitic conspiracy theory is the fact that although *Eleven New Cantos* expose all sorts of financial chicanery, it does not target Jews as conspirators. It is true that canto 35 is overtly anti-Semitic, but Jews are portrayed there as commercial exploiters, not as plotters for world domination. Even his favorite target in later years, the Rothschilds, are mentioned only once (in canto 40) and are portrayed as competitors of J. Pierpont Morgan (in a passage cribbed from Lewis Corey's *The House of Morgan*) and not as conspirators. The section was published in October 1934, but cantos 34, 36, 37, and 38 were published separately, the latest—canto 36—appearing in April 1934. Thus they were all written before Pound could have heard Coughlin's broadcasts and before he read *Money!* But some of them were written after he had been in correspondence with Kitson and after he had read Pelley. If he had been persuaded by Kitson and Pelley, *Eleven New Cantos* would surely have reflected their conspiracy theories as *The Fifth Decad* manifestly does.

Canto 46, in which he announces his "discovery" of the conspiracy, was published in James Laughlin's *New Directions in Prose and Poetry* in 1936. The chronology strongly suggests that the cumulative pressure of the conspiracy-based anti-Semitism of Pelley, Fack, and Coughlin pushed Pound over the edge into conspiracy theory—before he read Overholser sometime in 1938, two years after he had begun to publicly express credence in the Jewish conspiracy. His reading of *Money!* however, coincides with the appearance of denunciations of Jewish conspirators and with his announcement in canto 46 of his discovery of the perpetrator of the "crime" of usury: "Seventeen / Years on this case, nineteen years, ninety years / On this case" (231).

In *A Light from Eleusis* I took this passage to be a reference to his reading of Hollis's *Two Nations*. I now realize that Hollis was only a small part of the revelation to which Pound refers, though the Paterson item is from Hollis's *Two Nations*. At that time I was totally unaware of Pound's indebtedness to Pelley, Fack, and Coughlin. Hollis is more circumspect than Pelley and Coughlin in *Two Nations,* but like them he targets Jews as controlling world events: "the battle between capitalism and communism, so far from being the eternal struggle of our race, was in reality little more than a family quarrel between two Jews for the divine right to deceive mankind—between the Dutch Jew Ricardo and the German Jew Marx. And before the menace of a real challenge to the system—the challenge that has come in our day from President Roosevelt—even the family quarrel is forgotten" (130–31). This is pretty inflammatory stuff, especially in 1935, two years after Chesterton had renounced such talk in the light of Nazi racial policies. On the other hand, Hollis portrays Disraeli as a hero in the fight against the "usurocracy"—his term for the capitalist system as organized through bank credit in *Two Nations*—and even drew the title from Disraeli's novel, *Sybil*. Also, in contrast to Pound, Hollis was still in 1935 a strong supporter of Roosevelt and the New Deal.

Another change in Pound's enthusiasms between 1936 and 1942 that has not been much noticed by Pound scholars is his turn toward the Catholic church. It is not entirely clear what motivated this sudden affection for an institution he had long reviled, but it seems to have been because he perceived the Catholic church as a foe of usury, a feature Hollis stresses in *The Two Nations*. However, Pound's admiration for Rome was relatively short-lived. He had been hostile to all forms of Christianity as monotheistic and Jewish prior to 1936, and he reverted to that position after the war.

The turn to Catholicism was motivated by two distinct factors, one religious or cultural, and the other economic. The religious motivation derives from Thaddeus Zielinski's study, *La Sybille* (1924), a book Pound had Ivan Stancioff translate and publish in Noel Stock's journal, *Edge,* in 1956.

Zielinski's thesis is that Catholic Christianity—with its trinity and canon of saints—retains the core of ancient pagan religions: "we must agree that the Greeks and hellenized Romans were prepared in advance to become the followers of Christ, while the Jews were not. Prepared—by what? Evidently, by their religion, since religion is the question at issue. Now the religion of Greek and Roman was exactly what we mean by Ancient Religion" (2). Robert Casillo discusses this book at some length, characterizing it, not unfairly, as anti-Semitic and speculating that Pound read it as early as 1927, though he found no references earlier than the radio broadcasts of the forties (Casillo 71–75). It seems unlikely that Pound read Zielinski that early, since he habitually mentions whatever he was currently reading in correspondence, and I have found no mention that early. The 1926 letter to Richard Aldington on monotheism is strong evidence that he had not at that time read Zielinski. It seems likely that he read him about the time he began his flirtation with the church, that is, in the late 1930s.

The earliest reference to Zielinski I have found is in a 1941 radio speech in which Pound summarizes Zielinski's argument in terms very close to the passage cited above: "[Zielinski] speaks of the psychologic preparation for Christianity that was there in the Greek and Roman religions, both the religion of Delphi, that is of the cult of Apollo and in that of Ceres Demeter, Mater Dolorosa, and in less degree in some of the more ———— ———— cults" (radio speech 120, Doob 410; Doob's elision). It seems likely that Zielinski persuaded him that the religion of amor—which he had traced to the Troubadours in his 1912 essay, "Psychology and Troubadours"—went all the way back to the Eleusinian rites. Though Zielinski does not give any special prominence to Eleusis, he does mention the rites of Demeter as one of the pagan cults that informs Christianity, and Pound picks up this detail in the passage cited.

However, our interest here is not in Pound's religious beliefs, but rather Zielinski's recuperation of Catholicism as pagan and non-Hebraic, features he celebrates in a radio broadcast: "Zielinski offers a fairly complete list of prototypes, of the essentially Catholic beliefs, I say essentially Catholic because they are quite patently NON-Jewish, and ANTI-Jewish, and they are specifically the features of Catholicism which Protestantism has wiped out" (radio speech 120, Doob 411). Pound's conclusion is worthy of Father Coughlin: "today we are faced by a new INTERNATIONAL empire, a new tyranny, that hates and bleeds the whole world. I refer to the empire of international usury, that knows no faith and no frontiers. It is called international finance, and the Jew and the Archbishop in London are at work for that tyranny, trying to draft a universal religion in defense of the infamy of the usurers" (411–12).

Pound began to praise the Catholic church early in 1936—some months before he publicly manifests a conspiracy version of anti-Semitism—in "The Church of Rome." He begins with praise for the Vatican's practice of political neutrality and then lauds the church for "more than any organised body before or since" having taken "pains to determine a hierarchy of values." He goes on to praise Aquinas, the just price, various papal bulls on social justice, and Salmasius's history of usury (though Salmasius was a Protestant). He concludes:

> There is to my Mind a profound agreement between Douglas and the canonists. Not because Douglas meant to reach an accord, or knew he had done so, but because both were seeking and both found the truth. There is almost nothing in the Church's economic teaching which the [Rupert] Beckett shops and Rothschilds can face.
>
> The kind of religion which Lenin, *with absolute justice*, called the opium of the people, is the antipodes of the kind of intellectual daring which Dante admired and praised, when he called one of the great theologians "*santo athleta*", an athlete of the spirit. (*Ezra Pound's Poetry and Prose* 7:37. Rupert Beckett was the banker father-in-law of Neville Chamberlain. The great theologian is St. Thomas Aquinas.)

Douglas agreed with him, writing on 3 April 1936—in rare praise of Pound's journalism—that his article gets a hundred percent from him.

Characteristically, Pound seized upon this opening to push Rome on Douglas, reporting that he had been in touch with Hollis and also that he had interested an archbishop in Social Credit: "Am writing him a little Catholic news/ My archbishop was here two days ago. Explained why Vatican officers can't rush out and drag the Howly ChuRRRch into local political shindys. Lamented the death three years ago [1933] of the one Cardinal who might have DONE something. This Eminence used to complain that you MUST GIT BACK to the JUST PRICE. Which he had found in Aquinas. No library here or I wd. trail it. Am asking Swabey to do so." Pound then goes on to repeat many of the same points he had made in the "Church of Rome" article:

> The Archivescovo took away S. Cr. With that quote from the Encyclical. [. . .]
> The CHURCH can back up our MORALS/ anything we do inside the VOCABULARY of the Church can be APPROVED; Get that?
> The increment of association is PARTAGGIO, AS PARTAGGIO the Church is ALL for it. All bank loans are USURA/ damn it all if 12% with no proportional risk is USURA/, 70% and 60% and 30% gouge from the damn frawgs ARE USURA. (25 Feb. [1936], Pound Papers)

But Douglas did not take the bait, and Pound was left to do what he could on his own.

The archbishop was Por's neighbor and landlord, lived a block from Por's house, and frequently discussed economics with Por (Por to Pound, 21 Dec. 1935, Pound Papers). He was probably Monsignor Pietro Pisan, titular Archbishop of Costanza of Scizia (Redman 93). Monsignor Pisan got Pound published in the Vatican journal *Osservatore Romano* and sent him "a rattling good book on JUST PRICE" (Pound to Por, May 1936, Pound Papers). Pound encouraged Por (in an undated letter of early 1936) to cultivate the archbishop: "move on to Madre Chiesa/ [Mother Church] at least show it to the Archivescovo; to indicate that I am not settin waitin. But am givin the old Whore of Babylon [a common designation of the Church of Rome by American fundamentalists] a run for her money, against the god damn PROTS. [Protestants]" (Pound Papers).

Though Pound had long admired Dante, it would be a mistake to take that as evidence of a pro-Catholic bent on his part. He did not regard Dante as a Catholic writer, but as a closet heretic, like the Provençal Troubadours, whom he believed to be adherents of the Albigensian heresy (see Surette *Light* and *Birth*). Now in 1935, in a sharp departure, he begins to stress Dante's Catholicism, names papal encyclicals as founts of economic wisdom, and contrasts Catholics with Protestants and with the Rothschilds. All of this is remarkable in light of his previous and subsequent anti-Catholicism. As late as "Terra Italica" (1932) Pound regarded the Catholic church as ossified, though his remark reflects Zielinski's argument that it preserved pagan pantheism: "the ancient wisdom seems to have disappeared when the mysteries entered the vain space of Christian theological discussion" (*Selected Prose* 57).

I think it unlikely that Pound made a habit of reading papal encyclicals, so I suspect he got his information about them from Coughlin's radio speeches, which did frequently cite them on social and economic questions. Coughlin also cited one of Pound's favorite sections of the American Constitution, article 1, section 8, part 5: "Congress shall have the power to coin money and regulate the value thereof; and of foreign coin" (twice on 9 December 1934 and once on 10 March 1935, when he also spoke of the founding of the Bank of England; *Series* 59, 63, 207). If Pound missed those speeches, he would have found the relevant section of the American Constitution in *Money!* (22). The passage became a shibboleth for Pound, but the earliest mention of it I have found is in "Introductory Textbook," written as early as June 1938, well after he had read *Money!*

In the January 1935 broadcasts (which Pound praises in the letter to Por cited above), Coughlin launched his New Union for Social Justice and espoused Kitson's commodity money principles. He also made a particular point of denouncing the infamy of the state borrowing money from the banks. The following is a sample of what Pound would have heard on his shortwave radio on 6 January 1935:

> The very heart and soul, the motor of the new deal is the money question. Unless their constitutional privilege is removed from the bankers; unless their purple fountain pens are emptied and it be legislated that it is as illegal for them to create money as it is for you and for me to counterfeit it; unless this Congress has the fortitude and the sagacity to reclaim for itself the right and the duty to coin and regulate our money, the new deal will remain a noble but unsuccessful experiment on the part of man to destroy the worst brand of slavery that was ever perpetrated. (*Series* 116)

A little later Coughlin characterizes Alexander Hamilton as "the younger spiritual brother of Machiavelli" and goes on to bring the French and Russian Revolutions into his story as still other manifestations of cynical conspiracy (118–19). Coughlin closed with a call to Roosevelt and the Congress to fulfill a "new mandate for social justice," the New Deal having failed (121). The intervening speeches have not been printed, but the 27 January speech, "The Menace of the World Court," is devoted to Coughlin's opposition to America's entry into the World Court.

The conformity between Coughlin's attitudes and targets in his radio speeches and those newly adopted by Pound at the time he was listening to Coughlin is far too great to be attributed to coincidence. Pound's sudden interest in forging an alliance with Catholics is a consequence of the radio priest's casting his evil spell over him. In pursuit of a Catholic alliance, Pound urged Por to support G. K. Chesterton: "G.K. Chesterton is in Italy or coming/ you and rob/ Monotti ought to get hold of him/ Monot cd. do interview/ and stress the points of AGREEMENT" (Apr. 1935, Pound Papers). And we saw that he complained to Por in a letter of 21 June 1936 about an unidentified person's article that failed to give Chesterton his due.

Pound's contact with Christopher Hollis represents his major effort to recruit a Catholic economic reformer. Hollis was a follower of G. K. Chesterton and, like him, a convert. Pound first wrote to him just a month before his pro-Catholic article in *Social Credit* that praised Hollis for having dug out "a beautiful case of usury factive at 210 per cent. in the USA after the Civil War" ("The Church of Rome" in *Ezra Pound's Poetry and Prose* 7:37). Further comments on Hollis's *Two Nations* are found in Pound's "American Notes" column in February 1936, though they are not entirely favorable.

Pound's first letter to Hollis raises the question of the church and monetary reform: "ONCE the Church is SEEN to be profoundly right on money and credit, the way is open to the FIRST serious attempt to bring the Church back into leadership of occidental thought. Leibniz was the last OUTSIDER of [*sic*] [who] seriously thought of this possibility. [Cardinal] Newman was a professional. Ergo carries no weight with the phrfans [*sic*]. Protestantism due to ignorance (on BOTH sides); Bossuet merely a Times leader writer" (25 Feb. 1936, Pound Papers). He mentions the archbishop and near the end of the letter asks, a propos of nothing in particular, "What, if any, are your relations with Coughlin?" It would appear that Pound hoped to cobble together an alliance of Catholic economic radicals in a quixotic effort to influence events in the United States—much like his equally absurd plan to take over Social Credit in Canada after Aberhart's electoral success.

Hollis was less keen on Coughlin than Pound was. He considered the radio priest "quite embarrassingly ignorant," quarrelsome, and untrustworthy as a scholar, though he conceded that he was "on the side of the angels" in his criticism of the status quo (10 Mar. 1936, Pound Papers). Nor did Hollis agree with Pound's belief that the Union party's Lemke had a chance of success in the 1936 presidential election, though he agreed with Pound that it would be positive if he made a "good showing" (Hollis to Pound, 3 Sept. 1936, Pound Papers).

Pound responded with praise of Coughlin: "I think Coughlin says a lot more than he did. I mean the first six broadcasts this year contained a very large amount of clear statement/ immense act of popular education" (20 Mar. 1936, Pound Papers). Hollis was not persuaded, though he concedes in a later letter that Coughlin was useful to Roosevelt in that he diverted public attention from the radical nature of Roosevelt's reforms by denouncing him for not adopting a more frontal assault. Hollis hoped New Deal reforms would eventually subvert the credit system in a roundabout way (4 Apr. 1936).

Lemke made a very poor showing, bitterly disappointing Pound, who was vain enough to imagine that his advice could have made a difference: "Coug[hlin]. and co. seem to have erred. Waal if they hadda listened to papa !! CONfound 'em" (Pound to Hollis, 16 Sept. [1936], Pound Papers). After the election fiasco Coughlin is given less attention in the correspondence. The last mention is on 24 April 1937, which seems to have been prompted by Pound's reading of *Money!* "Coughlin seems to me to be printing useful information. I suppose there is no communication across the line from your camp to his" (Pound Papers).

Hollis and Pound disagreed over Roosevelt's policies. Stuck in Douglas's commitment to simple quantity theory, Pound regarded the mildly stimulative polices of the New Deal—such as raising the price of gold to thirty-two dollars an ounce—as inflationary. He attacked both Hollis and the New Deal in "American Notes" in February 1936: "Mr. Hollis's 'Two Nations' is an addition to general culture but he suffers as all these gunners after stabilization; he hath that air of pocus and hocus, Radbertian transnomenclation [*sic*] when he tells us that prices were STABLE over a long period when prices were progressively lower and lower and lower if measured by METAL." (*Ezra Pound's Poetry and Prose* 7:25). He goes on to criticize Philip Le Bel, Henry VIII (following Salmasius), and Roosevelt for "the fraud of devaluation."

Hollis tried, to no avail, to explain that prices could not be measured solely against gold and silver:

> I cannot even yet follow your point why it mattered that prices were declining as measured by metal in the Middle Ages. If other goods are increasing with rapidity and gold and silver is not increasing at all, it seems to me inevitable, whatever your policy, that the value of a lump of silver in other goods will increase. So long as, in order to discharge a debt, you have always to pay the same amount of silver by weight that matters tremendously, but, so long as the amount of silver that you have to pay is altered as the ratio alters, I cannot see that it matters. (Hollis to Pound, 10 Mar. 1936)

Pound repeatedly invited Hollis to visit him in Rapallo, and Hollis accepted the invitations warmly, but they never met. Their correspondence has more personal warmth than most despite their fundamental disagreements about economics. In particular, Hollis was critical of Social Credit and—even worse—praised Keynes's *General Theory* when it came out early in 1936. As with W. E. Woodward, Pound exaggerated his independence from Social Credit in his correspondence with Hollis, but he was unable to dissemble his hostility toward Keynes. Writing on 20 March 1936, he admits that Keynes has come over to their side, but will not give him any credit, pretending that he has nothing new to offer: "That scamp Keynes has caved in. I introduced him to Doug/ years ago. Fack also comments on K's taking 15 years to admit plain truth of Gesell. I wonder if Butch's vol. Was the last NAIL. Swindle damn well up. U P UP, when the tradition staked out and printed" (Pound Papers). Hollis was much more sympathetic to Keynes, remarking in a letter of 3 September 1936, "Keynes very bien pensant these days" (Pound Papers). Pound could not let that pass: "Keynes 'bien pensant' from WHOSE pt/ of view. St Nitouche?! 'Gesell

in the catacombs.' I introduced him to Doug, as I told you, about 1920"
(7 Sept. 1936, Pound Papers).

However, they were both profoundly antiliberal in political ideology.
Hollis responded positively to both the "Volitionist Economics" handbill
and *Jefferson and/or Mussolini*. Hollis's only complaint about the latter was
that Jefferson was too liberal for his taste:

> I have read not only chapter XXX but all other chapters of Jefferson and/
> or Mussolini with the greatest interest—mostly with agreement, though
> I am inclined still to think that there is a bit of liberalistic wash about
> Jefferson which bars him out from the highest marks. I think that it was
> excusable, at the end of the 18th century not to see what frauds liberals
> were, but that does not alter the fact that, absolutely speaking, it was an
> error. I wrote about him in my American Heresy twelve years ago and,
> though many of the expressions were crude, I do not know that I would
> alter my essential thesis. (4 Apr. 1936, Pound Papers)

He evinced no similar cavils about Mussolini's tyrannical tendencies. Instead, in the same letter he praised Roosevelt for his skill in manipulating the citizenry so as to implement Fascist policies in the United States:
"His [Roosevelt's] notion that you can get the virtues of Fascism without
its inconveniences, if you have two parties that are essentially the same and
let the people amuse themselves by changing the personnel from time to
time. Greatly struck by a remark of Cecil Chesterton to the effect that party
politics will only work when both parties are the same." A few months later,
he assured Pound that he was not hostile to Mussolini: "Nor have I any
objection to Mussolini—very much to the contrary" (1 Aug. 1936, Pound
Papers).

The relationship with Hollis did not sour; it was just broken off by the
invasion of Poland. In later years, however, Hollis hid his association with
Pound, much as Pound hid his enthusiasm for Coughlin. In his autobiography, Hollis gives a very misleading account of their relationship.
Speaking of his time in the United States, he wrote:

> I made at that time through my writings another strange friend [F. D.
> Roosevelt is the previous one], Ezra Pound. Ezra Pound was of course
> an enthusiastic supporter of Mussolini and imagined—I think with little
> evidence—that Mussolini's attack on the Money Power was of the same
> kind as that which I had exposed in *The Breakdown of Money*. I soon found
> the enthusiasm of his argument embarrassing. During the war I had at
> the Air Ministry the duty of monitoring foreign broadcasts and was a little
> dismayed to read one day in an extract from an Italian talk by Ezra Pound,
> "Who today in England dares speak of Christopher Hollis?" He obviously

took it for granted that I had been suppressed in the reign of terror that ruled war-time England—probably shot under 18B. I concealed the extract from my superiors at the Air Ministry and have never, I think, till this day, mentioned it to anyone. (*Seven Ages* 133)

Pound mentions Hollis three times in the broadcasts. None corresponds to this recollection. In one he complains, "Hollis has ceased to talk about 'the debts of the South to the City of New York being 200 million'" (radio speech 111, 1941, Doob 382). So far as I can make out Pound never read the book Hollis mentions, though he did read three others: *Two Nations, Foreigners Aren't Fools,* and *Not So Dumb.* He reviewed the first; Hollis sent him the other two and received comments on them. After the war Hollis abandoned economics and turned to literary scholarship. I attended a lecture he gave in Oxford in 1976 and asked him afterwards about his relationship with Pound, but on hearing the question, he simply turned away.

In contrast to the earlier correspondences we have examined, Pound's letters to Hollis are peppered with anti-Semitic slurs and a general presumption of agreement that Jews are manipulating world events for their own benefit. Hollis neither endorses nor condemns these remarks. Clearly he was not offended by them, for he not only continues the correspondence, but also repeatedly expresses a wish to visit Pound in Italy. But, on the outbreak of hostilities, Hollis was true to his nationality and returned to Britain to work in intelligence—apparently not under suspicion of harboring sympathies for the enemy.

The outbreak of war broke off the correspondence, but it did not cause Pound to alter his views. He remained persuaded that the war was orchestrated by the bankers and the Jews. Having absorbed the conspiracy theory poison of Coughlin's *Money!* he was lost. His "research" was henceforth directed at the exposure of the Jewish conspiracy for world domination instead of at solutions to the world's economic problems, as it had begun. He was stopped in this course only by his arrest on 2 May 1945.

His detention at Pisa, indictment for treason, and incarceration in St. Elizabeths Mental Hospital in Washington, D.C., as mentally unfit to stand trial caused several years of silence. But when he became active again—about 1950, though still in detention—his views had not changed. He still believed that the best explanation of World War II was that a Jewish conspiracy controlled the democracies and the communist countries alike, causing them to collaborate in blocking the Fascist revolution. This position is exactly the same as Father Coughlin's in *Money!* and in his radio broadcasts subsequent to Kristallnacht. Pound adopted Coughlin's analysis in 1936 and never abandoned it thereafter. Its absurdity needs no comment.

Even as a conspiracy theorist, Pound retained his adherence to the cultural program of early modernism—to take a putatively decayed and polluted culture and "make it new"; to take the *disjecta membra* of human culture and recombine them into an authentic *paideuma*. At first he had thought that the task of culture-creation was primarily one of recovery and restoration, of "making it new." But increasingly he came to think of it as one of cleansing and purgation. This move from restoration to purification is very much the reflex of his conversion to fascism and anti-Semitism.

In his "mature" view Pound saw the history of civilization and culture as a struggle between the donative and pagan culture of Greece and Rome and the exploitative and accumulative Semitic culture carried out in the bosom of Christian Europe. This bifurcation of cultural forces into warring factions is reminiscent of Nietzsche's Dionysian-Apollonian opposition, but it is not derived from Nietzsche—at least not directly. It has more in common with Yeats's historical schema as articulated in *A Vision,* whose second version, we should not forget, is prefaced with "A Packet for Ezra Pound" containing an explanation of Pound's epic (see Surette "Yeats"). As a young man he held much the same pseudo-Manichean cultural theory as Yeats, tending to identify the donative forces with artists and other creative individuals and the accumulative forces with clerics, merchants, and politicians. In that earlier form his views were not truly metahistorical, but rather a kind of class analysis of artists and others, and seem relatively harmless. After all a bifurcation of society into artists and others has been common amongst artists since the Romantic period—most especially of the avant-garde. Unfortunately, that relatively harmless bit of professional bias evolved into a metahistorical account of historical events based on racism and conspiracy theory.

Pound's later political analysis maps imperfectly onto his earlier cultural-aesthetic analysis. The alteration of the focus of his interest in Chinese culture illustrates the modulation that takes place. His early interest was founded on an admiration for the poetic and metaphoric nature of the Chinese written language as theorized by Ernest Fenollosa. Although Pound never abandons that position, his later attention is focused on the totalitarian political ideology of Confucius. Similarly, his earlier contempt for Protestant prudery and Catholic authoritarianism is replaced by an admiration for Catholic respect for authority and condemnation of usury.

The Cantos was originally conceived as a recuperative epic that would trace the survival and occasional efflorescence of the donative forces in world history. In the first thirty cantos Pound found those donative forces in Albigensian France, Quattrocento Italy, and Revolutionary America and located the exploitative forces in contemporary Europe and America. But as Pound became more committed to the totalitarian state, and more focused on the conspiracy of usurers, he began to lose his way, jumping back and forth in the poem between Italy and America. Ultimately Pound sought refuge from his uncertainties and passions in redactions of multivolume works—the Adams and Chinese cantos. The putative point of it all was to expose the malign effects of the accumulative forces (usury), which are alleged to have been attacking and suppressing the donative forces throughout human history such that they have survived only surreptitiously in a permanent resistance of artists. In this scheme artists both create and pass on the donative counterculture in their artworks.

The project of modernism was to make manifest the cultural nuggets of an archaic—or "permanent," as Pound would have said—and embattled *paideuma* (*Weltanschauung*) in works of art, thereby generating a renewed world culture (see Surette *Birth* for an elaboration of this view). Such a view was palliative for Pound during his confinement in St. Elizabeths. The defeat of the Axis powers and his own perceived martyrdom counted for him as further evidence that he and they stood for those donative forces that had been suppressed and perverted. In short, the debacle of the Fascist Era, the Third Reich, and Hirohito's empire only served to confirm his metahistorical fantasy. The view from St. Elizabeths is encapsulated in the fragment published as canto 116, in which he laments, "Muss., wrecked for an error" (815). Many scholiasts suppose that Pound is referring to some error committed by Mussolini, but my reading is that the error was that of Roosevelt and Churchill aligning themselves with the Soviet Union against the Axis powers.

Pound wrote nothing and saw very few people for a number of years after his confinement in St. Elizabeths. By 1950, however, his correspondence was in full swing once again, and he was working on translations from the Chinese and on *The Cantos*. But his days of journalism were over. One of the most extensive—and, until recently, entirely neglected—correspondences of the period is between Pound and Olivia Rossetti Agresti. Pound first made contact with ORA, as he called her, in June 1937, when he submitted an article on the fortunes of Social Credit in Alberta to the journal of the Italian Association of Joint Stock Companies, which she edited from 1921 to 1943. Unfortunately she found his Italian too "picturesque" and rejected the article. But Pound persisted, and she eventually published him. They became regular correspondents and life-long friends. She is mentioned at the head of canto 76 as a Mussolini loyalist: "'Will' said the Signora Agresti, 'break his political / but not his economic system'" (472).

Ten years Pound's elder, Agresti was never the object of an amorous interest on his part—nor he on hers. Nor was she drawn to him for his celebrity; they corresponded for several years before she discovered that he was a famous poet and before he learned that she was the daughter of William Michael Rossetti, niece of Dante Gabriel and Christina Rossetti, and first cousin of Ford Madox Ford, one of his mentors during his early years in London.

Agresti was born in London on 20 September 1875. She began a political life of sorts at the tender age of seventeen by publishing an anarchist journal, *The Torch*—with her thirteen-year-old sister, Helen—from the basement of their parental home in London. Through that enterprise she met and married—in 1897—Antonio Agresti, a Florentine journalist briefly exiled in London for political activities. They returned to Italy, where she lived until her death in Rome on 6 November 1960, not long after her eighty-fifth birthday. She was widowed young and earned her living from 1904 to 1918 as a translator for David Lubin. That collaboration was ended only by Lubin's death from influenza. She subsequently worked as a translator at the League of Nations in Versailles until she got the job with the Italian Association in 1921.[5]

Though the correspondence covers twenty-two years—from 1937 to 1959—our interest is in what it reveals about Pound's interests and attitudes in the cold war period. Judging from the correspondence, though Pound returned to his old anti-Catholicism, he remained virulently anti-Semitic, loyal to Mussolini and Hitler, and hostile to Churchill and Roosevelt. In short it reveals that his attitudes and beliefs froze in their 1936 position. The correspondence is particularly revealing because Agresti—although a Fascist herself—is not frozen in such attitudes and is not dominated by hatred as Pound clearly is.

Pound's letters to Agresti indulge frequently in vitriolic denunciation of Western democratic leaders as either Jews themselves or in the pay of Jews—and his manner is far more extreme than anything I have found in his prewar correspondence. The following comparison of World War II to the Crusades is a relatively mild example of his fulminations: "Yes, heroism, decency/ ALL excited by HIRED press to the wrong ends. Pawn yr/ castles and rescue the HOLY sepulchre from the Muslim. etc. KILL the germans, defend Damnocracy etc. ALL to profit of arms manuf/ and loan kikes. The decent motives which DO function perverted. History falsified" (letter 17, Tryphonopoulos and Surette 165). This assertion that the Crusades and World War II were both orchestrated by "arms manufacturers and loan kikes" through a hired press (or clergy, I suppose, in the case of the Crusades) is far more extreme than anything Pound expressed prior to the radio broadcasts.

We learn from this correspondence that though Pound was not a Holocaust denier, neither was he appalled by it; he persisted in his anti-Semitism in spite of the horror of Hitler's "Final Solution." After reading Fritz Hesse's memoir, *Das Spiel im Deutschland,* he wrote to Agresti in a spirit of exculpation, which, though offensive, is short of denial: "Even a man in Hesse{'s} position [he was a diplomat] did not know about gas ovens till Sept. *1944* and they were not particularly german, I mean not spirito del popolo/ *and* there were *none* in ITALY tho I have only seen ONE statement of that fact, forget if in Begnac or Spampanato/ also my geo-politik to use a large word was NOT germanic/" (letter 65, p. 119).

Another reference to the Holocaust was occasioned by a discussion of the Bible, which he characterizes as "the dirty jew book," and says he read it "from age of 6 to 17" (letter 85, p. 169):

> I consider genocide impractical/ and admit in theory each individual shd/ be judged on his merits.
> BUT the cathedrals rose when segregation was in fashion. (letter 85, p. 170)

Such a remark, which places the lives of millions of innocent people in the balance with aesthetic achievement, demonstrates the complete moral collapse to which Pound's metahistory had led him.

He is equally unwilling to condemn Hitler. A year earlier, reading *Hitler's Secret Conversations,* he praised Hitler for his recognition of the Jewish threat, conceding that he was crazy, but still preferable to Churchill:

> Crazy as a coot, as Mus/ noted on first me{e}ting him. BUT with extraordinary flashes of lucidity. He smelled the idiocy of judeo-xtianity, but had no basis either in Aristotle or Confucius.
> first impressions of quick perception/ Justification of germans who tried to bump him off/ AND of those who saw need of strong Italy to balance the Neitzsche-Wagner teuto-bobble wobble.
> On the whole, NO ethical basis. Not to say that Italy didn't produce a punk named Machiavelli. Lucidity without clarity. Churchill just the same [illegible deletion] kind of grabber and without any extenuating charm. (letter 69, p. 130)

These samples reveal two points that must not be evaded: first, despite the Holocaust, Pound did not back off from the anti-Semitism of his radio broadcasts; second, despite sharing the fantasy of a Jewish conspiracy with the Nazis, he rejects both their aesthetics and their "metaphysics"—derisively characterized in the letter as "Nietzsche-Wagner teuto-bobble wobble."

The disharmony of his aesthetic and political views is sometimes raised as evidence that Pound could not have been a Fascist or a Nazi sympathizer. Such a defense rests on the implausible supposition that a person cannot hold views that are inconsistent. Nonetheless, Pound's views are not spectacularly incoherent. It is true that his support of Mussolini—and then of Hitler—was in spite of their failure to adopt the economic and banking reforms he espoused. But it is consistent with his Confucian political theory that order and justice must *descend* from a wise and just ruler, as opposed to *ascending* from an educated and informed citizenry. Though he knew their views and policies did not coincide with his own, he hoped, quite implausibly, to persuade them to adopt his views. He had held the same hopes for Roosevelt and for Aberhart, as well as for all those correspondents he badgered mercilessly with his theories.

It would be wrong to characterize Pound's political behavior as irrational or even radically confused; it was, however, grotesquely naive and certainly lacking in the milk of human kindness. It was not a direct output of his economic views, though it was clearly motivated by them. His enthusiasm for Mussolini, for example, was proof against the almost uniform refusal of his fellow economic radicals to grant fascism any marks for its economic policies, as it was against Mussolini's total lack of interest in Pound's support and advice.

Pound's activities as an economic reformer placed him in association with men who were rabid anti-Semites, and he eventually succumbed to their paranoia. Pound was not led into anti-Semitism by Mussolini, for he was already given over to the disease by 1938 when Mussolini decreed his racial laws. Like Yeats, Pound had been antidemocratic and elitist from his youth—as, indeed, were most European artists of the day. And he was typical of his generation in his contempt for bourgeois liberalism. Mussolini skillfully appealed to such sentiments, while turning politics into words and gesture, that is, into theater. Hitler went Mussolini one better, with Albert Speer's design of his Nuremberg extravaganzas. Pound was foolish enough to suppose that such aestheticization of politics meant that artists could guide nations by proxy. Such a delusion is perhaps forgivable in a poet, but it is more difficult to forgive his failure to recognize the face of evil when it was bared before him.

Whatever theoretical armature we bring to bear on Pound's case, there is no evidence that he experienced a change of heart during his time at St. Elizabeths. An extreme instance of his intransigence is found in another comment on *Hitler's Table Talk* in a letter to Agresti: "The Hitler Conversations very lucid re/ money/ unfortunately he was bit by dirty jew mania for World DOminion, as yu used to point out / this WORST of German diseases was got from yr/ idolized and filthy biblical bastards. Adolf clear on the bacillus of kikism/ that is on nearly all the other poisons. but failed to get a vaccine against that" (letter 70, pp. 132–33). Obliged to admit that Hitler was the aggressor in World War II—something he had vigorously denied in the radio broadcasts—Pound is prepared to hold the Jews responsible for Hitler's aggression, attributing German expansionism to Hitler having been "bit by dirty jew mania for World DOminion." What can be said about such twisted thinking?

To get some perspective on the extent of Pound's intellectual and moral failure, we can contrast Agresti's attitude toward Hitler, remembering that she, too, regretted the triumph of the liberal democracies over Fascist Italy. She declined his offer to send her *Hitler's Table Talk* in no uncertain terms: "I look upon as Hitler as a madman, and a dangerous one; it is all very well to speak in a more or less flippant way of 'better deads', but when from such talk one sets down to really killing off all those belonging to such categories as one can lay hands on, it is a case of criminal lunacy" (18 Nov. 1953, qtd. in Tryphonopoulos and Surette 133). Distressingly, Pound was not prepared to surrender his admiration for Hitler, even in the face of the hostility of his old friend. He replied with a spirited—though totally unconvincing—defense of Hitler as a victim:

> Yes, my Dear O.R.A. BUTTT we shd/ ask WHAT kind of a bloody lunatic, and what druv him/ and NOT allow *ourselves* to be intoxicated by the very filth of propaganda which you so rightly deplore. The POSITIVE lucidities which revived the whole of germany by enthusiasm/ the 6 months blind in hospital knowing no one/ NO high connections/ the mass of kraut stupidity opposed to him/ . . . AND one must place pore Adolf in proportion to the two loathsome tops/ FDR and W.C. neither of whom EVER was under hammer of necessity, or in ANY misery, or suffered five minutes from sympathy with the multitude. NEVER five minute agony for the state of the people. (letter 71, p. 134. Hitler noted in *Mein Kampf* [266–68] that he had been hospitalized for blindness in 1918 after having been injured in a British gas attack at Ypres. The blindness lasted for only a few days, however, not six months as Pound claims.)

Even in 1953 Pound accepts Hitler's self-serving account of his heroic confrontation in *Mein Kampf* of malignant forces and still believes the Axis propaganda that portrayed Roosevelt and Churchill as evil warmongers.

Among Nazi and Fascist postwar apologists[6] it was standard to see the cold war as a continuation of World War II, which they were pleased to interpret as a struggle between bolshevism and the West, conveniently overlooking Germany's conquest and occupation of Poland, France, Belgium, Holland, Norway, and Greece. On this reading of recent history Churchill and Roosevelt were great blunderers, failing to aid Germany and Italy in their heroic struggle with bolshevism. Had they not committed that error, these apologists argue, the West would be safe. Wise heads finally prevailed, and an alliance was forged with Germany and Italy against the Communists (NATO), but—the argument goes—it was entered into too late. Prussia, Poland, Hungary, and Czechoslovakia had been lost to the Bolsheviks, and the rest of Europe was at risk of a Communist takeover. Of course, there had never been any possibility of an alliance between the Axis and the Allies, but it was a fantasy entertained by loyal Nazis before the fall of Germany and persisted afterwards. Pound shared this view and continued to believe, as did Coughlin and the Nazis, that Jews controlled Moscow as well as the democracies: "Of course Roose[velt] betrayed the world to Moscow/ there was one war on/ and the dirty work aimed at causgn making sure of a third/ with the U.S. and the occident in weak position and the kiko-russ on top/ god rot the lot of 'em/ includinge Weinstein Kirchberg [Winston Churchill]/ and the barber{'}s block/. Winston of Clowning St/ the Barclay Gammon of the political night club/" (letter 61, p. 111).

As bizarre and irrational as such views appear today, they were the stock-in-trade of the Goebbels propaganda machine and appealed to the Germans' deep sense of encirclement. They are reflected in Martin Heidegger's *Introduction to Metaphysics* (1935): "This Europe, in its ruinous blindness forever on the point of cutting its own throat, lies today[7] in a great pincers, squeezed between Russia on one side and America on the other. From a metaphysical point of view, Russia and America are the same; the same dreary technological frenzy, the same unrestricted organization of the average man" (37).

Western liberal democracies are indistinguishable from Eastern Bolshevik dictatorships when viewed from the lofty world historical perspective of Pound and Heidegger. Yeats, too, thought fascism and Nazism represented a stage in the world historical drama that he understood in his own idiosyncratic way. All three looked down with some contempt on those who could only see the superficial antagonisms of individuals, nations, and ideologies in the great conflicts of this century which they understood more profoundly from their metahistorical perspective.

Though unknown to one another, and appealing to different authorities, Pound and Heidegger held very similar cultural, religious, and political views. They both rejected modern, Christian (or post-Christian, if one prefers), Western civilization in favor of an authentic culture precariously surviving from an imagined archaic Greek *paideai*. Heidegger's guides were Nietzsche and the German romantic poets; Pound's were the Theosophists G. R. S. Mead and Alan Upward, the Polish classicist Thaddeus Zielinski, and other little-known and eccentric scholars (for a fuller account of Pound's metahistory see Surette *Birth*). For both men, the authentic tradition was pre-Socratic and Aryan. Both were anti-Christian— and on similar grounds. Heidegger regarded Christianity as a form of "onto-theology" (by which he meant a religion of transcendence as opposed to an immanentist or pantheist faith); Pound saw it as an infection of "clean" Mediterranean erotic-ecstatic polytheism by Semitic ascetic monotheism—though, as we have seen, he was for a time willing to accept Zielinski's characterization of Catholicism as more pagan than Jewish.

In the postwar period Heidegger singled out technology as a characteristic product of onto-theology, but in the thirties and forties he identified technology itself as the evil. This is a salient difference between Pound and Heidegger. Following Douglas and Dexter Kimball, Pound embraced the advantages of modern machine technology and even regarded the Technocrats as allies for a time. And he exploited radio technology for propaganda purposes, even boasting to Ronald Duncan (in 1940) that he had anticipated the radio "in first third of Cantos." However, in the same sentence he alleges that he "was able to do 52/71 because I was the last survivin' monolith who did not have a bloody radio in the 'ome" (Paige 442).

Rather surprisingly Pound complains in the same letter that "blasted friends left a goddam radio here yester. Gift. God damn destructive and dispersive devil of an invention. But got to be faced" (441). The friends were Natalie Barney and Romaine Brooks, who visited him on their way from Paris to Florence in flight from the Nazis (Wilhelm, "In the Haunt" 109). Pound's complaint is odd, since we know that he had been listening to shortwave BBC broadcasts and to Coughlin from early 1936 at least. Perhaps he listened in a cafe or bistro. In any case, this anecdote suggests that he is not as far from Heidegger's hostility to technology as one would have supposed.

Following Zielinski, Pound attributes idealism and transcendentalism to the Hebrews. Heidegger attributes these same "vices"—perhaps more accurately—to Plato:

> It was in the Sophists and in Plato that appearance was declared to be mere appearance and thus degraded. At the same time Being, as *idea*, was exalted to a suprasensory realm. A chasm, *chorismos*, was created between the merely apparent essent here below and real being somewhere on high. In that chasm Christianity settled down, at the same time reinterpreting the lower as the created and the higher as the creator. These refashioned weapons it turned against antiquity (as paganism) and so

disfigured it. Nietzsche was right in saying that Christianity is Platonism for the people. (*Introduction* 106)

Pound and Heidegger both excoriate Christianity for creating a gulf between the human and the divine. Pound's early mentors— Yeats and Mead—would not have disagreed.

We have seen that Pound adopted conspiracy theory in the late thirties after more than a decade of study in search of a consensus amongst radicals for a common course of economic and political reform. The Agresti correspondence reveals that his views remained unchanged during the St. Elizabeths period, if not for the rest of his life. He repeats in 1949 very much the same views we found him expressing for the first time in the late thirties after having read Zielinski: "The Church of Rome decayed, got steadily stupider pari passu as the jew books were put into circulation, and stupidities engrafted on the clean greek and roman ideas of the early Church" (letter 18, p. 24).

Later in 1949, or early in 1950, Pound returns to the question of Christianity in a long undated letter to Agresti:

> J.C. [Jesus Christ] indubitably had a good chunk of the true tradition, BUT the yidd already had Leviticus XIX/ so there is no use pretending those pious sentiments differentiate the Christer from the yitt/
> The bulk of jewish law is nothing but a wheeze, however, to jerk fines out of the populace for the benefit of the cohens and levis.
> Zielinsky has neatly shown that all the dogma worth a damn came from greek mysteries etc/ everything that built the cathedrals. (letter 23, p. 40)

Five years later he repeats much the same sentiment: "That ALL the clean ideas in Xtianity come via greece (earlier origin may be india) but at any rate NOTHING of the goddam kikes/ {vid} Tertullian, Gibbon, the classic authors/ slime always getting xtns/ killed off. FACE it" (letter 82, p. 162).

Pound, Heidegger, Mussolini, and Hitler all looked to an archaic past for redemption. Pound and Heidegger (like Nietzsche) wished to leap over the ancient roots of modern industrial capitalism, which they located severally in Aristotle or Socrates or Plato. Again like Nietzsche, they both believed that they had uncovered an ancient civilization overlaid by Christianity and modernity. Though neither Hitler nor Mussolini had any such lofty philosophical projects, they both cleverly exploited a widespread nostalgia for a more intimate and personal polity than was permitted— either by Christian self-knowledge or by liberal mass democracy and consumerism.

Communism, bolshevism, and revolutionary versions of postmodernism also reject modern industrial capitalism, but they look to the future instead of the past for redemption—in revolution or in an apotheosis of technology. Mussolini's signal contribution to conservative ideology was to dress in revolutionary clothing the widespread nostalgia for an intimate and human-scale past—a nostalgia Pound shared. He, too, held a restorative or recuperative view of revolution, as is clear from the slogan he adopted from Mencius, "make it new."

The future to which conservative revolutionaries like Pound and Heidegger or Mussolini and Hitler looked for redemption in this recuperative way did not come to pass. Less headstrong than Pound, Heidegger withdrew into a view of art as "technology":

> Because the essence of technology is nothing technological, essential reflection upon technology and decisive confrontation with it must happen in a realm that is, on the one hand, akin to the essence of technology and, on the other, fundamentally different from it.
>
> Such a realm is art. But certainly only if reflection upon art for its part, does not shut its eyes to the constellation of truth concerning which we are *Questioning*. ("The Question Concerning Technology" in *Basic Writings* 317)

Pound had expressed a very similar view in 1913: "The arts, literature, poesy, are a science, just as chemistry is a science. Their subject is man, mankind and the individual. . . . The arts give us a great percentage of the lasting and unassailable data regarding the nature of man, of immaterial man, of man considered as a thinking and sentient creature. They begin where the science of medicine leaves off or rather they overlap that science. The borders of the two arts overcross" (*Impact* 42). Heidegger prudently retreated from politics into poetry in the summer of 1934, when he saw that he could not form Nazism in his own image (Ott 293). Pound, on the other hand, advanced from poetry into politics, in the delusion that he could influence political events.

Amazingly, Pound never saw that his vigorous efforts in the political arena were almost entirely without result. Even more remarkably, he did not retreat a single step during the thirteen years he spent in St. Elizabeths, maintaining instead the conspiracy analysis of world history that he had adopted from Pelley, Fack, and Coughlin and found corroborated in Fascist and Nazi propaganda. That he persisted in those views even when it was against his own personal welfare to do so, and when he was no longer subjected to Fascist and Nazi misrepresentation, attests to the strength of his convictions and to his courage, but not to his wisdom or charity.

Notes

1. Coughlin was born in Hamilton, Ontario, and studied for the priesthood at the Basilian seminary in Toronto. He was teaching at Assumption College in Windsor, but decided to become a parish priest. The bishop of Detroit, who had befriended him, offered him a new parish in the Detroit suburb of Royal Oak. Always ambitious, Coughlin built a much too large church, which he dedicated to St. Therèse of Lisieux and called the Shrine of the Little Flower. He began his radio broadcasts to raise funds to pay for that folly. Of course, he soon discovered the power of radio and the appeal of political influence (Warren 21–23).

2. It was most shocking when he blamed the outrage on the Jews' alleged support of the reparations payments imposed by Versailles in his response to Kristallnacht in the broadcast of 20 November 1938 (Warren 155–57).

3. Coughlin is echoing the historical fantasies of anti-Semites such as Nesta Webster, whose 1924 *Secret Societies and Subversive Movements* is still a source book for anti-Semites and conspiracy theorists. For a discussion of Webster and Pound's relation to conspiracy theorists see Surette *Birth*. Coughlin's source was probably Gertrude Coogan, though she had read Webster (Warren 142–43), as had Pound.

4. Pound's failure to remember *The Modern Idolatry* may be attributed to Mark's dismissal of Douglas's A + B theorem (168–71), even though he was part of Orage's *New English Weekly* circle.

5. Olivia and Helen jointly wrote and published—under the pseudonym Isabel Meredith—an account of that experience called *A Girl among the Anarchists*. She also wrote a biography, *David Lubin: A Study in Practical Idealism.*

6. These include Fritz Hesse and Luigi Villari, whose works Pound read with care and commented upon in letters to Agresti. Villari wrote *Italian Foreign Policy under Mussolini.*

7. It is not clear whether "today" means 1935 or 1953, when the lecture was first published. It would have been more natural in 1935 to speak of Germany between the pincers of France and the United Kingdom on the one hand, and Russia and Poland on the other, so I assume this remark was added or revised in 1953.

Volitionist Economics

Which of the following statements do you agree with?

1. It is an outrage that the state shd. run into debt to individuals by the act and in the act of creating real wealth.

2. Several nations recognize the necessity of distributing purchasing power. They do actually distribute it. The question is whether it shd. be distributed as favour to corporations; as reward for not having a job; or impartially and per capita.

3. A country CAN have one currency for internal use, and another good both for home and foreign use.

4. If money is regarded as certificate of work done, taxes are no longer necessary.

5. It is possible to concentrate all taxation onto the actual paper money of a country (or onto one sort of its money).

6. You can issue valid paper money against any commodity UP TO the amount of that commodity that people WANT.

7. Some of the commonest failures of clarity among economists are due to using one word to signify two or more different concepts: such as, DE-MAND, meaning sometimes WANT and sometimes power to buy; authoritative, meaning also responsible.

8. It is an outrage that the owner of one commodity cannot exchange it with someone possessing another, without being impeded or taxed by a third party holding a monopoly over some third substance or controlling some convention regardless or what it be called.

[Gallup dates the handbill to sometime before 18 August 1934 (Item E. m).]

Works Consulted

Accame, Giano. *Ezra Pound economista: Contro l'usura*. Rome: Edizioni Settimo Sigillo, 1995.

Agresti, Olivia Rossetti. *David Lubin: A Study in Practical Idealism*. Boston: Little, Brown, 1922.

Ahearn, Barry. *Pound/Zukofsky: Selected Letters of Ezra Pound and Louis Zukofsky*. New York: New Directions, 1987.

Akin, William E. *Technocracy and the American Dream: The Technocratic Movement, 1900–1941*. Berkeley: University of California Press, 1977.

Allen, William R. "Irving Fisher, F.D.R., and the Great Depression." Blaug 560–87.

Arendt, Hannah. *The Origins of Totalitarianism, 3: Totalitarianism*. 1951. New York: Harcourt Brace Jovanovich. 1968.

Bacigalupo, Massimo. *The Formèd Trace: The Later Poetry of Ezra Pound*. New York: Columbia University Press, 1980.

Belloc, Hilaire. *The Servile State*. London: T. N. Foulis, 1912.

Bernstein, Michael. *The Tale of the Tribe: Ezra Pound and the Modern Verse Epic*. Princeton: Princeton University Press, 1980.

Bird, William. Manuscripts, 1923–63. Lilly Library. Indiana University. Bloomington.

Black, Stanley W. *Learning from Adversity: Policy Responses to Two Oil Shocks*. Essays in International Finance 160. Dept. of Economics, Princeton University, Princeton, N.J., Dec. 1985.

Blaug, Mark, ed. *Pioneers in Economics*. Aldershot: Edward Elgar, 1992.

Bleaney, Michael. *Underconsumption Theories: A History and Critical Analysis*. New York: International Publishers, 1976.

Bowley, Marion. *Studies in the History of Economic Thought before 1870*. London: Macmillan, 1973.

Bullock, Paul. *Jerry Voorhis: The Idealist as Politician*. New York: Vantage Press, 1978.

Cannistraro, Philip V., and Brian R. Sullivan. *Il Duce's Other Woman: The Untold Story of Margherita Sarfatti*. New York: William Morrow, 1993.

Casillo, Robert. *The Genealogy of Demons: Anti-Semitism, Fascism, and the Myths of Ezra Pound*. Chicago: Northwestern University Press, 1988.

Chace, William M. *The Political Identities of Ezra Pound and T. S. Eliot.* Stanford: Stanford University Press, 1973.

Chamberlain, Houston. *Foundations of the Nineteenth Century.* New York: Howard Fertig, 1968.

Clark, Martin. *Modern Italy: 1871–1982.* London: Longman, 1984.

Cohn, Norman. *Warrant for Genocide: The Myth of the Jewish World-Conspiracy and the Protocols of the Elders of Zion.* London: Eyre and Spottiswoode, 1967.

Collier, Richard. *Duce: A Biography of Benito Mussolini.* New York: Viking Press, 1971.

Cooper-Oakley, Isabel. *Masonry and Medieval Mysticism: Traces of a Hidden Tradition.* London: Theosophical Publishing House, 1977.

Coughlin, Charles. *Am I an Anti-Semite? Nine Addresses on Various "ISMS."* Royal Oak, Mich.: National Union for Social Justice, 1936.

———. *Eight Lectures on Labor, Capital, and Justice.* Royal Oak, Mich.: Radio League of the Little Flower, 1934.

———. *Father Coughlin's Radio Discourses, 1931–1932.* Royal Oak, Mich.: Radio League of the Little Flower, 1932.

———. *Money! Questions and Answers.* Royal Oak, Mich.: National Union for Social Justice, 1936.

———. *A Series of Lectures on Social Justice.* Royal Oak, Mich.: Radio League of the Little Flower, 1935.

Culler, Jonathan. "It's Time to Set the Record Straight about Paul de Man and His Wartime Articles for a Pro-Fascist Newspaper." *Chronicle of Higher Education* 13 July 1988: B1.

Dalton, Hugh. Introduction. Hiskett 5–9.

Davis, Earle. *Vision Fugitive: Ezra Pound and Economics.* Lawrence: University Press of Kansas, 1968.

de Kruif, Paul. *Hunger Fighters.* New York: Harcourt, Brace, 1928.

Derrida, Jacques. *Of Grammatology.* Trans. Gayatri Chakravorty Spivak. Baltimore: Johns Hopkins University Press, 1976.

———. *Writing and Difference.* Trans. Alan Bass. Chicago: University of Chicago Press, 1978.

Diggins, John P. "Flirtation with Fascism: American Pragmatic Liberals and Mussolini's Italy." *American Historical Review* 71 (1966): 487–506.

Doob, Leonard W., ed. *"Ezra Pound Speaking": Radio Speeches of World War II.* Westport, Conn.: Greenwood Press, 1978.

Douglas, C. H. *The Brief for the Prosecution.* Liverpool: K. R. P. Publications, 1945.

———. *The Control and Distribution of Production.* London: Cecil Palmer, 1922.

———. *Credit-Power and Democracy.* London: Cecil Palmer, 1920.

———. *Economic Democracy.* London: Cecil Palmer, 1920.

———. "The Mechanism of Consumer Control." *New Age* 27 (16 Dec. 1920): 78–79.

———. "Notes of the Week." *New Age* 24 (27 Feb. 1919): 270.

———. *Social Credit.* London: Cecil Palmer, 1924.

Dudek, Louis, ed. *DK: Some Letters of Ezra Pound.* Montreal: DC Books, 1974.

Dunlop, D. M. *The History of the Jewish Khazars.* Princeton: Princeton University Press, 1954.

Edmundson, Mark. "A Will to Cultural Power: Deconstructing the de Man Scandal." *Harper's Magazine* July 1988: 67–71.

Elsner, Henry, Jr. *The Technocrats: Prophets of Automation.* Syracuse, N.Y.: Syracuse University Press, 1967.

Eshag, Eprime. *From Marshall to Keynes: An Essay on the Monetary Theory of the Cambridge School.* Oxford: Basil Blackwell, 1963.

Farias, Victor. *Heidegger and Nazism.* Ed. Joseph Margolis and Tom Rockmore. Trans. Paul Burrell and Gabriel R. Ricci. Philadelphia: Temple University Press, 1989.

Fenollosa, Ernest. *The Chinese Written Character as a Medium for Poetry.* Ed. Ezra Pound. San Francisco: City Lights Books, [1920].

Findlay, Timothy. *Famous Last Words.* Toronto: Clarke, Irwin, 1988.

Finlay, John L. *Social Credit: The English Origins.* Montreal: McGill-Queens University Press, 1972.

Fischer, Klaus P. *Nazi Germany: A New History.* New York: Continuum, 1995.

Fisher, Irving. Assisted by Hans R. L. Cohrssen. *Stable Money: A History of the Movement.* New York: Adelphi, 1934.

———. Assisted by Hans R. L. Cohrssen and Herbert W. Fisher. *Stamp Scrip.* New York: Adelphi, 1933.

Flory, Wendy Stallard. *The American Ezra Pound.* New Haven: Yale University Press, 1989.

Frederick, J. George. *For and against Technocracy.* New York: Business Bourse, 1933.

Frère, Jean-Claude. *Nazisme et sociétés secrètes.* Paris: Culture, Art, Loisirs, 1974.

Friedman, Milton. "Bimetallism Revisited." *Commodity Monies.* Ed. Anna J. Schwartz. New York: National Bureau of Economic Research, 1992. 1:339–58.

Galbraith, John Kenneth. *Economics and the Art of Controversy.* New York: Random House, 1959.

———. *Money: Whence It Came, Where It Went.* London: Macmillan, 1975.

Galison, Peter. "Aufbau/Bauhaus: Logical Positivism and Architectural Modernism." *Critical Inquiry* 16 (Summer 1990): 709–52.

Gallup, Donald. *A Bibliography of Ezra Pound.* London: Rupert-Hart-Davis, 1969.

Gesell, Silvio. *The Natural Economic Order.* 1916. Trans. Philip Pye. London: Peter Owen, 1958.

Gibson, Mary Ellis. *Epic Reinvented: E.P. and the Victorians.* Ithaca: Cornell University Press, 1995.

Goodrick-Clarke, Nicholas. *The Occult Roots of Nazism: The Ariosophists of Austria and Germany, 1890–1935.* Willingborough, Northamptonshire: Aquarian Press, 1985.

Green, Roy. *Classical Theories of Money, Output, and Inflation: A Study in Historical Economics.* New York: St. Martin's Press, 1992.

Green, Timothy. "From a Pawnshop to Patron of the Arts in Five Centuries." *Smithsonian* 22.4 (July 1991): 59–69.

Hall, Donald. *Remembering Poets: Reminiscences and Opinions.* New York: Harper Colophon Books, 1978.

Harrison, John Raymond. *The Reactionaries.* London: Victor Gollancz, 1966.

Hastings, Beatrice. *The Old "New Age": Orage and Others.* London: Blue Moon Press, 1936.

Hatlen, Burton. "Ezra Pound and Fascism." *Ezra Pound and History.* Ed. Marianne Korn. Orono, Maine: National Poetry Foundation, 1985. 145–72.

Heidegger, Martin. *Basic Writings.* Ed. David Farrell Krell. New York: Harper and Row, 1977.

———. *An Introduction to Metaphysics.* Trans. Ralph Mannheim. New Haven: Yale University Press, 1959.

Heilbroner, Robert, and William Milberg. *The Crisis of Vision in Modern Economic Thought.* Cambridge: Cambridge University Press, 1995.

Hesse, Fritz. *Hitler and the English.* Trans. F. A. Voigt. London: Allan Wingate, 1954.

Heymann, C. David. *Ezra Pound: The Last Rower.* New York: Seaver Books, 1976.

Hicks, J. R. "Mr. Keynes and the 'Classics': A Suggested Interpretation." *Econometrica* 5 (Apr. 1937): 147–59.

Higham, Charles. *The Duchess of Windsor: The Secret Life.* New York: McGraw-Hill, 1988.

Hiskett, W. R. *Social Credits or Socialism: An Analysis of the Douglas Credit Scheme.* London: Victor Gollancz, 1935.

Hitler, Adolf. *Hitler's Secret Conversations, 1941–1944.* Trans. Norman Cameron and R. H. Stevens. New York: Farrar, Strauss, and Young, 1953.

———. *Mein Kampf.* New York: Reynell and Hitchcock, 1941.

Hobson, J. A. *Imperialism: A Study.* London: George, Allen, and Unwin, 1902.

Hofstadter, Richard. *The Age of Reform: From Bryan to F.D.R.* New York: Alfred A. Knopf, 1969.

———. *The Progressive Historians.* New York: Alfred A. Knopf, 1968.

Hollis, Christopher. *The Breakdown of Money: An Historical Explanation.* London: Sheed and Ward, 1937.

———. *The Seven Ages: Their Exits and Their Entrances.* London: Heinemann, 1974.

———. *The Two Nations: A Financial Study of English History.* London: George Routledge and Sons, 1935.

Huysmans, J. K. *La Bas.* Paris: Plon, 1908.

Hutchinson, Harry D. *Money, Banking, and the United States Economy.* New Jersey: Prentice-Hall, 1984.

Jahn, Janheinz. *Leo Frobenius: The Demonic Child.* Trans. Reinhard Sander. Occasional Publication of the African and Afro-American Studies and Research Center, University of Texas at Austin, 1974.

Jameson, Fredric. *Fables of Aggression: Wyndham Lewis, the Modernist as Fascist.* Berkeley: University of California Press, 1979.

———. *The Prison-House of Language.* Princeton: Princeton University Press, 1972.

Judt, Tony. *Past Imperfect: French Intellectuals, 1944–1956.* Berkeley: University of California Press, 1992.

Jumonville, Neil. "The New York Intellectuals' Defence of the Intellect." *Queen's Quarterly* 97 (Summer 1990): 290–304.

Kazin, Alfred. "The Fascination and Terror of Ezra Pound." *New York Review of Books* 13 Mar. 1986: 16–24.

Kenner, Hugh. *The Pound Era.* Berkeley: University of California Press, 1971.

Keynes, John Maynard. *The General Theory of Employment, Interest, and Money.* London: Macmillan, 1936.

Kimball, Dexter. *Industrial Economics*. New York: McGraw-Hill, 1929.

Kitson, Arthur. *The Bankers' Conspiracy! Which Started the World Crisis*. London: Elliot Stock, 1933.

———. *Industrial Depression: Its Cause and Cure*. London: T. Fisher Unwin, 1905.

———. *A Scientific Solution of the Money Question*. Boston: Arena, 1895.

Knox, Bryant. "Allen Upward and Ezra Pound." *Paideuma* 3 (Spring 1974): 71–84.

Koestler, Arthur. *The Thirteenth Tribe*. London: Picador, 1976.

Kuberski, Philip. *A Calculus of Ezra Pound: Vocations of the America Sign*. Gainesville: University Presses of Florida, 1992.

Kuhn, Thomas S. *The Structure of Scientific Revolutions*. 2d ed. Chicago: University of Chicago Press, 1970.

Labour Party Committee. *Report of the Labour Party Committee on the Douglas "New Age" Credit Scheme*. 1922.

Laidler, David. *The Golden Age of the Quantity Theory: The Devolopment of Neoclassical Monetary Economics, 1870–1914*. New York: Philip Allan, 1991.

Larson, Bruce. *Lindbergh of Minnesota: A Political Biography*. New York: Harcourt Brace Jovanovich, 1973.

Lauber, John. "Pound's Cantos: A Fascist Epic." *Journal of American Studies* 12 (Apr. 1978): 3–21.

Lehman, David. *Signs of the Times: Deconstruction and the Fall of Paul de Man*. New York: Poseidon Press, 1992.

Lentricchia, Frank. *After the New Criticism*. Chicago: University of Chicago Press, 1980.

Lewis, Wyndham. *Hitler*. 1931. New York: Gordon Press, 1972.

———. *The Hitler Cult*. 1939. New York: Gordon Press, 1972.

———. *Time and Western Man*. 1927. Boston: Beacon Press, 1957.

Lindberg, Kathryne V. *Reading Pound Reading Nietzsche: Modernism after Nietzsche*. New York: Oxford University Press, 1987.

Lindbergh, Charles A. *Banking and Currency and the Money Trust*. Privately printed, 1913.

Loeb, Harold. *Life in a Technocracy: What It Might Be Like*. 1933. Syracuse, N.Y.: Syracuse University Press, 1996.

Longenbach, James. "Matthew Arnold and the Modern Apocalypse." *PMLA* 104 (Oct. 1989): 844–55.

———. *Modernist Poetics of History: Pound, Eliot, and the Sense of the Past*. Princeton: Princeton University Press, 1987.

———. *Stone Cottage: Pound, Yeats, and Modernism*. New York: Oxford University Press, 1988.

Lunghini, Giorgio. Introduction. *L'ABC dell' economia e altri scritti*. By Ezra Pound. Turin: Bollati Boringhieri, 1994.

Macdonald, Alan Houston. *Richard Hovey: Man and Craftsman*. Durham: Duke University Press, 1957.

Macpherson, C. B. *Democracy in Alberta*. Toronto: University of Toronto Press, 1953.

Mairet, Philip. *A. R. Orage: A Memoir*. London: Dent, 1936.

Malthus, Thomas. *An Essay on the Principle of Population*. 1798. Ed. Anthony Flew. London: Penguin, 1985.

Mark, Jeffrey. *The Modern Idolatry: Being an Analysis of Usury and the Pathology of Debt.* London: Chatto and Windus, 1934.

Marsh, Alec. *Money and Modernity: Pound, Williams, and the Spirit of Jefferson.* Tuscaloosa: University of Alabama Press, 1998.

Martin, Wallace. *The New Age under Orage.* Manchester: Manchester University Press, 1967.

Martineau, Alain. *Herbert Marcuse's Utopia.* Trans. Jane Brierly. Montreal: Harvest House, 1986.

Marx, Karl. *Capital: A Critical Analysis of Capitalist Production.* 1867. 3 vols. Moscow: Progress Publishers, 1974.

Materer, Timothy, ed. *Pound/Lewis: The Letters of Ezra Pound and Wyndham Lewis.* New York: New Directions, 1985.

———. *Vortex: Pound, Eliot, and Lewis.* Ithaca: Cornell University Press, 1979.

Mathers, S. L. MacGregor. *The Kabbalah Unveiled.* 1887. New York: Oxford University Press, 1968.

McCormick, John. *George Santayana: A Biography.* New York: Paragon House, 1988.

Meyers, Jeffrey. *The Enemy: A Biography of Wyndham Lewis.* London: Routledge and Kegan Paul, 1980.

Michaelis, Meir. *Mussolini and the Jews.* Oxford: Clarendon Press, 1978.

Miller, Tyrus. "Pound's Economic Ideal: Silvio Gesell and *The Cantos.*" *Paideuma* 19 (Spring–Fall 1990): 169–80.

Minsky, Hyman P. *John Maynard Keynes.* New York: Columbia University Press, 1975.

Miyake, Akiko. *Ezra Pound and the Mysteries of Love: A Plan for the Cantos.* Durham: Duke University Press, 1991.

Mondolfo, Vittoria I., and Margaret Hurley, eds. *Ezra Pound: Letters to Ibbotson, 1935–1952.* Orono: National Poetry Foundation, 1979.

Moody, A. D. "Pound's Allen Upward." *Paideuma* 4 (Spring 1975): 55–70.

Morrison, Paul. *The Poetics of Fascism: Ezra Pound, T. S. Eliot, Paul de Man.* New York: Oxford University Press, 1996.

Mosse, George. Introduction. Chamberlain v–xix.

Muir, Edwin. *An Autobiography.* London: Hogarth Press, 1954.

Mullins, Eustace. *This Difficult Individual, Ezra Pound.* New York: Fleet, 1961.

Munson, Gorham. *The Awakening Twenties: A Memoir-History of a Literary Period.* Baton Rouge: Louisiana State University Press, 1985.

Mussolini, Benito. *Fascism: Doctrine and Institutions.* Rome: Ardita, 1935.

Nichols, Peter. *Ezra Pound: Politics, Economics, and Writing: A Study of the Cantos.* London: Macmillan, 1984.

Nietzsche, Friedrich. *The Birth of Tragedy and The Case of Wagner.* Trans. Walter Kaufmann. New York: Vintage, 1967.

Noll, Richard. *The Aryan Christ: The Secret Life of Carl Jung.* New York: Random House, 1997.

———. *The Jung Cult: Origins of a Charismatic Movement.* New York: Free Press, 1994.

Nordau, Max. *Degeneration.* 1895. London: Heinemann, 1913.

Norman, Charles. *Ezra Pound.* London: Macdonald, 1969.

Orage, Alfred R. *Consciousness: Animal, Human, and Divine.* London: Theosophical Publishing Society, 1907.

———. *Friedrich Nietzsche: The Dionysian Spirit of the Age.* London: T. N. Foulis, 1906.

———. *Nietzsche in Outline and Aphorism*. London: T. N. Foulis, 1907.

Ott, Hugo. *Martin Heidegger: A Political Life*. Trans. Allan Blunden. New York: Basic Books, 1993.

Overholser, Willis A. *A Short Review and Analysis of the History of Money in the United States*. Libertyville, Ill.: Progress Publishing, 1936.

Paige, D. D., ed. *The Letters of Ezra Pound, 1907–1941*. London: Faber and Faber, 1951.

Parker, R. A. C. *Europe 1919–1945*. London: Weidenfield and Nicolson, 1969.

Penty, Arthur J. *The Restoration of the Guild System*. London: Swan Sonnenschein, 1906.

Perkins, David. *A History of Modern Poetry*. Cambridge, Mass.: Harvard University Press, 1976.

Perl, Jeffrey M. *The Tradition of Return: The Implicit History of Modernism*. Princeton: Princeton University Press, 1984.

Perloff, Marjorie. "Fascism, Anti-Semitism, Isolation: Contextualizing the 'Case of E. P.'" *Paideuma* 16 (Winter 1987): 7–21.

Polanyi, Karl. *The Great Transformation*. New York: Farrar, Strauss, and Rinehart, 1944.

Popper, Karl R. "How I See Philosophy." *Philosophy in Britain Today*. Ed. S. G. Shanker. London: Croom Helm, 1986. 198–212.

———. *The Poverty of Historicism*. 1957. New York: Basic Books, 1960.

Por, Odon. *Fascism*. Trans. E. Townshend. London: Labour Publishing, 1923.

———. *Guilds and Co-operatives in Italy*. Trans. E. Townshend. London: Labour Publishing, 1923.

Pound, Ezra. *ABC of Reading*. 1934. New York: New Directions, 1960.

———. "American Chaos." *New Age* 17 (9 Sept. 1918): 449; (16 Sept. 1918): 471.

———. "The Atrophy of the Leninists." *New English Weekly* 2 July 1936: 227–28; 9 July 1936: 249–50; 16 July 1936: 272–73; 23 July 1936: 314–15.

———. "Banking Beneficence and . . ." *New Age* 56 (14 Feb. 1935): 184. Rpt. in *Ezra Pound's Poetry and Prose* 6:246–47.

———. *The Cantos of Ezra Pound*. New York: New Directions, 1995.

———. "A Civilising Force on the Move: The Bank Reform." *British-Italian Bulletin* 2 (30 May 1936): 3. Rpt. in *Ezra Pound's Poetry and Prose* 7:58–59.

———. "Declaration." *New Democracy* 2 (30 Mar.–15 Apr. 1934): 5.

———. "The Divine Mystery." Rev. of Allen Upward's *The Divine Mystery*. *New Freewoman* 1 (15 Sept. 1913): 207–8.

———. "Economic Democracy." *Little Review* 7 (6 Apr. 1920): 39–42.

———. Ezra Pound–Richard Aldington Correspondence. 1922–28. Humanities Research Center. Austin, Tex.

———. *Ezra Pound: Selected Prose, 1909–1965*. Ed. William Cookson. New York: New Directions, 1973.

———. *Ezra Pound's Poetry and Prose: Contributions to Periodicals*. Ed. Lea Baechler, A. Walton Litz, and James Longenbach. 10 vols. New York: Garland, 1991.

———. *Guild to Kulchur*. New York: New Directions, 1938.

———. *Impact: Essays on Ignorance and the Decline of American Civilization*. Ed. Noel Stock. Chicago: Henry Regnery, 1960.

———. "The Italian Bank Act." *British-Italian Bulletin* 2 (4 Apr. 1936): 4. Rpt. in *Ezra Pound's Poetry and Prose* 7:43–44.

———. *Jefferson and/or Mussolini.* 1935. New York: Liveright, 1970.

———. "Leaving Out Economics: Gesell as Reading Matter." *New English Weekly* 6 (31 Jan. 1935): 331–33.

———. Letters to William E. Woodward. 1933–37. New York Public Library.

———. "Letters to Woodward." *Paideuma* 15 (Spring 1986): 105–20.

———. *Literary Essays of Ezra Pound.* Ed. T. S. Eliot. London: Faber and Faber, 1954.

———. "Le Major C. H. Douglas et la situation en Angleterre." *Les Écrits Nouveaux* 8 (Aug.–Sept. 1921): 143–49. Rpt. in *Ezra Pound's Poetry and Prose* 4:167–71.

——— [as Bastein von Helmholtz]. "On the Imbecility of the Rich." *Egoist* 1 (15 Oct. 1914): 389–90.

———. Papers. Yale Collection of American Literature. Beinecke Rare Book and Manuscript Library. Yale University. New Haven, Conn.

———. *Pavannes and Divagations.* New York: New Directions, 1958.

———. *Personae: The Collected Shorter Poems of Ezra Pound.* 1926. New York: New Directions, 1990.

———. "Probari Ratio." *The Athenaeum* 94 (2 Apr. 1920): 445.

———. Rev. of *Credit-Power and Democracy* by C. H. Douglas. *Contact* (Summer 1921): 4.

———. "The Revolt of Intelligence." *New Age* 26 (13 Nov. 1919): 21–22; (11 Dec. 1919): 90–91; (18 Dec. 1919): 106–7; 27 (1 Jan. 1920): 139–40; (8 Jan. 1920): 153–54; (15 Jan. 1920): 176–77; (22 Jan. 1920): 186–87; (4 Mar. 1920): 287–88; (11 Mar. 1920): 301–2; (18 Mar. 1920): 318–19.

———. *The Spirit of Romance.* 1929. New York: New Directions, 1953.

———. "What America Has to Live Down" *New Age* 17 (22 Aug. 1918): 266–67; (27 Aug. 1918): 281–82; (12 Sept. 1918): 314; (19 Sept. 1918): 329.

The Protocols and World Revolution. Boston: Small, Maynard, 1920.

Reck, Michael. "A Conversation between Ezra Pound and Allen Ginsberg." *Evergreen Review* 56 (July 1968): 27–29, 84.

Reckitt, Maurice B. *As It Happened: An Autobiography.* London: J. M. Dent, 1941.

Redman, Tim. *Ezra Pound and Italian Fascism.* Cambridge: Cambridge University Press, 1991.

Robbins, Lionel. *Autobiography of an Economist.* London: Macmillan, 1971.

Robinson, Joan. *Economic Philosophy.* 1962. London: Penguin, 1964.

Roosevelt, Franklin D. *Looking Forward.* New York: John Day, 1933.

Rorty, Richard. *Contingency, Irony, and Solidarity.* Cambridge: Cambridge University Press, 1989.

———. "Taking Philosophy Seriously." Rev. of *Heidegger and Nazism* by Victor Farias. *New Republic* 11 Apr. 1988: 31–34.

Rossetti, Olivia, and Helen Rossetti [as Isabel Meredith]. *A Girl among the Anarchists.* London: Duckworth, 1903.

Rubinstein, William D. *The Myth of Rescue: Why the Democracies Could Not Have Saved More Jews from the Nazis.* London: Routledge, 1997.

Ruskin, John. *Unto This Last.* 1860. Ed. P. M. Yarker. London: Collins, 1970.

Salter, Arthur. *Memoirs of a Public Servant.* London: Faber and Faber, 1961.

Samuelson, Paul A. *Economics.* 1948. New York: McGraw-Hill, 1975.

Schorske, Carl E. *German Social Democracy, 1905–1917: The Development of the Great Schism.* New York: Harper and Row, 1995.

Scott, Peter Dale. "Anger and Poetic Politics in *Rock Drill.*" *San José Studies* 12 (Fall 1986): 68–82.

Selver, Paul. *Orage and the New Age Circle.* London: Allen and Unwin, 1959.

———. *Private Life.* London: Jarrolds, 1929.

Shaw, George Bernard. *The Sanity of Art: An Exposure of the Current Nonsense about Artists Being Degenerate.* London: New Age Press, 1908.

Sheehan, Thomas. "Heidegger and the Nazis." *New York Review of Books* 16 June 1988: 38–47.

Sherry, Vincent. *Ezra Pound, Wyndham Lewis, and Radical Modernism.* New York: Oxford University Press, 1993.

Sicari, Stephen. *Pound's Epic Ambition: Dante and the Modern World.* Albany: State University of New York Press, 1991.

Skidelsky, Robert. *John Maynard Keynes.* Vol 2: *The Economist as Saviour, 1920–1937.* London: Macmillan, 1992.

———. *Oswald Mosley.* London: Macmillan, 1981.

Sluga, Hans. *Heidegger's Crisis: Philosophy and Politics in Nazi Germany.* Cambridge, Mass.: Harvard University Press, 1993.

Smith, Adam. *The Wealth of Nations.* 1776. London: Penguin, 1979.

Smith, Stan. *The Origins of Modernism: Eliot, Pound, Yeats, and the Rhetorics of Renewal.* New York: Harvester Wheat Sheaf, 1994.

Sternhell, Zeev. *The Birth of Fascist Ideology.* Trans. David Maisel, with Mario Sznajder and Maia Asheri. Princeton: Princeton University Press, 1994. Trans. of *Naissance de l'idéologie fasciste.* Paris: Fayard, 1989.

Stock, Noel. *The Life of Ezra Pound.* New York: Pantheon Books, 1970.

Surette, Leon. *The Birth of Modernism: Ezra Pound, T. S. Eliot, W. B. Yeats, and the Occult.* Montreal: McGill-Queen's University Press, 1993.

———. "Cavalcanti and Pound's Arcanum." *Ezra Pound and Europe.* Ed. Richard Taylor and Claus Melchior. Amsterdam: Rodopi, 1993. 51–60.

———. *A Light from Eleusis: A Study of the Cantos of Ezra Pound.* Oxford: Clarendon Press, 1979.

———. "Yeats, Pound, and Nietzsche." *Paideuma* 20 (Winter 1991): 17–30.

Taylor, Overton H. *A History of Economic Thought.* New York: McGraw-Hill, 1960.

Terrell, Carrol F. *A Companion to the Cantos of Ezra Pound.* 2 vols. Berkeley: University of California Press, 1980–84.

Thatcher, David S. *Nietzsche in England, 1890–1914.* Toronto: University of Toronto Press, 1970.

Time: Almanac of the Twentieth Century. CD-ROM. New York: Soft Key International, 1995.

Toomer, Jean. *Jean Toomer: Selected Essays and Literary Criticism.* Ed. Robert B. Jones. Knoxville: University of Tennessee Press, 1996.

Tryphonopoulos, Demetres. *The Celestial Tradition: A Study of Ezra Pound's Cantos.* Waterloo, Ont.: Wilfrid Laurier University Press, 1992.

Tryphonopolous, Demetres, and Leon Surette, eds. *"I Cease Not to Yowl": Ezra Pound's Letters to Olivia Rossetti Agresti.* Urbana: University of Illinois Press, 1998.

Tytell, John. *Ezra Pound: The Solitary Volcano.* New York: Doubleday, 1987.

Upward, Allen [as 2031361]. *Some Personalities.* London: John Murray, 1921.

Viereck, Peter. *Metapolitics: The Roots of the Nazi Mind.* New York: Capricorn Books, 1961.

Villari, Luigi. *Italian Foreign Policy under Mussolini.* New York: Devin-Adair, 1956.

Voorhis, Jerry. *Confessions of a Congressman.* New York: Doubleday, 1947.

Walkiewicz, E. P., and Hugh Witemeyer, eds. *Ezra Pound and Senator Bronson Cutting.* Albuquerque: University of New Mexico Press, 1995.

Warren, Donald. *Radio Priest: Charles Coughlin, the Father of Hate Radio.* New York: Free Press, 1996.

Webb, James. *The Harmonious Circle: The Lives and Work of G. I. Gurdjieff, P. D. Ouspensky, and Their Followers.* New York: G. P. Putnam's Sons, 1980.

Webster, Nesta. *Secret Societies and Subversive Movements.* 1924. London: Boswell, 1946.

Weinroth, Michelle. *Reclaiming William Morris: Englishness, Sublimity, and the Rhetoric of Dissent.* Montreal: McGill-Queen's University Press, 1996.

Welch, Louise. *Orage with Gurdjieff in America.* Boston: Routledge and Kegan Paul, 1982.

White, Hayden. *Topics of Discourse: Essays in Cultural Criticism.* Baltimore: Johns Hopkins University Press, 1978.

Wilhelm, J. J. *The American Roots of Ezra Pound.* New York: Garland, 1985.

———. *Ezra Pound: The Tragic Years, 1925–1972.* University Park: Pennsylvania State University Press, 1994.

———. "In the Haunt of the Priestess of the Hidden Nest: A Tribute to Olga Rudge." *Paideuma* 26 (Spring 1997): 97–118.

Wolfe, Cary. *The Limits of American Literary Ideology in Pound and Emerson.* Cambridge: Cambridge University Press, 1993.

Woodward, E. S. *Canada Reconstructed.* Vancouver: Wrigley, 1933.

Yeats, William Butler. *Collected Poems of W. B. Yeats.* London: Macmillan, 1958.

———. *The King of the Great Clock Tower: Commentaries and Poems.* Dublin: Cuala Press, 1934.

Zapponi, Niccolò. *L'Italia di Ezra Pound.* Rome: Bulzoni, 1976.

Zielinski, Thaddeus. *The Sibyl.* Trans. Ivan Stancioff. *Edge* 2 (Nov. 1956): 1–47.

Index

Leon Surette has published *The Birth of Modernism: Ezra Pound, T. S. Eliot, W. B. Yeats, and the Occult; A Light from Eleusis: A Study of the Cantos of Ezra Pound;* and many articles on Pound and fascism. He has also edited, with Demetres Tryphonopoulos, *"I Cease Not to Yowl": Ezra Pound's Letters to Olivia Rossetti Agresti.* He is a professor of English at the University of Western Ontario.

Typeset in 10/12.5 New Baskerville
Composed by Jim Proefrock
at the University of Illinois Press
Manufactured by Cushing-Malloy, Inc.

University of Illinois Press
1325 South Oak Street
Champaign, IL 61820-6903

www.press.uillinois.edu